French Modern

French Modern

Norms and Forms of the Social Environment

Paul Rabinow

The University of Chicago Press
Chicago and London

The University of Chicago Press, Chicago 60637
The University of Chicago Press, Ltd., London

© 1989 Massachusetts Institute of Technology

All rights reserved. Originally published 1989 by the MIT Press
University of Chicago Press Edition 1995
Printed in the United States of America
01 00 99 98 97 96 95   6 5 4 3 2 1

ISBN 0-226-70174-3 (pbk.)

Library of Congress Cataloging-in-Publication Data

Rabinow, Paul.
    French modern : norms and forms of the social environment / Paul Rabinow. —
University of Chicago Press ed.
        p.   cm.
    Originally published: Cambridge, Mass. : MIT Press, c1989. Includes bibliographical
    references (p.   ) and index.
    1. Philosophy, French—19th century.   2. Philosophy, French—20th century.
    3. Ethnology—France—History—19th century.   4. Ethnology—France—History—
20th century.   I. Title.
    [B2185.R23   1995]
    944.08—dc20   95-35465
                                                                        CIP

♾ The paper used in this publication meets the minimum requirements of the American
National Standard for Information Sciences—Permanence of Paper for Printed Library
Materials, ANSI Z39.48–1984.

For Michel Foucault

Contents

Acknowledgments

The sources of this book are numerous; I can mention only a few here. The son of two social workers (who would have been surprised to know they were specific intellectuals), I grew up in a garden city, Sunnyside in Queens, New York, which demonstrated the possibility of a successfully planned urban social environment. Lewis Mumford, who lived in Sunnyside himself, agreed. After years of living and observing in other cities (New York, Paris, and Chicago), I was utterly unprepared, when I landed in Rabat, Morocco, in 1968 to begin my anthropological fieldwork, for the city's planned nature and its skillful, if ambiguous, juxtaposition of spaces. Since I was in Morocco to study rural religion and politics, and under my advisor's stern admonition that our role as anthropologists was to salvage disappearing Moroccan culture (in fact, only the Jewish and French colonial cultures were disappearing), I headed for the countryside; it was much later, still intrigued by colonial urban planning and its reappropriation by the Moroccans, that I returned to study Morocco's cities and the colonial period.

I gambled (and lost) that the end of the war in Vietnam would allow the possibility of scholarly exchange and research; this deception pushed me toward a historical project comparing French pacification strategies in Vietnam and Morocco. The project was narrowed to colonial city planning. I would like to thank Gwen Wright for her contribution as research historian on a 1980–1981 joint National Endowment for the Humanities grant for the collection of materials on the emergence of city planning in the French world.

The book in its current form was shaped by further research and reflection in France in 1983 and in 1986, when I presented some of these ideas as a visiting Directeur d'Etudes Associé at the Ecole des Hautes Etudes en Sciences Sociales. I am grateful for support along the way from the Howard Foundation, the John Simon Guggenheim Foundation, and the Institute of International Studies at Berkeley.

The work of Bernard Cohn and Michel Foucault most directly provided the training and framework within which my own work took shape. Bernard Cohn, at the University of Chicago, was teaching us about the relations of knowledge and power, spaces and colonies, long before I ever heard of Foucault. My encounter with Foucault, between 1979 and his death in 1984, was a decisive one on many registers. Foucault's death—cosmic grand larceny—robbed us of, among other things, his anticipated return to the analysis of modern society.

Literally scores of people have been helpful in many ways, and I wish to express my thanks for that aid. To mention only a few: François Béguin, Edmund Burke III, Katherine Burlen, Mary McCleod, Jean-Louis Cohen, Alain Desrosières, Daniel Defert, François Ewald, Jean-Pierre Gaudin, Christian Girard, Joseph Helms, Pamela Helms, Lynn Hunt, Jean Jamin, Michael Meranze, Thomas Metcalfe, Victoria Mukerj Annick Osmont, Alan Pred, David Prochaska, Alain Sinou, Anthony Vidler, and especially C. P. Seid. Two fledgling historians, Richard Gringeri and Marc Roudebush, provided invaluable support as research assistants along the way.

My greatest debt is to three friends, one in New York, one in San Francisco, and the third in Paris, whose intellectual and moral support, throughout the innumerable drafts of this book, kept me going. Their knowledge and wisdom is present throughout: Christopher Jeans, James Faubion, and Christian Topalov. As Aristotle almost said, friendship is the highest good.

Introduction to the Present

Par les seuls accords de ma voix
J'ai pouvoir de bâtir des villes.
—*Apollo, in René Descartes's opera, "La Naissance de la paix," written for the court of Sweden and performed on December 19, 1649[1]*

Saint-Simon's dictum that modern society would pass "from the government of men to the administration of things" has formed a leitmotif for French reformers, even though what was meant by "government," "men," "administration," and "things" has shifted over time, as have the relationships between these terms. This book diagrams some of those relationships, interpreted as elements in a history of the present. It is more concerned with a type of rationality than with daily experience: Apollo rather than Hera. Other books would be required to bring the story up to the present, to describe resistance to these developments, or to analyze the importance of the worlds out of which these reform schemes emerged and to which they ultimately returned (albeit in ways that remain devilishly hard to evaluate).

There is a consensus among historians that the period of 1940–1945 constitutes the chrysalis of the present French state, initiating an accelerated period of change in French society. The contrast between Vichy's ruralist, traditionalist propaganda and its introduction of a technocratic vision and institutions to implement that vision, should no longer seem paradoxical. Following France's stunning military defeat in 1940, amid penury, disorganization, rampant intrigue, and conflict, a new technical elite finally achieved an enduring structural role in the French state. The scarcity of basic goods, the destruction of the infrastructure, and most importantly the labor and industrial demands of the Germans, who were directly interested in imposing a more efficient, productive, and predictable organization on the French economy, all combined to facilitate the forced introduction of a form of directed economy and society. Massive industrial reorganization headed the agenda. Each sector of industry was assigned a Comité d'Organisation endowed with vast powers, composed of major industrialists and technicans under the banner of apoliticism and the pressing needs of the nation.[2]

The 1942 *Plan d'Equipement National* contained a comprehensive conception of "equipment" (one of those key symbols which is difficult to translate) amounting to the sum of social activity. Equipment included everything that was not a *don gratuit* of the soil, subsoil, or climate: "It is the work of each day and the country as a whole." While the notion of equipment contained in the *Plan* was still far from realizable in 1942, it nonetheless announced a powerful, technological literalization and expansion of a much older concept. The basic outlines of the Vichy technocrats' understanding of the national territory as a space on which equipment was rationally and efficiently distributed were incorporated by De Gaulle's technical advisors both during and after the war. Richard Kuisel argues that despite obvious, passionate, and deep political differences, Vichy and the Resistance shared certain assumptions: "Both sought a nationalist revival, social reconciliation, moral rehabilitation, a planned and more just economy and a dynamic state."[3] One could add a consensus on the need for a meritocratic elite above politics to direct the modernization process in the name of the public good.

A Modernist in Casablanca

In 1946, Michel Ecochard, an admirer of Le Corbusier endowed with previous urban planning experience in the Middle East, was named to direct Morocco's urbanism services. He wrote that Morocco, at the dawn of the twentieth century, consisted of less than five million beings, on a territory equivalent in size to France, who lived completely turned in upon themselves.[4] Ecochard's blithe attitude toward historical and ethnographic realities was not untypical of high modernism in architecture. History was imaginary; nineteenth-century European imperialism had ceased to exist. Ecochard saw instead Beings in a Territory.

The planning problem, as Ecochard saw it, was how to create a harmonious distribution of demographic and industrial elements throughout the territory. Repeating Le Corbusier's famous formula that to "renovate [aménager] the cities first you have to reorganize [aménager] the countryside," Ecochard proposed a national plan based on the decentralization of industry. He favored rural market centers and middle-sized cities as key tools for insuring a balance between economic development, demographic equilibrium, and political stability. Success lay in skillful planning, in that special combination of science and art implicit in the term "aménagement" (reorganize, renovate, clean-up, development), a second key symbol in the French discourse of reform. Following high modernist principles, Ecochard held that human needs were universal. He proceeded on the basis of a theoretical common denominator, ignoring variables of society, geography, culture, climate, and construction materials.[5] Perhaps inspired by Le Corbusier's *Obus* plans for Algiers, Ecochard proposed a linear extension of the existing industrial zone along the ocean, echoed by a strip of workers' housing running parallel to that zone but separated from it by some 800 meters. Ecochard advocated the mass production of housing units based on minimal universal needs; each consisted of two eight-by-eight meter rooms, a patio, and a W.C. The units could be extended indefinitely. He insisted that this *trame Ecochard* also provide for a fully developed social life, which amounted to pedestrian zones and schools. Plans were drawn for cities of 30,000 to 40,000, to be financed by the state and located outside Morocco's older cities.

Ecochard's plan was a failure; disproportionate industrial concentration in Casa continued to accelerate, as did the gap between coastal cities and the interior. Housing construction fell far short of the mark. Ecochard's efforts reinforced the spatial and social separation of Europeans, Moroccans, and Jews. Although a man of the left, Ecochard did not, in creating his plan, envisage Moroccan independence. His failure has been convincingly traced to his neglect, which bordered on contempt, of economic and political considerations. His refusal to acknowledge local practices should be added to the list.[6]

Environment: Aménagement, Equipement

In 1950, Claudius-Petit, Minister of Reconstruction and Urbanism, announced an ambitious *Plan National d'Aménagement du Territoire* establishing national norms through the specification of standards for equipment. During the 1950s a corpus of sociological, historical, and urban planning texts were transformed from journal articles and books into ministerial texts. The *quartier* was chosen as the sociological planning unit, and its architectural equivalent became the *plan-masse*. The *plan-masse*, the baseline form of the *grandes ensembles* (vast housing complexes built throughout France), was a technical transformation of a humanist interpretation of social life articulated by, among others, Robert Auzelle.[7] Using the language of the progressive Catholic circles around the journal *Economie et humanisme*, Auzelle argued that although much had been said about Man as Worker, the time had come to refine a humanist notion of Man as *Habitant*. Drawing on the latest advances in urban sociology, Auzelle's project sought to transform historical, sociological, and geographic insights into a method by which urbanists could combat what he identified as the central evolutionary danger facing modern society, *désagrégation*— literally "disaggregation."[8] To this end, he proposed a *Tableau récapitulatif des besoins des habitants du point de vue de l'Aménagement des Agglomérations* [Summary table of inhabitants' needs from the viewpoint of the development of urban areas]. Auzelle claimed to have overcome previous conceptions of urban organization: the sanitary orientation to the sun that had obsessed hygienists, the garden cities' reliance on the picturesque, and Beaux-Arts concern for formal grandeur and symmetrical axes. Although he cautioned against turning his theories into mechanically applied operational models, they lent themselves perfectly to that end. Auzelle's notion of *plan-masse* became an official state norm and form in 1958.

In 1959 the Minister of Construction published a technical program entitled *Grille des équipements nécessaires à un grand ensemble* [Grid of facilities needed for a major housing project], which established standards for the installation and equipment in a vast national housing stock under construction. Nothing here was startlingly new or innovative. The infrastructure of roads, health measures, water, electricity, lighting, gas, and telephone lines had already been established. The *Grille* supplemented these with a list of technical standards for the superstructure: schools; cultural and religious institutions; commercial, social, and sanitary institutions; sports; green spaces; administrative facilities; and parking. Although a technical program, the *grille d'équipement* was conceived equally as a social response to perceived inadequacies in previous housing. Delinquency and social dislocation, it was argued, could be overcome through *équipement*. The center of the *quartier* was defined as the site of the most equipment. Architects were assigned the task of creating an *image de la ville*. There was a total rejection of the organic city, which was composed, it was held, of unhealthy, inefficient, and uncontrollable accidents of history. In an important sense, the same view was held of social life. Once housing was considered as a generalized social and economic regulator, and once norms (cast as technical standards) were fixed by the state, the result was a technocratic articulation of a program for a society based on status rather than class. The impact of the national program was considerable: after 1960–61 it was integrated in all projects for organization of *zones d'habitation*. Its importance lay in its link to the unprecedented rate of construction and to the state's power to regulate this construction through an arsenal of laws. A remarkable consensus existed among professionals during the period from 1959 to 1968, when the greatest expansion occurred. No serious challenges were posed by professionals to the large, functionally-defined residential quarter, the necessity of regularized equipment, the specification of that equipment by experts, or its abstraction from local conditions.[9]

In the latest planning experiments, the *Villes Nouvelles,* French planners have turned away from the separation of work and domesticity and from their faith in the modernist architectural style, but not from their belief in norms or in the necessity of an environment scientifically regulated by experts. The goal was to construct semi-autonomous poles of attraction for the expected massive growth in population in the regions surrounding France's major metropolises. The initiative for the *Villes Nouvelles* represents one of the purest examples of the Fifth Republic's "voluntarism." Interdisciplinary terms of specialists, products of France's elite schools, working with the most up-to-date information, drafted plans aimed at achieving order and a nonsegregated social equilibrium. This massive effort represented a historically significant renewal of the positive discourse of urban life aimed at achieving a semi-autonomous combination of work, habitation, and leisure in a perfected environment.

This scale of operations was unprecedented. In the mid-1960s it was projected that by the year 2000, the population could approach five-to-six million people; each city would contain several hundred thousand inhabitants. The acquisition by the state of large plots of land, the coordination between adjacent communes, the linkages with regional transportation planning, and the implantation of industry all required a degree of planning and coordination far beyond what had been previously attempted. The challenge was as much administrative as urbanistic. The initiative started at the top with decisions made by the Prime Minister and passed on to the prefectures and elite teams of technical experts. The faith in form remained strong. In addition to including the latest technological and functional advances, the urbanism teams were directed to create a symbolism of urbanity and micro-spaces of sociability embodying the values of comfort, ease, and centrality. Perhaps, as the authors of the authoritative *Histoire de la France urbaine* coyly observe, the central limitation of the *Villes Nouvelles* was the myth of ecological determinism. Ambiguously echoing a long line of social reformers who will shortly be introduced in these pages, the authors conclude: "The material to be worked on is as much human behavior as the physical environment."[10]

The observation is coy because it is not clear whether the authors see the new towns as the end of an epoch or whether they are themselves calling for a new and improved post-modern Saint-Simon.

In his famous essay "The Painter of Modern Life," Charles Baudelaire presented one possible modern attitude toward modernity: "you have no right to despise the present." This dictum implies, at the very least, an anti-nostalgic attitude toward the modern world. Thus, while criticizing the banality, ugliness, and arrogance of Ecochard's boxes or the tracts of towers which have transfigured French post-urban domains is (with so much to validate it) an easy sport, it nonetheless opens the door on a variety of nostalgias. The current production leans either to celebrating the sociality of artisan communities, to lionizing bourgeois virtues, or to learning from Las Vegas, which, while no doubt satisfying to those who embrace and produce these images, offers little of substance to those who do not. Not despising the present by no means implies that the present is not, in many ways, despicable, but only that, as Baudelaire advised young writers, "Orgy is no longer the sister of inspiration." He recommends instead, though not without a certain irony, a substantial and regular diet. In 1868, Baudelaire wrote that tomorrow's achievements would arise from steady work "just as a readable writing style serves to enlighten and clear, and powerful thought allows one to write readably; for the time of bad writing is past."[11] One hundred and twenty years later, our perspective on the modern world is no doubt more tempered than Baudelaire's; in part for that reason our spleens are less full of bile and our prose is less poetic. Still, having no right to despise the present, we continue our work of writing its history.

Toward an Anthropology of Modernity

In "Norm and Form: The Stylistic Categories of Art History and Their Origins in Renaissance Ideals," Sir Ernst Gombrich argues that our modern periodization of styles—classic, romanesque, Gothic, Renaissance, mannerist, baroque, rococo, neoclassical and romantic—is both a symptom of and a mask for an underlying cultural crisis, the chasm that separates the classical and the nonclassical.[12] Gombrich demonstrates how the contemporary classification of historical styles derived from an evaluative position: one was either for or against the classical. Although the opponents of classicism were triumphant, and the debate lost its interest, the classificatory categories to which it gave rise remained in use. Much scholarly energy was then expended in seeking a scientific classification of form. Some historians sought universal morphological principles as the means to unify and ground the burgeoning historicist catalogue of difference. Others emphasized a plural unity within each of a multiplicity of cultural or historical periods; each era had its own internally coherent norm(s) and form(s). The discursive field opened by these debates is one element of what has come to be known as modernity.

In *The Order of Things* Michel Foucault employed an opposition of the classical and the nonclassical to interpret profound realignments in the discursive field of the human sciences. Modernity, he argued, emerged against the background of a cultural order in which the medium of representations made the project of ordering all things on a common table a coherent one. According to this history, the order of representations was shattered by the appearance of Man—that being who is both the subject and object of his own knowledge—marking one of those dramatic and unexplained ruptures that Foucault privileged during one period of his work. The unified medium lost its transparency, resulting in an unprecedented proliferation of human sciences. The age of anthropology dawned, characterized by the seemingly endless, if productive, succession of attempts to (re)discover a medium through which Man could grasp his own being. Foucault later complicated his understanding of modernity; he identified a field of power relations composed of both discursive and nondiscursive practices, which he called bio-technico-political. In English, welfare is a better term. Foucault was in the process of adding an analysis of welfare to Marx's analysis of capitalism and Weber's of bureaucracy, forming a third leg of modernity, when he died. This book continues the exploration, in its own way, of some of the contours of modern power and knowledge Foucault had begun to map. It is greatly indebted to his achievements but attempts to see him partially from the outside (outsides today seem only partial), from across the Atlantic, as one in a line of modern French social thinkers.

The debates about modernity are endless: since it has no essence, and refers to so many diverse things, it seems futile— or simply part of the modernizing process—to worry extensively about abstract definitions. It would seem more heuristic and more ethnographic, to explore how the term has been understood and used by its self-proclaimed practitioners. Other recent studies of modernity have masterfully dissected art, philosophy, science, politics, or aspects of the social history of daily life—obviously essential elements in an understanding of the contemporary world.[13] The focus of this book, however, is the middle ground between high culture or science and ordinary life (itself a typically modern distinction). It centers on a type of actor who, to quote one of the book's main protagonists, Hubert Lyautey (governor-general of Morocco from 1912 to 1925), can be appropriately called a "technician of general ideas." These men (for they are all men in this account) were the inventors and practitioners of one subset of the practices, discourses, and symbols of "social modernity," a term they often employed.

Most broadly, this book is about the emergence of certain practices of reason in France. In order to understand them I begin with the standard ethnographic assumption that we can analyze reason in the same general way we approach other ethnographic objects, i.e., as a set of practices bearing complex relations with a congeries of symbols. More specifically, it is about fields of knowledge (hygienic, statistical, biological, geographic, and social); about forms (architectural and urbanistic); about social technologies of pacification (disciplinary and welfare); about cities as social laboratories (royal, industrial, colonial, and socialist); about new social spaces (liberal disciplinary spaces, agglomerations, and new towns). In each of these domains, I describe the diverse constructions of norms and the search for forms adequate to understand and to regulate what came to be known as modern society.

It is important to clarify what is meant by norms. Clearly there has always been patterned behavior among human beings, as well as some type of indigenous reflection on that patterning. However, something new coalesced during the tumultuous period of change in Europe's demography, politics, social arrangements, economies, and philosophies that occurred at the end of the Enlightenment. Of course, philosophers had long proposed reform schemes; however, such "perfectionist" projects as Leibnitz's proposals for a universal language posited a definite point of completion. Georges Canguilhem isolates the beginnings of a modern type of normalization, one that was more dynamic, restless, and expansive, in medical institutions: specifically, he sees an Austrian imperial health commission of 1753 and its *sanitäts-normative* act covering medicine, veterinary, pharmacological, surgical, statistical, and demographic concerns, as paradigmatic. Not without a certain irony, Canguilhem identifies a normative revolution: "Between 1759, the date of the first appearance of the word *normal,* and 1834, the date of the first appearance of the word *normalized,* a normative class conquered the power to identify the function of social norms with its own uses and its own determination of content."[14] Regardless of who deserves the laurels for originality, something new and powerful was emerging on the historical scene.

The most general value in the name of which modern normalizing efforts have been justified is the welfare of the population. The project of understanding and regulating population has a long history, but it received a new impetus in the nineteenth century when the control of population was linked with the modern understanding of society. This link was provided by the new science of biology. The metaphoric transfer of concepts from a newly emergent physiology—function, hierarchy, and norm—to the social realm presented many conceptual and practical challenges for those seeking to intervene in and improve society. The search for a spatial localization of functions in society, similar to that found in the body, was a particularly bedeviling, if fertile, problem.

Although today we more or less accept "society" as a quasi-natural or universal term, in fact it began to acquire its current meaning in France only during the early decades of the nineteenth century. An ethnographic approach to society as the product of historical practices combining truth and power consists of identifying society as a cultural object, specifying those authorized to make truth claims about it and those practices and symbols which localized, regulated, and represented that new reality spatially (form is equally a cultural object). The problem that social thinkers, reformers, architects, engineers, and emperors posed for themselves was one of bringing both norms and forms into a common frame that would produce a healthy, efficient, and productive social order.

In the course of the nineteenth century, society slowly became to be seen as an object sui generis, with its own laws, its own science, and eventually its own arts of government. If an individual's action was a function not of his moral character, as liberals believed, but rather of his place within a social whole, then it made little sense to try to reform the individual separate from the social milieu within which his actions were formed and normed. The rise of "the social question" at the end of the nineteenth century in France was the correlate of the crisis of philanthropic reform and its associated moralizing, disciplinary technology (hailed by the 1869 strikes at model factory towns such as Le Creusot and Mulhouse), as well as of the purportedly liberal economic and social system in which they were embedded (symbolized by the government's crushing military defeat by the Prussians in 1870 and by the Commune in 1871). During the last two decades of the nineteenth century, a range of reform groups extending from Social Catholics to certain socialist factions attempted to map antagonistic classes onto a common space regulated by scientifically derived social norms. Charles Gide, one of the leaders of the social economy movement, captured this shift nicely in the image of workers washing up after work at a factory, changing out of their work clothes, and walking down the street identified not as a class but simply as men. Bringing such a world into existence required recasting century-long practices and assumptions about the nature of the individual, the state, science, space, and society. By the end of the century in France, social interdependence became the guiding symbol for a range of political, legal, and scientific discourses spanning the center of the political spectrum. Discursively, society no longer had an exterior.

Enter urbanism. Between 1899 and 1909, a group of Ecole des Beaux-Arts trained, prize-winning architects, of whom Tony Garnier is the most famous, articulated the French variant of modern urbanism. The secondary literature has stressed either Garnier's relation to the utopian socialist tradition of Cabet and Fourier or his role as a precursor of architectural modernism. I interpret Garnier's plan (read in the context of his cohort of prize-winning architects) as an urban parallel to Bentham's *Panopticon*. Foucault did not see the Panopticon as a Weberian ideal type, i.e., as the sociologist's generalized abstraction of various currents of empirical activity of its age; rather he emphasized an alternative use of such plans as strategic exemplars. To wit, Foucault suggested finding real schemas and following out their strategic uses—the transformations as well as the resistances they provoked—as a means of illuminating not a whole age but rather its particular nuclei of knowledge and power. The Panopticon was not the invention of the historian, although the interpretive importance given to it definitely was. In a like manner, Garnier's encapsulation of the principles of urbanism can serve as a grid of intelligibility, this time for modern welfare society. Its aim was not the efficient discipline of individuals, but the transformation of the socio-natural milieu into a healthy and peaceful environment. Urbanism's synthesis of historical and natural elements into an object—the planned city as a regulator of modern society—can be seen as one of the most complete examples of modernity. This synthesis was exemplary in its demonstration of man's ability to exploit, in a comprehensive functional form and in the name of the general welfare of the population, previously naturalized elements (geography, demography, and hygiene) as subjects of pragmatic knowledge; it was exemplary as well in its awareness of history (of monuments, styles, and cultures) as the ground on which society's future form could be legitimized. It earnestly embraced technological change. This stage in modernization, this attempt to balance technology with historical and natural givens, can be called, albeit clumsily, techno-cosmopolitanism.

Its triumph was provisional. The continuing search for more scientifically, spatially, and stylistically comprehensive means by which to represent and regulate a society devoted to efficiency, production, and the welfare of its population led to a second series of dissolutions and transformations. This second step, accelerated after the First World War, entailed the transformation of the object to be worked on from a historico-natural milieu into a socio-technical one. This new field could be called not simply *modern* but *middling modernist*. Once again, the book's focus is not on "high culture" nor the practices of everyday life, but on a middle ground where social technicians were articulating a normative, or middling, modernism. In their discourses, society became its own referent, to be worked on by means of technical procedures which were becoming the authoritative arbiters of what counted as socially real. Discursively, both norms and forms were becoming increasingly autonomous— freed from previous historical and natural constraints, defined by their own operations, and claiming universal status. This universalism, in turn, formed the ground of legitimacy for bypassing a political participation seen as short-sighted, self-interested, and destructive of the public good.

Pathos and Logos

The invention and coordination of, and experimentation with, spatial and social forms in the last two centuries has been characterized by an internationalization of social science and by reform, as well as by technology, colonization, and nationalism. This account, however, focuses only on the French variant. Its unit of analysis is not the nation, people, or culture, and even less some perduring "Frenchness." Rather, I attempt in this study to delineate the elements of one specific constellation of thought, action, and passion. The French historian of the life sciences Georges Canguilhem identifies a distinctively French concern (almost an obsession) in nineteenth-century life sciences: the belief that living beings and their milieux have no predestined harmony but are fated to struggle, through a disciplined and relentless effort of will, to adapt to constantly changing circumstances.[15] Canguilhem characterizes this situation as one of "pathos." This term, derived from the Greek word for passion, entered the French language during the sixteenth century as both a theatrical and a medical term. For the anthropologist, pathos is a key symbol. It became a cultural metaphor, as it migrated from its original site into other fields. The technical uncoupling of living organism and milieu could equally well have been interpreted (and was elsewhere) as "liberating," "tragic," "heroic," or "challenging." In France, the technicians of general ideas anxiously fluctuated between personal bitterness about the crisis of French institutions and culture and an unshaken faith in positive science. Although blocked in their efforts time after time after time, reformers like Lyautey (or thinkers like Foucault) railed venemously against their compatriots and against French society; however, they never took the path leading to *The Dialectic of Enlightenment* or what it was written to condemn. Borrowing a term from another ambitious German historian of philosophy and interpreter of the modern age, Hans Blumenberg, one might gloss this French ethos as one of "missionary and didactic pathos."[16] The understanding of social reality which yielded the pathos—its rejection of metaphysical solutions and the sense that society had no outside, but only margins—also produced a sense that there was no choice but to reform it. One had no right to despise the present; one had no place from which to despise the present.

Finally, there is the issue of the book's unorthodox form: *caveat lector*. While patience is a virtue, experimentation per se is not. However, as the book is not the study of a particular age, nor individual, nor field, nor class, nor region, nor city, nor nation, nor artistic movement, nor philosophy, very few models existed to aid the writer and now the reader. The writing itself constituted an experimental search for norms and forms appropriate to the conjuncture. A large roster of seemingly diverse topics are treated serially; their (partial) interconnections are made explicit only gradually. While the whole may seem too complex, the parts may seem too simple: readers may perhaps be frustrated when they encounter their own specializations. I hope they will be informed (and thereby compensated) when encountering the specialties of others. Copious illustrations might seem to be in order; after much spirited debate and reflection, I have decided to follow Hannah Arendt's dictum that "thinking is about the invisible."[17]

The narrative is given some unity by a roughly chronological progression of chapters. Breakdowns and irruptive events (epidemics, wars, strikes, and invasions) provided contingent but imperative catalysts (1832, 1869–71, World War I, and World War II) for shifts in constellations of discourses and practices. Throughout the book such events are used as narrative devices (and analytic tools) to highlight and reveal the successive coagulations of power and knowledge which form the heart of the chronicle. Thus, for example, the great cholera epidemic of 1832 dissolved received understanding in a number of different aspects of French thought and society, thus opening up a space for a new problematic. Through cholera's devastating ease of evasion of Paris' public health defenses, it brought central aspects of previous medical understanding crumbling down. Although the state and its medical authorities failed to stem the epidemic's ravages, they did succeed in accomplishing other significant things. Most importantly, medical commissions produced a detailed statistical analysis of the relationships of social class, housing, and disease in the Parisian population. The beginnings of a modern understanding of society as a historical/natural whole, as well as the beginnings of society as a target of state intervention—what has been called "the social"—can plausibly be situated at this historical conjuncture. It was on the level of knowledge, of a more precise and powerful analysis of milieu, with *conditions de vie* blending biological and social variables, that the cholera epidemic not only provided a clear impetus for change, but opened the way for new scientific discourses, new administrative practices, and new conceptions of social order, and hence ushered in a long period of experimentation with spatial/scientific/social technologies.

The book's narrative turns in part around a series of individuals—Hubert Lyautey (aristocratic dandy, military man, and colonialist), Joseph-Simon Gallieni (bourgeois, Republican, and pacifier), Emile Cheysson (engineer, statistician and philanthropic technician), Tony Garnier (provincial, urbanist, and socialist), Maurice Halbwachs (specific intellectual and sociologist), and Henri Sellier (socialist reformer and administrative technician). These actors are introduced not because they were the geniuses of their respective epochs (both terms, genius and epoch, are appropriately foreign to anthropological analysis), nor because they were typical of their culture (new understandings of "type" and "culture" emerged as both theoretical and practical objects through their efforts), but because each embodied and articulated, in diverse and often contradictory ways, an essential dimension of the French practice and ethos of social modernity. These men were neither heroes nor villains nor anonymous citizens. They were pragmatic technicians seeking to find scientific and practical solutions to public problems in times of crisis: hence they qualify as intellectuals. They might be called *specific intellectuals;* or, if one defines technocrats as those who direct the technicians, then these men are the forerunners of the technocratic society which emerged in France after the Second World War.[18]

This book could be called an ethnography of French pragmatic philosophical anthropology; or, less awkwardly, borrowing Pierre Bourdieu's felicitous expression, an example of "fieldwork in philosophy."[19] However, as we are arguably in a post-philosophic age, perhaps it is best described simply as a contribution to the emerging understanding of modernity.

The Crisis of Representations:
From Man to Milieux

In a treatise written in 1682, a certain Alexandre Le Maître, a French Protestant engineer working for the Prussians, proposed a particularly crystalline condensation of the elements of classical space.[1] Le Maître placed the capital of a hypothetical kingdom at the geometric center of a circular territory. All that moved—and circulation was an absolutely central concept and symbol in the Classical Age—was obliged to pass through the capital, where the sovereign could profit from, learn from, and regulate it. Le Maître's scheme was never implemented, although the spatial linkage of economy, society, and power was destined for a long career. Such utopian schemas for regulating a functionally organized whole, once unmoored from the metaphysics of representation, would provide elements and techniques for later non-utopian schemas of power, knowledge, society, and space.[2]

For Louis XIV and his court, appearance was being. Louis sought to build and run a court in which the complete ordering of life, the orchestrated *mise-en-scène* of every single gesture at court, and the correct public presentation of the most minute and what would later seem to be intimate acts, all aimed at the display of an elaborate hierarchy of relations. This hierarchy consisted of, was constructed from, and depended on the possibility of correct representations, of palpable form. The sovereign dream was of a realm in which, in every gesture, the order of the kingdom and the glory of the sovereign would be enacted: an endless opera.[3]

As the economy-minded Colbert discovered to his chagrin, this opera was a great deal more than a means of impoverishing the aristocracy. Louis, having constructed in his court the greatest spectacle of the century, believed himself to be its greatest actor. One of the absolutely essential skills of the king and of the aristocracy—in addition to hunting and rhetorical skills learned from Cicero—was dancing. Dance, it was held, modeled all of the body's movements and displayed them to the greatest effect. Every gesture, every movement, and every step was measured and studiously composed. Dancing, more than an adornment, was performed with high seriousness; it was a *fonction d'état* to which the court's aristocrats assiduously devoted several hours each day. These courtly dances were enactments of complex hierarchical status relations. Each player had his or her role, with its prescribed and proscribed moves. The elaborate ballets, adroitly or clumsily performed, in which these relations were danced paralleled the nobility's rhythms of daily life at court, itself only a slightly looser choreographic display of order.

Jean-Jacques Rousseau, in his *Lettre sur la musique française,* indicted the music played at court: its tones, its harmonies, and its pacing. In the name of the authenticity and integrity of the person, of social relations, and of the human heart, Rousseau railed against the baroque play of appearance. The Revolution put an end to sovereignty; Rousseau, as Foucault ironizes, hailed the modern age of individuality and social inclusion for all.[4]

Almost Modern: The Society for the Observation of Man

All three terms—Man, observation, and society—were in the process of changing meanings in the long threshold between the classical age and modern times (arguably between the French Revolution and the 1830s, although dates differ from country to country and domain to domain). Thus, Foucault's claim that there was a time "when the world, its order and human beings existed, but man did not," while occasioning polemics, does not differ substantially from the analyses of other scholars of the period.[5] Modernity, the era of Man, began when representations ceased to provide a reliable grid for the knowledge of things. Modernity was not distinguished by the attempt to study man with objective methods—such projects had already a long history—nor by the attempt to achieve clear and distinct knowledge through analysis of the subject, but "rather [by] the constitution of an empirico-transcendental doublet called man. Man appears as an object of knowledge and as a subject that knows."[6] How he sought to know the social world and himself as a social being capable of reform is central to this book.

What was meant by *société* was changing as well. When the court used the term, they meant "high society" in a status sense. (Rousseau often, if not exclusively, used it in a denigrating manner to refer to the same people.) Liberal economists employed the term for freely-entered-into contractual arrangements, for associations. The modern sense of society as a "whole way of life," to use Raymond Williams deceptively simple definition, was taking shape as well during this period.[7] What was meant by "a whole way of life," as well as how one might observe it, describe it, and finally improve it, constitutes another major theme of this book and of modernity as well.

In many ways the Society for the Observation of Man hovered between Enlightenment projects (and enthusiasm) for global understanding and their more troubled modern transformations. A discussion of its projects and activities serves to introduce aspects of the crucial themes of research, reform, and contingency. The Society is of interest on a number of levels. Epistemologically, Foucault identifies the Idéologues as occupying a special transitional place between the Age of Representations and the modern sciences of Man. More ominously, George Stocking has pointed to Georges Cuvier's famous research protocol for the comparative study of human physical structures as crossing another threshold of modernity, one leading toward later racist developments in nineteenth-century social science, i.e., scientific defense of fixed racial hierarchies. Recent studies have underscored the Society's historical significance as a forerunner of modern, fieldwork-oriented ethnography: the comprehensiveness of the descriptive project of other peoples through the systematic collection of social facts, as well as spatial and visual incorporation of those facts in scientific and pedagogic anthropological museums. The hopes for, dangers and partial successes of, and constantly renewed promises for the imminent construction of an empirical human science as the guide to understanding and improving first humanity, then society—"missionary and didactic pathos"—will appear in different transformations time and time again in this book.

The Société des Observateurs de l'Homme was founded during the first months of the Napoleonic period, in December 1799, with an aim typical of the Enlightenment in its scope and hopefulness: to study man's moral, physical, and intellectual existence so as to accelerate human progress and increase human happiness. Its motto was "Know thyself." The Société's approach to such knowledge—its insistence on avoiding the "spirit of system" through the gathering of facts based on observation and comparison—while itself not radically new, was nonetheless, we can now see, an indication of changes brewing at the time. Among its members were distinguished scientists and philosophers; biologists (Cuvier, Lamarck, Jussieu, and Geoffroy Saint-Hilaire); physicians (Cabanis and Pinel); explorers (Bougainville); and linguists and philosophers (Destutt de Tracy and Joseph-Marie de Gérando). Less illustrious members included its founder, Louis-François Jauffret (1770–1850), a naturalist and author of children's books. The Société's life span was a short four years. After Napoleon turned against the group, whom he dubbed the "Idéologues," and eliminated their stronghold at the Institut de France, the Classe des Sciences Morales et Politiques, the Société's days were numbered. Still, it constituted a significant incandescent moment, hovering on and illuminating one of many thresholds between the Enlightenment and modernity.[8]

The Société's projects—to study the childhood of a deaf mute, a Chinese man in a Parisian hospital, and the influences of different professions on the characters of those who follow them—resonate with the ring of the Enlightenment. The Idéologue program called for unifying the sciences of man and nature within a common epistemology based on the rectification of language. The program was a totalizing one that attempted to encompass all knowledge. Destutt de Tracy classified his program as part of a zoology with man at its center. The dream of scientific unity, under the banner of a purified and transparent language and a naturalist method, flared brightly one last time. The gap between this project and its fulfillment was much larger, and the time in which to accomplish it much shorter, than any of these optimistic men of science suspected when they put it forward with such enthusiasm.[9]

In March 1800 a certain Captain Nicolas Baudin (1754–1803), already a veteran of several scientific voyages, proposed to the Institut de France a project for a grandiose naturalist mission to the South Seas. Napoleon, himself a member of the Classe des Sciences Mathématiques et Physiques, approved a scaled-down version of the expedition. The Institut turned to the Société des Observateurs de l'Homme for aid in formulating its scientific agenda. Jauffret exuberantly welcomed the possibility of hailing "a new age in the intellectual history of mankind." The mission itself was rather a disaster, with the scientists bickering among themselves and with the crew, and with disease and rough seas contributing to a less than epochal accomplishment.

The Société's enduring achievements lie in its preparation of two programmatic memoirs drafted to guide the research of the ill-fated voyage: Joseph Marie de Gérando (1772–1842), recently returned from exile and recognized by the Institut for his work on signs, wrote *Considerations on the Methods to Follow in the Observation of Savage Peoples* and Georges Cuvier (1769–1832) wrote *An Instructive Note on the Researches to be Carried Out Relative to the Anatomical Differences Between the Diverse Races of Man.* De Gérando, echoing Rousseau's Second Discourse but proposing an empirical solution, opened his considerations by linking the egoism of the age to the general lack of serious attention to what man really is. As nature is the true master, he argued, the path to understanding is not through the construction of philosophical systems but through methodical observation. Savages, subject to fewer modifying influences, offered an excellent field for such observations. "The philosophic traveller, sailing to the ends of the earth, is in fact travelling in time;

he is exploring the past; every step he makes is the passage of an age."[10] If the pleasures of scientific understanding were not themselves sufficient to justify the enterprise, then the added joy, the "high feelings of philanthropy," of bringing progress and enlightenment to these benighted savages, themselves full members of universal society albeit in an inferior state, should suffice.

De Gérando's peroration urged the voyagers to spread Europe's enlightenment, not its passions, wars, vices, slavery, and egotism. He listed seven categories of faults that had flawed previous descriptions of savage peoples, ranging from incomplete observations, due to insufficient amount of time spent among the people, to hasty generalizations drawn from one atypical individual, to dubious analogies with Europe's customs, to the root failing: the lack of linguistic fluency. To remedy these shortcomings, de Gérando, following Idéologue procedures, outlined a systematic methodology for learning native languages, methodically moving from the simplest gestures to the most complex ideas. Language fluency would bring knowledge and community: "It is by learning their language that we shall become their fellow citizens."[11] The naiveté as well as the generosity of spirit involved in this program shine forth.[12]

De Gérando did not have a concept of society as prior to and constitutive of individuals. His method progressed from the physical environment, through the body, through sensations, and up to moral ideas; climate, food, physical strength, sleep, needs, cannibalism, clothes, illness, imbecility, physical education, and longevity; ideas of immortality and the like; attention, memory, foresight, reflection, reflective needs, and variety; the authority of the father, kinship and fraternity, women, modesty, love, marriage, divorce and polygamy, and the moral education of children; internal political relations, magistrates, external political relations, war, military art, arms, courage, peace, alliance, strangers, and hospitality; civil relations, property, and crime; economic relations, industry, domestication of animals, nomadism, tools, commerce, and amusement; population; moral and religious relations, virtues, affections, friendships, patriotism, religious ceremonies, priests, temples, idols,

tombs, and traditions. De Gérando thought it highly desirable
to bring back to France representative savages, one of each sex
and age—best of all, a whole family, an image of society in
miniature. Should the savages object, as was to be expected, the
"illustrious messengers of philosophy, peaceful heroes" should
regale them with accounts of the precious treasures of enlightenment. Even without such a trophy, the travelers should con-
sole themselves during the hardship they were sure to endure
with the thought of increased understanding, glory, and trade
for France, and of perhaps civilizing whole nations for
humanity.

The linked and complementary goals of universal enlightenment and universal commerce contained no space of opacity.[13]
De Gérando was no cultural relativist but a universalist preach-
ing progress which, with the aid of science, the whole species
might well attain. The philosophical presuppositions of the
Idéologues posited a common set of human capacities and responses. Human history led through stages to an increasing
perfection. Empirical investigation could specify details but not
really discover anything new about the overall pattern. Differences stemmed from alterable environmental conditions and
could be changed.

Georges Cuvier, in his "Notes instructives sur les recherches
à faire relativement aux différences anatomiques des diverses
races d'hommes," argued that the first steps in understanding
racial differences had barely yet been taken; in fact, during the
eighteenth century not a single detailed comparison of Negro
and white skeletons had been conducted. The possibility for
scientific comparison emerged only with the geometric method
of measuring skulls invented by Camper, which demonstrated
to Cuvier's satisfaction the physical differences among races.
The moral, intellectual, and artistic consequences of this diversity were less well known. Scientific progress required a disciplined collection of specimens. Anticipating that sailors might
view the preservation of skulls as barbaric, Cuvier advised the
captain to counter objections through a reasoned defense of
the usefulness of such practices to the advancement of science.
Cuvier acknowledged that exact description and the correct
preservation of remains might have to suffice. His research

protocol specified that portraits of all subjects should be painted in the same position, with their hair combed in the same manner, so as to reveal the foreheads as much as possible. All disfiguration, decoration, and jewelry should be ignored. Cuvier reluctantly admitted that systematic portraiture had its value, but longed for a methodical collection, especially of skulls, representing the fullest range of ages, sexes, and so on.

Cuvier and de Gérando went their separate ways. By 1817, after a series of bitter intellectual and institutional battles with Geoffroy Saint-Hilaire, Cuvier turned to deterministic racial explanations of levels of civilization, opening the way, as George Stocking indicates, for some of the less enlightened trends of the nineteenth century. The epistemological basis of Cuvier's conception of species as fixed and invariable was his firm belief that Buffon was wrong—nature was not composed of individuals upon whom classification was imposed, but rather of a series of "types." In the following decades, as we shall see shortly, the status of "types" became the focus of passionate debates about truth and value in both statistics and architecture. Symptomatically, de Gérando shifted his interests to social philanthropy, transferring the fruits of his pioneering work with savages to understanding and aiding those other others, the poor.[14]

Social Life: Spaces and Functions

Approaches to a modern understanding of society have vacillated between two poles: one has sought to capture man's nature through analyzing underlying, law-like universal mechanisms; the other has sought historical or interpretive methods adequate to the notion that knowledge was produced by men formed by certain historical, social, or economic conditions—that understanding and particularity were linked, that knowledge had a history, and that history was the means by which empirical understanding could be given adequate form. The sciences of man in the nineteenth and twentieth centuries are a litany of attempts to perfect one or the other of these approaches or, more ambitiously, to combine them in a grander synthesis. It was in the life sciences that this discursive field was first articulated.

A new attention to the terms function and hierarchy provided the transition from natural history as understood in the Classical Age to biology in its modern sense. The meanings of these terms changed as they moved from the conceptual field of physiology from which they derived, and were appropriated by social thinkers such as Saint-Simon in his sociology of industrial/scientific society, or by conservative thinkers like Lamennais, who worried about the disruption of historically grounded social bonds. Although each position was distinct, particularly in the beginning of the century, neither was stable; over time exchanges between and intertwining of the understanding of society as an organism to be modified and of society as a history to be interpreted became increasingly complex. By mid-century, thinkers on both the Social Catholic right and the non-revolutionary left concurred that norms of health could be objectively known; both agreed that the conditions of social existence constituted an object capable of pathology and hence of mortality. Disputes over specifying the normal and the pathological served to reinforce the reality of social self-understanding and reform in terms of norms.

Systematizing the work of Jussieu, Vicq d'Azyr, and Lamarck, Bichat defined physiology's task as the determination of the role of organs in the functioning of the general life system. Bichat maintained that the concepts developed in physics and chemistry to analyze matter were inappropriate for physiology, a science of living beings. He argued the existence of a qualitative change, a threshold in nature between living and inert systems.[15] His approach posed new questions about the status of life systems; all organs were not equally fundamental to life. The task of the science of comparative anatomy was to uncover the vital hierarchy of functions. This attention to the whole, to functions, and to life, however, revealed a tension in Bichat's physiology, "an opposition between the organs in general, which are spatial, solid, directly or indirectly visible and the functions which are not perceptible but determine as though from below the arrangement of what we do perceive."[16]

When the concepts of physiology were metaphorically transferred to the social realm, the search began for a spatial localization of functions. Georges Canguilhem argues that this search was particularly problematic when it came to the overall regulative function.[17] In the early decades of the nineteenth century, this quest was in its infancy. Utopian socialists sought to remake society anew from the ground of human nature; conservative thinkers sought to identify and strengthen those social bonds they interpreted as essential to stable relations of authority. Later in the century, more pragmatic experiments, whose aim was less to critique existing institutions—the distinctive characteristic of utopias—than to invent new social forms, were undertaken by a variety of reformers.[18] Before turning to these laboratories of social modernity, we must trace some of the scientific and practical developments which opened the way for "society" to become an object upon which experiments could be performed.

Natural Social History

After decades of political upheaval, social reformers at the center of the political spectrum saw the need to rethink and to strengthen social bonds. Not surprisingly, after the Revolution and Napoleon's reign, the first third of the nineteenth century was characterized by a massive outpouring of thought about continuity in human society.[19] Conservatives and reactionaries agreed that the defining characteristic of legitimate order was hierarchy. The only means to defend liberty against the social decomposition brought about by the twin modern perils—the State and egalitarianism—was the preservation of natural social differences in a functional hierarchy. The political liberty achieved by the French Revolution was a dangerous illusion. True liberty could not be decreed; it was rooted in tradition, confirmed through history, and authorized by God. Order and meaning had a transcendental source.

Conservatives and reactionaries like Félicité de Lamennais (1782–1854) and Louis de Bonald (1754–1840) agreed on the primacy of the social over the individual; both strongly opposed liberal contractualism. For them, social relations were the product of long-term historical processes. The whole determined the individual parts and these parts took their meanings only from their places in a social whole. Society was a quasi-organic being with its own laws, its own time, and its own bonds: "No government, no police, no order would be possible if men were not previously united by ties binding them in a state of society, that is, by shared beliefs conceived in reference to the idea of duty."[20] These imperatives, *relative à l'éternité*, were constants; only the content of political or civil society changed historically.

Lamennais was more modern than theocrats like de Bonald, who clung to a vision .of an archaic rural order, though modified by decentralized industrialization. While deeply opposed to both the revolution and Bonaparte, Lamennais nonetheless accepted the inevitability of industry and sought to control its consequences. He argued that a moral authority separate from the state was required for a healthy society; religion was the fundamental ground of society, its principle was order. In his *Religion and its Relations with the Political and Civil Order* (1826), Lamennais argued for the reestablishment of legal autonomy for the Church. Later he generalized this principle of the separation of spheres, formulating a hybrid form of liberalism: freedom from state control for social groups but not for individuals. He advocated a decentralized federalism based on the right to self-administration. Without the right of association, democracy became absolute despotism. Only intermediary bodies could curb the twin dangers facing France: individualization and totalization. Lamennais defended more than the rights of the Church. In his *Livre du peuple,* he pleaded for the workers' right to form associations as moral and social bulwarks against the brutal divisive energies certain to be unleashed in the coming industrial age. However, like those who led the Social Catholic movement later in the century, Lamennais discovered that Rome was less than enthusiastic about social reform. Still, he is important for having identified the autonomy of the social sphere as the quasi-natural basis for healthy order and for citing the importance of history as the locus of social legitimation for the coming industrial age.

Saint-Simon: Organized Functional Hierarchy

Although Enlightenment philosophers did not consider all men to be identical, they did construct social and political systems to strengthen political equality. Saint-Simon, and many others in the early nineteenth century, started with an emphasis on social difference and sought to make it a principle and a virtue.[21] A parallel counter-reaction against the primacy of reason emerged in many different forms during the first decades of the nineteenth century. Philosophers, reformers, and theologians argued for a view of humanity that gave a larger place to history, passions, aptitudes, and moral concerns. Saint-Simon proclaimed his abhorrence of all violent revolution, and searched instead for the means to a natural social order, one that would be hierarchical, harmonious, and voluntarily accepted because of its mutual benefits. France's problem, he held, was not that there were class differences but only that those differences were arbitrary. Therefore, the task was to discover a way to rebuild society starting from a solid starting point: mankind's natural capacities. By so doing, social differentiation would be peacefully accepted by all classes: the old Platonic dream of justice modernized. The social philosopher was to coordinate differences into a harmonious whole that would allow men to exercise their capacities to the fullest. The hierarchical organization of the social body and the healthy distribution of functions would produce a thriving totality within which each individual could happily and willingly find his place.

History for Saint-Simon had a telos: industrial, scientific society. In industrial society class conflict would disappear, but not the classes themselves. Classes would find their natural places, and their accidental attributes, such as mutual antagonism and misery, would wither away like the vestigial organs of Lamarckian zoology. The view that humans seek roles for which they are naturally suited was one Saint-Simon shared with contemporary conservative philosophers. However, what the theocrats defended as a religiously sanctioned order, Saint-Simon sought to ground in the latest advances of science. (Saint-Simon had his own religious schema and eventually returned to Christianity, albeit in a highly distinctive form.) Social hierarchy, according to him, should observe Bichat's three basic capacities: intellectual, motor, and sensory. Saint-Simon translated these capacities into social functions: a scientific elite whose task was to uncover the positive laws regulating nature and provide guidelines for rational action; an industrial class—by far the largest—divided into two groups, the workers and the administrative elite, who would run the temporal affairs of society, placing heavy emphasis on large-scale public works projects and on conquering nature through engineering; the third group was comprised of artists, poets, and ethical-religious leaders, whose role gradually grew in importance for Saint-Simon, reaching the pinnacle of the social hierarchy in his last formulations, since they would provide the humanitarian love bringing otherwise atomistic and antagonistic individuals together in harmony. The high administration of society by industrialists would have the advantage of overcoming the confusing multiplication of spheres of authority. Administration and spiritual authority would be unified, and the competition between scientists, religious leaders, and artists thereby overcome.[22]

Saint-Simon's was one of the first proposals to glorify engineers (being half-scientific and half-industrial, they seemed a promising hybrid) and to give them control over administrative and legislative power. He proposed a three-chambered parliament. The Chamber of Inventions was to be a central planning agency composed of 200 engineers, 50 poets and literary inventors, 25 painters, 15 sculptors, and 10 musicians. Its task was to arrive at a master plan for public works, emphasizing circulation. The Chamber of Review, composed of pure scientists, was delegated the right to examine all projects passed by the Chamber of Inventions as well as to invent a new, rational public education system and new holidays (Men's, Women's, Manager's, Worker's, etc.). Finally, an executive body of industrialists lodged in a Chamber of Deputies was charged with coordinating and financing public works projects. Insurance companies and savings societies had already developed means of equitable distribution and participation without elaborate administrations; so, too, would the new society.

Saint-Simon envisioned a harmonious and apolitical, but hardly static, society. Through the conquest of nature the possibilities for expansion and welfare were literally endless: there were marshes to be drained, woods to be cleared, roads to be cut, rivers to be tamed, and canals to be planned. Nestled in fifty thousand acres of the most picturesque sites in the land, Saint-Simon planned gardens, each containing a museum of the region's natural and industrial products.[23] The vision of a pacified world achieved through the scientific arrangement of society and the domination of nature, and crowned in a museum, is one we will encounter again. Indeed, Saint-Simonianism was to have a lasting effect; his ideas about banking, credit, and the financing of great public works (the railroads and the Suez Canal) took hold especially in the business world, and particularly among Second Empire industrialists.[24] However, rather more immediately, bio-social conditions of a very empirical sort became extremely problematic for theorists, administrators, and inhabitants alike during the cholera epidemic of 1832, to which we now turn.

The Cholera Epidemic of 1832: The Breakdown of Representation and the Appearance of Norms

The cholera epidemic of 1832, by evading Paris' public health defenses with devastating ease, and by its choice of victims, brought important aspects of previous medical understanding crumbling down and set the stage for a new understanding of social conditions. During the epidemic, sectors of the elite began to see the inadequacy of the discourses and practices of elements of the Classical order. The search for new explanations of pathology were literally forced on the administration. Although the state and its medical authorities totally failed in stemming the epidemic's ravages, the two did succeed in doing other important things. Most relevant to our discussion, medical commissions produced a detailed statistical analysis of the relations of society and disease among the Parisian population. This linkage of power and knowledge proved extraordinarily potent. These insights opened the way for new scientific discourses, new administrative practices, and new conceptions of social order, ushering in a long period of experimentation with spatial/scientific/social technologies.[25]

The cholera epidemic of 1832 was a watershed event. A number of elements—the destruction of the topographic understanding of disease, the production of detailed social statistics, and the construction of centrally administered local medical institutions—combined to yield the beginnings of an invigorated, "modern" set of welfare practices. The crisis saw the development of a model of intervention that was highly centralized yet which sought a finer distribution of a series of medical and observational facilities throughout the physical and social fabrics of French cities.

Milieu

In fact, the "city" was emerging as a new object of analysis and intervention. To understand why, some further background is required. By the 1830s some of the conceptual tools necessary for the emergence of modern social sciences and their object (society) were already at hand. By the second half of the eighteenth century, the term *milieu* had evolved from a mechanical term—the medium through which action takes place at a distance—into a biological one. Lamarck, borrowing from Buffon, who had systematized the neo-Hippocratic view of environmental influences with the Newtonian conception of *milieu*, forged *milieu* into a powerful and wide-ranging concept. Lamarck reinterpreted the influences obtaining between external conditions and individual living beings in a less mechanical, more interactive manner. In strong contradistinction to Classical usage, Lamarck postulated the absence of any initial harmony between living beings and the milieux to which they sought to adapt. Strictly speaking, for Lamarck, the milieu was exterior to the organism, a foreign environment that caused living beings to change and adapt.[26]

In Classical botany, *habitat* referred to the area inhabited by a particular plant species; a pre-existent harmony between the species and its habitat was part of the concept's definition. However, after the cholera epidemic of 1832, there was an important conceptual shift toward developing an understanding of pathology and of the lack of adaptation. An important substitution occurred. The term *conditions of existence* replaced *habitat*, which soon reappeared in the social realm with a new meaning, referring to environmental conditions that hindered harmony.

Pathological conditions were social and historical. Analysts postulated that the social environment constituted an essential mediation of the natural environment. Air, water, light, and circulation hardly disappeared as objects of inquiry and intervention; however, they were gradually assigned a subordinate role in a new conceptual order stressing social pathology. This emphasis opened up the possibility of postulating and elaborating norms for different milieux.

A confident report read to the Royal Academy of Medicine some six months before the arrival of cholera in France proclaimed: "Rich by virtue of its most advantageous geographical position, its gentle sky, its temperate climate, its fertile soil, its fortunate distribution of property in land, its universal industry, and its widely shared instruction, and on that account blessed also with a hygienic situation that leaves little to be desired in either the public or the private sphere, France hopes to be protected from this scourge."[27] The report reveals a number of key assumptions about the world. Nature and civilization were intimately interrelated. A nation's strength and health stemmed from its geographic position, understood most broadly, and from the degree of enlightened civilization it had attained:[28] an enlightened nation was a healthy nation. A French surgeon, inspector of the army health service and member of the Supreme Health Council, optimistically asserted in his 1831 *Mémoire sur le choléra-morbus* that France's topographical situation was so advantageous that she need not fear a cholera epidemic. His confidence was further bolstered by the rigorous quarantine methods adopted at the ports, indicative of what he regarded as the rational state of French medicine and hygiene, and above all of France's unsurpassed state of civilization.[29]

Cholera, after all, had appeared in India, and was often interpreted in the first part of the nineteenth century as the epitome of backwardness and disease. Cholera was an exotic production: "Its yeast was born or developed in the uncultivated, arid plains of Asia and in the rotting algae deposited by the flooding Nile; it ferments and warms itself amidst the residue of poisonous plants burned by the sun."[30] The Orient's fetid and putrefying earth stood in start contrast, of course, to

France's invigorating circulation. These natural advantages had, to use the contemporary vocabulary, "racial correlates." In the indolent and overheated Orient, despotism reigned; in the balanced climates of Europe, enlightened activity and enterprise flourished. The geographical and climatic conditions affected not only political constitutions but individual ones as well. A mutually reinforcing hierarchy of influences from soil to Enlightenment had made France the supreme representative of Civilization.

This is not to say that France had actually attained the harmony and vigorous health it was gallantly approaching. Contemporary observers were not blind to less than perfect conditions; the great influx of population from the countryside into Paris during the first decades of the nineteenth century was a source of much discussion and worry.[31] The physical manifestations of these industrial, social, and demographic changes were quite material: from overcrowded streets to overflowing sewer systems, to the transformation of the air above the city. Distinguishing new problems from old ones, and evaluating their effects, was a frequent topic of writers, journalists, travelers, doctors, and wits. Louis Chevalier underlined the combination of negative, often dire, presentations and underlying optimism. If the air had been allowed to circulate freely, and if the sun had been allowed to penetrate down to the street level and into courtyards, and if the water had flowed freely where it was needed, then Paris would have been a healthy city. For its topography was by nature salubrious and its civilization enlightened.

The topographic and climatological theories of the Classical Age had an explanation for epidemics. A doctor in 1751 presented a report on epidemics to the Société Royale de Médecine, the Académie des Sciences, and the Minister of War. The central factors identified for analysis were: temperature, dryness, humidity, atmospheric pressure, and wind direction. The principal culprit in spreading epidemics was the air.[32] These views led to attempts to improve the circulation and quality of air. More cubic air was allotted to hospital patients, and architects designed better circulation within hospitals; the pavilion solution was favored because it isolated patients with different diseases. Healthy air could be separated from foul. Certain sites considered to be loci of infection, such as tanneries, were moved to the outskirts of the city. From the early nineteenth century on, the Parisian subsoil was inventoried. This combination of geographic and geological ecology of fluids, however, paid little attention to the social dimension. The cholera epidemic put these principles in doubt. Devastating equally rich and civilized countries and poor and barbaric ones, overriding differences of topography and climate, sweeping past quarantine barriers at a single bound, the worldwide spread of cholera demolished one by one the criteria of the Classical science of epidemics.

Responses

Cholera was reported in India in 1826; in Persia in 1829; Russia in 1830; and in Poland, Hungary, Prussia, Germany, Austria, and England in 1831. It reached Paris in the spring of 1832, and by the time it ceased had left some 18,000 Parisians dead. The spread of the disease from India to France was well documented and much commented upon at the time. Standard public health measures had been taken to prevent its entering France: quarantine at the ports, a *cordon sanitaire* at the borders, and local health committees in Paris. These measures were prescribed by the French public health law of 1822. The law had been in draft for almost ten years when a yellow fever epidemic broke out in Spain in 1819 (and again in 1821), forcing its rapid application. Frontiers, particularly ports, were put under heavy surveillance. These were all standard Classical measures, a pure *police de santé:* establish a grid, systematically inspect its sections, separate islands of unhealth, clean up sources of contamination, isolate to avoid contagion, and enforce with the utmost rigor.

In 1832, the authorities employed two different but complementary types of public health tactics: *mésures sanitaires* (sanitary measures) and *mésures de salubrité* (health measures). The sanitary measures followed from quarantine tactics and contagion theory: direct bodily contact was the means of transmission, and thus the prevention of contact of bodies and substances became the basic defense. The second set of measures followed from an understanding of disease as infection: disease arose from and was strengthened in unhealthy locales and was then transmitted through the air. It followed that the sites of disease and the means of its circulation should be the primary targets of public health. Although the practice and discourse of contagion suffered a major setback when cholera spread through France, many of its tactics survived and were employed later in a different scientific context.[33]

Doctors who differed passionately about whether cholera was a contagious or an infectious disease could agree that preventive measures based on both theories should be put into practice. Medical authorities agreed that both preventive quarantine and the clean-up of particularly noxious sites made good sense. In July and September of 1831, a commission of the Royal Academy of Medicine and another of the army's Supreme Health Council went to Poland (a third was sent to Russia) to observe the epidemic firsthand. They advised attaching physicians to embassies in countries where cholera was appearing. Exact, scientific knowledge, not rumor and panic, were to form the foundation of government policy. Medical surveillance teams would be stationed at key points on France's borders; quarantine measures, such as the airing of cargo, were advocated. Certain goods were prohibited from entering France, although nothing was proscribed from entering cities. The measures were applied unsystematically and flaunted by rich and poor alike.

In Paris the Prefect of Police asked the General Council of Hospices to establish two committees, one for administrative measures and one for health measures. The health committee recommended a decentralized approach: markets were to be moved to the outskirts, public gatherings outlawed, and cholera victims' houses conspicuously marked. All of these measures, however, would only come into effect once the epidemic struck, if it did. Dissatisfied with the lack of active preventive measures, the government enlarged Paris' 1802 health council, which had originally been charged with investigating unhealthy industries, inspecting food, and evaluating the state of public spaces, and established a central health commission. The new body supervised twelve commissions—one for each of Paris' *arrondissements*. For reasons of efficiency, the *arrondissement* commissions were soon abolished in favor of commissions in each *quartier,* forty-eight in all. The local commissions were staffed by notables, local professional men aided by the police. Their task was to observe, compile data, and educate the people. The central commission wanted to know the number of neighborhoods and the size and nature of each. A detailed map of each *quartier* was produced and set within a larger map of the whole city. Mapping facilitated analysis; the whole city, down to the individual buildings on a street, was covered by a standardized spatial grid.

As the epidemic spread through Europe, the commissions pursued their investigation, urging a more vigorous application of standing public health measures: sewers were cleaned, more paving put in, fountains built, and garbage removed. Chloroform flowed in abundance. In the hospitals, prisons, and barracks, rations were increased and warmer clothes distributed. Interior walls were whitewashed and air made to circulate with renewed vigor. The investigation's detailed work was impressive; authorities found the state of Paris' public health, as scientifically displayed and quantified, depressing. During a two-month period close to a thousand sites were investigated, with nearly half revealing dangerous conditions. All of this was duly noted, but little action was taken. The government resisted spending funds. There was strong popular resistance, rumors of poisoning flourished, doctors moved about popular quarters in disguises, and health measures were ignored. Distrust of the government from the groups hit hardest was common, as was fear of the people on the part of the upper classes. Paris was bound together by panic, distrust, and hatred.

Life Conditions

The Commission proceeded systematically in its investigation of the causes of cholera. Weather was the first variable eliminated: neither temperature, humidity, barometric pressure, nor wind direction correlated with the spread of the epidemic.

Next, topographic differences—closeness to the Seine, degree
of exposure to sun and wind, height of each site, etc.,—were
explored, and they too proved inconclusive. The traditional
categories of neo-Hippocratic medicine proved worthless,
which is not to say that they were immediately abandoned.
More epicycles, as it were, were added: correlations with distant
volcanic eruptions and atmospheric conditions. But this was
mere hand waving.

The Commission extended its analysis into the social dimension, where its results were also surprising. No significant correlation between cholera and the population densities of *quartiers*
could be demonstrated. Moving beyond this traditional assumption, a micro-level analysis was attempted. Dwelling space
per inhabitant, per building, produced highly significant results. It was not the densities per se which proved conclusive,
but the quality of living conditions. At the heart of the matter
were social conditions conjoined with physical conditions: housing and social conditions proved to be the primary variable in
the localization of cholera.[34] "Social conditions" were broken
down into finer analytic units of work and domesticity, or
habitat. Occupation was the first category explored. Rentiers,
property owners, indoor merchants, and craftsmen were
largely exempt. Those who worked outdoors, such as furniture
dealers, were highly vulnerable. Of the 18,000 deaths, almost
11,000 were among artisans and wage workers, while only
5,000 were found among professionals, merchants, and members of the military. Money and comfort protected; poverty and
harsh working conditions made one vulnerable.

The detailed studies of cholera's spread throughout Paris are
landmarks in the history of social description. Both on the level
of popular experience and on that of statistical evidence, the
1832 epidemic demonstrated by the most pressing and horrible
existential evidence what Louis Chevalier has called the biological bases of class antagonisms.[35] Before cholera, it was known
that poverty and mortality rates in Paris could be correlated.
The cholera investigation refined the analysis: not only income
but life conditions, *conditions d'existence*, were now included.
Miserable conditions somehow provided an environment for

weakening the character and body of the poor, making them susceptible to illness. Pathology was understood as a function of micro-milieux, of an intertwining of biology and society.

Measures

Although statistical inquiries clearly demonstrated a relationship between the sanitary and housing conditions of the poor and mortality rates, it was pragmatically impossible for doctors to inspect and sanitize every household. Nor, short of revolution, was it possible to provide large numbers of people with good clothing, prevent the poor from eating inferior quality food, or stop workers from living crowded together in damp, low-lying places. Remedying living conditions in any systematic way would have required a truly massive effort on behalf of the poor, something the liberal government was not about to undertake. Instead, charity was increased. The king, his family, and his ministers set the tone through donations. Food was distributed. The Church activated its assistance facilities. Hospital space and physicians were allotted. However, some public hygiene measures, poor relief, and hospitalization were actually counterproductive. Cleaning sewers released noxious gases, charity stirred popular fear and anger, and medical measures taken in poorly administered hospitals were ineffective and were interpreted as efforts to sequester the poor. These essentially defensive measures were failures. The basic public health strategy adopted by those who could afford to do so was to flee: Paris witnessed a massive exodus of its bourgeoisie and aristocrats.[36]

Shortly thereafter a leading Saint-Simonian commented on a panicked nation: "The people of Paris were not made to serve as fodder for the cholera of Asia and to die like slaves in pain and terror. What good are all its hospitals, its doctors, its science, and its public administration? The city is a city of palaces and hovels: a few splendid quarters with colonnades and huge gardens closed to the man in work clothes and, in the center of this sumptuous enclosure, a sewer of narrow streets and dark, unhealthy buildings, as dank as dungeons, where those who toil come to catch their breath in fetid air. So, an epidemic arrives, preceded by cries of terror from two continents, and finds its prey ready-made, its victims huddled together and weak."[37] Some Saint-Simonian thinkers, closely associated with the prestigious Ecole Polytechnique, called for the equivalent of a technicians' *coup d'état*, arguing that only a planned and hierarchically coordinated effort was adequate to the crisis. Engineers could save France, but only if far-reaching changes in private property were undertaken. The public good must be given absolute priority. The situation demanded a fundamental physical and moral reshaping of France. The first step was a massive public works program: a comprehensive rail system would cover France so that any point could be linked to any other in twenty-four hours, massive canal construction projects would be instigated, wide avenues would be opened up in the most densely populated areas of the cities and ample water supplies provided for all.[38] More immediately, these Saint-Simonians prophetically advocated massive relocation of the poor to the suburbs, where they would find healthy conditions and new life.

The cholera epidemic catalyzed a new set of relationships, spurring a more precise and powerful analysis of the milieu focusing on *conditions de vie* that included local biological and social variables. The attempt to imagine, implement, and coordinate macro- and micro-reforms did not work very effectively in 1832. But the failure did not lead to the elimination of the strategy. The apparatus of finely grained observation of the social body—supervised by physicians, aided by architects, and backed by the police—in the service of the health of the population and the general good, had a long career ahead.

Nantes: Population in a Milieu

Empirical, statistical, and historical sociology, then, had begun long before Durkheim proclaimed its birth. Knowledge was so highly developed by the middle decades of the nineteenth century that a local doctor in the Loire port of Nantes produced a historical sociology of the city which ran to fifteen hundred pages, detailing every aspect of the city's social life, historical development, statistics, and industrial and moral topography.[39]

Among works of local erudition, *Nantes au XIXe siècle: statistique, topographique, industrielle et morale,* by Saint-Simonian physicians Ange Guépin (1805–1873) and Charles Eugène Bonamy (1808–1861), is a particularly outstanding example of the genre.[40] Guépin, born into a family of lawyers known for their ardent Republican convictions, passed the examination for the prestigious Ecole Polytechnique in 1823. Barred from entering, perhaps because of his father's politics, he stayed on in Paris, frequenting Saint-Simonian circles before entering medical school. His family's politics served him better in 1828, when upon his return to Nantes, he was appointed to a chair at the medical school. Guépin was an active reformer and co-founder of La Société Industrielle de Nantes, dedicated to the education and assistance of the poor. The Society's first act was to open a municipal road works program and create a medical service, library, mutual aid society, and training program for apprentices. Bonamy, another Paris-trained, Nantais doctor, joined Guépin in these activities. Both men had long medical careers, holding a variety of local posts, and both played active roles in the cholera epidemic of 1832 in Nantes. Although Guépin continued to participate actively in electoral politics, the main efforts of both men were trained on social and industrial reform grounded in the progress of science. They held what they claimed to be the first French Scientific Congress in 1833, as well as engaging in a variety of industrial and agricultural experiments, mixing business and science in search of a better society.

Norms: A Comprehensive Grid of Description

Guépin's *Histoire de progrès de la ville de Nantes* formed the core of his *Nantes au XIXe siècle* (1835) and his subsequent two-volume *Histoire de Nantes* (1839). The immediate model was Vicq-d'Azyr's study of medical topography. While these two doctors explicitly extended the work of Enlightenment medical topographers, they were also Saint-Simonians. They fully accepted the coming of an industrial society and embraced its progressive potential of remedying society's injustices. The incorporation of detailed historical and cultural descriptions of class differences in *Nantes au XIXe siècle* marks it as an important document in the history of the social sciences. The attention to cultural and social specificity arises, in part, from Guépin and Bonamy's medical work: their daily contact with all classes and their long familiarity with Nantes combined to produce a set of acute ethnographic observations. Their description is a totalizing one, taking the social life of Nantes as a whole and situating each of its social levels within that whole. In good clinical fashion, their analysis of constituent elements is presented in as exhaustive and precise a fashion as the current state of observation and calculation would permit. The use of quantitative data on all available questions (and the classification of those areas which deserved further study) was successfully combined with qualitative description based on personal observation. The book's aim was therapeutic; once the malfunctions, abnormalities, and pathologies were analyzed, the next step was to propose the requisite reforms—analysis, then intervention.

The book was cast as an epic story of progress, a rambling history of world civilization summarizing the mutual contributions of the Orient and the Occident, the characteristics of the races of France, the effects of the Roman empire, and the global movement of populations. Following this panorama, Nantes' geographic situation provided the setting for its historical and social character.[41] Every stone in Nantes was saturated with historical significance; the city's material structures provided mnemonic devices for recalling its collective memory and experience. The description of the city proper opened with an account of Nantes' administrative organization and an architectural description of its major church and Hôtel de Ville, followed by an account of the city's public squares and bridges. (Their pleasant quality, the historical events for which they provided the setting, and their role in the city's development.) The list continued: Nantes' public fountains; its minor churches; its cemeteries (a particularly rich source of personal sentiments as well as of civic, social, and political history); its educational institutions; its three newspapers, its abundant popular publications and almanacs; its scientific congresses; its Société Académique and Société Industrielle. Nantes was richly

endowed with civic and scientific institutions. It had its own
Société des Beaux-Arts; its Conseil de Salubrité and Ecole Secondaire de Médecine, as well as a regional medical association; its Ecole d'Hydrographie; its observatory; its Jardin des
Plantes; its public library and its *cabinets de lecture* (270,000 loans
per year); its scientific museum (a comprehensive listing of all
its fossil holdings) and industrial and commercial museum (appropriately located next to the primary school); its Musée des
Beaux-Arts; its theater; and its circus and riding school.

How Life Conditions Differed by Class

Doctors' duties were more than medical; the conditions which
produced suffering demanded public health remedies, not individual ones. The first step to reform was a detailed understanding of the milieux of each of Nantes' classes. Although it
would be possible, Guépin argued, to describe each family as a
class, this would be cumbersome. He proposed instead to clas-
sify by grouping individuals enjoying approximately the same
degree of wealth and comfort. Using this totalizing picture of
social, political, economic, and cultural variables Guépin arrived at eight classes: "the rich; the bourgeoisie (high, comfortable, struggling, impoverished); the workers (comfortable,
impoverished, destitute)."[42] Guépin closed his introduction sarcastically; lest anyone accuse him of fomenting revolution by
presenting a picture of a less than just society, the accuser
should know that the worker had no time to read, and furthermore that he was already intimately familiar with his own
poverty.

The Rich
The detailed richness of the volume's sociological observation is
suggested by its descriptions of the living conditions of classes
occupying the highest and lowest rungs on the social ladder.
The richest class was composed of landlords, high officials, a
few merchants, and even smaller numbers of doctors and lawyers. Their families were usually composed of four people:
father, mother, and two children. They occupied apartments of
ten to fifteen rooms located on the most fashionable streets.

Their houses were neat on the outside but not elaborately decorated, trim as if they had been planed down, and all similar. Inside they contained all available comforts, including plentiful windows that allowed light and air to enter and circulate, a luxury denied other classes. Their rooms were filled with the best that man could produce: luxurious carpets, pendulum clocks, stuffed cushions, chandeliers, and engravings. Servants could be called—through a system of bells—from any room in the house. Their children had individual tutors; it was fashionable to train these children in the arts—and some even had talent.

In the early spring, these families went to their cheery country houses along the innumerable rivers of the surrounding countryside. These villas might be far away, or, for those more socially inclined, close to Nantes. All of life's pleasures—music, paintings, billiards, and new novels—were enjoyed with leisure and confidence. Come the end of October, the rich returned to Nantes. A month of visits and house repairs preceded the social season: visits, dances, dinners, an occasional theater performance, and reading in comfortable reading rooms. Once a week there were music and dance evenings. Men suffered from the diseases of a full life: congestions, apoplexies, and gout; women, having devoted themselves more to the sentiments than to action, suffered from spasms, migraines, nervous disorders, and even madness. Though poorly understood, these maladies were real, not merely imaginary. The children of the rich had their own form of scrofula, which attacked their bones and produced deformations. Young girls, going from overheated ballrooms to freezing corridors, often had respiratory problems.

The Poor

The lowest classes, identified by *extrême misère*, received what can only be called unjust rewards in exchange for their work. For these people, living amounted to not dying: bread, wine, and no aspirations. They often lived below ground in terrible conditions: single large, cold, filthy rooms aired by tiny windows. The floors of such rooms were uneven and unpaved, and the rooms stank. They would be filled with three or four dirty beds usually without pillows or sheets; these were always dirty, because they were the only ones the family possessed. Cafe philanthropists made much of this class's drunkenness: what other choices, Guépin asked, were available? Children worked at an early age. Perhaps one quarter of those born lived to be twenty; those that survived were often vigorous.

Public Health
Guépin described Nantes' population of 87,529 (one-eighth of whom were listed as "mobile," without permanent quarters) and its institutions of public health. Between one of Nantes' poorest streets and one of its richest the mortality rates were in a proportion of 6:1. An examination of consumption patterns for 1834 indicated that a large part of the population was undernourished. A summary of the general medical situation followed: the diseases (gastro-enteritis and dysentery) that killed the poor were numerous. Better statistics—according to types of diseases—still needed to be systematically collected. Temperature, wind direction, and general weather conditions were listed in a graph without commentary. Guépin, turning his attention to Nantes' public health facilities, praised the Hôpital Général de Saint-Jacques located on the river at the edge of the city for its light, air, green spaces, and calm. He paid detailed attention to the architectural layout of the hospital and its administration. Patients were listed statistically and their rates of cure discussed: e.g., orphans were numerous and died at the same rate in Nantes as in Paris or Rouen. The other public and private clinics and hospitals of Nantes, from gymnastic spaces to maternal care, clinics, and public baths, were evaluated before turning to the condition of Nantes' bakeries. The states of butcher shops, charcuteries, and the slaughterhouse were likewise reviewed. On the day of Guépin's visit to the large and well-aired prison it contained only ninety-seven inmates, six of whom were political prisoners. Nantes had 600 registered prostitutes—necessary, Guépin reminded his readers, for the tranquility of family life. Guépin closed his study by listing the municipal taxes collected alongside expenses: upkeep of streets, markets, treatments for prostitutes, the national guard (twice that of the prostitutes), hospitals (six times the

national guard), charity, fellowships, libraries, the salary for the director of the theater, public fetes, the extinction of begging, a new primary school, an industrial museum, a school for the deaf and dumb, paintings and statues, stuffed birds (Guépin remarks no skeletons for the medial school or museum), and repayment of municipal loans of 1824 and 1830; no allowance was made for public fountains.

When one examines the list of expenses in the Nantes budget, one is struck by the extraordinary proliferation of services for the population, however inadequate and poorly delivered they may have been in reality. By the 1830s, there already existed an elaborate network of clustered nodes of power/knowledge, devoted to the care and regulation of the population and of a healthy society. Deeply involved in local and national issues, Guépin fought a lifelong struggle against a particularly reactionary right in the North. But he was not a revolutionary and did not believe in mass movements: "Our fathers have sung the harmonies of nature in every key; perhaps our sons will compose something for the bards of social harmony."[43] Guépin's program has a contemporary ring: the right to work, to housing, to a healthy retirement, and to schools, hospitals, prisons, and shelters.

Forms: Toward Regulated Growth

For centuries Nantes had been an active commercial center. The city boasted a number of monuments and engineering achievements but not overall plan.[44] In the first half of the eighteenth century, projects to facilitate circulation, improve health, and embellish the city had been proposed; concern over costs, however, stalled their implementation. During the later decades of the century, a wave of prosperity brought on by the growth of trade with America, particularly the traffic in cloth and slaves, once again stimulated interest among Nantes' merchants and officials in improving the city. The goal was the continuous growth of commercial activity in an efficient and embellished setting, rather than sovereign glory. A particularly literal attempt to reanimate the central city was put forward by an architect named Rousseau. Taking representation in its most literal sense, he designed a new quarter in the shape of a heart: clearly the most appropriate form to stimulate health, i.e., the vigorous circulation of goods, people, and air through the congested valves of the medieval city. Rousseau's plan never left the drawing board, although it did receive some praise.[45]

A series of rather less representational interventions guided the city's actual development. Nantes was fortunate to have a gifted architect in its employ. Mathurin Crucy was given charge of a host of projects and produced some of the finest neoclassical architecture and *ordonnances* (major streets, monuments, squares, a theater, and a stock exchange) in France.[46] The city was not conceived as a geometrically self-enclosed and representable unit. Rather, as its future prosperity depended on the vital, regulated flow of goods, people, and air, a series of *percées*, or widened streets facilitating the movement of heavier vehicular traffic, were cut through the older medieval lanes. The interior street network and the main commercial activities of the town could thereby be connected with a more extended network of circulation, both within the city and beyond. While this system of circulation increased activity, it also provided a means for the effective surveillance and control of such activity. Taxes could be collected, health measures enforced, and population movements controlled, all in a manner that maximized beneficial effects and minimized the nefarious ones.

The problem posed for the architects of Nantes was how to make a space that would promote regular and vigorous circulation. This was not simply a question of extending or perfecting an administrative grid of equal units, but rather of creating a flexible differentiation of space appropriate to specific functions and local particularities. For Nantes' bourgeoisie, space was not a neutral medium to be ordered *ex nihilo*. Rather, space was to be approached empirically, to be known in its specificity and to be used instrumentally. The search was for adequate forms, considered in their empirical relations with specific sites; for information on the demographic, commercial, and social characteristics of the already existing population; and, most innovatively, for means to guide the potential future development of these diverse human and geographical particularities, now acknowledged as resources to be regulated and maximized.

Crisis of Representations: Architecture, From Type to Style

The classical vocabulary of architectural forms entered into crisis in the 1830s. César Daly (1811–1894), founder of France's first major architectural magazine, *Revue générale de l'architecture et des travaux publics,* argued that the classical European consensus that antiquity was the unique standard of form—"the absolute doctrine of art, without regard for real life, the country, the race, or the era (or) the materials used"— had yielded the most unfortunate of results.[47] Once ancient models were seen as only one among many possible solutions to a given architectural problem, the meaning of style in architecture gained an entirely new value, or more accurately, took on value. Ultimately, the debate was not merely over form, decoration, or even art; the real problem was social. As Daly put it: "Modern society, powerless to express through art a harmony among souls that no longer exists, and powerless to attribute a fixed meaning, the same for everybody, to the fundamental forms of architecture [is] without the power to create, and is constrained to borrow."[48] This crisis posed a new problem for architects: what was the most appropriate style for a modern society?

Architectural Type: Its Historicization and Formalization

In order to understand this crisis of architectural representation, we must first take a detour into the question of type. In classical theory, the architect's task was to invent representations corresponding to Nature's perfection. This was more than a simple classificatory device; correct representation of nature provided the basis for order, beauty, and truth. The right type provided the architect with a standard by which he could evaluate all construction. A dictionary of 1727 defined type as "figure, shadow, representation."[49] Nature or God provided already perfected forms that architecture was to represent. The most famous example of this, one that actually appeared rather late in the classical age, was the primitive hut of the Abbé Laugier.[50] Laugier proposed the simplest and most natural of models: "Man wishes to make himself a dwelling which covers him without burying him. A few fallen branches in the forest are the suitable material for his design. He chooses four of the strongest that he raises up vertically and disposes in a square. Above them, he places four others horizontally; and on these he raises others which slope and come together at a point on two sides."[51] As Anthony Vidler points out, in the frontispiece of the second edition of 1755 the posts have become trees, miraculously growing in a perfect square.

Architecture's task was to represent correctly the origins of a building and to make its function a visible and legible part of its structure. Within this framework, it was reasonable to assume that building types could be codified and techniques for representing their characters taught. Jacques-François Blondel (1705–1774) did just that, listing among others: theaters, halls for dancing and festivities, vauxhalls, cemeteries, colleges, hospitals, charnel houses, hotels, exchanges, libraries, academies, factories, fountains, baths, markets, fairs, slaughterhouses, barracks, town halls, arsenals, and lighthouses. Blondel's theory endured well into the nineteenth century, forming the basis for many Beaux-Arts prize competitions. There was less consensus about his codification of appropriate character—prisons should be terrible and public markets masculine. The fate of these codifications was somewhat troubled, although it was a long time before the notion of appropriate character disappeared entirely. The last glorious flowering of representation rose forth in the work of the visionary architects Boullée and Ledoux. Ledoux sought to enlarge the classical vocabulary so as to capture new social and industrial forms. He designed giant drains for housing river surveyors, giant barrels for housing the work and recreation of barrel makers, and cosmic spheres for the humble shepherds of human flocks.

Just as reaction quickly set in against the Société des Observateurs de l'Homme, so, too, the official academy responded crossly to these visionary projects. Antoine-Chrysotome Quatremère de Quincy (1755–1848) attempted a reformulation of the theory of character as a way of blocking what he saw as individualistic abuses of representation creeping into French architecture. Repeating criticisms he had made as early as 1788, but which he set down in canonic form between 1825 and 1830 in his comprehensive *Dictionnaire historique d'architecture*, Quatremère attempted to resurrect the traditional repertoire.

Architecture was to give to each building its appropriate character. "The art of characterizing, that is to say, of rendering sensible by material forms the intellectual qualities and moral ideas which can be expressed in buildings; or of making known by means of the accord and suitability of all the constituent parts of a building, its nature, propriety, use, destination; this art is perhaps the finest and most difficult to develop and to understand."[52] Quatremère then systematized these attributes in a scheme that remained largely in place at the Ecole des Beaux-Arts throughout the nineteenth century. Discussing types produced by the ancients, he was on the firm ground of tradition; with the appearance of new social types stemming from new uses, problems arose.

Type: Uniform Representation

A different kind of synthesis was achieved on another front. A major scientific advance played an important role in undermining one dimension of the classical theory of type. One of the founders of the Ecole Polytechnique, Gaspard Monge, published in 1795 a *Géométrie descriptive*. Its appearance marked an important turning point in the history of representation and contained significant implications for architectural practice and teaching.[53] Although elements of geometrical projection had been part of architectural drawing since at least the sixteenth century, these procedures had not been formally and comprehensively synthesized. Monge invented a system to map three-dimensional objects through descriptive geometry onto a two-dimensional space that then could be translated into algebraic representations. Engineers at the Ecole Polytechnique were trained in descriptive geometry. New codifications such as Jean Rondelet's *Traité théorique et pratique de l'art de bâtir* of 1802, designed for practitioners and not theorists, were frequently consulted. Understanding that particular materials, sites, and general situations would require specific applications of his general rules, Rondelet sought to wed detailed empirical considerations to elegant mathematics.

This marriage of technique and abstraction was brought to perfection in the work of Jean-Nicolas-Louis Durand (1760–1834). In 1794, Monge hired Durand to teach architecture within the department of applied geometry. Durand, who had learned his trade in the atelier of Boullée and eventually carried off a Second Grand Prix in 1780, was no stranger to official architectural doctrines and practices. Recognizing that departmental engineers were doing more building than architects (constructing hospitals, prisons, barracks, arsenals, bridges, and lighthouses), he developed a course to teach them the trade in two years. For Durand, the purpose of architecture was utility, not beauty, pleasure, or any other metaphysical ideal. His codification, published between 1802 and 1805, of the elements of architecture—walls, columns, and openings—their combination into intermediate units—porches, stairs, and halls—and their combination into complete ensembles (towns), enabled the engineer-architect to meet any problem. Everything, character included, turned on function and economy. As Durand put it: "Suitability demanded that the building be solid, healthy, and comfortable, economy that it be as simple, regular and symmetrical as possible."[54] Decoration, the symbolism of the Orders, and styles were of little or no interest to Durand. He did not so much challenge the neoclassical style per se as redefine the problem to be solved.

Durand elaborated a systematic presentation of the elements of architecture and their combination based on geometrical form and mathematical drawings. He sought a characteristic form for each building type, based on function. The first step was to make a comprehensive collection of historical materials of every genre. Building plans were organized according to species, eventually yielding, it was hoped, a kind of natural history of architecture. Durand arranged his building types on graph paper, side by side and drawn to the same scale, to represent a progression from primitive to refined. An architect-historian, J. G. Legrand, wrote the historical complement to Durand's graphic representations. Although history was not taught at the Ecole Polytechnique, progress, as Anthony Vidler nicely observes, certainly was; Saint-Simon was meeting with Durand's students across the street from the Ecole.

The next logical step was taken by a student of Ledoux named Dubut, who produced a book of house types from which his clients could choose. The plans were not fixed but could be transformed in a number of ways without losing their basic symmetry. Form and technique were separating. Type was now purely a question of the inner workings of plan and distribution in their myriad logical variations. Style, in this system, was decoration applied externally to the structure; being inessential, it could vary at the whim of the client, who chose from an eclectic catalogue of styles made available in part by a great outpouring of historical and cultural studies of other times and places. The same logic (in an inverse sense) also applied to public buildings such as prisons. While Ledoux had devoted his attention to the correct representational form of, say, a courthouse, panoptic prisons demanded no 'style' except functionality.[55] What had once been a unified theory of type in French architecture thus, broadly speaking, split in two. While Durand and his engineers proceeded on their functionalist way, the Beaux-Arts architects—having accepted into the core of their curriculum and practice the essentials of Durand's approach to functional typology—continued debates about style.

The Neo-Grec: Historicizing Form

The official lifespan of the Parisian Ecole des Beaux-Arts extended from 1819 to 1968. However, its predecessor, the Académie Royale d'Architecture, one of the last of the great Royal Academies, was founded in 1671.[56] From its founding, the principal charge of the Academy was theory—the formulation of doctrine—rather than directly pragmatic concerns, although the latter were obviously included. A student at the Royal Academy attended lectures, but he learned to design in the studio of a master to whom he was apprenticed. This pattern continued to characterize French architectural training; an apprenticeship system producing intense personal loyalties both to the master and to fellow apprentices was combined with universalist speculation on the nature of architecture's principles.

Students were ranked at the Ecole des Beaux-Arts through a series of competitions, or *concours*. These were of two types: *esquisses* requiring one drawing submitted after twelve hours and *projets rendus* usually requiring three large drawings done over two months. The pattern of training students to produce a sketch of a whole project rapidly under test conditions and then to work out the details without major revisions in conception was extremely influential in the formation of Beaux-Arts architects and their architecture. Exercises testing the student's abilities in construction were also important. A series of six *esquisses* and six *projets rendus* formed the heart of the program. These were open competitions devoted to compositionally complex projects, usually the kind of civic buildings a Beaux-Arts architect would eventually hope to build: schools, museums, hotels, and theaters.

The crowning achievement was the Grand Prix de Rome competition. There were three steps in the competition: in March, the student was required to produce an *esquisse*, often a facade. Shortly thereafter, he was required to produce a second, more detailed *esquisse*, to be completed in twenty-four hours and devoted to a more complicated compositional problem such as placing the building in a larger setting. The official architects of the Institut de France would choose eight finalists. The third and most demanding step began immediately thereafter and lasted until July. The program was usually for a monumental public building such as a museum, a cathedral, or a university. First, second, and third places were chosen, with the winner gaining great prestige. He was sent by the government to the Villa Medici in Rome for four or five years to study the monuments of antiquity. Upon his return he would usually be chosen as an official Architecte du Gouvernement and receive commissions for public buildings. The only other honor remaining for a Prix de Rome winner was to be elected to one of the lifetime architectural positions at the Institut.

The hallmark of the architecture of the Ecole des Beaux-Arts was composition. This involved not only the design of ornament or of facades, but "of whole buildings, conceived as three-dimensional entities and seen together in plan, section and elevation."[57] Typically, a student was asked to design a monumental building on an unencumbered site. This meant distributing the relations of interior spaces and exterior volumes along symmetrical axes. The simplest form was two axes intersecting at right angles in a major central space, the whole being compressed inside a circumscribed rectangle. Given a set of fixed, if broad, compositional techniques, the Beaux-Arts architect was confronted with the task of adapting the specific building's functions to these principles. Said another way, the problem was posed entirely in terms of solving a compositional problem harmoniously. This meant applying the given principles to a specific building; social, cultural, and geographic considerations were by definition beyond the scope of the problem. Formal and technical techniques were not the subject of explicit theorizing at the Ecole des Beaux-Arts. Rather, they were taken for granted as part of the practice of the profession as it was taught directly to students in the ateliers. Part of the explanation of the enduring influence of these techniques on French architecture lies precisely in their status as untheorized Kuhnian "skills."[58]

Style and History

If the technical compositional principles of the nineteenth-century Ecole des Beaux-Arts were relatively stable, there was nonetheless controversy over their meaning. In fact, the nineteenth-century history of the school was consistently marked by strife, most of it turning on the relations of style and history. Among the most important of these battles was the reinterpretation of architecture, history, and style posed by Henri Labrouste (1801–1875) and his so-called romantic or "neo-Grec" companions during the 1820s and 1830s. The terms of the debate set the conditions for Beaux-Arts arguments for the rest of the century. A historicized structural and decorative diversity were not only acknowledged but made central by the neo-Grec architects. Form and content were differentiated and played off against each other; difference and history were introduced into the heart of architecture. At least superficially, this synthesis was quickly rejected; both Viollet-Le-Duc and his rivals at the Ecole des Beaux-Arts reacted against the neo-Grec style, but its diagnosis of architecture's problems was to take center stage.[59]

Labrouste won the Second Grand Prix in 1821 and the First Grand Prix de Rome in 1824, and arrived at the Villa Medici in January of 1825. The newly recodified rules for the Prix de Rome winners in architecture stipulated that the pensionnaires were to travel through Italy, so as to acquaint themselves with "the different styles, the varied arrangements of the monuments, and the means of construction employed."[60] For the Academy's architects this meant classical Roman models and their Renaissance variants. The students' *envois* each year were to demonstrate mastery of these models. Each spring the *envois* were exhibited at the Villa Medici and in the fall at the Academy in Paris. The students' work was annually reviewed by the Institute and publicly evaluated in the press. The work of the first three years formed a unit comprised of a series of analytic exercises, mainly of details of Roman buildings. These exercises grew in complexity, so that by the fourth year the student attempted to reconstruct a complete building. The content and principles of evaluation were fixed and represented the basic elements of architectural value.

Labrouste's *envois* for the first three years—seven drawings of parts of the Temple of Antoninus and Faustine in Rome, details of the Column of Trajan, the Column of Marcus Aurelius, and the Arch of Titus in Rome, and five drawings comparing the Colosseum and the Theater of Marcellus, were well received by the Academy. In his fourth year, he chose for his project the site of Paestum. The choice was unusual; Labrouste was the first pensionnaire to choose a Greek site and the last one to do so for fifteen years. Labrouste had traveled to Paestum, in southern Italy, as well as to Sicily, in order to experience Greek architecture directly. His *envois* aroused the fury of the Academy in Paris and particularly that of its Secrétaire Perpétuel, Quatremère de Quincy.[61] Upon receiving Labrouste's drawings, Quatremère launched a campaign to prohibit travel outside of Rome during the pensionnaires' first three years. For Quatremère and his colleagues, the danger was that young architects might, in the presence of non-canonical examples of architecture, arrive at erroneous conclusions about correct form. In the case of Greek architecture, it was not so much a question of the architecture itself as of its interpretation. For the Academy, Greek styles represented the infancy of classicism; hence Roman buildings were always preferred to

Greek ones. A small number of models would provide the young architect with all the inspiration and complexity he could possibly need.

Quatremère and his fellow Academicians were not wrong in sensing danger; once the canon was expanded, even to Greece and Republican Rome, the floodgate was opened. Labrouste's drawings of Paestum are generally taken to be the most important expression of this revolt, described by Viollet-Le-Duc as a revolution brought about on a few sheets of double-elephant paper. In fact, when Labrouste returned to Paris in 1830, he was paraded on the backs of students during the July Revolution. It was not just that Labrouste presented polychromy in the drawings (Hittorff had already done so in 1824 without causing major controversy); nor the simple fact of presenting Greek buildings, as that too had been done previously, although it had not met with enthusiasm; nor the specific choice of Paestum per se, as Paestum had been drawn several times in the eighteenth century after its rediscovery in the 1740s. Viollet-Le-Duc explained the excitement: "Labrouste did not deign to look at Greek antiquity through the classical lens, (this) revolution undermined the academic foundations of family, property and religion."[62] What, then, was the new lens that Labrouste used?

In his *précis historique* Labrouste suggested that the Greek architects had built the temple in response to local conditions, and not as an exemplification of the universal principles of architecture. Labrouste sought to explain each detail as a response to the specific requirements of material, program, and site. His interpretation of Paestum stressed its Greek qualities; he did not mention any classical ideal. For missing structural or decorative details Labrouste examined other Greek temples on his travels in Sicily rather than, as would have been customary for a Beaux-Arts student, examining Roman models. The provincial Greek examples, Labrouste argued, were more informative because they shared a cultural world with the architects at Paestum, whereas the Roman examples did not. For Labrouste, buildings were an expression of a culture as much as the exemplification of true and eternal principles of beauty.

Labrouste paid particular attention to the effect of the use of local materials on construction techniques. He further irritated the Academy by attempting to understand how the decoration of buildings was integrated with their uses: "We may assume that the ancients customarily renewed the decoration of the monuments at certain consecrated times, or it may be that religion prescribed that custom."[63] In classical architectural doctrine, the true principles of architecture were found in the Orders. Each Order, it was held, contained its own characteristic expression. Labrouste, however, interpreted temples done in the same order as being functionally different. He thereby saw use, function, and plan as more important than the Orders themselves. This was sacrilege. In sum, Labrouste sought a cultural and pragmatically functional explanation, rather than a metaphysical one, for every aspect of the temple.

Labrouste further attacked the Academy's canons by asserting that the structure and decoration of the temples at Paestum were absolutely unified. He contrasted the "firmness of architecture" in Greek temples with the "extreme delicacy" of their decoration. He argued that decoration could be an important dimension of the meaning of a particular building and not, as was usually asserted, just its Order. Finally, Labrouste considered the earliest temples the most pure. This too was heresy, for the Academy taught that there was, by definition, a progression toward the purity of Rome. Labrouste's subtext was revolutionary: the earlier forms were pure, the later ones academic and decadent. Any dogmatic insistence on the use of certain forms could only exhibit a loss of principle; sterility and decadence were signs of academic old age. There was no ideal in classical idealism. Meaning did not inhere in the forms themselves, and their mechanical reuse only signified spiritual decay. History, not nature, was the soil from which architecture sprang: positivist fact, not generic form.

Labrouste's fifth-year *envoi* from Rome in 1829 was a bridge, called *Pont destiné à réunir la France à l'Italie*. The final year's project was added by the Academy to allow the student, as he prepared to leave Rome, to display the summa of his learning. The student was free to choose his topic, as long as it fit into the general rubric of "a public monument appropriate to the customs of France." The fifth-year *envoi* was the limbering up exercise through which the Prix-de-Rome winners began the process of translating their studies of Roman monuments into the context of nineteenth-century France. Labrouste's choice, a double-arched bridge with single-arched triumphal entries at both ends, was a common enough subject, but once again he chose to treat it in a highly provocative manner. Although his bridge used classical decorative elements, they were greatly reduced and sparsely applied. The Academy objected. Once again, it had perfectly understood Labrouste's challenge; he had chosen a style that was more Etruscan than Roman in its arches, proportions, and general decoration. As a culminating project it was simply too provincial and too restrained. The Academy objected to the absence of further buildings, such as fortifications, officers' barracks, customs houses, and warehouses, that would constitute the "vast composition" required of the fifth-year *envoi*.

By choosing pre-Roman (Etruscan) or extra-Roman (provincial) models for his final drawings, Labrouste's attack on the classical canon was clear. By orienting his drawing so that one could see only "France" engraved, he was clearly leaving Italy behind. The areas of both countries were barren; one found neither the grandeur and monuments of Italy nor the greatness of France, which the Academy expected and demanded to be extolled. Labrouste did not design a bridge connecting two eternal civilizations, but one connecting two land areas.

2

Modern Elements:
Reasons and Histories

The crisis of representation occurring in the 1830s in disciplines concerned with social norms and in architectural forms was not readily resolved, if resolution involved constructing the new, stable, and synthetic vocabulary sought by the actors themselves. A central thesis of this book is that modern discourses are characterized by enduring instability and only momentary coalescences which are soon contested. A variety of discourses—clustering around the poles of the mechanical, efficient, and standardizing, versus the cultural, social, and historicizing, and all the force lines in between—embodied not so much contradictory or paradoxical opposites as a distinctive and dynamic equipollent field. The rationalization of spatial practices accompanied the appearance of a historicist discourse. An absorption (almost an obsession) with meaning as historical joined with regularized topography, provided the ground for the century-long debate over the pluralization of forms and norms.

This chapter explores three important domains in which these processes are readily identifiable. In social statistics, social ecological and probabilistic approaches emerged together and constituted a field in which debate flourished for the next century. In architecture, throughout the middle decades of the century, Viollet-Le-Duc and his contemporaries fought to the death over the differing weights of reason and history in modern architectural form; a thin and complacent doctrine of neoclassical eclecticism was the institutional winner and was enshrined at the Ecole des Beaux-Arts. In city planning Louis

Napoleon and Baron Haussmann rebuilt or, better, "regularized" vast sectors of a Paris bloated by a surge in population.
Meanwhile they catalogued the city they were destroying, giving "monuments" new meaning and laying the groundwork for
a different understanding of the city, space, and society.

Norms and Numbers

The use of numbers in solving social problems was obviously
not entirely new at the beginning of the nineteenth century.
Speculation on the need for quantitative understanding of the
population had been part of seventeenth-century Cameralist
political thinking. The Enlightenment abounded in projects for
the mathematization of social understanding: e.g., in the 1720s
the Abbé de Saint-Pierre proposed the creation of a central
bureau for the collection and analysis of statistics. In Germany,
Leibnitz proposed a detailed plan for a similar centralization of
administrative numbers. In France, criminal statistics had been
collected before the Revolution—e.g., an ordinance of 1670
asked the *procureurs du roi* for a trimestral account of offenses—
but such efforts were sporadic.[1]

Condorcet's introduction of calculus into statistical methodology and his plans for the perfection of mankind through
massive public health programs marked another important
step in applying an increasingly powerful and sophisticated science of numbers to public policy.[2] Condorcet's friend, Philippe
Pinel, applied his suggestions by attempting quantitative evaluations of the treatment of mental patients at the famous Parisian Salpêtrière Hospital. Pinel insisted on the importance of
maintaining accurate records of each patient so as to facilitate
long-term studies and more rigorous comparison.[3] It should be
underlined, however, that these projects were rarely carried
through with any sustained coherence, and few data of scientific value, worthy of comparison and testing, were produced.[4]

By the end of the eighteenth century, the term "statistics" was
beginning to replace the then current "political arithmetic." In
1817, the French Academy of Science defined statistics as a
"science of facts" concerned with collecting the data of civil
society and contrasted it to political arithmetic, the application

of mathematical analysis to political economy.[5] By 1848, political arithmetic would pass from the scene, and statistics would become the state's numbers. In between lay what is generally referred to as statistics' "age of enthusiasm."[6]

A professionalization and regularization of population statistics, linked to a range of reformist projects, occurred during the first decades of the nineteenth century.[7] The most important professional journal of the period was unquestionably the *Annales d'hygiène publique et de médecine légale*. The *Annales* set broad goals for itself that extended far beyond studying and curing illness; its stated aims included aiding legislators and magistrates in the formulation and interpretation of laws and acting as a watchdog over the maintenance of public health.[8] Four of the eight members of the editorial committee were members of Paris's Conseil de Salubrité (formed in 1802 and extended to France's main cities during the 1820s).[9] The *Annales* was not directed at popular education. Rather, it functioned as a diffusing mechanism through which physicians and administrators were kept abreast of the latest technical developments. It provided a vast repository of international information on public health matters. All the leading French specialists published work in the journal. The effort to provide a collection point for all work on a problem, as the first step to its solution (which often never occurred), was characteristic of many regulatory movements throughout the nineteenth century. The importance of the *Annales* was that it opened a discursive space linking the systematic study of hygiene, statistics, and the social world. It represented the institutionalization of the scientific break with neo-Hippocratic orthodoxy.

Two of the most famous social statisticians of this period, Louis-René Villermé (1782–1863) and Adolphe Quételet (1796–1874), demonstrate in different ways the emerging importance of norms as the privileged means of understanding and defining society. Two related, though not identical, conceptions of society are embodied in their work, a comparison of which shows the major cleavages of statistical work at this time and the tacit convergence on redefining society in terms of norms and health. Both thinkers were troubled by an unresolved tension between searching for a totalizing understanding capable of quantitative formalization and the awareness that individualizing specifications, necessary for the methods to be accurate and effective, were, if not absent, at least elusive. Put another way, there was a significant gap between the object "society," as it was given form by statistical methods, and the effective reality which it supposedly adequately represented. This gap would serve as the motive for further studies. The scientific importance of Villermé's and Quételet's technical statistical work for the advance of that field of inquiry was not great. However, their impact on social theory and eventually on social reform efforts is another matter.

Social Ecology

Villermé developed a statistics based on biological analogies, very much concerned with the interrelations of society and nature. Villermé began his career as a military surgeon, serving ten years with Napoleon's armies. In 1819 he published important statistical evaluations of recruits. His attention shifted to public health questions, and in 1820 he published an important study on prisons—*Les Prisons telles qu'elles sont, et telles qu'elles devraient être*—based on extensive visits to the prisons as well as on quantitative evaluations. As late as 1822, Villermé attributed the pathology of French hospitals to the bad circulation of air, as had eighteenth-century theorists.[10] Villermé worked with other well-known figures of the emerging public health movement on the population survey of Paris, the *Recherches statistiques sur Paris et le départment de la Seine*, the first volume of which appeared in 1821. A massive amount of data was compiled to serve as the base for the most sophisticated and theoretically advanced contemporary statistical work. The *Recherches* contained within its folds work proceeding from both Quételet's social physics model, in which means and covariations were established through the formalization of quantitative series, and a biological-ecological model drawing on physiology and anatomy for its concepts and seeking to develop an understanding of society as a whole composed of interrelated and interrelating functional parts. Villermé was the leading practitioner of the second mode.

Villermé pursued investigations of criminality and delinquency throughout the 1820s. Perhaps his most influential work of this period was his *Mémoire sur la mortalité en France dans la classe aisée et dans la classe indigente*, first presented in 1826.[11] Drawing mainly on data from a Parisian survey, Villermé demonstrated strong differences in mortality rates between rich and poor quarters; he showed that the same correlations held even more strongly for specific sections of these neighborhoods and even for certain streets; he found the same correlations for French departments. Seeking the cause of the correlations, Villermé statistically tested proximity to rivers, climatic conditions, and types of soils. These factors proved statistically insignificant, as did the width of streets, height of houses, gardens, direction of winds, and the purity of water; even population density alone did not correlate with mortality. Villermé concluded that the covariation of death and revenue showed that the classical explanations of sites and infections, contagion and air, were less revealing than analysis of social conditions. There was no escaping the conclusion that a milieu formed through the interrelations of natural and social elements and capable of providing conditions for social pathology was a much more complex affair than had been previously understood.[12]

Villermé's most famous work, *Tableau de l'état physique et moral des ouvriers employés dans les manufactures de coton, de laine et de soie*, published in 1840, was a comprehensive account of the textile industry.[13] The product of six years of intensive research that included many direct visits to centers of textile production, *Tableau* combined both statistical and qualitative observations, the latter drawn from Villermé's use of key informants. His conclusion that the workers' plight had been slightly improved by philanthropic measures drew fire from socialists, who pointed out the miserable state in which these workers continued to live; his criticism of child labor practices drew fire from liberal industrialists. Villermé's *Tableau* led directly to the last large-scale official inquiry into major problems in France as a whole: the study of agricultural and labor conditions commissioned by the National Assembly in May 1848. The work was poorly done, methodologically marred, and largely skewed in favor of officials' views. Having called for a general inquiry into workers' conditions throughout the 1840s, the socialists shifted their tactics after 1848 and sought instead an institutional base in a Ministry of Labor. The calls for inquiries now came from the right, in part as a stalling tactic. Socialist opposition to such research continued until late in the century. Empirical studies would remain a predominantly right-wing practice in France throughout the nineteenth century.[14]

William Reddy has shown how misleading many of Villermé's statistics really were, despite their almost unquestioned acceptance throughout the nineteenth and twentieth centuries. He reveals Villermé's use of the rhetorically powerful device of textually juxtaposing seemingly hard statistics and the supposedly first-hand depiction of misery, to support a specific moral vision and to instantiate it in a genre of social description. Reddy shows in detail how Villermé included or excluded data to bolster his vision—which is not, of course, to accuse him of lying. Contradictory evidence was supplied with a background of "breakthrough" passages in which a vision of poverty arising from remedial, individual moral weakness was incisively articulated. Villermé's work became the model for descriptions of the urban poor; observers may well have traveled to this city or that, but their prose repeated time and time again the same commonplaces about "the poor." These tropes and the social understanding they embodied then moved into literature; during the course of the century they migrated leftward, from spokesmen for neo-conservative social philanthropists like Villermé, until they eventually formed central tropes of the socialists.[15]

Types: L'Homme Moyen

Adolphe Quételet sought the foundations of a true science of man, an expression becoming commonplace by the 1830s, in identifying predictable regularities of man's physical, intellectual, and moral life. A Belgian, Quételet came to Paris in 1823–24 to work at the Astronomical Observatory, where he encountered France's most brilliant mathematicians, who were at that moment making important advances in probability theory. Quételet's first statistical work, *Mémoire sur les lois des nais-*

sances et de la mortalité à Bruxelles of 1825, was undertaken to improve the statistics available to insurance companies. The regularity of the numbers he found convinced Quételet that he had discovered the laws of nature.[16]

Introduced to Villermé by none other than the illustrious Fourier, Quételet eventually shifted his focus to social questions. Expressing his admiration for the work done in the *Recherches statistiques sur la ville de Paris et le département de la Seine*, Quételet used the same approach in his study of criminal propensities, claiming to prove that moral facts were just as regular as physical ones. However, France's criminal statistics were neither complete nor collected in forms allowing adequate comparison. In the 1830s, Quételet shifted his inquiries to marriage patterns, birth and death records, and the like, where he could get more reliable results. The shift constituted both a methodological improvement of the mathematical reliability of the data and a shift from pathological to normal social facts, i.e., socially normative in a positive sense. Linking the normal and the pathological was one of Quételet's most significant achievements. More accurately, the invention of statistical tools dependent on and made possible through a conception of social regularity, which could be mapped along a continuum from the normal to the pathological, represented an important shift in social understanding.

It is worth emphasizing that Quételet rarely employed sophisticated mathematics in his statistical work and that he neither invented nor employed other than the crudest sort of evaluative tools.[17] If one were writing a history of progress in statistical methods, one would pay more attention to works such as Poisson's (1781–1840) on French juries, in which the author used probability theory to predict verdicts, or other more directly mathematical advances. But this is not my aim.[18]

For Quételet, using astronomy as his model science, the theory of probability was the cornerstone of the sciences of observation. Nature was law-governed. Following the method he was to use in all his subsequent inquiries, Quételet sought to demonstrate that he could discover mathematically representable regularities, as long as a sufficiently large sample was available. He thought of these regularities as expressing underlying types. Quételet began his search to uncover and describe human types with studies of physical stature. He wondered if there was for each people a typical, representative build.[19] He argued that the great artists of the past sought to represent human perfection by combining existing traits into a type whose proportions they found beautiful. Quételet attempted to provide these intuitions with a solid mathematical foundation; probability theory would provide the basis for the true, the good, and the beautiful. He first measured chest sizes in Greek sculptures and then convinced important political personages in Belgium to have the chests of army recruits measured. The two sets of proportions matched. When these figures also correlated with visiting Chinese and captive Ojibwah Indians, Quételet felt sure he had uncovered the true human type. His findings pointed to a human commonality; a sufficiently large sample would provide the type for the whole human species: "The average man, instead of representing the type of the beautiful and the good in relation to his own period, would represent the type of the beautiful and the good absolutely and in the most general sense."[20] What artists had found through genius, modern statistics would provide through mathematics.

Almost precisely at the moment when the concept of type, which had supported the canons of French architecture during the entire Classical Age, was being undermined by new ideas and new historical research, it was being redefined statistically by Quételet, although not without some regret, some lingering confusion about its normative, in the singular, weight. Reviewing the scientific literature devoted to the topic of size and growth, Quételet found only Buffon's discussion of growth in young men. But Buffon's study was not sufficiently rigorous. Quételet insisted that the only way to study individuals was as indications of general characteristics of a population. To do this one had to ensure that the individuals under study were thoroughly normal.[21] Quételet studied the systematic variations in body size in a homogeneous population. While plotting his figures, he discovered that they came out in the form of a Laplace-Gauss bell-shaped, binomial curve of errors. In order for the curve to come out as precisely as it did, Quételet concluded that the distribution had to be the consequence of random effects acting on individuals. The more measures one took, and the more they conformed statistically to the Laplace-Gauss curve, the more interfering and accidental effects on the type could be eliminated. Following this insight, Quételet arrived at his famous notion of *l'homme moyen:* "The proof of the existence of an average man is given in the manner in which the numbers obtained for each dimension measured (waist, head, arms, etc.) gather around the mean according to the law of accidental causes."[22] Man, without knowing it, was subjected to divine laws. Probability theory, brought to perfection by Fourier and Laplace, revealed the workings of those laws.

For Quételet the *homme moyen* was no abstraction; he existed in the world. Quételet equated the notion of statistical frequency with the norm: the distributions did not represent an arithmetic mean to which it would be perfectly plausible that no beings corresponded; rather, Quételet claimed to have isolated an ontological regularity which expressed itself on the curve. For Quételet human traits, as Georges Canguilhem observes, were not normal because they were found frequently, but were frequent because they were normal, and in that sense normative for a given way of life. One could consider sicknesses, Quételet concluded, as greater or lesser deviations from the normal, healthy state.[23]

A recent history of statistics evaluates Quételet's contribution to the growth of the science as modest: his social physics was completely unworkable, his use of mathematics elementary, and his calls for charting the changes in *l'homme moyen* unheeded. His contribution lay, it is argued, in his subsequent influence on others, in his shifting the focus from concrete causes to larger wholes governed by their own internal laws. This would have salutary effects on population biology and initially comforted liberals who thought that intervention in society was a transgression of natural processes to be avoided as much as possible.[24] This point is made in another way by a second historian: Quételet's normal curves lacked discriminatory power; they fit too many cases too well. Quételet's studies—and those following his method, dubbed "Quételismus"—basically validated, in a new vocabulary and with the appearance of scientific rigor, already existing schemas of classification.[25]

While valid, what such evaluations miss is the sea changes taking place in French conceptions of the real. Quételet's work marked a major step away from natural law and from all related moral, psychological, or metaphysical theories which gave an absolute primacy or independence to the individual. Society was becoming an object sui generis, with its own laws, its own science, and eventually its own arts of government. If the individual's normality and pathology were a function not of his independent moral state but rather of his place within a social whole, then it made little sense to try to reform him separately from reforming the social milieu within which his actions were formed and normed. This is not to say that all the disciplinary techniques aimed at moralizing or controlling individuals described by Foucault disappeared (many are still with us), but only that society was becoming the object to be understood and reformed. The use of statistical approaches to social problems posed the problem of finding forms through which to present this understanding, just as the century-long search for new architectural forms was perplexed about the norms of modern society that these forms were supposed to embody and represent.

Forms and Styles

From Labrouste's challenge to the Academy's understanding of the importance of Rome to his denial of the absolute primacy of the Classical Orders, his separation of Classical decoration from structure, and his use of iron in construction, a number of elements of French architectural thinking and practice were isolated and shown to be independent. The relations of structure, history, and style seemed increasingly problematic. One consequence of the dissolution of architecture's ability to represent character and order was a move toward a kind of humanism of intent (architecture should draw on many models and should serve wider interests: the architect's subjective genius was glorified) and a growing professionalism in practice (everything was open to technique, and the architect's technique was to produce what the client wanted). All styles were made available.[26]

The battle over architectural styles in the nineteenth century is a story of the attempt to relate style, structure, and society within a common frame. There was relatively little disagreement about structure. Whether it was the Ecole des Beaux-Arts itself, the Ecole Polytechnique, or rebellious and innovative architects like Labrouste and Viollet-Le-Duc, the matter of structure, of building techniques, and even of the use of new materials, was not particularly controversial—it was their meaning that was contested. The battles over styles were battles over the social. The fact that the problem of style could not be solved meant that the problem of architecture had not been solved. Starting in the 1850s, French art and architectural historians developed the periodization with which we still work. Stemming from the Neo-Grec and the Gothic, the acceptance of other periods and cultures became more general and more organized. Architects undertook vast, detailed, and systematic descriptions of the structural and decorative styles of the past. Historical restoration and a "rationalist" position appeared together in French architecture. Between 1840 and 1860 the historical school produced a massive repertoire of historical styles in technical and scientific terms, thereby making them accessible to reproduction. The true historical nature of classical antiquity, as opposed to its Renaissance reconstructions, as well as Viollet-Le-Duc's successful reinterpretation of the Gothic, were eventually accepted into the canon, although debates continued to rage about the significance of each. Attention then turned to studies of more "exotic" building styles—Chinese and Persian—completing the inventory of styles available for imitation in such treatises as Leonce Reynaud's nineteenth-century *Traité d'architecture* (1850–1858), a manual to which many referred.[27] Academic respectability, stylistic eclecticism, and theoretical exhaustion reached a climax in the teaching of Julien Gaudet (1834–1908), who held the Chair of the Theory of Architecture at the Ecole des Beaux-Arts from 1894 to 1908. Gaudet advocated the teaching of classical doctrine. However, he redefined the classical: "Everything that deserves to become

classical is classical, without limits in time, space or school
. . . everything which has remained victorious in the struggle of the arts, everything that continues to arouse universal
admiration."[28]

Viollet-Le-Duc: Rationalism and Historicism

While there was general agreement in architectural circles
about the importance and inevitability of new technical advances, there was also a broad consensus that changes in materials and construction techniques did not offer a sufficiently
coherent stylistic base for modern building. Nineteenth-
century discussions turned on the correct way to unify style and
technique. These two currents were joined in the work of Emmanuel Viollet-Le-Duc (1814–1879). His project to save the
architectural patrimony of France was not an isolated antiquar-
ian or nostalgic enterprise. Its aim was Janus-faced; the principles of architecture that provided the groundwork for the
future of French architectural development lay, according to
Viollet-Le-Duc, in the proper uncovering of the technological
and cultural genius of the past. He sought scientific principles
of restoration: the Gothic cathedrals interested him for their
complexity and brilliance, not for their mystery. His first methodological principle was that one should not touch any monument without preliminary study. The historic conditions of the
style had to be fully documented, then the specific vicissitudes
of its construction, and finally, the site itself. Viollet-Le-Duc's
credo was: respect the system's own logic; each building is the
result of a rational underpinning. The genius of the artist always developed from a coherent structural system—a system
linked to a world vision and a culture.

Archaeology, for Viollet-Le-Duc, was a comparative anatomy
of antique and modern monuments. The particular logic of
each period contributed, when part of a larger comparative
method, a step toward a universal structural method. But this
was not modernism; the goal was not pure form but a system
that could only be fully apprehended by placing it within its
own cultural and historical time. The problem was how to combine historicism and rationalism in a new form that allowed

them to coexist and thereby reveal a new type of truth. This alternation between the attempt to ground the nature of architectural principles by uncovering historically sedimented meanings and the firm belief that there were rational principles given for all time was, as we have seen, characteristic of many areas of nineteenth-century inquiry.

Viollet-Le-Duc learned his trade and forged his doctrine through a rigorous case-by-case study of France's architectural heritage and through commissions from his powerful friends. He never attended the Ecole des Beaux-Arts, having decided instead as a young man to tour France and draw its medieval buildings—he effectively provided his own atelier and training. He traveled and drew in the French countryside for five years (1831–1836) before extending his travels and education to Italy. In 1839, a friend of his family, Prosper Merimée, the Inspecteur Général des Monuments Historiques, offered Viollet-Le-Duc the task of restoring the cathedral at Vézélay. This opportunity launched Viollet-Le-Duc on his famous life work. In a continuing working relationship with Merimée, who named his Inspecteur Général des Edifices Diocésains in 1853, Viollet-Le-Duc was in a position to analyze, catalogue and reconstruct France's architectural heritage.

Viollet-Le-Duc was an ardent regionalist and demonstrated how the particularities of local conditions and history were intimately tied to regional customs and architectural styles.[29] After years of work in historical reconstruction, most importantly at Vézélay and at Notre Dame, Viollet-Le-Duc articulated, beginning in 1854, the detailed defense of his rationalist position in his *Dictionnaire raisonné de l'architecture française du XIe au XVIe siècle*. A clear presentation of its essential points is found in the first of his two-volume *Discourses* of 1860. He proposed

to inquire into the reason of every form—for every architectural form has its reason; . . . to call attention to the application which can be made of the principles of ancient Art to the requirements of the present day: for the arts never die; their principles remain true for all time; humanity is always the same;—however its customs and institutions may be modified, its intellectual constitution is unchanged; . . . it is moved by the same desires and the same passions; while the various languages it employs do but enable it to express in every age the same ideas and to call for the satisfaction of the same wants.[30]

The quote maintains an uneasy balance between claiming that architecture has a grounding in eternal, rational principles—"that there is a nature of human knowledge that determines its form and that can be made manifest to it in its own empirical contents"—and claiming that genius in art arises from particular historical and cultural embodiments—"that there was a history of human knowledge which could both be given to empirical knowledge and prescribe its forms."[31] Viollet-Le-Duc's lifelong goal was to invent a language which would allow both of these poles to coexist and be given full expression.

Viollet-Le-Duc's rationalist belief that forms derive from structural determinants made all of architectural history available to renewed examination and reevaluation. For him, ancient art no longer had absolute primacy; there could be no a priori decision as to what forms were the most appropriate. As circumstances and problems varied, so too did architectural solutions. Viollet-Le-Duc did not hold that architecture was a simple expression of a culture.[32] Art, like Reason, had a certain autonomy, because it arose from the functioning of a human faculty. Art was not reducible to either the political conditions of a people, or to the state of its sciences. The Greeks, for example, were often mistaken on questions of anatomy, and their political institutions were far from perfect. While modern governmental machinery was superior to that of ancient Greece, "this does not prevent the Iliad and the Odyssey from maintaining their rank as superior to all other poems, either of the past or of the present. Hence we may conclude that Art is not dependent on the political state of a nation."[33]

Having strenuously argued for the rationalization of architectural understanding and practice, Viollet-Le-Duc also sought to relativize architectural history: "Art does not reside in this or that form, but in a principle,—a logical method. Consequently no reason can be alleged for maintaining that one particular form of art is Art, and that apart from this form all is barbarism; we are justified in contending that the art of the Iroquois Indians or that of the French in the Middle Ages may not have been barbarous."[34] By means of this pluralizing historical move, a vast field of possibilities opened and the potential for a new unity was established.[35] Once historicism had dissolved the absolute authority of the ancients by revealing the principles underlying their work, the path was cleared for rediscovering a French style rooted in a uniquely French genius. He argued that the French, having the same topographical, climatic, spiritual, and social conditions as their ancestors, should rationally favor the Gothic. Viollet-Le-Duc was not calling for academic imitation of past models—in his eyes that would have been substituting one irrationality for another. New techniques and new conditions existed; it was rational to learn from the Gothic, but not to copy it slavishly. Viollet-Le-Duc did think, however, that he had recaptured an architectural system which was both historical and rational. Nonetheless, the historicist acid that his rationalism exuded was corroding his privileging of a single historical style, no matter how "French" or how "rational" that style might be.

The Reforms of 1863

Although Viollet-Le-Duc did open an atelier near the Ecole in 1856, he soon found that he did not like teaching, and the atelier lasted only a few months. He returned to his ambitious restoration work and to publishing his ideas and theories on architecture in his massive *Dictionnaire raisonné de l'architecture française du XIe au XVIe siècle* and *Entretiens sur l'architecture*. Viollet-Le-Duc had been introduced by his friend and mentor Merimée to Louis Napoleon and Eugénie before the *coup d'état*. He continued to move in these circles throughout the Second Empire.[36]

Partially under Viollet-Le-Duc's influence, the government issued a report in 1863 calling for a major reorganization of the Ecole des Beaux-Arts.[37] The goal was nothing less than the seizure of the school and the French Academy in Rome. Four of the six professors were dismissed; new chairs were established; a director responsible to the Minister of Beaux-Arts was appointed; three official ateliers in architecture (each with an appointed professor) were established; the maximum age for the Prix de Rome was lowered to twenty-five; a new jury system and Conseil were established to design and judge the competitions; a government stipend for four years, of which two were to be spent traveling, was instituted; and the director of the French Academy in Rome was made responsible to the Ministry of Fine Arts. As was to be expected, reaction was violent. Some compromises were made, but most of the reforms were instituted on January 14, 1864. The central issue was control over the appointment of professors at the Ecole; this power was taken over by the government. More diversity was instituted and the scope of the curriculum broadened. Some appointments, such as that of Pasteur to the chair of geology, physics, and chemistry, received widespread approval.

The most controversial appointment was that of Viollet-Le-Duc himself to Professor of Art History and Aesthetics. The Ecole's traditional and architecturally conservative doctrines were clearly under attack. Viollet-Le-Duc's first lecture, on January 29, 1864, turned into a fiasco. He delivered an extremely pedantic talk on the influence of civilization on art. From the first and continuing until the seventh—and last—lecture, raucous student demonstrations followed each performance. In March, Viollet-Le-Duc resigned. Hippolyte Taine was named to replace him and assumed the position in January 1865 with a series of lectures on Italian painting. He was enthusiastically received by the students, thus marking the end of the crisis and of the government's attempt to institute major reform of the Ecole.

Paris: The City

By the 1850s, the conditions of housing, health, circulation, and infrastructure (water and sewage) in Paris were appalling. Paris had very few large streets; the major east-west and north-south axes were insufficient; the major exterior roads leading to the ports of Paris quickly diminished in size and accessibility within the city, and they were poorly linked, uneven, and crammed with traffic. The central market, Les Halles, had become practically inaccessible by the middle of the nineteenth century.[38] Paris's population had increased from 580,000 in 1805 to 1,274,000 in 1851 and would rise to over 2,000,000 by the end of the Second Empire. The terrible housing and hygienic conditions of the poor had only worsened with the large influx of population, especially in the old, central quarters. There was no regulation of the innumerable, cramped living quarters in the courts behind the controlled facades. Cholera reappeared in 1847, 1848, and 1849.[39] The Saint-Simonian Victor Considérant commented darkly in 1848 that Paris was "a great manufactory of putrefaction in which poverty, plague, and disease labor in concert, and air and sunlight barely enter. Paris is a foul hole where plants wilt and perish and four out of seven children die within a year."[40] Officials were fully aware of the need to extend the state's control of public health beyond the street, but a combination of popular resistance and Liberal governments ensured that this was very slow in happening.[41]

From as early as the fifteenth century, urban order in France had been conceived in terms of three elements—the house, the street, and the city—and the problem of how (legally, aesthetically, financially, socially, politically, and medically) to relate them. The state and society met at the street. De La Mare's *Traité de police* contained numerous street regulations: the length and size of streets, *police des bâtiments* (i.e., materials), the height of houses, dangers, fires, cleanliness, movement, decoration, and embellishment of public ways were all prescribed. These royal police regulations concerning space were the entry point of procedures for state intervention into social life. The eighteenth-century French state's concern with fixing a floating and dangerous population gradually turned into a politics of health, opening a discursive and institutional field for experimentation which continued to expand almost indefinitely to the present. By the end of the eighteenth century four major trends could be identified: (1) the increasingly important role of the state, in which, however, other authorities (scientific, architectural, and medical) played major roles as consultants; (2) the public nature of debate: truth was no longer esoteric, and its authorized spokesmen multiplied; (3) population as an object of scientific inquiry and administrative control; (4) the search for techniques for containing and curing disease (as well as other social problems) and the thematization of, and experimentation in, prevention of diseases.[42]

Haussmann's Predecessors

The Comte de Rambuteau, appointed Prefect of the Seine in 1833, had initiated a number of projects which Louis Napoleon and Haussmann were later to magnify and bring to fruition. Rambuteau's reign marked a new willingness to intervene in the central fabric of the city rather than to follow the more traditional methods of placing external limits on city growth or attempting to control the populace through incarceration. Many of the proposed street changes were taken from the 1793 *Plan des artistes* drawn up during the convention that produced Paris' overall street scheme.[43] Widening of streets was proposed, as was the standardization of street widths (five categories were established); a general plan for Paris's sewers was drawn up, and water distribution was improved. Timidly following the *Plan des artistes,* conceived for a Paris without railroads and less than half its current size, Rambuteau's achievements were necessarily limited.

Rambuteau's changes were initiated within the context of a major policy debate about the city's markets. Les Halles had been at its site on the Right Bank, across from Ile de la Cité, since the Middle Ages. With the appearance of railroads in the 1830s, the amount of produce coming into Paris increased substantially, to meet the vast increase in population of the first half of the century. In 1842 the government declared the provisioning of Paris a matter of public order. Rambuteau argued the economic, political, and medical advantages of maintaining the market in its centralized location, even though the only way to do so would entail major changes in surrounding streets. After a lively debate, during which the need for some form of long-range planning for Paris was recognized, the commission concurred and voted to begin work in 1847. The events of 1848 brought a halt to even these timid efforts. In 1851, the City Council approved the plans for the market extension and street improvements, although for financial reasons the start of work was delayed until 1852, by which point Louis Napoleon's coup d'état had taken place. On June 22, 1853, Louis Napoleon appointed a new prefect, Georges Haussmann.

Haussmann: Regularization

The physical changes that Louis Napoleon and Haussmann (1809–1891) implemented in Paris over their eighteen-year collaboration are unquestionably the most substantial Paris would know between the Revolution and the Second World War. If there is general agreement that these changes were important, there is little agreement as to their exact significance. Leonardo Benevolo, in his standard *History of Modern Architecture*, labels Haussmann's efforts "neo-conservative town-planning," while Françoise Choay emphasizes what she calls Haussmann's "regularization."[44]

The phrase "neo-conservative town-planning" is seductive. It contains, however, an ambiguity: the phrase implies a forerunner, conservative town planning. Certainly, there had been a baroque ordering within cities (grand perspectives, symmetrical distribution, and attention to monuments) but it is questionable whether this should be called urbanism in the modern, technical sense, in that it was unable to accommodate change and was not geared to industrial society. Although a more detailed discussion of urbanism is reserved for later chapters, suffice it to say that Haussmann's goals extended far beyond the glorification of the sovereign, while not yet attaining a full articulation of social conditions. As has been pointed out repeatedly, Louis Napoleon's regime had political and police objectives; it also had a clearly defined sense of the economic and medical importance of the circulation of goods and men, as well as elements of an aesthetic program. Choay argues that Haussmann's neoclassicism can be separated from that of his predecessors by several traits: its gigantic scale, out of proportion with baroque sensibilities; its strict regularity and uniformity, which opposed classical conceptions of order; its privileging of autonomous, individual monuments; and finally, its systematic use of urban parks as both aesthetic and hygienic instruments.[45] Benevolo gives a telling example of this disparity: the boulevard de Strasbourg, leading up to the Gare de l'Est, was 2.5 kilometers long, making the railway station invisible from Châtelet at the other end.[46] Despite the scope of their intervention, Haussmann and Louis Napoleon lacked a normative project for the ordering of the social milieu—any direct and plausible attempt to link norms and forms—precisely, it will be argued later, what defines modern urbanism.[47]

Haussmann approached the city as a technical object to be worked on, improved, and regulated. To this end, one of his first efforts was to establish a detailed and comprehensive plan of Paris. The fact that it took a year to complete indicates the degree of specialization, administrative hierarchy, and technical proficiency demanded for such a task, as well as the previous paucity of adequate technical tools. The top priorities were hygiene and circulation. Regional geologic studies of water supply led to the implementation of a successful plan for clean water and the efficient elimination of waste. Circulation meant opening wide avenues, connecting them to squares or places, and establishing further connections with smaller arteries. Haussmann's roads were straighter, longer, and wider than ever before; sidewalks were greatly expanded and more gas lamps placed along them. The avenues allowed for circulation of cars, people, air, and street light and provided greatly enlarged green spaces. Haussmann approached the distribution of park space in terms of the numbers of inhabitants, the distance from other parks, the general distribution of parks across the city, and beauty. With less success, he sought to establish a decentralized distribution of medical care in Paris. However, he did build a number of large, peripherally located mental hospitals, the most famous of which was Sainte-Anne. He proposed a plan for the equal distribution throughout the city of schools of all levels, and of municipal administrative offices, churches, and theaters. In addition to more traditional monuments, the new railway stations formed major points of articulation for the remodeling of Paris. The city's seven major stations formed a grid around the old city but were poorly linked to the center city and to each other; connecting roads were made a top priority.

Choay argues that Haussmann retained a static, and hence archaic, conception of the spatial framework of the city and of the social order, one fundamentally at odds with the logic of the emergent industrial, technocratic, and administrative rationality of capitalism. Marcel Roncayolo adds that within this structure Haussmann sought a capitalism of the stock market and commerce, maximizing the circulation of goods, men, and money, rather than a capitalism of the factory and its disciplines.[48] Haussmann and Louis Napoleon understood Paris as a political, economic, and technical object, but not yet as a social one.

History and Eclecticism

In 1832 Guizot reestablished the Académie des Sciences Morales et Politiques with five sections: philosophy, ethics, legislation, political economy and statistics, and history. The history section was cast as "philosophic history," distinct from the erudite history of the Académie des Inscriptions et Belles-Lettres. Other major institutional projects accompanied this renewed surge of enthusiasm, debate, and combat over the meaning of France's history. Villermé was himself elected to the political economy and statistics section of the Academy; yet only Michelet, among major historians, was directly interested in his work or that of others concerned with the social dimensions of contemporary France. It was only outside the Academy's hallowed walls, among the Saint-Simonians, doctors, and administrators, that such research was given due attention.[49]

The first half of the nineteenth century was a period of intense interest in history. By the July Monarchy of 1830, Paris had employed two full-time historians to document past policies, laws, and regulations. Special attention was paid to monuments as auxiliaries of historical studies.[50] Haussmann ardently rode the wave of historical passion; he founded a series of publications entitled "General History of Paris," established an archaeological and historical department at the Hôtel de Ville, used new methods of photographic documentation, supported independent scholars doing historical research on Paris, searched for old maps as part of a project to reconstruct the history of the city's topography, and underwrote a major project to complete a block-by-block documentary reconstruction of the whole city.

The creation of a Parisian historical museum, housed in the Hôtel de Carnavalet, was motivated in part by the desire to reach a larger public. As the Baron Poisson, its creator and a close friend of Haussmann's, put it, its goal was to place a material history of objects alongside written history. Serving as a center of documentation, it accompanied and facilitated Haussmann's destruction (done with a clear conscience) of many old buildings. Haussmann boasted that he was thoroughly documenting the Paris he destroyed. It is worth underlining that neither Paris's urban fabric nor its domestic architecture qualified as sufficiently historical to be included in the museum or identified as a target of preservation. Haussmann was supported in his attempts to isolate Parisian monuments from their urban context by the Historical Monuments Office, which had been inspired by Viollet-Le-Duc. Beyond scholarly circles, there was very little opposition to Haussmann's demolition policies until the late 1860s. When opposition did arise, it was arguably due, at least in part, to the increased historical awareness which Haussmann's work had encouraged. However, with the destruction caused by the events of 1870 and 1871, these criticisms remained muted, and it was only under the Third Republic that a strong preservationist movement appeared.

The Beaux-Arts anxiety over style was paired with a practical exploitation of diversity in the explosion in luxury buildings for the bourgeoisie, which characterized the second half of the century. Viollet-Le-Duc built villas as well as restoring cathedrals. During a period of far-reaching spatial changes in Paris, orchestrated by Haussmann, vehement debates raged at the Ecole des Beaux-Arts; but these discourses remained disparate and distinct. To give one small but not insignificant example, Neil Levine's massive thesis on Henri Labrouste, which devotes hundreds of pages to the architectural debates of the mid-century and which is itself a classical monument of scholarship, barely mentions Haussmann. Style and the city remained epistemologically separate, if physically intermingled, domains.

By mid-century, however, attempts were made to link the debates over style, technique, society, and history that were prominently carried on in the most successful and influential French architectural journal of the nineteenth century, the *Revue générale de l'architecture et des travaux publics*, founded and edited by César Daly and lasting from 1840 to 1889.[51] Daly was sympathetic toward efforts to reform French architecture, championing Labrouste's attacks on Beaux-Arts orthodoxy. Although Daly himself was not a confirmed partisan of a particular school, he was a fervent believer in the existence and significance of the connections between style and society. Society was changing, and so too, Daly believed, must architecture. The *Revue*'s contents were broad-ranging and eclectic, spanning technical construction details, aesthetic theory, archaeological reports, and accounts of the latest buildings at the World Expositions. Daly was innovative in publishing accounts of new materials, procedures, and systems of heating and ventilation alongside aesthetic discussions of ancient monuments. The *Revue* advocated technical advances, but it also held that changes in materials and construction techniques did not offer a sufficiently coherent stylistic base for modern building. Even those who were enthusiastic about the new building materials like steel, glass, and concrete maintained that art had its own prerogatives which could not be subsumed under mere technology.

The logo of the journal reveals art and science mediated by history. Daly's positivist faith rested on the belief that a new style would emerge once a scrupulous scientific study of the past uncovered the laws of historical development. One of the *Revue*'s main purposes was to make the history of architecture better known to architects, to aid in the search for new and appropriate styles. Daly was aware of the dangers of eclecticism but saw it as a useful tool in preparing the ground for the emergence of a new and vigorous style. The term eclecticism was linked to the philosophic doctrines of Victor Cousin, which he had formulated early in the century but summarized in his 1853 work, *Du vrai, du beau, du bien* [Of truth, beauty, and the good]. Cousin advocated a systematic survey of all past philosophical systems; by choosing the best parts of each, he hoped, a superior system would emerge. As architectural candidates for such a synthesis, Daly successively presented the Neo-Grecs and Viollet-Le-Duc, as well as the new industrial structures constructed at the international expositions. Recognizing the fragility of such an approach, Daly made a distinction between organic and transitional periods. The second half of the nineteenth century was a transitional period; the mere recognition of this historical fact, he argued, was already a significant step forward. Daly's positivistic faith required that an answer soon be found.

3

Experiments in Social
Paternalism

As we have learned from Michel Foucault, Robert Castel, Michelle Perrot, and others, philanthropic and scientific reform efforts through the 1870s focused on the articulation of spaces of discipline and moralization. Their common aim was to form a *prévoyant* worker, a monogamous family, and a conflict-free, hierarchical social order. Noting that the word "normal" first appeared in official French usage in 1854, Perrot reminds us that working-class families at mid-century were seen to be in crisis only from the perspective of the discourses of normality.[1] In the 1860s and 1870s, normalizing techniques were applied in separate but parallel ways to the home and to the work force, but not yet to the city. Modern urbanism and the totalizing social planning it embodied were born only at the end of the century, when a form was invented that combined the normalization of the population with a regularization of spaces.

Liberal Limits

Louis Napoleon and Haussmann, though conscious of the problem, implemented almost no programs aimed at industrialization, workers' housing, and the suburbs. Haussmann renovated and disengaged circulation points for goods—docks, stations, stockyards, and storage points—but did very little direct planning for industry per se. The regime's lack of effective action on housing for the working class and the poor in Paris was even more pronounced. Although Haussmann succeeded in requiring the facades of Parisian apartments to be cleaned every decade, he could not pass a provision to limit qualitatively or quantitatively the dwellings built on lots behind these buildings, which were sites of extensive substandard housing. Liberal ideas of the sanctity of property and the fear of workers' associations continued to block any effective response to this social problem, despite Louis Napoleon's personal interest in such questions.

A good example of these limits was the question of expropriation. Before 1789 expropriation had been a royal prerogative. The first effective change came with the law of May 3, 1841 (incorporating a principle established in 1807), which expanded the expropriation powers available for public works. The 1841 law, written and implemented for the massive railroad projects of the 1840s, was restricted in its applications within Paris. An important extension of the principle of expropriation was made by Louis Napoleon in the law of December 25, 1852, which allowed expropriation for *Grands Travaux* (large-scale public works) by executive decree. Essentially, the strategy consisted of borrowing on the surplus value generated by the upgrading of property. In an important decision of December 27, 1858, the Conseil d'Etat ruled that the city no longer had the right to resell the land which it had expropriated for public works. This right was given back to individual property holders, and the city denied the general revenues, even though the works it had undertaken had generated the surplus value in the first place. Speculation increased dramatically.

The other structural block was the lavish expropriation damages paid by juries to their peers. Maurice Halbwachs's detailed study, *Les Expropriations et le prix des terrains à Paris de 1860 à 1900,* remains an invaluable discussion of the social and economic consequences for Paris of these decisions. After 1860, with expropriation juries granting consistently higher awards than the government, the costs of acquiring land rose sharply.[2] A growing piecemeal speculation in land and housing taking place on the periphery paralleled major speculation in the center city. Private developers, mainly small ones, were left to their own speculative devices and received little or no aid for infrastructural necessities. The great growth of the Parisian suburbs throughout the second half of the nineteenth century went unregulated.[3] Yves Lequin makes the important point that both Haussmann-type operations and the planned workers' cities represented only a miniscule fraction of the growth of housing and the general development of French cities during the nineteenth century. The growth of cities in the heyday of liberal capitalism was not planned, and its history remains to be written. Christian Topalov makes a parallel point for the twentieth century.[4]

During his London exile Louis Napoleon had followed the English reform movements with some interest. Prince Albert, in 1848, had placed the issue of the housing needs of the poor into the full light of public attention by commissioning a set of model houses for the London World's Fair. The architect of these houses, Henry Roberts, published two books on the subject—*The Model Houses for Families Erected by Prince Albert* in 1851 and *The Dwellings of the Laboring Classes* in 1853—which greatly impressed Louis Napoleon, who immediately had them translated into French.[5] Viollet-Le-Duc wrote the introduction to the French edition of Roberts's book. In an oft-quoted passage he proclaimed: "It is a great honor to be deemed worthy of going to Rome; it is to one's credit to return bearing the drawings for some palace destined to embellish our cities, but he who finds or propagates the means to drive away the dampness which makes such a large number of the homes of urban or rural workers so unhealthy, that person will earn the recognition of the whole country and create a source of inexhaustible satisfaction."[6] In 1849, Louis Napoleon, inspired by Roberts's ideas, offered 50,000 francs for workers' housing, a sum that was increased in 1852, after the confiscation of Orléans property, to 10,000,000 francs (nine-tenths of which was never accounted for). He directly financed the building of a residential complex for 500 people, the Cité Napoléon. Largely because land was too expensive in Paris for single-family houses, Louis Napoleon proposed a high-density block housing 200 families and a smaller number of single men.[7]

The plan posed problems of social control for authoritarian liberals that were clearly laid out by Villermé: "How do we prevent these unfortunate encounters of a large number of people going up and down the same staircase each day, traversing the same hallways, seeing each other at the door of those bathrooms unfortunately shared by several unfamiliar families, where one should be the most hidden from view?"[8] The Cité Napoléon included four buildings of three to four stories, with 170 individual dwellings of two rooms and a kitchen, and a number of single rooms for single men. Flats were grouped around central galleries. Located on the ground floor were community facilities for day care, laundry, baths, and health care, as well as shops, workshops, and common meeting rooms. Regulations for the Cité Napoléon contained 100 articles, including mandatory hours at which workers were to return home and mandatory school attendance for their children. Fear, rigidity, and a police mentality informed these disciplinary features to such an extent that the Cité was referred to by workers as a barracks. Despite the terrible shortage of housing in Paris, only the most desperate workers accepted the city's provisions. Several of the working-class delegations to the Parisian Universal Exposition of 1867 were quite articulate in their disapproval of Louis Napoleon's projects. They accused the philanthropists of constructing quarantined quarters; they countered with a proposal for a government tax on vacant apartments to force down rents and increase the number of available units. The Cité Napoléon was a failure; boycotted by workers, by the 1880s it had become a bourgeois residence.[9]

Louis Napoleon had originally planned to build a similar complex in each of Paris's *arrondissements,* but opposition was so widespread that the plans were abandoned. Opposition came from all establishment quarters. Proposing workers' housing was equated with advocating socialism.[10] Villermé rejected them for inflaming class hatred and encouraging depravity; he lamely expressed a hope for private industrial initiative as a solution to the housing problem. Given the chorus of disapproval and the cost of urban land, as well as the political and legal impediments to state social programs, no further steps were taken in Paris during the Second Empire to address workers' housing needs. The problem, however, did not go away; nor was it totally ignored. Its most important and coherent theorist was Frédéric Le Play; the most important laboratories of paternalistic social spaces were Mulhouse and Le Creusot.

Le Play: Social Science and Social Reform

Frédéric Le Play (1806–1882), an extremely influential (if personally unsuccessful) social reformer, was a metallurgical engineer actively concerned with the social consequences of industrialization. Politically, he sought to create an alternative to liberal individualism, revolutionary change, and the reactionary advocacy of preindustrial society. In search of a moral science of order and reform, he focused on strengthening family bonds within a hierarchical society in which an elite of the wise and the informed would assume the responsibility of ensuring a happier and more harmonious social order.[11]

Le Play is best known for his pioneering, detailed monographic and comparative studies of workers. *Les Ouvriers européens* consists of monographic accounts (thirty-six in the first edition, of 1855, and fifty-seven in the second, of 1878–79) of workers' families and budgets throughout Europe and beyond. A recent scholar claims that the study "represents the first instance of large scale empirical research based on a standardized method that combined both observation and quantification (placing) the study of family structure and work relations in different types of societies."[12] Le Play's scientific aim was to develop a comparative classificatory system of the family. His political aim was to provide a scientific basis for a harmonious industrialized society. The data were collected between 1829 and 1855; after 1855, Le Play turned to an active public life.

Student, Scientist, Reformer

Le Play saw his life as divided into three periods: student, scientist, and reformer. Born in Normandy in 1806, he was sent to live with a rich uncle in Paris, where he was introduced to conservative Catholic, Restoration ideas. The contrast of Normandy and Paris for Le Play was a shock, providing a source of reflection on the multitude of differences between rural France and Paris. As with so many others, while continuing to proclaim the virtues of the rural and provincial life, he left its supposed

virtues behind for more exciting Parisian prospects. Returning
to Normandy upon his uncle's death, Le Play refused a local
position. Instead, he returned to Paris in order to continue his
studies. Admitted to the Ecole Polytechnique in 1825, he dis-
liked the abstract teaching (including the Saint-Simonian doctrines of many of his fellow students) and harsh discipline. He
transferred to the Ecole des Mines where he graduated in two
years with the highest honors ever accorded.

The Revolution of 1830 was a major turning point for Le
Play: "France has had ten governments since 1789. Each had
been ushered in and subsequently overthrown by violence.
When I saw the blood spilled by the July Revolution (of 1830), I
dedicated my life to the restoration of social harmony in my
country."[13] The remedies, he hoped, would be found through
a more exact and empirical study of social conditions. He entered a period of nonpolitical activity lasting until the 1848
revolution. Le Play, while sharing some Saint-Simonian social
concerns and emphases on technology, nonetheless differed in
important ways in his analysis and remedies of France's problems. One of Le Play's most insistent rhetorical tropes was his
attack on the a priori and abstract nature of the Saint-Simonian
theories. Echoing the critiques of the Société des Observateurs de
l'Homme, Le Play insisted on facts, not systems: "While I was
carrying out my apprenticeship as an engineer, I did not know
where I would find the remedy to the ills of society; but after
acknowledging the sterility of preconceived ideas, I was sure of
one thing: that in the science of society as in the science of
metallurgy, I would not believe that I had found the truth until
my ideas could be based on direct observation of facts."[14]

Le Play was named director of the statistical bureau of metals
in the Ministry of Public Works in 1834 and carried out extensive surveys of the state of the industry. One of his major interests was to extend the collection of government statistics on
industrial production to include details of the private lives of
the workers. As part of his official duties, in the next ten years
he made research trips to the major European countries and to
Russia to examine the social and technological state of industry
in each, emphasizing the comparative dimension of all sociological facts as well as the importance of linking micro-level dimensions with his macro-level grid of family evolution. In 1848 Le

Play was nominated inspector of the Ecole des Mines. In addition to the technical curriculum, Le Play developed courses on the administration and sociology of mines for future engineers. During the twenty-five years of his teaching at the Ecole des Mines he was granted six months' leave each year for research, providing him with time for gathering the massive data compiled and analyzed in his *Les Ouvriers européens*.

Neither a socialist nor a liberal, Le Play advocated an elitist hierarchy in which men of science, drawing on the accumulated wisdom of local authorities, would institute humanitarian social reform in the interests of a more harmonious society. Those institutions promoting cooperation between classes he supported, those calling for struggle, he opposed. He was strongly opposed to Spencer's individualism and to Darwin's naturalism; he considered De Tocqueville's *Democracy in America* to be the most dangerous book of the century, because it advocated equality. Le Play's diagnosis of France's problems was sweeping:

The bonds of patronage have been broken and individualism has a free hand; commercial competition has become a struggle for existence and rages unchecked by the traditions of former years. Only the strongest can resist its assaults; the others succumb. Outstanding individuals advance to the front ranks: they rise higher and higher and reject the troublesome obligations which the old regime imposed on them with regard to the weak; and the feeble, left to their own resources, sink lower and lower. Thus, social inequality develops, dragging after it a cortege of selfishness, suffering, hatred and envy.[15]

On both moral and analytic grounds, he opposed Adam Smith, Utopian Socialist evolutionary thinking, and Quételet's statistical laws. He divided the blame for the evils of modern society equally between the encyclopaedists and the utilitarians of the eighteenth century. While he criticized the ahistorical and asocial bases of liberal and universal schemes, he also distanced himself from the correlation statistics of Quételet. Not only did these lack a comparative dimension, they ignored individual action.

Le Play shared the conservative analysis of the crisis of modern society as one of relations of authority; authority, cooperation, and stability had to be restored in the family and work place if France was to regain its health. Industrialization was inevitable; there could be no simple transposition of earlier social structures onto the present. Change had to be understood and accommodated, or France would not achieve social peace. Le Play's undertaking can be best understood as an attempt to render empirical and operational certain pillars of conservative doctrine: the family as the elementary, moral cell of society; society as a hierarchically organized entity; the functional necessity of institutions; and the importance of history in understanding and directing social change.

Le Play had become acquainted with the tradition of German descriptive statistics (which included family budgets) in his travels to Germany and particularly to the University of Göttingen, where this mixture of geography, history, law, political science, and public administration was still being taught. He organized a course in descriptive statistics at the Ecole des Mines and carried out his own investigations using its categories. The key indicator of the health or sickness of the prevailing social conditions was, he thought, the strength of moral ties (i.e., authority relations). His researchers inquired into: commitment to worship and to religious instruction; the state of general and professional education; general laws on marriage, widowhood, and single life; laws on prostitution, legitimate and illegitimate births, and abandoned children; a summary of the judgments of various courts; and principal laws covering individuals unclassified in society's ranks and without known professions.[16] Through comparative macro-correlations of social institutions, and a fine-grained attention to the moral ties and private life of social groups, he hoped to develop technologies that would accommodate and strengthen the ties appropriate to both the general structural conditions of modern industrial society and the particular historical and social settings of different groups.

Monographies: Totalization and Individualization

Le Play was perhaps the first to distinguish between workers, the poor, and the criminal classes.[17] Other social reformers, such as Parent-Duchâtelet, had interviewed Parisian prostitutes, and Villermé had certainly used empirical methods in his studies of working class conditions. Le Play sought a research technique that was both more particular and more comprehensive. The focus of his inquiry was the comparative conditions of the European working class. He departed from many other conservative thinkers in not choosing the peasantry (seigneur/serf or master/servant pairs) as his social and moral yardstick of authority relations. For Le Play, the working class occupied a strategic position in modern society. While still possessing elements of peasant culture, it was also the most exposed to the ravages of new industrial conditions. Workers suffered the most under industrialization, yet their welfare was crucial to the emergence of a harmonious state of social relations. The habits and customs of the working class were the reservoir of an important set of moral bonds. Le Play sought to establish with scientific precision which of these bonds were worth strengthening. Outside of the family, he was most concerned with the patron/worker relationship. Workers were directly subject to the influences of their environment, since they lacked the means to alter or resist the combined influences of the soil, the climate, and human history. The combination of social importance and environmental passivity made the workers strategically crucial subjects of study and reform.

Le Play began with the elementary structures: "If we want to recapture the mentality of the past and thereby gain a thorough understanding of the present situation of the working classes in the West, the best way to proceed is to study conditions in countries where the agricultural and industrial techniques, the organization of labor and the natural relations of the various social classes remain like those which existed in France in past centuries."[18] Although new conditions would prevent the exact reduplication of these social relations, social science, through comparative historical study, could nonetheless gain important insights into healthy hierarchical arrangements.

Le Play opted for intensive study of a relatively small number of workers' families set within a macro-comparative frame. He was highly critical of previous government-sponsored inquiries (particularly those following the 1848 Revolution). Their bad design, he argued, combined with an administrative personnel who did not appreciate the importance of correct method, had produced inaccurate information. Le Play worked out a systematic series of questions explicitly designed to limit the bias of the investigator and to provide a comparative frame for the data. Questions provided a means by which the investigator could demonstrate to the worker "the public usefulness of its goals and the spirit of self-sacrifice which inspires the observer."[19] Le Play advised presenting little gifts and flattery to facilitate the flow of information. Researchers were advised to let the worker talk as much as possible; to recount theories; to dwell on favorite subjects; to wander while the interviewer carefully recorded all this personal information. Only by a thorough understanding of the private sphere of human relations, Le Play argued, could a full understanding of the differences between social groups be scientifically classified. Statistical comparisons missed the most essential aspect of social activity, the private realm.

The guiding purpose of the inquiry was diagnostic. Le Play sought a scientific means of assaying the state of essential moral bonds; the moral atmosphere of the home was the vital indicator. He sought techniques for producing families who were thrifty, *prévoyante*, and disciplined. "No matter where we look in Europe today, the heads of most families lack foresight. Sometimes only an insignificant minority have developed this quality. Consequently each social system must provide special mechanisms to make up for this moral deficiency. These mechanisms are usually found in the relationships which link workers to masters, communities and voluntary associations."[20] Le Play argued that society advanced ineluctably in complexity as well as individuation. In the face of change society could choose external means for maintaining order, or internal restraints: "The external law which regulates actions can only become less repressive if the internal law of the soul becomes more so."[21]

Along with many liberals, Le Play saw distinct limits to social engineering. Total reconstruction of society posed the greatest danger: the destruction of moral bonds. Le Play, like many other French thinkers, then and now, saw the attempt at remaking the whole society as the major danger of the Revolution. The role of the reformer was to work on material that was already there; a mining engineer did not create minerals, he mined them. The strongest material, as it were, had to be set correctly so that the whole social edifice would stand harmoniously. This material was "the elite" or "social authorities." Each community contained its social authorities: "Individuals whose private lives can be considered models; who demonstrate an outstanding propensity for good, regardless of race, condition and social system; who by the example of their households and their workshops (as well as strict observance of God's law and the customs of social harmony), win the affection and respect of all those who surround them; and finally, who make well-being and peace reign in the community."[22] As Le Play did not assume that all members of a class embodied these virtues, the identification of the true social authorities became an important task of social science. Le Play drew a sharp distinction between this social elite and the ruling class. When the two coincided, the result was a prosperous and healthy period; but frequently, the ruling classes and the elite were separate groups. Under Louis XIV, for example, decadence was the primary impulse, establishing the conditions for the horrors of the eighteenth century and the Revolution. Certain people seemed to have the ability to adjust to new circumstances, to carry forward older social traditions, without decadence. The belief that the more powerful and prominent figures in a community are morally superior and best represent general values is an enduring assumption of conservatism; superior morality and talents are held to be the basis of social legitimacy. Le Play thought that the elite could be identified and its influence strengthened. The social skills embodied by this group, however, could not simply be fabricated. The role of the reformer was to articulate the means of identifying and sustaining a new elite for modern society.

Reform: Universal Expositions

Les Ouvriers européens was published in 1855 under the official imprimatur of the Imperial Press of Louis Napoleon. Le Play's pretensions for it were impressive: "It contains social facts which establish the truth, the scientific method which allowed me to discover them, and the plan of reform that I derived from them."[23] In 1856, Le Play was appointed to the Conseil d'Etat, thus beginning his third, or reformist, period. Le Play's books of the next fifteen years were essentially condensations of his massive *Ouvriers* supplemented with reform proposals. In 1856 he created the Société Internationale des Etudes Pratiques d'Economie Sociale, with Villermé as its first president and including other leading figures such as Emile Cheysson, director of the Creusot steel works (to whom we turn shortly) and leading actor in the introduction of statistical methods in France.

Again and again, Le Play emphasized the importance of training the elite in new methods to enable them to act knowledgeably and effectively. He dedicated his book *La Méthode sociale* to this elite. It was "intended for the ruling classes who, in accordance with the tradition of the great races, desire to prepare themselves by systematic journeys to fulfill in worthy fashion the obligations imposed by the supervision of domestic households, rural and manufacturing workshops, neighborhoods, local government and great national interests."[24] Although Le Play failed to influence social legislation, his role in a series of Universal Expositions did present the opportunity to have his models widely disseminated. Le Play accepted official posts at the Universal Expositions of 1849, 1851, 1855, 1862, and 1867 and used his position, particularly when in 1867 he was appointed Commissioner-General, to propagate his views. He first drafted a report, for the steel section of the 1849 fair. He played a slightly more active role in the famous London Exposition of 1851, as a member of the French commission. Louis Napoleon, after his seizure of power, looked to the 1855 exposition as a showcase for the imperial pretensions of his regime. However, a war with Russia, mismanagement, and bad planning delayed the opening. Le Play was called in at the last minute to take over as Commissioner-General. He managed to pull together a credible showing, thereby attaining public prominence. He organized a competition for the most successful industrial patron; the prize was won by Jean Dollfus at Mulhouse. Among other innovations Le Play instituted awards for workers and foremen. Spurred by the suggestions of Jerome Bonaparte and a group of former Saint-Simonians, Le Play helped organize systematic meetings of workers at the expositions. These had been first initiated in London (as a spur to the formation of the First International).

In 1863 Louis Napoleon named Le Play head of the 1867 Exposition to be held in Paris. Le Play instituted a new category of awards for harmonious and moralizing industrial relations. The jury was composed entirely of government officials, church officials, and industrialists. It is fair to say that the majority of French industrialists was hardly more enthusiastic about these philanthropic schemes than were the more revolutionary workers. With at least tacit governmental support, Le Play insisted on unofficial representation for trade unions, which were still illegal. He provided free travel arrangements for workers from the provinces, had barracks-like housing constructed, and even paid a small stipend to workers coming to the fairs. Those workers were asked for and submitted their own evaluations of the competitions and of the state of labor relations in general. They criticized the lack of union representation; they emphasized the absolute necessity for industrialists to provide workers with a living wage; they criticized the apprenticeship system; and they demanded freedom of association, the end of the *livret* or workbook system, more education and health benefits, and compulsory arbitration.[25]

At the Paris exposition, the prize for the most successful industrial patron went to a certain von Diergardt, owner of a silk and velvet mill at Viersen in Prussia. His mill provided schools, a pension system, free education, and other model provisions. While hardly standard in the practical world of industry, these programs were accepted among reformers and a small group of industrialists. Von Diergardt, however, went further in providing security of employment, encouraging loans for workers to buy housing, and encouraging women to work (although not in the factory)—all favorite provisions of Le Play's own reform schemes. Community relations and savings were given the most attention as keys to preventing labor strife. In his evaluative report on the 1867 Exposition, Le Play argued that the work and expense was too great for a temporary exposition. He urged, to no avail, the establishment of a permanent exposition located in a town outside of Paris, so that education and exchange of information on labor relations could take place with more regularity. Such a center of information and debate—the Musée Social—was formed at the end of the century, under the direction of reform-minded industrialists and their allies. As we will see, the Musée Social spearheaded the drive for modern urbanism in France.

Rural Industrial Laboratories

Industry during the Second Empire continued to follow the eighteenth-century pattern of locating in the countryside, away from the major metropolises. The city and industry remained separate spatial entities.[26] The housing and planning schemes implemented in the city of Mulhouse in Alsace were awarded numerous commendations, highlighted as models at international expositions, and much discussed then and now in the scientific literature. Designed by Protestant industrialists, these experiments embody the nascent art of paternalistic liberalism.[27]

At the end of the eighteenth century Mulhouse was already an industrial center employing some 8,000 workers, including a large community of foreigners. Reorganization came with industry; the city's gates were taken down in 1809, and suburbs began outside the old city; the Rhône Canal was strategically engineered to pass through the southern part of the town; land was allotted for industrial development; the water system was reworked to accommodate industry; and the railroad appeared in 1842. The town's class segregation intensified as the city grew. Mulhouse's bourgeoisie moved out of the overpopulated center city to a new quarter, conceived in 1826 for some 200 luxury houses (only one-third of which were ever built). The promoters were the leading families of Mulhouse; the model was a neoclassical imitation of prestigious Parisian quarters, laid out around a formal garden and closed to the non-bourgeois. The symbols of liberal capitalism were placed in the town's central square: the Société Industrielle de Mulhouse, the Chambre de Commerce, and the stock exchange.

From this bastion of provincial liberal capitalism emerged one of the most important loci of reform thought and practice in the nineteenth century, the Société Industrielle de

Mulhouse. Founded in 1825, its stated aims were to advance industry, raise it to the state of a science, and encourage the spirit of enterprise while proposing projects of public utility to the state. These enlightened Protestants proposed schemes for education, baths, health services, mutual aid societies, savings banks, pensions, asylums for the old and infirm, and precautions against work accidents.[28] Under the initiative of the industrialist Jean Dollfus, the Société Mulhousienne des Cités Ouvrières was founded in 1853, with both private and public funds, to guide the construction of workers' housing. The first decision concerned the choice between a large block of flats and separate houses. Although the former were more economical, they had social disadvantages and were unanimously rejected by the advisory committee at Mulhouse:

The convenience and cleanliness of a man's lodging have a greater influence than might be thought on the morality and well-being of the family. If we can offer these same men clean, attractive houses, if we can procure for each man a small garden, where he can find pleasant and useful employment, where caring for his own small harvest he can learn to value that feeling of ownership which Providence has instilled in us all, shall we not have solved one of the most important problems of social economy? Shall we not have contributed towards strengthening the sacred bonds of the family, and rendered a true service to this class so worthy of concern, to our workers and to all society?[29]

For the first time, an *autorité sociale* had recognized the legitimacy of workers' comforts and needs, previously acknowledged only for other classes.[30]

Mulhouse represented a laboratory situation in the sense that it was the product of comparison and experimentation, involving careful consideration of construction materials and criteria of economy and hygiene, social criteria for the layout of rooms and of the collective space as a whole. Mulhouse workers' housing was designed by Emile Muller, who was chosen because of his familiarity not only with local housing conditions but with other solutions to housing questions in Europe. A two-bedroom house with a garden (1,300 square feet, calculated to grow vegetables worth two months' rent) was rented to workers at about half the going rate. These houses, and their spatial grouping, were conceived to create an environment which would inculcate moral habits of domesticity, responsibility, and punctuality. In return for the low cost, the worker had to agree to maintain his vegetable garden, send his children to school, pay his debts, make a deposit in his savings account each week, and contribute to a health fund (from which he received medical care). All the plans provided for running water, a toilet, specially demarcated spaces for eating and sleeping (assuring the separation of parents and children, boys and girls), and a common room. Communal services were also provided including baths, a swimming pool, laundry, schools, shops, a library, and medical facilities. The whole complex of houses was located adjacent to the textile manufacturers. A street plan separating the main traffic from subsidiary traffic routes provided the basic grid pattern for the development.[31]

The Mulhouse reformers sought to force individuals to be virtuous in order to gain entry into liberal society. Workers were visited regularly by committees who inspected their houses and awarded prizes for order, cleanliness, and general upkeep.[32] By 1867, over a thousand such dwellings had been built.

Le Creusot: Regulation and Distribution

The town of Le Creusot in Burgundy was a much-observed laboratory for industrial and social experimentation. Its directors, the Schneiders, friends of Louis Napoleon, were highly placed throughout the Second Empire, and their efforts were rewarded at the international expositions. Le Creusot can be seen as a larger-scale experiment sharing the principles of Mulhouse but placing more emphasis on profit, advocating more "advanced" social schemes, and possessing a less fully disciplinary *encadrement* than Mulhouse's social paternalistic efforts.[33] Discussion of Le Creusot introduces Emile Cheysson, whose work on statistics and the reformulation of social liberalism later in the century provides an essential bridge to the emergence of modern urbanism and planning.

Between 1782 and 1785, the most modern steel plant in Europe had been constructed in Burgundy at a site called Le

Crozot. The site was rich in coal, and the foundry constructed there soon attracted other enterprises, including a royal glass-works. Although the Revolution and its associated economic crisis induced the factory's failure, the stage was set for its development as one of France's major steel and metallurgy sites. In 1826 the old factory was purchased and renovated. The manufacturing space was enclosed behind an extended wall, new wells were dug, and an interior rail system was installed. The major forge was resituated so as to link up directly with the regional railway system. These changes destroyed the older symmetrical, classically-inspired architectural space of the manufacturing compound. New functional considerations replaced the distribution of buildings according to a representational plan. Although the movement toward functional space was piecemeal, once it was underway, the classical distribution of spaces was gone forever.

During the expansion years of mid-century, the industrial space became less urban, developing in accord with an industrial logic of transport, multiple and efficient use of buildings, and a spatial coordination geared to increased production. Between 1836, when the Schneider family acquired the firm, and 1855, when the process of rebuilding was completed, there was a progressive evacuation of nonproductive functions at the factory site; by 1855 there were no remaining trees. New types of industrial buildings and a new distribution of them produced a flexibility and interchangeability of function as well as a capacity within the buildings for the expansion of individual units.

With the increase in industrial production at Le Creusot, the population soared from 1,300 in 1826 to 13,000 in 1855. Growth imposed the problem of lodging the work force. At first, the factory owners simply duplicated the eighteenth-century, military-style organization of workers under strict surveillance and control. Old industrial buildings were reconverted into barracks. These two-storied constructions had small rooms on the top floor for bachelors and one-room apartments for couples on the ground floor. For a time, these barracks lodged all those working at the factory except local peasants still living in their villages. The first major step away from the barracks solution was taken in 1825 with the introduction of a sort of half barracks, half individual residence, a model directly imitating a Welsh mining town. In good disciplinary fashion, the building was designed to minimize workers' sociality and to maximize and strengthen family interactions. Although elements of rural housing typology were integrated into the design, they were moralized for city life (e.g., each domestic unit had its own entrance and shared no space with its attached neighbors).

The town itself grew in a basically unplanned fashion, following speculative investments, although the Schneiders used a variety of regulative measures to shape its development. Philanthropic, paternalistic institutions of social hygiene were financed by the Schneider family and centrally sited around their new residence in the old royal glassworks. It was only toward the end of the Second Empire that partial attempts were made to coordinate the three spaces (industry, town, and institutions). It is important not to construe piecemeal changes as a strategy coherently planned from the start. The "inflationist" view of industrial towns as fully-formed embodiments of a strategic intent must be tempered by a more complex and fragmented picture.[34]

The Schneiders built a school in 1837, financed by obligatory workers' contributions to a Caisse de Prévoyance and "gifts" from the owners. The school included training for the factory; its teacher was paid one-third of the salary of a worker. The Schneiders also built a church, a town hall, and a post office, grouping them around their own imposing residence. The paternalistic, social-hygienic intent involved would be hard to dispute and its effects easy to overestimate. Schools, for example, were undeniably intended to play a moralizing and disciplinary role. Although schooling was not obligatory, a child who had not gone to school was ineligible to work in the factory. Homogenization of the population was certainly another goal. Emile Cheysson, director of Le Creusot, captured both dimensions when he argued that schooling aimed to: "inculcate in every mind respect for authority . . . to efface in Le Creusot those class distinctions which no longer correspond to anything real and which still offend legitimate sensibilities."[35] There was more than one path to social peace; Cheysson saw a need not

only for obedient and efficient workers, but for educated employees, and above all, for some commonality on which to base
non-antagonistic social relations.

The first public buildings were simply the old factory structures converted to new uses. The new hospitals and schools
followed plans derived from recently established international
standards; they had no explicit historical or stylistic references.
Prize-winning architects trained at the Ecole des Beaux-Arts
who were awarded commissions for state buildings followed J.-
N.-L. Durand's method of drawing all buildings on the same
scale, allowing for a uniform system of types based on function.
During the course of the nineteenth century, administrative
buildings, hospitals, and schools were standardized. The
churches were the only buildings by architects and the only
ones marked with signs of architectural historicity. The mid-
century phenomenon of technological experimentation took
on an international dimension through the medium of the Universal Expositions. Le Creusot was one of the main producers
of steel edifices and frames for state projects under Louis
Napoleon, and later for the colonies. The techniques used in Le
Creusot's own industrial architecture were echoed in many of
these constructions: perhaps the best known is the Galeries des
Machines at the Universal Exposition of 1878. Its revealed
structure, its potential for modular expansion, and its interior
rail link for machinery all paralleled technical solutions developed for Le Creusot itself.

New types such as workers' housing constructed in accordance with the normalizing recommendations of hygienists,
building technicians, and industrialists were produced.[36] The
Schneiders did not undertake a comprehensive housing program. Only two housing complexes for workers were built at Le
Creusot, and they were built, at least in part, to be presented
as models at the Universal Expositions of 1867 and 1878.
Schneider was anxious to present an exemplary social achievement at the 1867 Exposition Universelle. Le Creusot's La Cité
de la Villedieu offers an example of a complete and coherent
morphology: a formal geometric space produced a formal
equality; no differentiation, characteristic marks, or urbanity
intruded. One hundred five single-family houses were con-

structed on identical geometric parcels and placed in exactly the same place on each plot. A homogeneous space of economy and hygiene replaced the street as the organizing principle.[37]

The Schneiders' goal was to have workers build their own houses. But by 1869 only 24 percent of the households were worker-owned. Although the Schneiders may not have actually built the town of Le Creusot, they certainly regulated its development through intervention in the real estate market. This enabled them to control the direction, pace, and character of urban growth. Their control of the credit market was also important; credits for construction were made available to workers seeking to build their own homes, but in amounts sufficient for a very small minority of workers. Although a great deal of discussion ensued over the need to instill morals in working-class families, very little housing was built for this class during this period. The only group for whom the Schneiders did systematically provide housing were the higher-level company employees, and in the long run, it was this group who was best suited to his self-regulatory, self-policing model. Politically, the promotion of a local *petite bourgeoisie* of artisans, storekeepers, and salaried employees, was intended to form—and was successful in forming—the stable, conservative backbone of the town. This "elite," having already made the *prévoyante mode de vie* their own, and having the income to afford houses in the first place, spread the model of the single-family house beyond its intended limits and used it to different social ends.[38]

Until 1854, Le Creusot was covered by a series of regulations following the classical *ordonnance:* placement, alignment, and height. Property owners were required to construct sidewalks. Some streets were straightened. A marked definition of public and private domains was evidenced in the requirement of closable doors for all entrances giving onto the street. As most of the workers at the factory were still closely connected to peasant, rural spatial practices, *ordonnance* at this level did define an urban milieu. The application of technical procedures of regularization and hygiene drawn up by specialists characterized the period from 1855 to 1867. New regulations included the interdiction against building in courtyards and alleys and the requirement of septic tanks; by 1863 all construction plans had to be approved by the company. Fire insurance was required to receive credit.[39]

A form of prezoning evolved in Le Creusot: the factory was gradually cleared of habitations; the living quarters were to some extent regularized; and the majority of the city's *équipement* (hospital, church, school, and civic administrative buildings) was localized. This constituted prezoning and not zoning, because there was no overall plan guiding these operations. The rationalization of industrial space in the name of efficiency first defined the overall distribution of spaces; then hygienic and regulatory considerations were progressively—if partially—articulated, and finally even less comprehensively implemented. These processes were not yet linked by a common vision.

Resistance: Social Demands

The amplitude of the strikes that swept France in 1869 was as unexpected as it was traumatic for police and patrons alike.[40] Many of the tools forged to create social and economic order were double-edged. Thus, most workers, having passed through the Schneiders' schools, were literate. The primary demand of the strike was for more representation in running the Caisse de Secours, the mutual-aid fund. Workers' demands were diverse: they requested precise details on the administration of their funds, stipulated that fired workers be allowed to serve on its board, and asked that certain foremen be fired. When the vote on worker participation in the Caisse unexpectedly went against the Schneiders by a margin of almost four to one, they were enraged. Eugène Schneider hurriedly returned from Paris and closed down the factory, even allowing the steel furnace to be shut down. The Minister of the Interior sent some 3,000 troops to occupy the town. Twenty-five strikers were sent to jail; several hundred workers were fired and black-listed by other steel plants; schoolchildren were given homework assignments on the horrors of the strike; and "delinquents" were chained and paraded through the streets. The judge who presided at the trial of these individuals intoned: "In the midst of a community until now loyal and trusting, and which has suddenly become ungrateful, a strike whose causes are unknown breaks out. This is the blackest ingratitude toward a management which has been exhaustive in its efforts and unsparing of its budget to spread well-being and education in this industrial enterprise so admired abroad."[41] The strike was a failure, as were contemporary strikes at Mulhouse and other model factories. However, the "social question" put on the agenda by industrialists like Schneider, had now become part of the larger political agenda. Some industrialists, including Emile Cheysson at Le Creusot, realized that the form of social technology aimed at forcing discipline and morality on workers was, by itself, inadequate to the task of ensuring social peace.

New Elites:
From the Moral to the Social

In the late 1860s French faith in progress was at its pinnacle. The Saint-Simonian doctrine holding that states evolve from warrior to industrial stages—in which competition in industry and science replace war—seemed to have been verified by the Suez Canal, the railroads, and the great popular success of the universal expositions. Complementing this faith in progress was a belief that among all nations, France most fully embodied these historical trends. Chauvinists—after all, M. Chauvin was French—did not so much hate as disdain foreigners.[1] Confidence in France's military strength was particularly high. On the left, a strong residual current of faith in the "nation in arms" remained; on the right, there was blind confidence in the Imperial army, as a bulwark against exterior aggression and the potential internal dangers posed by the masses. A strong current of antimilitarism, supported by the Freemasons, opposed jingoistic militarism more than the preparedness of the French army. Little critical attention (on the part of either the military or the general public) was paid to rethinking technical questions of arms or strategy. Warning signs were largely ignored. The Prussian victory over Austria at Sadowa in 1866 was commented on but not given close scrutiny. Only Edgar Quinet and a few others saw it differently: after Sadowa Quinet wrote of a new world coming into being: "This is another race of men making its appearance."[2] A few observers noticed that the universal military service instituted in Prussia implied that a whole nation could be militarized and made to serve nationalist goals.

The challenge and threat posed by the power and modernity of that new race would soon impose itself on numerous domains of French life.

After the wave of strikes in 1869, the defeat by the Prussians in 1870, and the shattering events of the Commune in 1871, important segments of the conservative *classes éclairées* began to face up to the obvious fact that far-reaching changes were not only necessary but inevitable in almost every sphere of French life. For conservative groups, the gradual stabilization of the Republic and an undeniable turn to the left by the end of the 1870s, together with the disappearance of realistic hopes for a monarchy (capped by the death of the Comte de Chambord in 1883), signaled their own loss of power and authority. The parliamentary elections of 1881, in which the Republican majority reached 81 percent, dispelled any lingering doubts about the durability of the Republic. The *coup de grâce* was delivered by Pope Leo XIII in his famous *Rerum Novarum* 1891 Encyclical, which urged French Catholics to accept the Republic.

To many conservatives the political makeup of the nation seemed dangerously leftist, implying endless demagoguery, division, and the decline of France. Although the Paris Commune had been crushed militarily, it was clear that revolutionary sentiment as well as the conditions that had produced it still existed. Many conservatives concluded that some accommodation of the Republic was inescapable. From this it followed that they too would have to participate actively in new reform processes, which they no longer controlled. At this juncture, given the conservatives' poor showing in the elections, parliamentary politics hardly seemed the most promising course to social reform.

Hubert Lyautey: A Modern French Hero

One of the most important issues under discussion was France's problem in producing new elites. The theme of a meritocratic elite was, and still is, a recurrent one in modern French social history, but its contents and contexts varied. Conservative reformers sought not simply to overcome a conjunctural crisis but to devise a means to guide French society for generations to come. One figure who linked the worlds of reform and reflection was Hubert Lyautey (1854–1934), future Maréchal de France, head of the Protectorat in Morocco from 1912 to 1925, and certainly the colonial figure most written about in modern times. In a celebrated call for reform, he wrote: "Rather than hateful violent war, which fruitlessly divides brothers, political parties, and classes, to substitute peaceful and fertile research on the problems posed by the industrial revolution of these times. Does there not exist a cadre in the military sense of the term, by nature capable of more sensible actions than the others, and if such a cadre exists, is it not the first to be imbued with the necessity and urgency of social responsibility?"[3] It was hoped that the political dangers of revolution from below and the petty parliamentary paralysis of the bourgeoisie could be avoided through the identification and institutionalization of an elite. There was a chance, Lyautey and others believed, that through the creation of new social techniques, France could successfully enter the modern world on a par with its rivals.

Many biographies of Lyautey open with an evocation of his aristocratic and rural upbringing—even though he grew up in Nancy, and moved to Dijon and then to Paris, when his father was named Ingénieur en Chef at Versailles. Lyautey's youth was more intimately connected with urban settings than with any *vie de château*. As the branches of the Lyautey family came from different regions, André Gide's famous reply to Barrès about *enracinement* applied to Lyautey as well. The nostalgia for a rural elite and a harmoniously hierarchical world embedded in this myth are clear; more distinctive and more modern is Lyautey's own literary self-creation, which, at least most of the time, he knew to be one of his most important weapons. The (self-)construction of Lyautey as aristocrat in search of a nation worthy of his virtues is striking when contrasted with the textual destiny of General Gallieni, inventor of pacification theory and practice and Lyautey's commanding officer in Indochina and Madagascar. Gallieni was a bourgeois and an ardent Republican who neither commissioned biographies nor cultivated the Parisian salons. Although Gallieni certainly belonged to the new elite Lyautey sought to invent, he remained in the textual shadows. He never engendered a cult; the left had other heroes.

The women in the Lyautey household were devoutly Catholic, and the men were military, being imbued with an ethic of state service. Lyautey's grandfather had been Ordonnateur en Chef des Armées de l'Empire and sired three generals. His father became an engineer after attending the elite Ecole Polytechnique and the prestigious Ecole des Ponts et Chaussées. Conservatives rather than reactionaries, the Lyauteys faithfully served France, and not its passing governments.[4] Much symbolic capital had been invested in Lyautey's fall from a balcony, at the age of two-and-one-half, while he was watching a military parade in Nancy. His back badly damaged, requiring corrective surgery and a brace, the boy was solicitously attended to by the women of the household, and became high strung, sensitive, and willful. The young man's will to survive, his self-discipline, and his natural grace enabled him to overcome his handicap and to achieve strong character and eventual glory (and strengthened the metaphoric identification with the French nation). A further recurrent element in the biographies, significant for this narrative, is the depiction of the young Lyautey kneeling in his garden, assiduously building cities (not chateaux) in his sand pile, joining his father's engineering talents with the artistic flair of a precocious urbanist.[5]

Aristocracy, for Lyautey and his biographers, while rooted in race and environment, derived validity from an elitism based on service, merit, and grace. Lyautey's fundamental distinction was, to use the modern jargon, between an elite of ascription and one of achievement. He expressed utter contempt for his aristocratic friends whose concerns were limited to guns and horses: "From the beginning I have always been drawn to the social elite on the one hand, and to the peasant and the worker on the other, and completely alienated from the mediocre, envious petit bourgeois from whose ranks come the majority of those who govern us today."[6] The key word was *petit*. All the ambiguities, the hatred, the confusions, the paternalism, and the fear so common in the right during this period are captured in this quote; uncommon, however, was the insistent undertone that only major change, only reform at the top, would save both France and his class.

Social Catholicism, Social Works

Having recovered his physical health, Lyautey attended the preparatory school for the Ecole Polytechnique and the military academy of St-Cyr. Perhaps out of respect for family tradition, he chose St-Cyr, where he discovered "a barbarous land where the material and the superficial are the idols one worships."[7] Discouraged by the anti-intellectualism, blind emphasis on drilling, spiritual sterility, and lack of fraternity, "this eternal tedium, this loathing, this vexation," Lyautey turned away from the majority of his cohort of rich, complacent officers.

While attending a lecture with his small circle of ardent, high-minded Catholic friends, Lyautey experienced his first major spiritual and social engagement. The lecture was given by Albert de Mun, who was in the process of organizing Catholic action groups to address social questions. De Mun and his close friend, René de La Tour du Pin, were joint founders of the Oeuvre des Cercles Catholique d'Ouvriers, an organization devoted to improvement of and fraternization with the working class.[8] The crucibles from which these groups emerged were the events of 1869, 1870, and 1871. In the war, both de Mun and La Tour du Pin had quickly been taken prisoner. As officers were garrisoned in comfortable compounds (similar to a pension), they had ample time to meditate on the causes of France's humiliation. Both concurred that the basic weakness was moral. A book by Emile Keller, *L'Encyclique du 8 décembre et les principes de 1789*, provided them with the analytic elements they were seeking. The book (in the mode of Taine) was an attack on the French Revolution for destroying the foundations of authority by promoting the insidious idea that the individual was master of his own fate. Keller argued that the spread of these revolutionary sentiments was responsible for the serious decline of social bonds, and consequently of all community. Keller was elaborating on a papal encyclical, the *Syllabus of Error*, issued by the conservative Pius IX in 1864, which sought to address the new spiritual needs of industrial society. Individualism was the problem, and hierarchical community was the answer.

After the armistice, de Mun returned to Paris in time to witness the outbreak of the Commune and to participate in its suppression. He was struck and confused, however, by the Communards' extraordinary bravery—comparison with the manner in which his own soldiers had confronted the Prussians was inevitable—as well as by their hatred of the bourgeoisie. De Mun testified to a parliamentary inquest into the origins of the Commune as follows: "The evil from which our society suffers derives from two causes. On the one hand there is a profound hatred of the upper classes by the working class, and on the other a complete apathy among the bourgeoisie for the welfare of the workers and a complete lack of ability on their part to distinguish error from truth. Between the classes there is today a profound abyss that can be filled only by time and by a better moral education. I do not believe that force alone can bring about any amelioration."[9] In 1871, de Mun, his brother, and the Marquis René La Tour du Pin formed the Oeuvre des Cercles Catholique d'Ouvriers, essentially a series of meeting rooms in which games, concerts, schooling, free meals, limited loan arrangements, and obligatory religious observance were combined, in an attempt to create a public space in which France's warring classes could come together and discuss the nation's problems.

In order to understand the call for elitist reform that de Mun and his spiritual, aristocratic Catholic friends put forth in the 1870s it is necessary to look back briefly at the development of the church's relations to social questions in nineteenth-century France. Systematic attention on the part of the Church to the plight of industrial workers is usually linked to the Société de Saint Vincent de Paul, founded in 1833 by Frédéric Ozanam. The Society was distinctive both for having acknowledged the existence of a problem and for developing a system of local organization, parallel to but not identical with that of the Church itself. Its success produced its downfall. In 1861, Napoleon III, frightened by its organizational reach, dissolved its central council. The Society survived in a diminished form, regrouping after Napoleon's downfall. The Société de Saint Vincent de Paul, however, never looked beyond charity to the causes of poverty and disorder.

Neither the Society nor Le Play's attempts at social organization (after 1870 he established the Unions de la Paix Sociale to bring workers and patrons together) succeeded in finding an organization or ideology which both the Church and the conservatives could accept. When the liberal and socially minded Pope Leo XIII came to power in 1878, he was faced with a French Catholic Church that was embracing increasingly phantasmagoric schemes for a return to a Gothic society of hierarchy and absolute order, exactly at the moment when the Republic was moving toward the center. The brightest new recruits, like Lyautey, realized that more modern and sophisticated methods had to be invented. Although Zeldin mocks the fact that "its purpose was as much the salvation of the souls of these students as that of those they assisted," Lyautey and his friends realized that saving the souls of aristocratic youth was not an easy or irrelevant task.[10] In 1874, at the age of twenty, Lyautey was enthralled with Le Play and claimed to have memorized all of *La Réforme Sociale*. He soon abandoned his faith in the moralizing paternalism of both de Mun and Le Play, seeing their proposed solutions as part of France's problem. The settings for Lyautey's loss of faith were visits to two different cultural and political contexts: Algeria and Italy.

Orientalism

Upon completing his military training in 1878, Lyautey received two months' official leave. Still an ardent Social Catholic, he planned to accompany René de La Tour du Pin on a sort of pilgrimage to the exiled Comte de Chambord in Austria. Surprisingly, when his best friend, Prosper Keller, made a counterproposal to go to Algeria for six weeks, Lyautey accepted. The decision foreshadowed his future: he would focus on the colonies, their political and social questions, and not on the monarchy, the Church, or aristocratic good works. In the coming years Lyautey distanced himself from each of these pillars of French conservatism.

Like any young officer of his class and generation, Lyautey was familiar with the major contours of Algeria and its colonial history. However, his connection was closer than that of many others, as several members of his family had fought in Algeria in the early days of the conquest, and stories of their exploits were familiar household tales. He was anxious to experience the country firsthand. The two young men first visited Constantine, in the east. Lyautey's immediate reactions were predictably Orientalist: "The train station in Constantine: horse-drawn trolleys, civil servants, gas-lit boulevards; but beyond this European prose we can already visualize the Arab interiors where three or four white figures, crouching around the Moorish coffee urn, are smoking."[11] Given the obligatory tour of the Bey's palace and the winding streets of the Arab city, Lyautey enthusiastically embraced what could be called the initial moment of an Orientalist progression. Rehearsing the standard clichés, Lyautey's reaction was nonetheless positive: "First evening in Constantine: at last some local color: what a dream out of the *Thousand and One Nights!*"[12] Lyautey moved quickly from the guidebook monuments and curiosities to a more refined, highly textualized appreciation of the Orient's sensuality, as embodied in Delacroix or Flaubert: colors, sounds, smells, bodies, notebooks, and sketch pads. Although he soon encountered everything he hated in France, there were exceptions; one young officer, an amateur archaeologist, provided a scholarly appreciation of local surroundings.

Visiting the site of a large Roman city, Lambese, Lyautey was impressed by the Imperial urbanism; the military, economic, aesthetic, and hygienic wisdom of the choice of site. The uninspired manner of French military engineers too often neglected those features in their placement of towns and forts. Adjacent to the Roman ruins was a French prison. "I never look at these brutal institutions without wondering if they are truly the supreme invention of society. I cannot believe that within those walls there is only the brute beast and that regular whipping is the best discipline. The guards, as everyone admits, are as bad as the criminals, with their trafficking, etc. I am ashamed to find myself here."[13] To this young aesthete, everyone caught in the web of these institutions—guards and prison-

ers alike—seemed destined for the same ruin. After a tour of
the tribal areas, Lyautey and Keller reached Algiers. Lyautey
was again impressed by the site but repulsed by what the
French had built on it. "There is nothing but shoddy goods and
pastiche from the elegant Moorish woman to the vendor of
Turkish pipes made in Paris. Even the palaces, hardly re-
touched and truly beautiful, have taken on the irritating air of
European museums."[14] Europe's eclecticism mirrored its vul-
garity, casting a shadow over the light and vitality of the Other.
The young lieutenant, imbued with the glow of Orientalism
and perhaps other memories, returned to France to take up a
dreary regimental life.

Form and Civilization: Second Visit to Algeria, 1880–82

In October 1880, Lyautey's regiment was transferred to Algeria and stationed in Orléansville, a small garrison town.
Founded in 1845, Orléansville was typical of the several hundred towns and villages in Algeria built during the nineteenth
century by French military engineers: over half were cast in a
checkerboard pattern oriented by the compass points. Defense
was the primary consideration: surrounded on three sides by a
trench and fortified wall and on the fourth by a steep incline,
the town of Orléansville was well protected. An adjacent village, La Ferme, was laid out with similar Cartesian regularity.[15]
Lyautey's reaction to Orléansville was unequivocal: "As for local interest, nothing. A Frenchified town, asphalt and shops, a
few Arabs still, but unfathomable, inaccessible, and for the
most part completely corrupted by our presence."[16] Urban
form and its civilizational consequences reflected each other
perfectly. Lyautey attributed the monotony of the town's plan
to a general failing of French civilization: "Ah the prefabs! the
prefabs! the single-minded spirit of the French civil servant."[17]
The levelling effects of French bureaucracy were embodied in
the dreary towns its engineers had distributed over the Algerian countryside; a soulless provincial monotony complemented the tasteless pastiche of Algiers.

The Home

Renting an apartment on the bluff overlooking the Arab settlement below, Lyautey initiated a pattern he would follow

throughout his life. He decorated his home (always using the English word) in an exotic style, in this instance, à l'arabe. In this highly coded space, Lyautey wrote, reflected, entertained, and displayed his social and cultural distinction by separating himself from the majority of his fellow officers. For the rest of his life, whether in France or in the colonies, one of his initial acts was always the construction of an exoticized, cosmopolitan home.

As the duties of an officer were comparatively undemanding, Lyautey regularly went to the local Bureau Arabe to pass the morning listening to cases, gossip, and complaints. Visiting local caids and other tribal leaders became a regular source of pleasure and information, providing Lyautey material for yet another equation of spatial and civilizational qualities. "The tents stand before us; no longer the monotonous, rigid military camp, but command tents that the caids have pitched for us at each stop, colorful, varied lopsided fabrics made into verandahs."[18] He began Arabic lessons, advancing, he thought, toward a truer understanding of the realities of Algerian life. His world was still manichean and Orientalist. The negation of French life led to the positive valorization of the Arab. One was whole and manly, the other empty, fragmented, and sexless (there was no female in Lyautey's world). These initial formulations provided him with a matrix of sensual experiences and analytic elements by means of which he could sharpen his criticisms of French society. Wholeness no longer lay in the neo-Gothic visions of the French past, but in Arab civilization.

In March 1881 Lyautey was transferred to the offices of the Etat-Major in Algiers. Suffering a violent reaction to the sterility and stultifying constraints of bureau life, he found that his second visit confirmed his vehement distaste for French Algiers. Accepting money from his family, Lyautey chose a sumptuous villa overlooking the city and bay. His family connections gained him immediate entry into Algier's most exclusive colonial social milieu, which he found stupid, sterile, and artificial. "It is we who have the air of barbarians in the midst of barbarians. Our prescribed mores, our Parisian houses, our customs, seem as offensive here as vulgar failures in art, wisdom, and understanding."[19] Society, form, and intelligence comprised a whole that was either civilized or barbaric, degenerate or life-giving. If Lyautey had contempt for the limited and boring life of his fellow officers and the local French elite, he reserved a scathing hatred for other sectors of the colonial population, and above all else, for the press (who throughout his career returned the favor).

How would an Arab not feel exasperated? Not a single day passes in which this disgraceful tainted thing known as the Algerian press does not debase him, promise his destruction, deny him any sense of honor, loyalty, intelligence, or aptitude. Pretty maxims for all-out egalitarians and so-called liberals, men with plenty to say about universal brotherhood . . . and since, after all, we cannot destroy an entire people, I conclude that unless we return to a more civilized, humane, and sensitive system, the insurrections will continue to occur like clockwork.[20]

Lyautey warned of the political dangers inherent in the social destruction French colonization had wrought: it had dissolved all local social forces, leaving only a disintegrated powder for the French to govern. The answer was to start anew, to create new men: simultaneously soldiers, engineers, architects, school teachers, farmers, and who knows what else. Engineers must become poets; archeologists, economists; and military men, visionaries.

Re-Orient: Beyond Nostalgia to the Social

In the fall of 1882, Lyautey returned to regimental life, beginning a dark period of stagnation. His career, off to a rapid start, stalled, as he remained at the rank of captain for a decade. Suffering from a profound nervous exhaustion and irritability, the word "tedium" returns time and time again in his letters. His open disdain did not endear him either to his fellow officers or to the military hierarchy. Barely reinstalled in France, Lyautey asked for, and was granted, a leave of two months to go to Rome. Although officially charged with drafting a report on the reorganization of the Italian cavalry, his real mission was to contact Pope Leo XIII and the Comte de Chambord for his aristocratic friends. Lyautey found the Count disappointingly intransigent on the Republic and the modernization of French society. His death in 1886, and the subsequent exile of all pre-

tenders to the throne, marked the end of monarchist hopes for
all but the most fanatic. Granted an audience with the Pope,
Lyautey took the last communion he would for decades, in the
Sistine Chapel. His religious faith was in crisis. Already dis-
abused of his respect for the army, seeing clearly the lack of a
plausible monarchist alternative, and sobered by the pope's acceptance of the Republic and the worldly decadence of the high
clergy, Lyautey gave himself over (both in Rome and then in
"Proust's Paris") to a sort of dandyism.

Italy and North Africa have been objects of articulate Orientalist discourse.[21] Lyautey devoured Rome's artistic treasures,
especially the architecture. Taine's writings in hand, he repeated the standard clichés about climate, creation, and politics, concluding that small aristocratic Republics were in every
way superior to large democracies. Slaves did the work, aristocrats occupied themselves with the arts, war, and public affairs.
In the modern world, "we are confined in categories, by careers, and woe to he who tries to escape. Social classes have
been suppressed, but the division into specializations that has
replaced them is equally intolerant and tyrannical."[22] While
remarkably indulgent—classes no longer existed for him in
1883!—Lyautey nonetheless shared none of the contemporary
nostalgia of both right and left for occupational groupings.
Lyautey's diagnoses spared neither himself nor his generation:
"Our beautiful and vibrant generation of 1873. What a bank-
ruptcy. We lacked a guide; de Mun absolutely confused us, and
led us down the wrong path, which is, in sum, an impasse. This
is also his school's problem; they are ideological Jacobins; they
are wrapped up in an absolute idea; as for realistic possibilities,
they just sneer."[22] Lyautey displayed courage and consistency
in generalizing Taine's critique of the French Revolution to
include conservative Le Playists, identifying their rigidity and
fanaticism as cultural processes which had led France to
decadence.[23]

By the end of his first contact with other societies, Lyautey
did have, in larval form, the elements of a strategy for renewal.
He knew what he hated. Having found elements of wholeness
in Arab society, he sought to recast them in a form appropriate
to modern society. Lyautey advanced beyond stereotyped for-

mulas to articulate a more modern understanding of cities, culture, and society. Beyond the compatibility of high art and small aristocratic republics, Lyautey identified another harmony: the specific character of meridional architecture, which was so well adapted to the local climate and mentality. Naples had achieved the integration of family structure and beauty appallingly absent in European Algiers. Not all European cities were failures—the vernacular had historical lessons to teach. On another trip to Rome Lyautey was impressed by the use of architectural monuments in the social life of the city. Exultant at the potential for more than stylistic pastiche in old cities, Lyautey identified historical layering as a potentially productive source of social vitality. Later in Morocco, Lyautey would turn his reflections on the social importance of restoration into a pillar of his pacification policy.

Stationed in Tours, Lyautey frequented the highest Parisian literary and social circles. Searching for a spiritual ideal, Lyautey chose a new mentor, Vicomte Eugène-Melchior de Vogüé. In his *Remarques sur l'exposition du centenaire* of 1889, de Vogüé contrasted two Frances, two *races d'hommes:* those of Notre Dame (Christian, loyalist, and backward-looking); and those of the Eiffel Tower (Republican, anticlerical, and idealist, who willfully ignored the treasures of the past). France had to overcome this division. Quoting de Tocqueville and Chateaubriand, de Vogüé argued againsts his conservative friends' sentimentalism; the march of science and secularization was inevitable. The crisis of modernity was social; the challenge was to invent new forms for society.

Change in the Military

France's crushing defeat at the hands of the Prussians in 1870 made it obvious that military overhaul was mandatory. To understand the state of the army in 1870, a little background is required. It was only in 1583 that the army was brought under royal control, regular pay instituted, and time limits of inscription fixed. A long process of professionalization, Weberian rationalization, and Foucaultian discipline accelerated under Louis XIV, who placed control of the army in the hands of civilians. During his reign there emerged a discourse of discipline and machine-like regulation of the body; the representation of the soldier as a controlled parallelogram of forces replaced that of the heroic warrior. It was only after another defeat by the Prussians, however, that disciplinary measures began to be widely enforced. Choiseul, named minister in 1761, instituted a series of reforms closely modeled on those of Prussia's Frederick the Great. The model soldier was expected to display not only complete obedience but the ability to perform complex maneuvers. Techniques to achieve individual bodily discipline and drilling of squadrons became important requirements for an army whose military strategy had become more offense-minded. The steps that transformed the professional army of Louis XIV and his successors into the revolutionary nation-in-arms are well known. The army became a laboratory for the nation; by forging an army, one forged a militant and disciplined citizenry. This potential was the great strength of modern democracy.[24]

With the return to power of conservative forces after the defeat of the Napoleonic armies, hierarchy and absolute obedience became military virtues par excellence. Soldiers were trained to be apolitical and to obey commands blindly. The *Règlement sur le service intérieur* of 1833 instructs: "Discipline constituting the principal force of an army, it is essential that each superior officer obtain from his subordinates complete obedience and continuous submission. One doesn't obey the man, one obeys the rank."[25] Politics were to be removed from the army, and the militarization of society ended. Conscription was abolished. In order to separate the army from the people, terms of military service were lengthened to as much as eight years. In 1835, Quételet, basing his work on Buffon's inquiries and Villermé's expansion of those studies, provided guidelines for choosing recruits at the optimum age, size, and temperament to maximize the strength of the army while minimizing the loss of strength in the general population.

The French army was undergoing major transformations in its social composition and becoming more conservative. The savage repression of the Commune culminated the century-long reversal of the army's place in the spectrum of French public opinion. The Napoleonic army had been seen as a carrier of democratic and nationalist hopes, and consequently, until 1848, it was held in high esteem by the left and mistrusted by the right. From 1848 to 1871, the army came increasingly to represent and enforce order and a conservative social hierarchy. French tactics until 1870 emphasized complicated group maneuvers. When some military officers began to question these tactics, after the Prussian success of 1866 and with the appearance of new, more powerful and accurate weapons, old timers such as Charles Lyautey, Hubert's uncle, accused them of disloyalty.[26]

Unlike the Prussian army, the French officers had not formed a distinct caste. In fact, because of the army's image as a progressive enclave, the officer corps had been drawn from a wide spectrum of the middle and upper-middle classes. With the establishment of the Third Republic in 1871, and increasingly during the course of the 1870s, numbers of conservative Catholics in the aristocracy and haute bourgeoisie began sending their sons into the military corps. Previously, the choice of a military career had not been a high priority for many of these families (which is not to say that they were absent from the command posts of the military). However, the army became increasingly Catholic, conservative, and defensive with the laicization of and increasingly firm Republican hold on other institutions. In the early years of the Third Republic, the number of candidates for St-Cyr almost trebled, and the proportion of noble names in the officer lists rose dramatically. Loyalty to the corps became the highest virtue; army prerogatives were jealously guarded. Social relations, in terms of family connections and proper manners, counted heavily.

Toward a Social Army

The military defeat of 1870 had put the army's technical and organizational abilities under highly critical public scrutiny and led to a number of technical reforms in the military academies. Aristocratic officers like Count Albert de Mun viewed the state of the army as a reflection of a decadence spreading in France, and Lyautey shared this view.[27] Despite the turning inward and defensiveness, despite its crushing defeat and savage repression of the Commune, the army enjoyed curiously high prestige during the 1880s. Across the political spectrum (excluding the extreme left, which was pacifist during this period), the hopes for a renewed and vigorous nation—able to reunite a divided France—focused on the army. Even as ardently Republican a figure as Gambetta could place high hopes in the army as the locus of the nation's moral regeneration.[28]

Figures as diverse as Lyautey and Jean Jaurès, however different their backgrounds and ultimate goals, analyzed the task confronting the army in similar terms. Just as Lyautey acerbically criticized the officers of his own class and political persuasion for their refusal to meet the new social challenges posed by the conscript army and changing times, so too Jaurès criticized the revolutionary socialist flank of C.G.T. pacifism at its height in the 1880s. Jaurès challenged the syndicalists of the extreme left and the officers of the extreme right in terms Lyautey could well have used. Both Lyautey and Jaurès agreed that it was only through a new, symbiotic, mutually reinvigorating exchange between society and the army that France could be regenerated. Lyautey could certainly have endorsed Jaurès's call to the recalcitrant and disdainful of the officer corps to accept the Republican order. The resources for a modern France lay within French society; the problem was to invent a means of forging the social ties that would make them flourish. It was only through the production of active social relationships, which demanded the recognition of responsibility and dependency on both sides, that the French army as well as French society would prosper.[29]

The Social Role of the Officer
One of the clearest formulations of the need for reform is found in an article Lyautey published in the *Revue des Deux Mondes* of March 15, 1891. Lyautey had submitted the article at the request of de Vogüé, a stalwart of the conservative, socially conscious journal. Military regulations required written permission for an officer to publish anything dealing with such controversial matters. Lyautey knew that his suggestions were not shared by the upper reaches of the officer corps, and so he

published them anonymously. The article created a stir, bringing Lyautey worldly success as well as official reprobation. Lyautey began his article by underlining the critical problems found in all areas of contemporary French life. France's great uneasiness and loss of direction, he claimed, were particularly palpable to those who came into contact with the generation about to make its entry into professional life. The best youths were affronted by the pervasive spirit of dilettantism, of the sterile chatter of those in power. Against this lassitude and self-aggrandizement, Lyautey called for a *rude et féconde* social action. He was obviously not calling for general social mobilization: only through a reform of the elite could France be saved from decline, sterility, and—always looming (at least in certain quarters)—revolution.

Lyautey called for a manly, meritorious, and selfless cadre; this call could only be read as an attack on the officer corps. He was not painting the entire canvas of France black; there were positive signs of effort and renewal. The Church, industry, the university, and even the press had positive elements which afforded Lyautey a glimmer of hope. These elements needed to be identified, strengthened, and unified. Diverse individuals had recognized the need for unifying, collective action. Lyautey singled out Albert de Mun and his Catholic workers' circles, Ernest Lavisse and his reforms at the Sorbonne, and E. Melchior de Vogüé. None of these three was attached to political parties; representing conservative, Republican, and liberal tendencies, each was committed, above all else, to the nation.

While Lyautey's letters made clear his criticism of the army's pettiness, its over-attachment to routine, its antagonism toward any intellectual or social questioning, and its generalized rigidity, he felt that, at least among the new officers, change was possible. A potential route to reform, Lyautey explained in his article, was the institutionalization of a conscript army, beginning in 1872 and strengthened by the 1889 law requiring three years' service. With the institution of universal military service, all healthy French males would be obliged to undergo training.[30] This law assigned the 20,000 members of the officer corps the tutelage of these recruits. For Lyautey, a good deal more was at stake than military matters, which were no longer separable from social concerns. In an argument paralleling those put forward by others for school reform, Lyautey asserted that Frenchmen's attitudes toward authority needed to be reshaped in order to save the nation. The stakes could not be higher. The recruits could leave the army with a heightened national consciousness and, more importantly, with a respect for authority that would endure throughout their lives and extend to all aspects of their social existence. The other possibility was that the army could exacerbate the class, regional, and religious differences already plaguing France. Social pacification and a stifling of the smoldering class hatred throughout the French nation could be achieved, Lyautey held, if a positive experience of authority in the name of a larger good were demonstrated in the army.

New Techniques

Lyautey's goal can be seen as a reactionary call for order or as a naïve, if generous, plea for uplifting philanthropism. However, the innovative means he proposed—which are rather more innovative and less naïve than they might appear—belie such views. His program constitutes an important interpretation of what a conservative order would look like in the modern world, as well as a sketch of the social technologies required to achieve it. Lyautey portrayed an army strangled by a complex of practices that had become counterproductive and characterized by the increasingly refined techniques of *dressage*. Disciplinary drill had become a counter-rationality unmoored from its explicit strategic objectives and blind to newer threats. The system was a self-enclosed training ground, more relevant to horse training than to meeting the Prussian threat or internal strife. This conception of drill, order, and hierarchy had been turned into a doctrine of Christian duty encased in a code of honor. The rhetoric of obedience could reach lyrical, if absurd, heights: "That which is highest, most beautiful, most worthy of admiration in our modern societies is certainly the peasant transformed by the law into an infantryman. Poor, he protects the rich; ignorant, he protects science. At the drop of a hat, he crosses seas to die without a murmur, without even knowing the cause of the war."[31] What worried Lyautey was that even after the crushing defeat by the Prussians, the consolidation of the Republic, and the institution of universal service, sentiments of this order could still be taken seriously.

Lyautey too drew on a Christian vocabulary, though of a different sort—stressing pastoral rather than disciplinary themes. In the coming period, Lyautey argued, it was the officers corps, rather than the soldiers, who had to develop and accept a Christian mission of *patronat, de devoir social* (social duty). The officers corps remained an archaic and sclerotic anomaly; it needed to adopt new practices. But, Lyautey urged, this change could be easily accomplished by infusing the army with a new pastoral consciousness while modernizing the technical aspects of military procedure. The pastoral component defined the officer's role. For three reasons, the officer was in an ideal position to fulfill a social calling. First, he shared the physical existence of his men (Lyautey never underestimated the pleasures and advantages of physical proximity and spiritual ties—they were in fact highly formative of his own character, first among the Christian brothers at the Chartreuse monastery, where he had his first religious experiences, and among his fellow soldiers). Second, the officer's motives were untainted; unlike industrialists, the officer drew no personal profit from his men's labors. Third, the same military regulations governed both the officer and his men; there was a superior authority to which they all submitted. This combination of physical proximity, common purpose, and disciplined conduct was ideal for the creation of a cohesive and efficient group.

Modern pastoral care required a new degree of knowledge. Lyautey cited a cavalry officer who boasted that he knew every detail about the state of his horses, but could barely remember the names of those who served under him. In the hagiographic biographies of Lyautey, this passage is often interpreted simply as a call to greater compassion; but in fact it was equally a call for greater knowledge as a means to achieve better results. Such knowledge entailed more than familiarity; it indicated detailed sociological comprehension. In order to penetrate the recruits' characters, so foreign to most officers, one was obliged to conduct "a veritable investigation, making the most of their contacts at local recruitment centers, writing to local officials, gathering information about their families, their ancestors, their aptitudes, ambitions, and moral physiognomy."[32] Effective pastoral knowledge turned on a precise and attentive individualization. Gathering this knowledge was not a one-time, once-and-for-all affair. Understanding was a dynamic process which demanded continuous operation: daily routine had to be rethought and reorganized. Unutilized moments—marches, meals, chats, and rest periods—offered the officer the greatest potential for advancing his understanding and increasing his men's allegiance and respect. The more attentive to detail, the more observant he was, the easier it would be for an officer to reach his men and to establish more firmly the bonds among them. The true role of the army was education, not war. Since wars were less and less frequent, it was unlikely that an officer would fight more than once in his career. Social peace was the true vocation of the modern army.

Pacification: From the Moral to the Social

In December 1891, Lyautey was invited by Paul Desjardins, an earnest young Catholic friend, to participate in the creation of a new movement, the Union Pour l'Action Morale. The movement's goals were as ecumenical as they were vague. At first, Lyautey was attracted by the aim of creating an organization tying together men from different milieux. He proposed a slightly different name, Union Pour l'Action Sociale. In one way the difference was minimal; in another, it offered a precise indication of the growing gap between Christian humanist circles and modern social thinkers. Lyautey soon had second thoughts. He resigned, citing personal reasons: his "casual moral standards," leaving him insufficiently pure to serve as a model for Christian youth. Underlining that he was not married, he worried that his private life could compromise the Union. However, more pertinent was a growing suspicion that he no longer saw the principle of modern action as "the religious sentiment of social solidarity."[33] He wrote to Desjardins that of the two currents present in the Union—the social and the moral—he unequivocally placed himself in the former.

However—and this was the crux of the matter—the work Lyautey had been engaged in for the last year—"an attempt at social pacification by the army, through a transforming of its inner life"—had shown him that although there could be moralizing effects from changes in social arrangements, these effects constituted only side benefits. The importance and modernity of such changes lay elsewhere; the force of this new social technology lay precisely in its ability to separate social effects from the moral character of those running society. The techniques of efficiency rested neither on the virtue of the officers nor on the morality of the soldiers. Lyautey's object was social: "It is not moral in form; the good that results from it is for absolutely material, down-to-earth organizations, and it can be put into practice with an absolute efficiency by agents who are in no way moral, much less virtuous."[34] The theory of pacification and the rise of modern planning rested on the differentiation of these two spheres. Lyautey was consistent and almost prophetic when he wrote to his Christian friends: "I will remain a friend to all of you; I will no longer be your colleague."[35]

In October 1894, Lyautey was assigned to Indochina. Earlier biographies interpreted this as an exile, whereas recent ones deny any sanction for his article by the high command, but all agree that Lyautey, thirsty for action, was overjoyed with the prospect of finally escaping the crushing boredom of garrison life. On the thirty-seven-day steamer trip to Indochina, Lyautey absorbed the shipboard conversation of the old colonial hands: a sustained and unabashed criticism of the metropolitan administration. Part of this colonial vulgate was a disparaging comparison of the French with the English colonies. From Colombo to Singapore, Lyautey singled out element after element of English superiority: pragmatism, devolution of powers, and local initiative. He was astonished by the barracks of the Lincolnshire Regiment in Singapore: set in a park outside the city were bungalows placed in a verdant setting, game rooms, sports fields, space, air, and comfort: "My head is swimming at the sight of all my ideas put into practice; these are then not just utopias; somewhere there really does exist the cheery, welcoming, open quarter which furnishes a complete life in which things are done with a smile, where men are humans and not ragged convicts stuck endlessly sweeping deadly courtyards under the curses of warrant officers."[36] The contrast with the French barracks in Saigon could not have been starker; aside from verandas, these were the same buildings he had just left in France. He counted 12 faucets for 800 men. Lyautey exulted over Saigon's large, palm-lined avenues and its sumptuous villas set in tropical gardens. Better yet, the Governor General, a certain Jean de Lanessan, had read and heartily approved of his article. One of the leading neo-Lamarckian biologists in France, de Lanessan had a clear idea of the relations between biology, military tactics, and colonization. De Lanessan had not brought Lyautey to Indochina by accident.

5

Milieux: Pathos and Pacification

The assimilation of Darwinism into official French science was slow. The causes of this delay were diverse, ranging from simple French chauvinism to the more complex barriers provided by the internal structure of biological discourses. The particular coloration of what can only loosely be called Social Darwinism took a distinctly French cast quite different from that of other nations. The humiliating defeat by the Germans hardly put the French in a position to adopt readily Victorian hierarchies or mythological German races as matrices of history. For many Frenchmen, the key to the German victory was science. Typical of one such current of thought was Emile Algave, who opened the first postwar issue of the *Revue scientifique* by saying: "We can hope for revenge only by taking from Germany the weapons which have conquered us. It is thus on the terrain of science that we must first fight, in order to prepare the struggle on the other fields of battle, because it is science alone which produces victory today [and] also regenerates society, since modern society rests on the applications of science"[1]

Ernest Renan prophetically warned that Germany had opted for a *politique des races* that would lead to zoological wars of extermination "analogous to those which various species of rodents or carnivores participate in to survive."[2] The French response was to redouble faith in science as a means of overcoming crippling political fights, of unifying the nation, and finally of strengthening the French race. However, when General Gallieni instituted a *politique des races* in the colonies, he meant something much more environmentally based and much more malleable than the German sense of the phrase.

Darwin in France

Although the strictly biological reception of Darwin's work falls
outside the scope of this book, a brief introduction is necessary
in order to situate later discussions of Social Darwinist, or, more
accurately, neo-Lamarckian, movements in France during the
Third Republic.[3] This latter current of discourse (and practices) forms an essential background to the migration of the
concepts of *milieu* and *conditions de vie* from physics to biology,
to demography, to sociology, to geography, and, finally, to urban planning.

It took three years and at least six contemptuous rejections
by publishers before *Origin of Species* received its first French
translation. Not only was the translation highly inaccurate, it
was accompanied by a polemical introduction. Darwin forfeited
his royalties in order to facilitate the publication of another
French translation; even so, it did not appear until 1873. Darwin was also consistently passed over—rejected six separate
times—in favor of French scientists, in his applications to the
Académie des Sciences. It was not until 1878, nineteen years
after the publication of *Origin of Species*, that he was finally
elected a foreign correspondent of the Academy and even then
it was to its botany, not its zoology, section that he was
assigned.[5]

Yvette Conry, following the methodology developed by Canguilhem and Foucault, analyzes in great detail the structure of
conceptual fields in a number of sub-disciplines of contemporary biological (and physical-anthropological) discourse. She
demonstrates how each of Darwin's major concepts was either
rejected in France or altered to such a degree that it could no
longer be called Darwinist. Once this translation into "French"
concepts was accomplished, and once Darwin's thought was
extended to other domains, the resistance dissipated.[6] It should
be remembered as well that neo-Lamarckianism was not simply
a chauvinistic French aberration, but emerged in an international setting. There were parallel debates in America at the
end of the nineteenth century, and the movement's leading
theorist was the German Ernest Haeckel. In France an important part of the debate among biologists took place among the

evolutionists. Although differing passionately on points of interpretation, the warring camps agreed on the necessity of fighting the church and other anti-evolutionist forces. At least until Weismann's publications of 1893, the center of debate was not the inheritance of acquired characteristics because all evolutionists, including Darwin, accepted this notion.[7]

Broadly speaking, there were two main, competing models of environmentalist thought in France: one largely static and classical, the other interactive and transformationist. The first, which dominated French biology in the first half of the century, was associated with Cuvier. In this view the world was constituted by relatively stable environments in which well-defined species occupied well-defined ecological niches. Spatial or geographic thought was paramount in this understanding of nature. Nature was construed as a spatial order in which and through which taxonomic relations could be displayed. There existed a coordinated and harmonious relationship between a physical place—*le lieu métaphysique*—and its associated ecological niche. This harmonious relationship arose from either a divine hand or a metaphysical order. In this static, natural economy, there was neither place nor need for an active principle of self-regulation. Thinkers of this school were shocked by Darwin's notion of niche, in which a species provisionally occupied a territory in which it had no natural, i.e. preordained and harmonious, right to be. A hostile environment constituted through struggle and aggressive appropriation had no place in the older conceptual and cultural fields.

The concepts of *milieu* in biology and *conditions de vie* or *modes de vie* in geography played central roles in the articulation of a conceptual field bringing space and society together into a historically situated relationship. Canguilhem underlines several extremely interesting consequences of the transformist concept of milieu. First, the concept resulted in a fundamental decentering of the understanding of nature and society. There was no longer a fixed center—given by God and Nature—capable of being represented. There was no graphic whole; rather, the milieu was a homogeneous and continuous space. This space of processes could not be represented by a geometrical figure (e.g., the circle or sphere of earlier representations). The milieu was no longer a preordained place, but simply the "between" of two places, *mi-lieu,* a relational system without metaphysical grounding.[8]

This decentering led to what Canguilhem incisively identifies as a persistent dualism in French biology. Lamarck proposed a mechanistic conception of the milieu and a vitalist one of the organism. One was basically passive and the other active; although they continually interacted, a fundamental gap remained between them. Canguilhem characterizes Lamarck's position as one of fundamental pathos: an active organism seeks endlessly to attach itself to its milieu, which is fundamentally indifferent to its survival: "Life, said Bichat, is the ensemble of functions that resist death. In Lamarck's conception, life resists solely by deforming itself in order to survive."[9] The active was the normal, and the norm of action was flexible, adaptive, and self-regulating organization.

Neo-Lamarckianism

One of the leading neo-Lamarckian proponents was the same Jean-Marie de Lanessan (1843–1919). De Lanessan began as a Navy *aide-médecin* in Indochina in 1868. He then returned to Paris, received his *agrégation,* filed his thesis, and was named to the Faculty of Medicine, where he made a name for himself as professor of natural history. He led a study mission to Indochina in 1886, was elected deputy from Lyon-Vaise and Governor General of Indochina in 1891, and served as Minister of the Navy from 1899 to 1902.[10] De Lanessan was one of the leading figures in the Third Republic who opposed Darwinism and Social Darwinism.[11] In many ways, he was typical of the period: an acknowledged and accomplished scholar and expert in several fields, who also led a highly active and successful political career. It was evident that he thought of the various domains in which he worked as interconnected. However, today his work has been parceled out either to those working on the history of biology or to those specializing in political and colonial history. It is only by reintegrating his production that his lifework—and the discourses, practices, and strategies of the period—regains intelligibility.

De Lanessan was one of the main spokesmen of the comprehensive science of the milieu. Drawing on eighteenth-century theories of climates and places, but updating them to account for changes in a whole array of sciences, this line of thinkers problematized the correlations of organisms and their environments as the key to advances in biology, sociology, and social reform. De Lanessan was a prolific author, producing over twenty books on topics as diverse as the evolution of pine trees, French colonial doctrine, and the history of the German Empire. The central theme in all of these works was the ceaseless transformation of living beings. On this topic, in his home discipline of general biology, de Lanessan's views varied little from the publication of *Le Transformisme* in 1883 to his grand synthesis, *Transformisme et Créationisme*, of 1914. Like so many other late nineteenth-century thinkers, de Lanessan was in search of comprehensive, synthetic views linking diverse realms of human activity. De Lanessan saw no contradiction between fact and value. His values, he believed, were based on universal laws, and consequently could hardly be in conflict with the facts. He was avowedly Republican, materialist, and vehemently anti-clerical.

De Lanessan cast his *Transformisme et Créationisme* in epochal form, retracing the major steps of mankind's halting discovery of the truth. The history of truth was one of struggle, and each step marked an advance of science (truth) over religion (superstition), of materialism over spiritualism. Civilization had dawned when Chaldean priests began the systematic observation of nature. The Hebrew doctrine of divine creation—Genesis—was the origin of religious thought, and signalled a major defeat for truth. If the enemy of naturalist cosmology was religion, the enemy of physicalist investigation was metaphysics. In the fifth century B.C., Ionian scientists reopened the door to the systematic investigation of animals, plants, and natural processes. Strict materialists, they eschewed doctrines of creation *ex nihilio* and of spiritual transmission. This promising beginning was blocked, however, by the rise of metaphysics: doctrine replaced observation, and a powerful elite operating in its own interests again halted the advance of science.

In de Lanessan's scheme the ancient world reached its
apogee with Aristotle, the true founder of transformationist
biology and naturalist observation. Aristotle devoted himself to
systematic observation of animals and to zoological collection,
developed a comparative anatomy, refused any recourse to divine substance, and pointed out the importance of environment. Most importantly, Aristotle laid the groundwork for the
science of transformation by setting man in the animal kingdom. The triumph of Christianity brought about the dark ages.
Transformationism lay dormant, and creationism had its long
day. Roman civilization is barely mentioned. Twelve hundred
years of Western history are covered in twelve pages. Modern
science was born with Descartes, who showed that the body
could be understood entirely in mechanical terms. However,
the Jesuits intimidated him into drawing too sharp a line between animals and men, even though the refutation of this
religious doctrine is actually present in his *L'Homme et la formation du foetus*. Linnaeus, who was on the verge of understanding
the continuity of species, lacked the courage to confront the
church. The time was ripe for a new synthesis: "A man was
needed who was at once an experienced physicist, a naturalist
who had studied a great number of living beings, an extraordinarily wise philosopher, and someone audacious enough to
have confidence in his own genius."[12]

Georges-Louis Leclerc de Buffon (1707–1788) was such a
man; de Lanessan considered him the greatest French genius
of all time.[13] Buffon demolished the dogmas of the Catholic
Church: divine creation and the belief that beings exist today in
the form they have always taken. Buffon demonstrated that
nature was a material whole composed of indestructible
molecules animated by life, which, entering into relations with
the environment, formed complex beings that lived, died, and
reintegrated into that environment. Plants and animals received nutrition when this animated matter penetrated the
body; development was a result of more extended nutrition;
reproduction occurred because of an overabundance of matter.
Although de Lanessan conceded that Buffon erred on details,
he believed that he had discovered nature's principles; neither

Darwin nor anyone else had found anything new. As nature was material, unified, and continuous, it followed that the classification of species was a convenience for scientists, and not a fact of nature. Nature contained neither classes nor genres, but only individuals. There were (or could be) intermediary forms between every species. Canguilhem remarks that once nature was cast as a continuum, the possibility of normalization was established. The question remained which norms would provide the common measure.

There were obviously regularities as well as differences in nature. If these were not fixed, and if they were not distributed in natural classes, then the question was: How had they occurred? Buffon's answer was milieu: climate, food, and conditions of life. He had demonstrated, to de Lanessan's satisfaction, that the highest state of diversity was produced not by nature, but by man's art of domestication. Cats, like men, responded to their environments, becoming bigger, stronger, and more courageous in cold climates, more civilized and gentle in temperate climates, and weaker and uglier in hot climates. For Buffon, the essential difference between men and animals was that humans could adapt actively and consciously to an existing environment: human beings could alter and improve their milieu. Diversity marked an advanced state of civilization; simplicity was a sign of backwardness.

As Michèle Duchet has shown, Enlightenment anthropology was a key element in conceiving and justifying many of that period's colonial projects.[14] De Lanessan's neo-Lamarckian update followed in the same tradition. The example de Lanessan used to confirm Buffon's thesis of adaptability is instructive: take two Indochinese men from different villages (having the same food and climates), make one a sailor and the other a rifleman; after a few years, differences will appear; the sailor will become muscular and his character European; the rifleman will grow thin and become peaceful. The explanation lay in food (sailors eat French food) and milieu (the villager imitates and is influenced by his French mates). The figure who provided the tools for understanding the importance of such transformations was Buffon's student, Lamarck.

Buffon's courageous physicalism and his destruction of metaphysical and religious dogma opened the way for Lamarck's work. Jean-Baptiste Pierre Antoine de Monet de Lamarck (1744–1829) was born into the minor nobility in Picardy and educated at the Jesuit College of Amiens. He joined the army, and after an injury settled in Paris around 1770, where he worked in a bank and attended scientific lectures. His two passions were meteorology and botany. His *Flore française*, published in 1779, was considered a masterpiece. His work on meteorology was not as well received, but was central in forming his views on the interactions between living beings and the environment.[15]

Lamarck met Buffon at the Jardin du Roy, and the latter became his friend and patron, employing Lamarck as his son's tutor. Buffon's patronage enabled Lamarck to pursue his research, to move in the leading scientific circles of the day, and to enter into the Académie Royale des Sciences in 1779, which provided him with a state pension. Although his political opinions were not pronounced, they were sufficiently acceptable, and Lamarck survived the Revolution (Buffon died in 1788). In 1793, as part of a reform at the Muséum d'Histoire Naturelle, Lamarck was awarded one of the twelve chairs (insects and worms) established to cover the whole of the natural world. His work on fossils led to an interest in geology, and by the late 1790s he was convinced of the scientific importance of the environment as a key to changes in species. What Lamarck meant by the environment, however, needs some explanation.

Georges Canguilhem, in his important article "Le Vivant et son milieu," shows how the term "milieu" migrated from Newtonian mechanics to zoology in the second half of the eighteenth century. It was Lamarck who took the abstract, singular noun and pluralized it. For Descartes, action occurred only through direct contact between objects. For Newton and classical Newtonians, milieu provided both the problem and the answer to the nature of action at a distance. Ether was the medium, the milieu, that carried energy from one object to another. Newton, in his *Optics*, extended the scope of the term to the human body in his explanation of sight: light traveling through the ether into the eye caused a contraction of the muscles. This was the first description of an organic action caused by the action of the milieu, i.e., a purely physical explanation. D'Alembert and Diderot use the term "milieu" in exactly this fashion in the *Encyclopédie:* water was the milieu in which fish moved.

Buffon's use of the term was taken from two disparate sources. He enthusiastically accepted Newton's cosmology. He also adopted the ideas of the *anthropogéographes* like Montesquieu who, drawing on the continuous line of Hippocratic theory in the West, postulated relations of climate, place, body, and society in order to explain the diversity of men and races. Although Lamarck initially adopted a mechanistic sense of the term, he always used it in the plural. He called the action of outside conditions on a living being *circonstances influentes.* Conditioning circumstances constituted the genus of which climate, place, and milieu were species. In his *Philosophie zoologique* of 1809 Lamarck introduced an important mediating term, "needs." The organism was both vital and active in its relationships with its milieu, and not merely the passive receptor of stimuli. Changing circumstances implied changing needs, and changing needs implied changing actions, which in turn altered the organism. For Lamarck there was no a priori harmony between an organism and its circumstances. Adaptation was active, not a mechanical event or a teleology; survival was an effort to adapt to a foreign environment. Climate and place were thus dethroned as major categories (at least in their classical senses) during the nineteenth century, while milieu progressively gained importance (both as a concept and as a metaphor), as it spread across a large and disparate group of disciplines, from biology to sociology.

In *Philosophie zoologique,* his magnum opus, Lamarck brought his system to its fullest expression. Lamarck shared with his contemporaries in natural history an acceptance of the Great Chain of Being, the unity and hierarchy of forms in nature. Although there was agreement on the unity of nature, great diversity existed in the specific explanations of its elements, their origins, and finalities. According to de Lanessan, Buffon assigned Lamarck the task of refuting the Church's doctrine of the immutability of species. Lamarck developed a classificatory approach based on the complexity and hierarchy of functions. In strong opposition to Linnaeus, Lamarck adopted Buffon's emphasis on change and on the arbitrariness of classificatory devices as means of overcoming the static nature of previous schemes.

The methodological canons of the Idéologues helped Lamarck make the transition from the natural history of the Classical Age to Biology.[16] His *Philosophique zoologie* began with the more complete animals (those with the most highly developed and differentiated vitality) and searched for their more primitive and basic expressions in progressively less-developed animals. He discovered the building blocks of nature by moving down the animal series; he then presented the animal world as nature's sequential elaboration of higher forms beginning with the most basic elements of life. Lamarck's classification was based on complexity of function. This led him to see men as more complex than, but not qualitatively different from, other living beings.

Previously, natural order had referred to a static pattern of relatedness. This issue formed the basis of the famous dispute between Lamarck and Cuvier on the changeability of species. Lamarck held that levels of increasing complexity and degrees of kinship in nature were not merely classificatory but were the results of specific, identifiable, historical changes.[17] Lamarck published his lectures, and it is possible to date his first public statement that species—like everything else in nature—change, as being made in 1800. Although Life was the central concept in Lamarck's system, he rigorously sought to strip the notion of any metaphysical or religious residues. Life was physical; matter was passive, life active. Whereas inert matter displayed only properties, organisms possessed faculties; "faculties" was the name Lamarck gave to powers derived from life: "Life is an order and a state of things in the parts of every body which possesses it; it allows them to execute organic movements."[18] The essence of the organism lay in its ability to do things; ordinary matter just existed.

But Lamarck was not satisfied with the more standard eighteenth-century mechanistic, physicalist views, and sought to distinguish levels of complexity in nature by isolating levels of organization. He was confident that once this double step (of accepting both change and organizational complexity) was made, the threshold to a comprehensive science of life—biology—would have been crossed. Lamarck consistently maintained that although, as the science of living organisms, biology dealt with the most complex order of organization in nature, it could never be separated from the study of the earth and atmosphere. Together these two comprised nature, the totality of *circonstances influentes*. Lamarck's theory, then, was composed of the following propositions: nothing in nature was constant; organic forms gradually developed from each other and were not created all at once in their present states; and the laws governing living things had produced increasingly complex forms over long periods of time.

How had differentiation occurred? Lamarck, following Buffon (although he made, through his fossil studies, a more complex and specific case for their importance), isolated two key variables: time and favorable circumstances. Nature then, for Lamarck, was characterized by change, multiplicity of milieux, and endlessly shifting interrelationships among these elements. For de Lanessan, Lamarck's major addition to Buffon's theory was a more complex and refined understanding of the relationships of environment and living beings, and of the effects of that environment on individuals. Living beings for Lamarck—and this was the thesis which made him famous and infamous—changed as their situations or habits changed. The organization of habits was the only thing transmitted across generational lines. In keeping with his radical materialism, de Lanessan retained the concept of an ether as the medium of this transmission. This ether was composed of atoms whose contact caused motion and alteration.[19]

Darwin's true ideas, de Lanessan concluded, came from his predecessors. The idea of the evolution of natural beings according to simple laws was discovered by Buffon and Lamarck, as was the idea that variations in living beings were produced by usage. The struggle for existence was also a Lamarckian idea. Transformism was French. Darwin's only original ideas (i.e., on heredity) were false: natural selection was a secondary phenomenon; it conserved but did not create variation. Lamarck's genius, for de Lanessan, was established; nineteenth-century biology had merely filled in the details. Among those details was the relationship of society and nature.

De Lanessan wrote a popular pamphlet on the struggle for existence, of which, not surprisingly, Lamarck was the hero.[20] Although Darwin's doctrine had been exploited by power seekers eager to use science to condemn the socialists' belief in cooperation, de Lanessan would demonstrate that association and the struggle for existence were found at every level of natural organization. In a chapter on "The struggle for existence and the association for struggle in minerals," de Lanessan demonstrated that even rocks struggled for existence with their milieu. At the edge of the sea, rocks were being worn away by the waves, eroded by lichen, and broken by roots. The rocks, however, were not defenseless. They were hard; they grouped together; a scrupulous observer would see that they formed an association, with outer rocks keeping the sea from the inner rocks.

Reactionary politicians had argued that the family was the basis of society. For de Lanessan, vegetables proved the falsity of this claim: an oak dropped its acorns; initially the soil and shade it provided were beneficial for the growth of the young saplings. However, as the young matured, the same qualities which had once nurtured them now inhibited or even destroyed their growth; e.g., light was blocked out. While these conditions were detrimental to the young oaks, a variety of other plants installed themselves amid the warring family. It was this diversity which saved the oaks. If, by accident, birds transported the oak's seeds to another part of the forest, the oak would survive. Although strength counted in the battle to survive, intelligence became an increasingly important element. Only the development of social life protected the weak from the strong. Nature's lesson was that diversity, complexity, and motility were the elements of survival; successful transformation depended on association and intelligence. De Lanessan drew republican conclusions from his reading of nature's message: education was society's arm in the battle for survival; private property, through its creation of castes, crippled a more just, i.e. fluid, society. If association through intelligence was the means, progress and *bien-être* (well-being), for the individual and the species, were the goals.

In 1886 de Lanessan, who had served briefly in Indochina in his youth, was asked by the French government to head a study mission to that region. He produced an encyclopedic defense of colonialism, identifying its sociological and natural causes, chief among which was migration and the consequent incessant struggle over fertile and temperate lands.[21] During the tertiary epoch there had existed a harmonious balance between sea and land, vegetation and animal life. For unexplained reasons, the planet began changing: harmony was broken, mountains appeared, seas expanded, and new continents formed. Living beings were cast out in a migratory search for new niches: Lamarckian pathos. Eventually a new synthesis was achieved; blessed with a climate that was neither too hot nor too cold, Europeans built better houses, designed better clothes, and produced greater intelligence. While the possibilities for industry and science under modern conditions were limitless, these same advances led to ferocious competition for materials and markets. Colonies were now necessary to survival, but Europeans were incapable of living in the extreme climates of those colonies. It followed that only a small group should be sent out to direct this vital work.

De Lanessan's preface was followed by a detailed colony-by-colony synthesis of history, climate, geography, and ethnography. Each colony had to be organized on the basis of scientifically-established particularities of climate, customs, and political organization. Indochina, de Lanessan argued, had an underlying unity which had been ignored by the administrative demarcations of North and South imposed by colonials; its agriculture, industry, and commerce would prosper as soon as security was ensured, communication routes were increased, and the population grew. Not remaining at the level of generalities, de Lanessan presented a detailed analysis of the comparative merits of canals, roads, and railways in aiding circulation and increasing the flow of goods and men.

Liberal Geography

In order to understand the changes in social description taking place in the last decade of the nineteenth century, one must first introduce the French geographical movement. Today French geography is known for its emphasis on *modes de vie:* embedded, long-term, patterned interaction between natural and social life (a subject to which we return in the next chapter). There was another type of French geography, now buried by the triumph of Paul Vidal de la Blache's human geography, which had close links to the liberal political economists as well as to the nascent colonial lobby from which they drew much support.

In the geographical sciences, as in so many other fields, the defeat of 1870 caused a profound shock, stimulating both conceptual and institutional renewal. Many different criticisms were aired: the press charged that French officers had been poorly trained in map reading and frequently lacked familiarity with local terrain.[22] Reforms were incumbent. Geography, the reformers held, should form an integral part of the new school curriculum, as technical training and as a major means of forming nationalist and Republican sentiment. The sense of crisis was particularly acute among Republican and progressive geographers, who attributed the French military defeat to the superiority of German science, and consequently looked to Germany for answers to the question of how to rebuild French institutions. If the left tended to imitate German models so as to compete with them more successfully, much of the right rejected them as foreign. Traditionalist and reactionary currents valorized differences, pluralism, and localism, in opposition to what they understood as the centralizing, leveling influences of the Jacobin state. Although elements of regional decentralization were present in the work of post-Revolutionary reactionaries like de Bonald, conservatives generally tended to prefer occupational to territorial representation. By the end of the century, however, a renovated conservatism took a spatial turn. Expanding Le Play's monographic approach, geographers sought to demonstrate how place influenced work and hence the family. Before doing battle, both the social-spatial Le Playists and the human geographical Vidalists had to dispose of the reigning school of French geographers, who were linked intellectually and institutionally to liberal political economy.

The Société de Géographie de Paris, formed in 1821, was for the next fifty years the center of geographical activity in France. Largely a society of amateurs, it was dominated by armchair geographers devoted to collecting and diffusing accounts of travel and adventure. After 1860, under the leadership of Chasseloup-Laubat, Minister of the Navy, the Society increased its links with colonial activities by calling for expansion, promoting lectures on potential colonies, and even sponsoring expeditions independent of and often opposed to official French government policy, like that of Francis Garnier to Tonkin in 1873, intended to force the hand of a reluctant government—and often succeeding in this aim.[23] Linking the themes of national honor, commercial prosperity, and the interests of science, the Society prospered. Chambers of Commerce became logical places to house these three functions. By 1876, Paris, following Lyons and Bordeaux, formed its own Société de Géographie Commerciale. By 1884, France had the most geographic societies (26, with 25 periodicals) with the most members (18,000) of any country in the world.[24]

The emergence of powerful colonial lobbies greatly facilitated geography's cause.[25] The Comité de l'Afrique Française, formed in 1890, had among its regular supporters the leaders of scientific reform: Paul Leroy-Beaulieu, Jules Siegfried, Emile Boutmy, and Paul Vidal de la Blache. A Comité du Maroc, headed by Eugène Etienne, was formed in 1904, with Eugène-Melchior de Vogüé and Augustin Bernard playing active roles. The Comité du Madagascar included Emile Levasseur as a charter member; the personal links and overlaps of this group, as well as its high-level connections, were obviously instrumental in its success. By the end of the century, the Société de Géographie was no longer a research center, having been displaced by Vidal and his school, but it remained important for its colonial connections and for the publicity it generated for geographical concerns.

As early as 1871, Jules Simon, Minister of Public Instruction, asked Auguste Himly and Emile Levasseur to conduct a survey of the teaching of history and geography. Himly, a liberal Protestant, held the chair of geography at the Sorbonne from 1862 to 1863.[26] Levasseur held the chair of Géographie, Histoire et Statistique Economique at the Collège de France beginning in 1868 and also taught at the Conservatoire National des Arts et Métiers and the École Libre des Sciences Politiques. Along with Paul Leroy-Beaulieu, Levasseur was a leading member of the school of liberal economists interested in historical, statistical, and social studies. An active participant in the group of social statisticians led by Bertillon, he was one of the first to introduce quantitative methods into geography. In addition to his links with the Republican *Revue internationale de sociologie*, he joined the Le Playist Société d'Economie Sociale, where he met Emile Cheysson, an important propagandist for modern statistics, former director of Le Creusot, and future founder of the Musée Social.

Noting the importance given to geography in Germany, Levasseur and Himly, in their 1871 *Rapport général sur l'enseignement de l'histoire et de la geographie*, called for an increase in the number of chairs of geography at the university level. They identified the secondary level of French education as the worst in terms of material conditions (lack of maps and textbooks) and quality of training for instructors. The reforms proposed by Levasseur and Himly met with more success in primary and secondary schools than at the Sorbonne. Although this blockage constituted a problem for the science's legitimacy, geography's institutional entry was significant in this time of great educational expansion. The creation, in 1879, of Ecoles Normales to train teachers initiated an era of reform aimed at creating informed citizens for the Republic; in 1881 a law was passed making primary school education free and one in 1882 making that education obligatory and separate from religious instruction. Teaching manuals became central vehicles for dispersing Republican ideology, but also for propagating liberal doctrine.[27]

The school of liberal economists professed a doctrine of updated Saint-Simonianism, in which the industrial and moral developments of nations were closely linked. Liberals saw geography as a subsidiary of political economy, providing the elementary data on material life. Geography, in a famous phrase, formed the "art whose science is political economy."[28] What better place to test these fledgling sciences of the environment than in the colonies? The man brought to Vietnam by de Lanessan to pursue the policy of scientific pacification he had experimented with in the Sudan was Joseph Gallieni.

Gallieni: Republican Discipline

The discursive construction of Joseph-Simon Gallieni (1849–1916) complements Lyautey's textual persona. Although also the son of a military man, Gallieni's family's hero was Voltaire, not Louis XIV. Gallieni's father, a teacher in Milan, had fled the Austrians, joined the French army, risen in its ranks, and finally retired to Saint-Béat in the Pyrenees, where he became mayor. The Gallienis embodied the success narrative of secular Republican France: joining the French nation by choice, rising through merit, assimilating, receiving public acknowledgment, and devoting themselves to the service of the nation. A standard biography of Gallieni, by Lyautey's nephew Pierre Lyautey, opens with a Tainesque evocation of the physical and spiritual affinities of Gallieni and his birthplace. Born at five in the morning on April 24, 1849 in "a house with a high slate roof, built against rock. Near arid peaks, accompanied by the sound of streams along the gray cliffs and amid tiered vineyards, this Saint-Béat offers a mix of grace and savagery."[29] Although approaching parody when taken to these extremes (Gallieni's father, after all, was from Milan), the mutual influence of character and environment were at the center of an important current of French thought in biology and geography. This view provided the basis for the theory and practice of pacification developed by Gallieni first in Africa, then (with Lyautey) in both Vietnam and Madagascar, and which reached its apogee during Lyautey's term as Governor-General of Morocco from 1912 to 1925.

Despite his family's laicism, the young Gallieni was sent to the famous Jesuit school of La Flèche, and then to St-Cyr. He graduated in 1870 and was immediately sent to the front, where he was taken prisoner. Transferred to Germany, Gallieni's daily life was closer to a lycée existence than to that of a prisoner: studying, eating well, and living in a pension. Like de Mun, Gallieni's captivity provided a formative interlude. Mastering the German language, he systematically studied the nation's history, ethnography, and geography. The war's lesson, he concluded, was not to hate the Germans but to learn from them. From his German crisis Gallieni underlined the themes of discipline, science, order, distrust of politicians, and contempt for the press. Released in 1874 after four years of captivity, he returned to France with his own translation of a German book on military tactics under his arm.

Gallieni's war experiences confirmed his populist Republican sentiments. Although undeniably sympathetic to the left, he avoided public allegiances: "I am only a soldier."[30] Comfortable in English, German, and Italian, he kept his journals in several languages, devouring information from numerous sources. Gallieni presented himself as having a passion for detailed documentation, an extraordinary patience, and a broad culture: the disciplined professional. Whether in the colonies or in France, he scrupulously devoted an hour a day to literature and philosophy: "Master of himself; a perfect stoic by daily practice, his daily existence is methodical, organized. To Lyautey, boiling with impatience during battle, he recommended sketching or reading Stuart Mill. 'I have never been affected by emotion.' "[31]

Like Lyautey, Gallieni was uncomfortable with the officer corps in France, and found solitude and freedom in colonial life. Although deeply cultivated, Gallieni was a practitioner par excellence, a doer and not a theorist. He was a rigorously anti-metaphysical, Third-Republic positivist. His two favorite authors were Voltaire and Spencer. Reserved and tenaciously duty-oriented, Gallieni disapproved of the frivolities and compromises of worldly life. He forged a reputation as a solitary, inscrutable chief, making his own decisions without consultation, commanding respect through his self-control and technical competence, rather than through charisma. A believer in a clearly demarcated hierarchy of command, Gallieni presented goals to his officers, and left them with the task of accomplishing these goals without further interference or assistance. The result was often a strong loyalty. Although married, Gallieni left his wife behind in France during his long colonial stints; abstemious, vegetarian, and obsessed with work, his values were organization, motion, and self-discipline in the service of science, progress, and the French nation. Gallieni was an ascetic missionary of the Third Republic.

The Berlin Conference of 1884 and the subsequent treaties of 1885 opened the floodgates of imperial expansion in Africa. In 1886, Gallieni was appointed Commandant Supérieur du Soudan Français. With a secular, Third-Republic missionary zeal Gallieni stressed the crucial importance of French education. Civilization and the French language formed an inseparable couple; Sudan's elite would be civilized through learning French.[32] Gallieni's universalist, rather thin conceptions of society and of colonization paralleled one another. Although his efforts in the Sudan contained all of the major elements of pacification in embryo (schools, roads, markets, and security), it was really only in Tonkin that Gallieni had his chance to put these elements into practice. He left the Sudan in 1888, returning to Paris, as a thirty-eight-year-old lieutenant colonel, to take up a post at the Ecole de Guerre. In Paris he led a kind of semi-bohemian existence, holding court at a creamery on the Rue Cardinal Lemoine among students and a mixed lot of Parisians passionately engaged in literary, political, and social discussion, which Gallieni, eating his vegetarian fare, followed but in which he did not engage. His next assignment was to be in Indochina.

A renewed aggressiveness on the part of the Ferry government in 1883 led to a rupture with China over spheres of influence in the northern provinces of Vietnam. Ferry asked for and received from Parliament substantial funding for a military campaign to annex these provinces. A display of strength by a French flotilla succeeded in intimidating the Vietnamese emperor into signing a treaty giving the French direct administration over Northern Vietnam. China responded by sending arms to rebels in the northern mountains. France forced China to negotiate a treaty in 1884 recognizing French influence and promising restraint. Although the treaty was not respected, it was nonetheless significant to future Vietnamese-Chinese relations. In March 1885, a celebrated incident occurred at the Northern outpost of Lang-Son. A scouting party under Brière de l'Isle, who had been Gallieni's commander in the Sudan, was ambushed. The commander (apparently drunk) panicked and ordered a retreat, even though the Chinese had already pulled back. Brière sent a famous telegram to Paris—"I hope, whatever happens, to be able to defend the [Tonkin] delta"—and Ferry's ministry fell. Despite this debacle, China signed a new treaty on June 9, 1885 recognizing French rights. With a four-vote majority in Parliament, the French sent Paul Bert to be the new Resident General of Annam and Tonkin as of January 1886. At the same time, de Lanessan was dispatched to conduct his fact-finding mission. The elements were in place for the neo-Lamarckian pacification of Tonkin.

Before entering into a discussion of pacification, a small digression is in order. Responses to pacification are not the object of this book any more than is the efficacy of the pacification strategies described. This is not because the response or the effects are, or were, unimportant—quite the contrary—but because it would take another book to do them justice. Still, it seems worthwhile, from time to time, to expand a parenthesis and approach these experiments from a broader perspective. David Marr characterizes the period of 1885 to 1897 as a crucial transitional period, during which traditional political forms were undermined and the groundwork laid for the revolutions of the twentieth century.[33] This period has been interpreted as one of anarchy and piracy, rather than proto-rebellion and transformation.[34]

Vietnamese hopes were raised after the French retreat from Lang-Son, but quickly dashed when the Chinese signed a treaty abandoning them to the French, after all—a shocking abdication of Confucian responsibility toward a client state. This abdication, this legitimation of the barbarian, put Vietnamese mandarins in a terrible double bind: they had either to accept the humiliation of becoming a French protectorate or challenge the Chinese to change their policy. On July 5, 1885, the young king of Vietnam, Ham Nghi, fled from Hue to lead a resistance movement, marking a turning point in the history of Vietnam's response to foreign intervention. By fleeing the capital, the king legitimated resistance to colonialism and de-legitimated future collaborationist Vietnamese monarchs and mandarins. Although the king's flight was militarily unsuccessful—he was captured and executed in 1888—his actions made all subsequent Vietnamese resistance to the French respectable. Although the king's opposition to colonialism was based on Confucian principles, his flight gave resistance at the village level a new cast. Popular Vietnamese resentment and rage were diverted from the collaborating monarchy to the French.

Authority had collapsed. In 1890 most of North Vietnam's midlands and highlands were essentially autonomous, containing a congeries of ethnic Vietnamese—remnants of Chinese, Nung, Thai, Muong, Meo, and other tribal groups—none of whom owed firm allegiance to anyone above the district or provincial levels. When Gallieni and Lyautey entered these provinces, they faced a highly fragmented arena, one in which resistance had not found a cultural or political form sufficient to unite the various groups in a higher-level federation or coherent program. The French were correct in recognizing that these groups were relatively autonomous but were simplistic and self-serving in labeling them all pirates. The most celebrated of the pirate-rebels of Northern Tonkin was De Tham, the "tiger of Yen-The," who had earned a Robin Hood reputation for aiding poor peasants. Lyautey's claim that De Tham represented a piracy exploitative of the natives, and not insurrection against French intervention, is at the very best a self-serving exaggeration. Even if De Tham was not a proto-Ho Chi Minh, he did have a social base.[35]

Neo-Lamarkian Pacification: The Physiocrat's Society

With the appointment of de Lanessan as Governor General in 1891, the methodical plan for the progressive occupation and pacification of the country was set in motion.[36] Military regions were established and plans made to create roads, railroads, villages, hospitals, and markets. The construction of an infrastructure for a new society was underway. By the late 1880s, the French more or less controlled the heavily populated, rice-growing Red River Valley around Hanoi. The mountainous regions to the north, leading to the Chinese frontier and populated by tribal groups and scattered villages, remained uncontrolled throughout the 1880s. As France had been drawn into Indochina by the lure of lucrative trade with China, it was essential that these regions be secured. The French at first attempted to organize a sort of protectorate system in which local leaders received support and compensation in return for guaranteed security. This policy was unsuccessful.

Gallieni arrived in Indochina in August 1892, and by December 1892 de Lanessan had assigned him responsibility for the turbulent military province of Lang-Son. Gallieni demanded complete authority to coordinate military and administrative operations, threatening to resign unless his demands were met. Overruling strong opposition from his own administration, de Lanessan granted him full powers. Gallieni carefully prepared a full-scale military attack which succeeded in routing the rebels. The victory, he concluded, was due to precise tactical preparation (including mapping and supply lines), the successful performance of his subordinate officers and their troops, and the (at least tacit) support of the local population, without whose acquiescence his supply lines would have been cut, and the element of surprise eliminated. Gallieni was confirmed in his self-image as liberator of the population when he discovered notebooks filled with documentation of tax exactions left behind in haste.

Having scored an initial military victory, Gallieni moved quickly to complete pacification of the region. Mapping was first: "An officer who has successfully drawn an exact ethnographic map of the territory he commands is close to achieving complete pacification, soon to be followed by the form of organization he judges most appropriate."[37] Gallieni had a restricted conception of ethnography, the term meaning for him little more than the geographical location of groups. He also had a minimalist military eye. His topographic descriptions portray sites either as of military importance or as picturesque. He was obsessively concerned with the strategic implications of the landscape—including its inhabitants. He saw the world instrumentally and assumed the natives saw things the same way. Every group (*agglomération*) of individuals, races, tribes or families represented a sum of interests; the art of pacification lay in manipulating those interests. Gallieni was thoroughly convinced that if the French could succeed in freeing the peasants and tribal groups from heavy tax and labor exactions, they would remain loyal. There were only the most casual asides about more standard ethnographic realities—such as that the Mans didn't like villages—Gallieni's interest was infrastructural and instrumental. In village after village, he covetously and proudly noted every new bridge and road built; the French were spinning a growing spider's web of installations—and Gallieni was the spider.

Roads were the key; without them there could be no movement of troops, no commerce, and ultimately no society. Gallieni was adamant that posts be constructed in durable materials, to demonstrate that the French intended to remain permanently. He ordered a masonry blockhouse built on a high outcropping overlooking the Chinese border. The post served a triple function: to observe both sides of the border, to provide solid military security, and to function as a representation of France's enduring presence. All of these measures fell within a coherent if rather limited conception of conquest, human motivation, and social organization. Describing a meeting with one of the pirate-rebel leaders, Gallieni argued that signing a peace treaty was in everyone's self-interest, as it was good for commerce. Although Gallieni basically distrusted the "feudal" warlords, he was pleasantly surprised to meet a Chinese warlord with whom he could drink (mediocre) champagne and discuss the need for peace and markets.

Gallieni was a strong believer in a *politique des races,* that is, in letting the local social groups rule themselves. If the area was pacified, and if there was no outside interference, then there would be no problems: society would operate naturally. In Tonkin the problem was the rapacious and arrogant mandarin class, who ruled without knowing the languages and customs of the people. The feudal system had to be dismantled. Gallieni urged that de Lanessan reinstall a tribal system in the north. A trial run proved his point; as soon as the former chiefs were reinstalled, security was reestablished. Gallieni was deadly serious. His method of verifying his success (developed in the Sudan) was as simple as it was shocking to the regulars of the French administration in Hanoi: he armed loyal villages. Only when the natives were willing to defend themselves would pacification work. Lecturing a group of Tho tribal chiefs, he observed: "Little by little I saw their expressions change as I laid out my plans: rapid closing of the frontier, construction of blockhouses, building a system of roads passable at least by draft animals, arming the villages and even a distribution of beef, buffalo, and grain to those villages, destroyed by the pirates, that wanted to rebuild. And their satisfaction was clear to see when I produced cases of rifles and bullets and presided over their distribution."[38]

Gallieni's approach to the French was equally skeletal: a constant surveillance of his own subordinates and an insistent incitation to progress. In Tonkin, Gallieni orchestrated his basic strategy: conquer strategic points, construct blockhouses, and animate markets. As soon as the fighting stopped, each village was to be rebuilt with a market and a school; all useless destruction was to be avoided. Pacification rested on the artful combination of politics and force. Gallieni was literal about these principles. The truest sign of pacification was the peaceful animation of roads and markets.

If the sign of civilization was a busy road, the sign of modernity was hygiene. The Chinese, after all, had also animated commerce and secured the roads. The French had higher standards to meet. Gallieni noted some success in French-controlled public spaces but was dismayed at the poor hygienic state of domestic spaces. He wrote of a border town: "The streets are clean. As for the houses, they seem to be as dirty as on the other side of the border. Animals and people live together pell-mell in a promiscuity which is common in these regions."[39] Gallieni was no cultural relativist; his standards were universal. The general lack of hygiene, the negligence of the domestic, and the refusal to separate humans and animals, were not tribal traits worthy of respect but simple indications of a lack of civilization.[40]

In a pacification army, each soldier had to be capable of playing multiple roles, of transforming himself from a legionnaire to an architect, of replacing his rifle with surveying equipment, and of displaying versatility, enthusiasm, and adaptability in the most trying circumstances. Just as the natives wanted peace and commerce, the French soldier wanted to put his numerous abilities to work. Gallieni's view of the perfect modern soldier is captured in an anecdote he recounted of an Alsatian recruit assigned to a remote lookout point. Sitting alone in his post, his only complaint was that there was so much fog he could not keep anything under observation. Near the Chinese border one officer was growing strawberries.

Gallieni returned from Northern Tonkin to the Red River Valley, where he found everything active and productive: trains and boats moving, people working, and the land under cultivation. The next step in pacification was to create new needs. First, one induced the rulers and their wives to adopt European clothing; others would soon imitate them. The natives had to learn French; a well-designed educational system would produce, in one generation, a pacified and devoted population, one thoroughly open to French ideas. Gallieni attempted to put these ideas into effect in Madagascar, where he was called to serve as Governor General.

Upon arriving in Saigon in November 1894, Lyautey dined with de Lanessan, whom he credited with providing him with the fundamentals of his own colonial doctrine. Meeting Gallieni for the first time in Hanoi on December 10, Lyautey was flattered by Gallieni's compliments of his *Rôle social*. Although their class backgrounds and styles of life differed, their opinions on matters from pacification to French politics meshed surprisingly well. Lyautey's arrival in Indochina coincided with the unfolding of the Dreyfus affair. Both Gallieni and Lyautey remained reserved, and refrained from choosing sides. The affair reinforced Lyautey's views of the shortcomings of the higher ranks of the army, as well as his new reservations about the Catholic Church. He expressed his disgust at the anti-Semitism of the crowds, drawing a connection between them and the anti-aristocratic crowds of the French Revolution. He saw in both instances demagogic political manipulation and the failure of the elite to provide leadership. These fears were confirmed when Parisian intrigue succeeded in having de Lanessan recalled.

Lyautey was named to head the four northern provinces of Tonkin, which had been Gallieni's fief. Lyautey embraced Gallieni's simplistic political and economic views as well as his more sophisticated military ones. Compared to Gallieni, Lyautey displayed some awareness of the complexity of mandarin rituals and of the coded dress of Chinese warlords. He expressed open contempt for the Vietnamese mandarins and their "nero-isms," as well as for the Vietnamese people who obeyed them. While reserving a particular disdain for mandarins who had been to France, he was totally silent about those who led the resistance. He found the colonial French vulgar. As in Algiers, he crafted a home: *décor chinois,* lavish entertainment, "boys" in white vests, and opium. After Gallieni left Indochina, Lyautey remained in Hanoi as head of the military cabinet of Governor General Rousseau. In this post he formulated the general principles of colonization he would later implement in Morocco: protectorates, not directly annexing territories; commercial exploitation without large numbers of colons; use of local elites to support French rule, rather than the destruction of those elites; and association of cultures, rather than assimilation to the French model. Pacification had been given only a limited, and primarily military, test in Indochina. Madagascar presented the possibility of more complex experimentation.

Madagascar: Royal Modernization

Although the ancient history of Madagascar is complex and barely known, suffice it to say that waves of immigration, a sparse population, and relative isolation produced a congeries of different cultural and political systems on the island. At the beginning of the nineteenth century, one of the most important kingdoms, the Imerina (named after the Merina people), began a century-long process of consolidation and expansion. Under king Radama I (1810–1828), they expanded out from the cen-

ter of the great island and began systematically conquering
neighboring peoples, greatly aided by English arms and technical advice. English and Norwegian Protestant missionaries
opened schools and succeeded in converting some of the aristocrats. These schools also furnished candidates for the new
bureaucracy, which eventually succeded in controlling perhaps
half of the territory of the island.[41]

A fervent anti-European reaction marked the long reign of
Radama's widow, Ranavalona (1828–1861), who was brought
to power by high-ranking military officials. The missionaries
were expelled and their schools closed. In many domains,
Ranavalona's reign constituted a return to traditional forms
(although elements of technological modernity in manufacturing, the army, and the bureaucracy were retained) carried out
in a new context and to such extremes that even a sympathetic
observer has called them caricatures. Court intrigue and execu-
tions marked the end of Ranavalona's reign: some 200,000
people out of a population of 1 million were purged in public
ordeals. The transformation of rituals of truth previously applied only sporadically to individuals into a means of purging
populations is itself an element of social modernity. Surprising
parallels can be established with the rise of missionary influence
in Vietnam, its expulsion, and the growth of bureaucracy that
occurred during the Nguyen dynasty.[42]

Radama II, the queen's son, came to power in 1861. The
change of regime provided a point of entry for the French, who
had gained some influence in Radama's camp through their
role as technical advisers on manufacturing. However, the king
was assassinated in 1863, bringing a military caste to power. For
the rest of the century, a series of powerful and adroit queens
ruled the island. With the return of the Europeans came a
return to Protestantism. In 1869, the queen and her husband
(the prime minister) were baptized. Protestantism was made the
official state religion. This decree stirred protest on the island;
the royal power responded by destroying all the chief talismans
of the kingdom. The traditional basis of Merina society was, if
not destroyed, severely damaged. After 1869, every national
politician who had previously spoken for the devotees of the

talismans either converted to Christianity or was dismissed from national politics.

The policy of centralized government was pursued vigorously. A series of attempts were made to place officials responsible to the central government in every large village, culminating in the appointments of village governors between 1886 and 1889. Over half of the adult male population was classified as permanent soldiers. The importance of the court was such that the population of the capital swelled to almost 100,000. A contemporary historian observes that Imerina after 1869 closely resembled a colonial society. It was ruled by an indigenous elite, but one so distant from its citizens in taste, means of subsistence, and religion as to be quite foreign. That elite was committed to encouraging the economic development of its subjects and to improving their morals. It would be hard to overstate the corruption and viciousness of the Merina kingdom in its last years.[43]

The French had established a trading post on the southern coast as early as 1642, but serious imperial efforts on their part date only from the early nineteenth century, when they engaged in an elaborate and bitter rivalry with England over influence in the Imerina court aimed at acquiring control of the island. The French fought a losing battle with the English Protestant missionary lobby during the early part of the century, only to triumph at the end of the century when the European division of Africa at the Berlin Conference of 1884 gave them a free hand in Madagascar.[44]

The main lobbyists for French intervention were the colonials on the nearby island of Réunion, who depended on Madagascar's laborers for their plantations and who saw their prosperity and security directly linked to French control of the larger island. The combination of leftist opportunist support for the colonial lobby and Catholic support for the missionaries wielded effective pressure. In 1883, following rejection of French claims to the northern ports, the office of the Ministry of the Navy (charged with colonial policy) was briefly taken over by a Réunionais colonial. This episode resulted in the hasty dispatch of warships to Madagascar. Although the

French met with initial success, Jules Ferry's Tonkin fiasco resulted in a major dampening of French enthusiasm for colonial expansion.

Orchestrated pressure from colonial interest groups again mounted in France, culminating in a vote by the Chamber of Deputies in November 1894 to send a force to Madagascar. The troops landed on the northwest coast in 1895. Although meeting little military resistance—the major battle cost the French seven lives—the invasion was poorly planned (the armored wagons the French had sent were totally unsuited to the terrain), and the 200-mile march to the capital took nine months. During this period, one-fourth of the 20,000 troops died from disease, as quinine had not been stocked. On October 1, 1895, a treaty was signed establishing a full protectorate. As soon as the capital was captured, the French expeditionary army began to disband and return to Europe. Madagascar was annexed on June 20, 1896. But the island was already in revolt. The remaining talismans were resurrected and an organized conservative movement, in the strict sense of the term (i.e., one calling for a return to traditional astrology and monarchy) spread across the island. As the movement's central concerns lay elsewhere, it remained unclear during the spring and summer of 1895 whether the revolt was pro- or anti-French. This disunity was to prove costly for the islanders, as it directed energies to internal politics rather than toward preparing to combat the French.

And how did the French view the Malgaches? Throughout the nineteenth century, a Gobineauesque typology of races, invented by explorers and clergy, provided the basic grid of interpretation. For example, Alfred Grandidier, the future author of the encyclopedia on Madagascar, wrote in 1872: "The Merina have a respect for authority, the spirit of obedience, the habit of work, and, above all else the social organization characteristic of the races that grow out of the yellow trunk."[45] Habits and social organization arose from a racial fount. Given this grid, European accounts of the Merina were characterized by a fundamental ambivalence: they were seen as more civilized than the other peoples of Madagascar but more tyrannical and treacherous as well. The coding of the Merina as tyrants, as

Oriental despots, enabling the French to label themselves liberators of the tribes of the island from the domination of the corrupt Merina; of the Merina from their English advisers; and, finally, of the Merina from themselves.

The work of such thinkers as Gustave Le Bon was influential in propagating a view of fixed hierarchies and dangerous others. Given this perspective, the most that could be hoped for was a certain moralization and domestication of the natives. Such views were quite common among settlers, as were more virulently racist attitudes.[46] Missionaries adopted an evolutionary framework; after a moralizing apprenticeship, the Malgache were promised entry into Christianity and universal values. This position led to an emphasis on elementary discipline and Bible training, Missionary pedagogy essentially infantilized the Malgache, whose souls were nonetheless believed to be redeemable. Missionaries did not aim at assimilation, which, it was held, only produced poor imitations of European vices.[47]

This racial-civilizational grid was transformed during the pre-conquest period of 1880–1895 into a political description. Madagascar contained the Merina dominators, the tribes whom they dominated, and those who escaped this domination. Ethnographic descriptions increasingly included an evaluation of the group's probable attitude toward French intervention.[48] The Merina remained the unassimilable term: dominated dominators. With the conquest the discourse changed from one of war to one of power: the Malgache became subjects of power, and objects of knowledge. The Merina reduplicated the civilized/savage distinction within Madagascar. Among the non-Merina peoples were those who were docile and those who were aggressive, i.e., opposed to the French.[49]

By the 1890s French scholar-administrators were tracing a more supple grid of objectification, one capable of incorporating all the peoples of Madagascar in a common framework, despite differences in origin and historical evolution. One commentator, perhaps too literally, dates this new phenomenon as beginning precisely with the appearance, several months before the military invasion, of the *Guide pratique du colon et du soldat à Madagascar*. The *Guide pratique* was written in 1895 by geographer Emile Gautier, Lyautey's guide in northern

Madagascar, professor of geography at the University of Algiers and later one of the leading colonial specialists on the Maghreb.[50]

The French Protectorate period, which extended from October 1, 1895, to September 27, 1896, was brief but important for future developments. The expeditionary force, following instructions to use the local power structure as much as possible, established parallel systems of Merina officials and French advisers. Gautier was placed next to the Malgache Minister of the Interior. Administrative personnel in the center of the island were reinforced, and fixed salaries were instituted for these officials. Special attention was paid to reinforcing the "commune" *fokon'olona,* particularly in its responsibilities to the central government of controlling order. In the short run these measures were futile, as revolt spread throughout the island and French forces proved insufficient to stem it. In the long run they constituted the basis of French administrative policy.

Madagascar reanimated debate in France over whether to adopt an assimilationist policy (its Republican partisans demanded the abolition of slavery as a condition for French intervention) or a protectorate system (advocated by those, like Hanotaux, Minister of the Colonies, who believed it cost less and was more effective). The protectorate system was given scientific sanction by Alfred Grandidier, president of the Société de Géographie and the erudite specialist on Madagascar (whose son later traveled with Lyautey during his conquest of the south, just as Gautier traveled with Lyautey in the north). The opposite camp, the annexationists, were led by the colonists on the nearby island of Réunion, who put forward mainly commercial arguments concerning the closing of the island to competitors in trade, but who also argued that annexation would be militarily more efficient. They were supported by the major groups of the colonial lobby. Paul Leroy-Beaulieu, the influential colonial theorist and propagandist, argued for a mixed plan of external control and internal protectorate. This position won the day. A law of annexation was voted on June 20, 1896, and Gallieni was called in to coordinate the full conquest of the island.

Gallieni: French Modernization

Gallieni had been back in France only a few months before being named to the post in Madagascar. He rapidly informed himself on the military situation and carefully read the geographical work of Grandidier. Echoing a long French tradition of debate on Oriental despotism, Gallieni accepted Grandidier's migrational account of the peopling of Madagascar.[51] Gallieni arrived in Madagascar in September 1896 to face a general state of insurrection. The French task was conceptually simple: substitute organization for revolt through a flexible administration that respected tribal differences. The means were at hand: pacification with unity of direction in each military command; the largest possible initiative left to commanders at the local level; a progressive and methodical occupation of the country; the establishment of permanent military posts; the use of force only when political means failed; and attention to communications through the construction of roads.[52]

On September 30, 1896 a light column had entered the capital, Tananarive. The queen was forced to accept a French protectorate. The Merina administration was left in place, its army only partially disarmed. However, the revolt continued. Although the military subjection of the "fetishist" rebels proved to be relatively easy, Gallieni was impressed by their bravery—a virtue, in his eyes, distinctly lacking among the Merina troops. In February, other revolts—against the Merinas—sprang up. Incidents multiplied: Europeans were killed and supply routes around Tananarive cut off. A double revolt was in progress, the tribes against the Merina tyranny, and a proto-nationalist revolt (including the Merinas) against Europeans. The first victims were English missionaries and the Malgaches they had converted.[53] Gallieni decided a show of force was required to symbolize French resolution. After consultations with Emile Gautier, the government's Madagascar specialist, Gallieni arrested two high-ranking court officials, one a noble from the court party, and one a commoner from the old government's party. The two were charged with treason and, after a mock trial, shot in public.

Putting into effect his *tache d'huile* (drop of oil) strategy, Gallieni surrounded the capital with a ring of fortified posts. As in Indochina, he took the risk of arming the villages within the pacified perimeter. From this network of outposts and secured villages, the French moved outward, establishing a series of temporary but well-protected posts. The country was divided for the time being into military territories and smaller administrative-military circles which supposedly corresponded to local geographical, racial, and administrative units. Local commanding officers were given almost totally free rein in applying the policy, and many abuses followed. Gallieni approached the countryside as he had in Vietnam. If it was hilly, he calculated the difficulty of transport; if it was wooded, he wondered about the value of the wood; if it was sparse, he considered whether it could be used for grazing land, and whether the people would be good laborers. In his published reports, one finds maps with docile groups of natives pictured below.

The day before his entry into the capital on September 26, 1896, Gallieni abolished slavery. However, as land remained in the hands of former masters, the ex-slaves remained structurally vulnerable. The abolition of the "feudal" regime of landholding on April 17, 1897, which Gallieni vaunted as an advance of civilization and economic productivity, changed little in the short run, and even facilitated the adaptation of the ruling castes to the new situation.[54] Similarly, the old *corvée* (forced-labor) system was abolished, and replaced by state-controlled labor obligations. Malgache who worked regularly for French colons were exempted. Gallieni was proceeding cautiously. Speaking in the third person, he said of himself: "He was to proceed methodically, taking into account the mental traits of a population descended from Orientals, who atavistically bent by an absolute power were unprepared, especially as concerns work, to understand from one day to the next a regime of full and complete freedom."[55] In February 1897, Gallieni ordered the abolition of the monarchy. The queen was exiled. Gallieni moved the kings' remains from the holy town of Ambohimanga, twelve miles away, to Tananarive (Antananarivo). Close to 30,000 people followed the coffin, singing "unspeakably sad songs." The royal coffins were opened and their goods placed in the queen's palace, which henceforth served as a museum. The remains of the royalty were buried in new tombs where they still are today.

By May 1897, the pacification of central Madagascar was completed to Gallieni's satisfaction. Pacification then entered stage two: the physical and intellectual development of the conquered people, amelioration of their social state, and the economic exploitation of the country through native labor.[56] The first and most pressing problems were rampant disease and chronic underpopulation. An English hospital was requisitioned, and clinics, a campaign of vaccination, and medical propaganda were proposed. Within a few months, Gallieni reported, the influence of witches had noticeably diminished. Choosing his symbols carefully, Gallieni established a school, locating it in the ex-queen's palace. The school's purpose was to begin training Malgache personnel in French, enabling them to serve as teachers, interpreters, and functionaries. Although recruitment to all higher-level schools was by competitive exam, Gallieni particularly sought out non-Merina functionaries. Although hardly elevated, the rate of education in Madagascar was three times higher than in Tunisia.[57]

Gallieni moved quickly to establish an administrative structure based on nine services, the heads of which served on an administrative council under the Governor General. In the center of the island, the Merina administrative hierarchy was left largely in place, but under strict French control. There were no institutions on the island representing either the Malgaches or the French. The tax policy was the central instrument of both control and socialization. As all French colonies had to fund their own budgets, heavy taxation was a necessity. Gallieni was a firm believer in the progressive, socializing benefits of taxation as a means of teaching work discipline. For those unable to pay, Gallieni continued the system of thirty days' required labor. He instituted the Torrens Act system of land registration (such as had been used in Australia by the English) advocated by French reform groups, which required written deeds, and which in Madagascar as in Morocco occasioned much abuse.

The French divided Madagascar into provinces headed by powerful French *chefs de province*. Gallieni sought to correlate these provinces (as well as lower-order administrative divisions) with existing regional and ethnic unities. The provinces were conceived as future economic regions. If the role of the province was basically geo-economic, the role of the eighty-four districts was political. The French district head was advised by a committee (nominated by the *chef de province*), of property holders, farmers, and businessmen. They met at least three times a year and were charged with representing local opinion. This was the sum of representative democracy. Gallieni established a commission composed of French and Malgache legal experts to propose a new administrative model. In March 1902, the commission recommended continuing what they took to be the traditional organization rather than imposing the French commune model. The reform was intended to create an active, if controlled, engagement of natives in the administration and development of what Gallieni was forthright in calling "our new possession."

In principle, the lower limit of direct French intervention was the *fokon'olona*. *Fokon'olona* means literally "grouping of persons"; perhaps the best translation is *deme*.[58] Georges Condominas defines these groups as follows: territorially-based patrilocal clans localized around an ancestor's tomb and providing religious unity.[59] As in Vietnam, the status of local communities was the product of older social forms and rather recent history. In both countries, the consolidation of power and expansion of an important dynasty, with its own administrative bureaucracy, coincided with, and was shaped by, the cultural and political penetration of Europeans. Of course, the early nineteenth century was a time of administrative, legal, and ethnographic reorganization in France as well. As in Vietnam, the *fokon'olona* was first identified as the French sense of municipal community, i.e., a territorial unit whose rights and obligations were cast as delegated from the king.

The Napoleon or Charlemagne of the Merina was Andrianampoinimerina (1787–1810), who faced his own task of pacification. Andrianampoinimerina administered the territory either by strategic placement of his clan members and allies or by tutelage over smaller kings and nobles of conquered ethnic groups. During the course of the nineteenth century, the conquering clans acquired a territorial base and public representation both of their (fictive) unity and attachment to the land and the king. Regional administrators, hierarchically organized, reported directly to the king. The elements of the transformation of Madagascar into a modern state were in place. A highly rationalized ranking system was organized; units divided into 10, 50, 100, and 1000 subjects were created for the purpose of taxation and forced labor.

The ministers instituted a series of intermediary links between the clan based local unit and the sovereign. These included a system of information-gathering at the local level, and a veritable surveillance and reconnaissance system (including a prize for denunciations); a strictly enforced collective responsibility—a collective moral status—for duties, crimes, and forced labor completed the control. The *fokon'olona* remained the fundamental unit linking the local level to the court and bureaucracy, and increasingly assumed responsibility for regulating social life. Soldiers were provided with pensions, in return for which they were expected to return home and act as government agents. Some 6,000 of these retired soldiers returned to their *fokon'olona*s to act as government information agents concerned with all dimensions of social life, from divorce to the abuse of power by local nobles. This *amis du village* system opened the door for widespread abuse to the extent that, by 1881, a new level of control was introduced to keep watch over the surveillants. Reform produced more bureaucracy; the code concerning the *amis des villages* contained 305 articles.

The steady march of bureaucratic centralization—or at least of attempts at bureaucratic centralization, as the real extent of implementation of these reforms is unclear—was broken by the French-Malgache war of 1883.[60] Merina attention to external affairs loosened the state's grip on the local levels, where substantial resistance began to manifest itself. Faced with foreign dangers and recognizing the precariousness of social support for the Merina kingdom, the prime minister in 1884 issued new ordinances for the *fokon'olona* which officially encouraged self-government.

Gallieni's Republicanism, as well as his pacification strategy, favored the democratic veneer of the *fokon'olona*. He instituted legislation which conceived of the *fokon'olona* as a territorial unit rather than a kinship or ritual grouping. The head of the *fokon'olona* was picked by the province head from three names presented by the community. He retained the right—for security reasons—to temporarily appoint someone not on this list. The representative was more of an administrator than a politician. He was charged with general surveillance as well as the collection of taxes (from which he was paid). Highly controlled forms of minimal local consultation were proposed. Local budgets were never allocated to the *fokon'olona*. Collective responsibility was assigned to each *fokon'olona;* its members could be fined proportionately for not fulfilling this. Although collective responsibility was a principle foreign to French law, Gallieni argued for the advantages it provided in terms of security. Collective work obligations were also retained, although Gallieni specified that these should be restricted to matters of local collective concern, such as the repair of dikes, roads, and rice fields. Collective responsibility was enlarged, not to increase local autonomy but to facilitate the central administration's work of local control, surveillance, state labor, and taxation, all of which were administered at the lowest levels by the natives themselves.

Lyautey: Social Forms or Social Dust

In his letters, Lyautey expressed strong reservations about Gallieni's policy towards the Merina, characterizing it as authoritarian and inflexible. Lyautey was assigned to pacify the southern third of Madagascar. Most of his detailed report, submitted to Gallieni at the end of the campaign, was given over to topographic and tactical descriptions of the military campaign. He emphasized the fundamental importance of the ethnogeographic situation; his constant preoccupation was avoiding "a confusion of units and concentrating each one in a neatly determined region."[62] At the end of his text, in a small section on native policy, Lyautey offered a synoptic description of cultural diversity which must be considered among the classic pages of colonial literature. As he saw it, all the major types of human social organization were juxtaposed in this sprawling southern region, which stretched over 500 kilometers in length.

A half-century before Lévi-Strauss's celebrated use of the metaphor in *Tristes Tropiques,* Lyautey exulted in the socio-geologic panorama: "One sees layered before one, like a geological section, all the ages of history."[63] Several Merina at the northernmost tip of the territory were, "in costume and habitat as well as in intellectual assimilability and education, at the most advanced stage of modern civilization. Some are already at the level of the French bourgeois."[64] These modern Merina occupied an outpost in the territory of the Betsileo group, whom Lyautey compared to peasants in Brittany living scattered across the countryside, working their own homesteads, surrounded by gardens, and subsisting on corn and potatoes. Continuing south one seemed to traverse ten centuries. The Bara were feudal, ruled by a single caste proud of its genealogies and its traditions. Their chief lived on his fief with his warrior clientele. Further south, among the Tanala, Lyautey imagined himself in the Iliad; tribes, assembled for oratorical contests behind kings whose prestige depended on their rhetorical abilities as much as on the force of their arms, engaged in Olympian contests of strength and physical prowess as well as presentations of cattle. Finally, at the southern reach of the island, were the Antadroy, who still lived in prehistoric fashion. Their social organization was rudimentary, comprised of anarchic groups of warriors who spent their time fighting over herds of barely domesticated animals kept for superstitious, not economic, reasons. The people lived in crude huts without beauty or order; they had no currency.

Such diversity could not possibly be ruled effectively by a uniform administrative policy. The protectorate system was the best solution; the reason for its superiority was social: "Each time we find fully formed ethnic groupings, local institutions, our highest priority should be to protect and utilize them. Otherwise, we find ourselves faced with nothing but social dust; then it will be years, if not centuries, until our administration can reconstitute a solid base."[65] Lyautey was a conservative: ethnic groups and their social institutions were products of long histories. Far less optimistic about the potential of social engineering than Gallieni, Lyautey saw government as more of a social art than an engineering feat. The existing social practices were a given, and were ignored only at great peril to both science and government.

For Lyautey, the French love of names and systems was a menace in the colonies. The key to the colonial role of the army was flexibility, "the right man in the right place" (a phrase frequently used by Lyautey in English).[66] This meant not just having the requisite military or civilian skills but combining them in a new form of pragmatic administrative talent. The essential divergence from standard military procedure lay in the fact that this organization was established before the conquest, not after it. Everyone, from the foot soldier to the highest officer, knew before he moved into a region that he would have to live there after he had pacified it. Each would be trained to understand that careful preparation, while less dramatic than large assaults, was infinitely more productive. A road, for example, became not only a line on a map plotting invasion, but marked the way to a future market. Would a soldier, knowing that he had to live in a village, be as quick to burn it? Building a road was often more complicated than firing a cannon at a village. In a new colonial army, patience would be classified as heroism. Gallieni and Lyautey dreamt of new men, who were not merely soldiers but who constituted "above all a collectivity, a reservoir of foremen, leaders, teachers, gardeners, farmers, all ready with no further expense from the metropolis, to be the first cadre of colonial improvement, the first initiators of the races for whom we have the providential mission of opening the industrial, agricultural and economic way and, it must be said, a higher moral life, a fuller life."[67] In Algeria, Bugeaud had built communities in which civilian life was militarized down to the smallest details; Lyautey proposed the reverse: the civilianization of military life.

For slightly different reasons, Gallieni and Lyautey concurred on the importance of symbols of stability. Gallieni, more in line with British imperial ideas, insisted on their demonstrative effect, while Lyautey saw that representations not only stood for order but were a fundamental ingredient in its realization: "It is that in fact we are not the masters of the minds of the natives. We must never forget that the native doesn't like to 'change the face of things,' if I may be permitted the expression; but that provided that the 'face' to which he has become accustomed remains the same, he is indifferent to which regime keeps it that way."[68] Not sharing Gallieni's faith in the inevitability of progress and the benefits of modern civilization, Lyautey was more pessimistic about French domination: "It is not necessary to create the illusion that our domination is agreeable to them. Even if it is permissible to hope that the evolution of our civilization and the disappearance of the generations that knew independence will lead to an acceptance of the regime we have imported that is complete and without ulterior motives, we are not yet at this point in any of our colonial empires."[69] This is an impressively clear-headed evaluation of the French empire in 1902. Of course, Lyautey was not questioning the colonial project, only its potential success.

Van Gennep and Lévy-Bruhl: Social Science and Policy

New social sciences were coming into existence in Europe. Their leading practitioners unabashedly vaunted the utility of each. Lamenting the rudimentary state of knowledge concerning Madagascar, Arnold van Gennep in *Tabou et Totemisme à Madagascar* claimed that previous social descriptions had been amateurish and frivolous, providing only the illusion of scientific work (he made no mention of Gautier, nor of the twenty volumes of Grandidier's encyclopedia). Van Gennep confidently postulated the necessity of modern social science to the success of colonialism: "The in-depth study of half-civilized societies is a prime necessity for whoever wants to make the work of colonization durable."[70] Better science was the means to better colonial government. Only a more complex, theoretically sophisticated analysis—one approaching social facts as systems—van Gennep argued, would remedy the situation.

Previous analyses had started with values that prevented them from appreciating the social bases of religious phenomena. While Christian missionaries had found elements of monotheism at the base of the island's religions, others, like Tylor and Andrew Lang, denied that savages had any notion of a Supreme Being. Neither argument was scientific: in order to evaluate primitive forms of religion and morality, one had to move beyond good and evil. Scientific comparisons had to be institutional, comparative, and functional. Society, and not race, religion, or diffusion, was the true object of study; social facts had to be rigorously treated sui generis as social facts. One of van Gennep's general conclusions bore directly on colonial policy. The natives in Madagascar were not insufficiently social, as some held, rather they lacked the individual development required for modern society because they were *too* social. Modern society, aided by modern social science, showed that the task of colonizers was to focus on individualization rather than totalization—an opposite but complementary situation to the one faced by reformers in France.

Lucien Lévy-Bruhl was as sanguine as van Gennep about the emergence and future utility of sociology.[71] Moral life, according to Lévy-Bruhl, could be understood correctly only by employing scientific method. Knowledge reached the level of science when the practical arts from which it had arisen were left behind and all subjective, mystical, and metaphysical dimensions eliminated in favor of objective description. History and anthropology demonstrated the rich diversity of human society; the belief in a universal human nature was the residue of a religious belief in the soul. There was no universal man. The only condition under which a universal moral system could exist would be a unified world society. As moral facts were law-governed social facts, moral practices could and should be made objects of scientific study. It was then and only then that the relations of theory and practice could be reorganized. The history of moral theories showed the minimal effect they had had on moral practices.

Lévy-Bruhl distinguished his scientific approach from that of Utopians and social reformers. Their well-meaning efforts were devoted to the reorganization of society, but were not based on objective study of social reality. In the future, reformers would be subordinated to sociologists. Although the process of scientific guidance was only beginning, there had already been some successes, e.g., transformists' theory. Biology had demonstrated the slow rate at which change took place. Historically, collective sentiments had changed, almost accidentally, as an effect of changes in the economic or religious realms. The next step in this evolution would be to change them scientifically. As the march of science was ineluctable, Lévy-Bruhl was certain that science, once it grasped the laws of social life, would resolve "most moral conflicts and enable us to act in the most economical and efficient fashion on the social reality in which we find ourselves immersed."[72] A steady accumulation of scientific knowledge concerning education, assistance, and unemployment was leading inexorably to the constitution of a sociologically based social hygiene. Lévy-Bruhl warned that although social sentiments were the hardest ones to change, giving scientific form to moral representations was the only path to the rational construction of norms for modern society.

6

From Moralism to Welfare

When Lyautey hesitatingly declined to join his Christian friends' Union for Moral Peace, sociologically speaking he was both insightful and blind. His insight lay in recognizing the cultural, social, and political movement away from moralizing, philanthropic, liberal understandings of the world (and their associated techniques of order) and toward social ones. It was clear to Lyautey that France was facing a crisis and that new approaches were mandated. His conservatism, and hence his blindness, lay in his residual personalism. As a technician of general ideas, Lyautey identified the need to reconceptualize and regulate human relations. Although realizing that the moral dimension of ties between recruits and officers or between colonizers and the colonized was no longer operative, he continued to think in terms of individuals and dyadic relationships. He shifted the emphasis from instilling morality in the recruit (or colonized, or worker) to the duty of the officer. Lyautey also, like de Tocqueville, understood the need to provide a more socially powerful glue for human relations than individual self-interest or economic efficiency. Both men saw that the modern world would be post-moral, at least as far as morality had traditionally been understood in the West. With some regret, both believed that virtue provided too feeble a support for man in modern society. While de Tocqueville proposed a sociologically functionalist theory of religion, Lyautey sought to articulate a social role for his new meritocratic aristocracy.[1]

In France during the last decade of the nineteenth century many other groups were struggling with similar problems. This chapter explores attempts to rethink and formulate policy for a society based on unities other than individuals. Candidates included *populations,* identified by statisticians' analytic procedures; *regions,* defined as enduring historico-natural entities; *social law,* articulated as a return to a Roman republican system operating between the individual and the state; *social solidarity,* defended as the organicist, quasi-naturalist ground for political action; and *municipalities,* chosen by reform socialists as the arenas in which social justice could be achieved. At one level, these discourses and practices were empirically quite disparate. On another level, they revealed a certain commonality; drawing on what they defined as historical and natural elements, they strove to create a discourse that would transmute these elements into social understanding and social policy. These reformers saw such an undertaking as central to confronting the crisis of modernity. I will now outline the various elements under study; the next chapter describes how they were synthesized in the discourse of modern urbanism.

The Search for the Social

The rise of the "social question" in France at the end of the nineteenth century corresponded with the crisis in philanthropic reform (with its associated moralizing, disciplinary technology) and with the purportedly liberal economic and social system in which it was embedded. During the last two decades of the century, a range of reform groups extending from Social Catholics to non-revolutionary socialist factions attempted to map antagonistic classes onto a common space regulated by social and scientifically derived norms. Moving toward such a world required recasting century-long practices and assumptions about the nature of the individual, the state, space, and society. The period between the International Exposition of 1889 (where the Grands Prix were awarded to the paternalistic efforts at Le Creusot and associated Social Catholic variants) and the International Exposition of 1900 (held under the banner of Solidarity, a discourse of social interdependency that spanned the center of the political spectrum) marks the beginning of a major shift in the discourse of the social sphere. Just as these groups were arguing that society, and not the individual, constituted the *real*, so too the state (along with new social sciences) was beginning to replace both the church and industry as regulator of social relations. As Madeleine Rébérioux put it, the welfare state was not yet in place, but by the turn of the century it had at least become possible to conceive of it.[2]

Liberal thought and practices centered around the protection of the quasi-natural laws of the market and around the individual and his or her virtues and vices. The linchpin and target of the assistance system was the morality of the worker, a concept rooted in the liberal view of individual responsibility. For philanthropists, there was a direct link between inculcating moral habits—above all of responsibility and *prévoyance*—and the amelioration of social justice. Economy and morality went together; social economy studied voluntary, contractual relations between individuals and the social institutions which resulted from those relations. Attempts to solve the social question turned on techniques designed to modify the society's practices, or *moeurs*. The sovereignty of the market relieved the patron of any legal obligation to his workers; they had no right to work and hence no right to compensation for unemployment, accidents, or other such "misfortunes." Although this position was logically consistent, it was socially and politically vulnerable; philanthropy, after all, aimed at social peace as well as coherence. The schema presupposed, among other things, continuous employment, which could not be taken for granted during the depressions of the 1880s. Another major change was the movement of industry out of the countryside and into the areas surrounding major cities. The advance of capitalism, with its anonymous structure, increasingly undermined the personalist conception of political relations that characterized the patronal model. Finally, many leading industrialists were finding the older model costly and inefficient.[3]

Emile Cheysson: Governing the Normal

After the strikes at Creusot (and other model locations), the search for new arts of government accelerated. When a chapel erected by Social Catholics at Montceau-les-Mines was burned in 1882 during a worker revolt, even leading Social Catholics like de Mun had to admit that the model was not working. With the law of 1884 legalizing unions, and thereby officially bringing three organized actors to center stage—patrons, unions, and the state—liberal premises had to be rethought. The Pope's famous *Rerum Novarum* encyclical of 15 May 1891, which called for social justice, marked yet another step away from strict liberalism and reactionary Church doctrine. The problem of how to govern within an industrial democracy was still posed, at least initially, in terms of the social control of workers. How should society be organized to avoid violent outbreaks? What spatial organization would underlie and accelerate the emergence of the new society?[4] The target of new discourses, however, was less the marginal or pathological elements of society and more daily life viewed across a wide social spectrum. For an array of interested parties, the problem was becoming one of constructing and regulating a new social field of everyday relations in an industrial, scientific, and democratic—i.e., modern—world, of regulating the normal.

Le Play died in 1882, leaving an important group of followers. In 1885 his legacy was split between those emphasizing the methodology of the social sciences and those who, while not neglecting social science, emphasized social reform. The social science group was marginalized by the triumph of Durkheimianism. By the end of the century, having lost its scientific centrality and its social and political bases, this group withered away.[5] After the Commune, the Unions de la Paix Sociale were organized with the goal of lowering class antagonism by stationing Le Playist observers and mediators in working-class neighborhoods. Their journal, *La Réforme sociale* (founded in 1881), was devoted to sociology and to commentary on political and social questions. A group of (heavily Protestant) followers of Le Play, interested in social reform, clustered around *La Réforme sociale*. Their institutional vehicle was the Société d'Economie Sociale. The Society had previously been headed by Villermé, then by Armand de Melun, and finally by Emile Cheysson, who joined in the 1860s and served three terms as its president. Although the Society too lost out in the scramble for the establishment of departments of sociology in the university system, this group found another niche, the newly formed statistical bureaus of the government.

The movement beyond philanthropic models of discipline and social economy did not happen overnight. Some of the hesitations, overlaps, and contradictions involved are seen in the career of Emile Cheysson (1836–1910). Cheysson was an engineer, a disciple of Le Play, a director of Le Creusot, a founder of the Musée Social, and an important innovator in institutionalizing statistics in France, a well as a participant in almost every major reform effort during this period, from the League of Anti-Alcoholism to the International Congresses on Industrial Accidents. Cheysson had attended the Ecole Polytechnique and the Ecole des Ponts et Chaussées. An active engineer throughout his life, Cheysson worked on river and road projects before joining Le Play at the 1867 Exposition Universelle, where he was director of machinery. He underwent a kind of conversion at the Exposition, embracing Le Play's social philosophy as the path toward peaceful unification of society and industry. After the exposition, Cheysson taught administration at the Ecole des Ponts et Chaussées before being called upon to organize the grain rationing in Paris during the German seige of 1870.[6] The war and the Commune raised the question of industrial society for Cheysson. When Schneider asked him to become director of his factory at Creusot, Cheysson accepted, and held the post from 1871 to 1874. In this "grand laboratoire" Cheysson experienced at first hand and invested heavily in the techniques of patronage, building schools and workers' housing, instituting a pension system for widows, and making other similar gestures. He advocated more worker participation in decisions concerning their own social welfare, as a means of reinforcing *prévoyance*. After leaving Le Creusot, Cheysson returned to Paris, where he directed the Bureau of Maps and Plans for seven years, and actively participated in renewing cadastral mapping of the entire country. Actively involved in a wide range of reform issues, Cheysson joined the Société d'Economie Sociale and held the chair of political economy at the Ecole Libre des Sciences Politiques from 1887 to 1901. He was elected president of the Société de Géographie in 1896.

Although he advocated social insurance laws that inaugurated far-reaching changes in the social field, Cheysson
never fully abandoned the patronal model. In a talk he gave in
1897 to the Société des Ingénieurs Civils, entitled "Le Rôle
Sociale de l'Ingénieur," Cheysson reaffirmed the liberal credo
"every economic issue is a moral issue as well."[7] He expressed
no doubt that the techniques (to use his term) of patronage
(pastoral attention plus social science) were the ones most
suited to bring about social peace. The new scale of industrial
production had severed the personal ties between patrons and
workers. Cheysson enthusiastically accepted technical advances
in industry, but was frightened by the democratization of
public opinion.

Types and Norms: Clinging to the Referent

Central to the Le Playist world view was the notion of the family
as the elemental unit of social relations—the fundamental
milieu for the individual—and the unique product of particular historical and environmental relations. To apply the new
methods of statistical distribution (worked out by Galton and
Pearson in England and known to Cheysson) to family relations
necessitated a leap Cheysson was not ready to take.[8] For Cheysson, the goal of studying the family was to reveal the type upon
which normative evaluations could be made: "The budgets of
Siberian, Chinese, and French families are juxtaposed on the
same grid, but it is impossible to make quantitative comparisons
since each family is an individual case resulting from an infinite
variety of customs."[9] The family, understood in modern statistical terms, was not a "type," but only one of a possible set of
differentially distributed, structural variations. Galton had
shifted the emphasis from the mean as the object of statistical
analysis, revealing an underlying unity (identified by Quételet
as the type), to the field of differences in which individual traits
were distributed. Both the democratic equation of individuals
and the anonymous distribution of traits were morally unac-
ceptable to Cheysson. Galton's method was systematically mis-
interpreted by Cheysson in an effort to save the type. It would
only be in the next generation (after the First World War) that
the implications of Galton's statistics and the social reality they

represented would be understood and integrated into both science and reform programs. A group of socialists clustered around Maurice Halbwachs and Henri Sellier fully abandoned the understanding of the norm as an expression of an underlying type and pursued the social and scientific implications of welfare and sociology as guiding norms around which social agglomerations could be evaluated and organized.

Cheysson made important additions to Le Play's monographic method, extending it beyond the family to the workshop and the rural commune. In this capacity, he established an important, mutually influential connection with the Marquis de Vogüé, Lyautey's patron, who was active in the *Revue des Deux Mondes* as well as the Société des Agriculteurs de France. Together, they initiated sociological studies of life in France's rural communes. In addition to fostering a new range of monographic approaches, Cheysson was one of the leadering figures in the organization and propagation of statistical methods in France. He became an important personage at the Ministry of Public Works during the years between 1874 and 1885. In 1881 he served as president of the Société de Statistique de Paris, where he helped coordinate and consolidate (across different governmental agencies) existing collections of data and argued forcibly (and successfully) for the inclusion of more industrial statistics. The result was the creation of a Conseil Supérieur de Statistique in 1885 and the Institut International de Statistique in 1886.

Combining these twin sociological interests, Cheysson attempted in the late 1890s to modernize Le Playist methodology through systematically joining statistics and monographs. The role of the monograph was to describe a subject (individual, family, workshop, commune, or nation); the role of statistics was to insure scientifically the subject's typicality.[10] Cheysson cited the example of a study done in 1889 by the Ministry of the Interior on mutual-aid societies; among the thousands in France, forty were selected as typical. He underlined the central point: "It is the typical that is the true essence of the monograph."[11] Modern observers had more to rely on than their own intuitions. They were guided by the synthetic statistics assembled by the government in its administrative inquiries, which facilitated the choice of subjects for monographs. Cheysson argued that this approach guaranteed the scientific validity of the subject under study, by assuring its representativeness without sacrificing the insights gained from the on-site contact with workers and peasants monographic inquiry necessitated. The type chosen for the monograph should most closely approximate the "end to which the milieu tends in which individuals develop."[12]

Social Economy 1889: Almost from Types to Norms

The problem of how to represent this material to a larger public so as to move them to action was high on Cheysson's agenda. The social technologies proposed by the Le Playists formed the core of the exhibits at the Universal Expositions of 1867 and 1889. For Cheysson, the social economy exhibitions marked an important milestone in the history of social science because they made clear the common concerns, shared by all six hundred entries, and the diversity of solutions for achieving social health. Although many of the philanthropic and disciplinary elements of the exhibitions at the 1867 Exposition were not abandoned, subsequent events forced them to be modified. Cheysson saw the need to gain wider public support. At the 1867 fair, a jury composed only of notables had judged the exhibits; greater efforts had to be made to extend the participation in and understanding of social progress to the general public. The 1889 Exposition included more exhibits of healthy industrial relations conceived not for specialists but to educate the public. How could one present institutions? How could one represent abstractions? The point of the exposition, Cheysson argued, was for workers to see that the true state of society had been misrepresented; progress toward a healthy and harmonious industrial society was being achieved on many fronts.

In a written guide to the exposition prepared for the readers of *La Réforme sociale,* Cheysson explained that although the most impressive theme of 1889 was the history and progress of machines, it was men who were responsible for these wondrous machines. People wanted to know: Who was the worker who made these machines? How did he live? What were his relations with those who directed him? Did this worker suffer in the same way as those who built the pyramids? Cheysson assured his audience of industry's humanity, praising the exhibits for showing how model industrial establishments provided all the workers' needs and responded to every crisis, from cradle to grave. He noted the juxtaposition of the modest buildings housing the social-economy exhibits and the replica of Angkor Wat, with its shining gilded towers, which stood directly across the way, a representation of "the Orient fixed in its immobility of forty centuries; on the other side, the West churning with all the problems of the modern world."[13] The time, he noted, was not yet ripe to confront the danger posed by this juxtaposition. He proposed instead a visit to the Exposition of Social Economy, to see how the West was doing.

Upon entering, the visitor was greeted by a pyramid honoring English cooperatives and an exhibit by an insurance company. Then came a street of model houses occupied by "good worker families who are in their proper place in these houses, so that one cannot imagine these homes without their families."[14] While this form of representation and the philanthropic discourse dovetailed, the rest of the exhibit confronted other modern problems not representable by the literal depiction of a subject and its milieu, i.e., the type case. Originality in the 1889 Exposition was found in the hygiene exhibits: the visitor, upon entering, was struck by the large quantity of graphic material covering the walls. While the architectural and Beaux-Arts galleries, housing paintings and drawings, were nearly empty, and while it had been predicted that the hygiene exhibits would suffer a similar fate, these predictions proved false. Visible in these figures and charts were the central concerns touching on the happiness and morality of families. Statistical representation of trends and distributions within populations, charts and graphs of savings banks, pension systems, and death and birth rates of the population were presented. The real subject of the hygiene exhibits was a statistically normal population. Yet types still played the representative role.

As opposed to the 1867 Exposition (which emphasized assistance), the social hygiene exhibits of 1889 shared a common concern with *prévoyance*. Cheysson underlined the distinction. Assistance was directed at helping the weak and wounded, those already fallen. While its motive was worthy, assistance was nonetheless dangerous: it actually increased misery by weakening moral resolve. *Prévoyance* accomplished the opposite: "It gives as much as it receives; it strengthens rather than weakens moral verve; it uplifts rather than depresses; it respects the independence of the one who practices it while joining force with the efforts that assure the security of his future."[15] Forward-looking reformers demanded health, not dependency; hygiene, not disciplinary measures. A population's social health was easily read on charts of worker stability (gauged by lengths of stay at given factories). Good relations were a technical question requiring constant attention. The model patron was a certain Frederick Engel. Engel had assembled a complete arsenal of social weapons to help the worker in life crises (sickness, accidents, old age, and death), as well as facilitating his normal life through savings, housing, and food. Workers were themselves following a similar path of *prévoyance* with the proliferation of cooperatives, savings funds, mutual-aid societies, and banks. The state was appropriately absent; its role, Cheysson argued, should be limited to the collection of accurate statistics, particularly on consumption patterns (which would lead to a wage policy).

Since, as Michelle Perrot had shown, over 80 percent of the strikes in this period turned on salary demands, information on workers' budgets and consumption patterns was vital to any arbitration claiming scientific neutrality.[16] The state's response to the social question was to create the Office du Travail in 1891. Placed within the Ministry of Commerce, Industry, and Colonies, the office received an official mandate to collect information on work conditions both in France and abroad. This consecration constituted an important step: a specific part of society—workers—now had their own research bureau within the state organization. The bureau was run by Le Playists. Just as Le Play had been a sort of counselor to the prince *vis-à-vis* Napoleon III, so too the Le Playists in the last decade of the nineteenth century played a key, if less visible, role in shaping the expanding French state. Later, the Office du Travail, which included La Statistique Générale de la France, would become a stronghold for a group of socialist intellectuals with a different conception of statistics and society.

Beyond Liberalism: From the Factory Town to the Suburbs

The population of Paris rose nearly 50 percent between 1861 and 1896, an increase of 840,000 persons. In the 1870s, after the upheavals of the war and the Commune, Paris experienced extremely rapid population growth. More than a quarter of a million people came to the city in the five-year period between 1876 and 1881.[17] This growth was largely due to in-migration, with only 25 percent of heads of households in 1886 having been born in the department of the Seine and only 5 percent of the city's population comprised of foreigners. Most of these in-migrants were poor and settled in the peripheral eastern sections. Rents soared, evictions mounted, and the famous Daumier drawings of the hated landlord seemed to represent adequately popular opinion of the day.

Jacques Bertillon, head of the Bureau of Municipal Statistics in Paris, standardized the collection of data for the census of 1891. He demonstrated once again (with more sophisticated statistical methods) a chronic shortage of housing, a high percentage of overcrowding, and unhealthy housing in the poor sections. The structural picture the census depicted closely resembled that of the 1830s. The 1850 law and philanthropic experiments had, statistically speaking, accomplished almost nothing for housing, though they had made major advances in the normalization of statistics.[18] Nor had the broad lines of housing reform discourse changed significantly. A proposal in 1883 for a law implementing the 1850 law, backed by the Minister of the Interior and public hygiene specialists, never even got to a vote. In 1887 a new law was proposed which included mandatory examinations of housing by outside specialists; another required a health code for new buildings. Both measures were defeated.[19]

France passed only two major pieces of housing legislation during the nineteenth century, one in 1850 and one in 1894. Throughout the second half of the century, Catholics, socially minded liberals, and socialists were deeply divided on the importance of and appropriate form for social legislation for housing; each of these major social actors had a wing that worked vigorously, if largely in vain, for social legislation, and each had a wing which opposed giving priority to social legislation over charity, the market, or revolutionary political activity. Just as the revolutionary socialists grouped around Jules Guesde saw no need for housing reform, arguing that it was a palliative diverting the attention of the working classes from the need for more total change, so too advocates of laissez-faire principles left no means by which its advocates could incorporate housing reform.[20]

In France, one current of reformers was drawn from the upper reaches of the socially conscious industrial world; this group sought to modify the strict liberal principles of the day to accommodate some form of social action. Georges Picot (1838–1909), a judge, historian, director of the Railroad of the South, and future permanent secretary of the Académie des Sciences Morales et Politiques, was, with Jules Siegfried, the leader and co-founder of the Société Française des Habitations à Bon Marché, organized in 1890. During the early 1880s Picot became interested in the housing problem. In phrases that could have been lifted directly from Villermé, Picot railed against both state intervention and workers' cities, "deplorable barracks containing the phalanstery of misery and crime."[21] Picot argued for single-family houses, located on less expensive suburban land near Paris, made available and accessible through the creation of an affordable transportation system. His proposal was innovative in its relocation of worker housing to the suburbs.[22] Even the most ardent proponents of the single-family house for workers in the Société d'Economie Sociale acknowledged, in a report of 1880, that no more than 4 percent of working-class families could afford even subsidized housing.[23] Emile Cacheux, one of the leading housing specialists in this camp, proposed partial state intervention at the lower end of the market. The gradual shift of the locus of reform efforts from factory cities and urban casernes to suburban areas continued to dominate the discourse of housing reform in France for the next hundred years.

Jules Siegfried: Reform Legislator

Along with Emile Cheysson, Jules Siegfried (1837–1922) was the leading figure among the reformers of the Société d'Economie Sociale. Born into a Protestant textile family from Mulhouse, Siegfried made his fortune during the American Civil War by investing in the cotton market. With the annexation of Mulhouse to Germany in 1870, Siegfried moved permanently to Le Havre. Now quite wealthy, Siegfried left most of the business matters to his brother, and launched an energetic career of philanthropic work. Socially active, he set up a housing society and workers' club; politically active, he advanced from deputy mayor in 1870 to mayor in 1878, and became a deputy in Parliament in 1885.[24] An ardent Republican, Siegfried was extremely well connected in the upper reaches of the government and in influential business circles. As a member of the Union des Amis de la Paix Sociale, the Le Playist offshoot, he also had ties to the Social Catholic movements.

In Le Havre, Siegfried incorporated some of the experiments carried on at Mulhouse into a more urban context. For example, he emphasized the provision of a social space, a setting where workers could gather and find diversion and recreation. Siegfried was particularly involved in housing reform. A preparatory conference for the Workers' Housing Exposition was held in Paris in late June 1889. Siegfried opened the congress with a resounding speech proclaiming that workers' housing was the answer to the social question. "Do we want to make people happy as well as true conservatives; do we want to fight misery and socialist errors at the same time; do we want to ensure order, morality, political and social moderation? Then let us create workers' housing!"[25] Although the barracks arrangement continued to be attacked as the root of moral decay and socialism, the practical limitations of the single-family house with a garden schema forced the congress to explore other possibilities. The participants reluctantly acknowledged the need for multi-residence buildings, provided interfamily sociality could be minimized.

The Exposition of 1889 provided the impetus for reform experts to meet and discuss common proposals. An entire

street of different model houses was constructed to complement the International Housing Congress organized by Siegfried and Picot. Following the Exposition and the Congress (the
first housing law was passed in Belgium in 1889, followed by
one in England in 1890, and a third in Austro-Hungary in
1892), Siegfried formed, in February 1890, the Société Française des Habitations à Bon Marché (French Society for Low-
Cost Housing). The name had originally been "Habitations
Ouvrières" (Worker's Residences). This change acknowledged
that "petits employés" were the target group most likely to be
able to afford (and desire) such lodgings. Still reluctant to call
for state intervention, Siegfried underlined the transmission of
information as the group's most important function. The association was to be a clearinghouse for plans, model houses, and
leases; it was strictly to refrain from lending money or buying
land, as well as from all religious and political activity.

Siegfried put forward a proposal for a housing law on March
5, 1892, which drew heavily on the experiences of the juries at
the Exposition and on laws passed in other countries, especially
in Belgium. The tax advantages for builders, savings banks,
and local housing committees instituted in Belgium were heartily endorsed, whereas the government subsidies and interventions included in the English law were too close to socialism for
Siegfried's comfort. The initial parliamentary reaction was favorable. The law specified that to be eligible for a house, a
worker could not already possess one, and that the value of the
house could not exceed the level set for each commune. The
home owner had to be insured to guarantee the mortgage for
his family. The legislation adopted a Le Playist feature on inheritance, making it hard for heirs to sell the property to a
third party as long as any family member made a claim to retain
it. Building societies were granted some tax concessions. But,
most important, a certain number of organizations were
granted permission to put a percentage of their funds into such
construction enterprises: 20 percent for charitable institutions
and savings banks. Socialists argued that the law tied workers to
specific locales and heavy financial burdens, thereby reducing
their ability to strike. Nevertheless, the law went into effect in
1894.

As in 1850, there were only minimal means established for implementing the scheme. The law provided little more than faith in private initiative. The first step, once again, was to survey housing needs. The task was given to France's prefects, who carried out their mandate in a desultory fashion. Savings banks simply would not lend the necessary money: one-seventh of the legally allowable funds were actually lent; few houses were constructed. By 1900, the liberal principles of many of the partisans of the HBM were weakening, and they were beginning to accept the inevitability of state intervention. In 1891, the government proposed a set of public health laws (passed eleven years later in 1902) which laid the legal groundwork for the eventual enforcement of a hygienists' reform program.

The Musée Social: Social Technocrats

Due largely to the efforts of Cheysson and Siegfried, the Musée Social was founded in 1894 at a moment when a shaky if expanding economy, increased labor militancy, and the crisis of the disciplinary model made the necessity of social action clear to those hoping to preserve the capitalist and Republican order in France. The twin aims of the Musée Social were to gather comprehensive comparative information on social questions—particularly on working-class life—and to work toward an understanding of and legislation for social peace. Its members included labor leaders, social scientists, industrialists, colonialists, and religious leaders. Tracing their lineage to the exhibitions on social economy at the 1867 and 1889 Universal Expositions, its founders shared much of the Le Playist social scientifically-founded model of intervention. They parted company, however, over the modernization of liberalism. Charles Gide called instead for a "school of solidarity" opposing both leveling socialists and atomistic liberals.[26]

At the 1889 fair Cheysson had put forward the idea of a permanent exposition of social economy. In 1893 the Minister of Commerce, Jules Siegfried, proposed a permanent Musée d'Economie Sociale. Not all the credits were granted, but funds were found for a modest exhibit at the Conservatoire des Arts et Métiers. Failing to secure sufficient government backing to insure its future, the planners sought private sources of support instead. The leaders—Siegfried, Say, and Cheysson—interested the Comte de Chambrun, the reforming owner of the Baccarat crystal works. At his factory de Chambrun had instituted a day-care center, a medical and pension fund, funds for orphans' support and workmen's compensation, free baths and showers, a dispensary, a music society, a library, regular religious services, and a free school of industrial design; his factory remained free of labor unrest.[27] In March 1894, Chambrun agreed to donate the necessary funds to get the Musée Social started. By the end of August, after an unusually short delay, the Musée Social was recognized by the cautious Conseil d'Etat as being of public utility. The Musée Social, aided by its powerful networks, got off the ground quickly, setting, in Cheysson's words, the "machinery for social peace" in motion.[28] The Musée's original board was diverse: Albert Gigot, former prefect of Paris police; Paul de Rousiers, arms lobbyist and Le Playist activist who brought his work to labor relations and was active in the International Society of Social Science; Robert Pinot, businessman and later secretary-general of the powerful Comité des Forges (the iron and steel producers' organization); Léopold Mabilleau, a specialist on labor relations who had organized a society in Caen to build workers' housing, as well as an employment bureau and a temperance society; Anatole Leroy-Beaulieu, younger brother of the liberal economist and propagandist.

The Musée Social constituted a conservative but not reactionary group; it was a sort of enlightened industrialist meeting hall for those who understood the necessity of social change. The leaders of the Musée Social sought to overcome paralyzing electoral alliances by forging a coalition concerned with work and environmental issues. The Musée achieved relative autonomy from these groups exactly to the degree that its leaders used their technical expertise on social problems, that is, attempted to unite technicians, industrial patrons, and workers' groups instead of the usual ruling-class alliance with the petite bourgeoisie. The Musée addressed the social problems of the day under the banner of science. In chemistry or physics, Cheysson argued, no one would pretend to proceed without experts. The same logic held in social matters, where the complexities were even greater. Good wishes and pious sentiments no longer sufficed; modern techniques and correct organization alone guaranteed results. The Musée's self-proclaimed role was technical, not doctrinal. To this end its founding statutes proposed that the Musée contain: a permanent exhibit of social economy, a library, an information bureau for social questions, a technical consulting service, a service of popularization, study missions in France and abroad, publications, and special prize competitions. Cheysson likened the Musée's role to a lift-and-force pump (*une pompe aspirante et foulante*) collecting and spreading information. Léon Say called it the Experimental Museum for the world.

Beyond Liberalism: Solidarity

Although by the mid-1880s the Republic had been consolidated, its political limitations were immediately apparent. Parliamentary deadlock and its consequent frustrations demonstrated the representativeness of the Republic as well as the profound political cleavages in French society. In the elections of 1885, the so-called opportunists held one-third of the seats, the radicals an almost equal number, and the conservatives the remaining third, producing a balanced—and hence deadlocked—situation. Frightened by General Boulanger's attempted coup, the radicals returned to the fold and cooperated with the opportunists in the elections of 1889, thereby saving the Republic. Zeldin argues that "the long term significance of Boulangism is that it confirmed that, in a crisis, the republic would show itself to be conservative rather than attempt innovation, and that although its oratory was all about justice, its instincts rated stability more highly."[29] The Church rallied to serve the Republic, even if local priests did not. Once the crisis passed, parliamentary fragmentation and blockage returned. To many observers, extra-political solutions to the conflicts and cleavages in French society seemed imperative.

A new doctrine—solidarism—designed to address these intractable conflicts attracted widespread attention from ex-monarchists, socialists, and center radicals. Analysts agree that the movement was an eclectic one. It has been ironically referred to as quasi-socialism; another gibe stated: "It is like a radish, red outside and white within."[30] Not everyone, however, took the movement so casually; Poincaré remarked that solidarism's "beguiling and reassuring formulas did not conceal its extreme and sometimes dangerous, almost revolutionary theories."[31] The common problem was providing an objective basis for social ties.[32] By the end of the century in France, interdependence had become the guiding symbol for a range of discourses about society and nature. Durkheim's 1896 *Division of Labor in Society* is today the best known expression of this current, although in its day it was not the most important. Hayward emphasizes that the details of a social program based on solidarist principles were not really worked out by Durkheim and that much of what he said on the subject was published only posthumously.

The leading exponents of the doctrine were the politician Léon Bourgeois and the jurist Léon Duguit. The core of the doctrine was simple: the social whole was greater than its parts and formed a *sui generis* reality. Processes of individuation began with the whole. Bourgeois, the son of a watchmaker, became the spokesman for solidarism. He transformed the platitude that men were not free individuals, that all men were indebted to others—to parents, to language, and to history—into a legal and social tool. Solidarism had two main concepts: quasi-contract, the idea that overt and explicit consent was not required for all contracts, because society had prior rights; and social debt, the notion that contract was not voluntary but arose from preexisting obligations to others. Social debt was prior to and had a higher value than social right; both individual and social progress depended on its repayment. With the idea of a collective social debt, political responsibility and injustice were dramatically transformed. Solidarity was not to be based on the sentiment of culpability; its ground was scientific. The state's task was not the radical transformation of power relations but a regulation and enrichment of social ties in the name of general equity.

Bourgeois systematized the doctrine in a series of lectures given at the Ecole des Hautes Etudes Sociales in 1901–2. The leading thinkers of the Third Republic publicly united behind the banner of solidarism.[33] The guiding principle, emphasized time and time again, was the belief that society was greater than and existed prior to its individual parts. France needed a new organizing concept. Justice, as a legal term, had lost its vitality. Charity expressed condescension and hierarchy. Fraternity was nothing more than a sentiment. The modern era demanded a scientifically grounded concept; solidarity was the answer. Although solidarity was linked to Christian charity, the metaphysical underpinnings of charity disqualified its use in the modern world. Solidarity was a "positive" fact: men existed on this earth in association with one another. The force of the idea was that it removed social bonds from the battlefield of politics. Once science established the primacy of interdependence, a consensus would surely emerge on collective social effort. What was the guiding theme of solidarity? "It is the amelioration of the living conditions of its participants, conforming to an idea of justice, in a quasi-fraternal association. Note that in this kind of association there are neither benefactors nor beneficiaries."[34] Solidarity did not demand superior commitment nor moral stature: self-interest was sufficient. Once set in motion, the machine would be self-regulating.

Bourgeois followed the opening presentations at the Ecole with a series of three conferences on the meaning of solidarity.[35] He began by rehearsing solidarism's modern scientific lineage, its ascension from the political to the scientific. Gide had given the term its modern meaning by equating life with interdependence. Since interdependence held not only in the biological realm but in the economic and social realms as well, social science had a double task: to conduct inquiries into the division of labor and the exchange of services, and to bring these insights to the public's attention. Science demonstrated the necessity, and morality the conditions, of common action as a duty. Justice was not natural. Nature was *a-juste;* justice was precisely what was added to nature by men. Although interdependence was natural, its transformation into justice required a conscious, voluntary act. Freedom was the recognition of this social debt and its transformation into a duty. Bourgeois repeated his two themes over and over again: the scientific fact of interdependence; the moral duty to make society just.

In his second lecture, Bourgeois posed the question: In what did the morality of solidarity consist? First, it entailed an extension of the concept of responsibility. Responsibility had previously been understood only as an individual matter; solidarism transformed it into a social one. The law was beginning to appreciate the weight of the milieu in determining action. Only when conditions of equality were reestablished could justice be served. Social debt aimed at reestablishing this equivalence. But what was the social? "Social" meant more than merely the brute fact of association. A man was not truly social unless he was aware of his dependence on society and actively accepted his debt to others. Social life depended on mutual consent to mutual protection against mutual risk. The solidarist doctrine was the opposite of Rousseau's: Rousseau began with contract; the solidarists ended with one. The social contract was the culmination of a conscious agreement signaling the ascent from the realm of force and necessity to that of freedom. Since the highest stage of sociality was mutuality, it followed that the mutualist contract would be the road to social peace. Through a socialization of risk guaranteed by, but not created by, the state, the conditions of justice were made possible. Insurance companies had done just that; society should follow their example.

If this was socialism, then it was of a new type, one starting from collectivism and moving toward individual liberty. Neo-Kantian socialism combined the liberal economists' notion of freedom with the socialists' concept of justice. Bourgeois was careful to underline his differences from the socialists on a number of points: respect for private property but especially the question of the State. The State was not an end in itself but only a protection. Its main role was to apply sanctions to violators of the common quasi-contract. Risks, not property, would be socialized.

Society as Cooperation and Consumption

Two different attempts to go beyond Bourgeois' neo-liberal views of social organization, while remaining within the horizon of a solidarist perspective, were presented at the Ecole des Hautes Etudes. M. F. Rauh, of the Ecole Normale Supérieure, asserted that Bourgeois and socialists agreed on ends but differed on the means of attaining them.[36] For Rauh, Bourgeois placed too much emphasis on the role of law and State sanctions; socialists approached the matter in more positive, concrete social and institutional terms. Interpreted harshly, Bourgeois' social justice could be seen as only a democratic form of the old state charity practiced under the Ancien Régime. Socialists proposed making justice not only an organizational, but a positive task: "The socialist system contrasts with Mr. Leon Bourgeois's system as hygiene and preventive medicine do with ordinary therapy, which cures an illness after its onset."[37]

According to Rauh, the error of moving from the top down was not restricted to Bourgeois and the radicals; some socialists still clung to these archaic positions. Socialism had two distinct lineages: one erroneously emphasized centralization; the other correctly amplified the just and democratic organization of society. Rauh was critical of Marx and Engels' doctrine of centralization of production and of their goal of communalizing and redistributing wealth. Instead, Rauh, following Proudhon, advocated a mixed and decentralized economy. The best path was not nationalization of the means of production but democracy: in the factory, by means of councils and open discussion; among industries, by a coordination of efforts. Socialists, Rauh urged, must create a future in which the citizen would feel as free in the factory as in the voting booth. To reach this socialist society, democracy needed to be rethought in the light of modern social science and the principles of solidarity. Socialists too frequently envisaged the transition to the Social Republic as either violent or as engineered by state legislation. Both of these Jacobin conceptions, however, were negative; the modern socialist task was to develop positive alternatives, such as cooperatives and mutual societies. Most important, for these changes to take hold in society, change had to come not merely from the top. Solidarist thinkers of quite divergent political persuasions concurred on this point. Both Gide and Karl Kautsky agreed that a federation of cooperatives was possible; they differed only on the means of achieving it. Gide believed in individual effort; the socialists believed in greater organization.[38] Socialist solidarity consisted in economic democracy based on autonomous local production, on democratic social law based on the right of society to regulate the redistribution of goods, and on a state whose only function would be to regulate democratically controlled local cooperatives operated on the basis of democratic social relations. This program was being tested electorally, socially, and administratively in the municipal socialist movement.

Charles Gide sought a path diverging from those of both neo-liberals and socialists.[39] Economists offered three naturalistic models of social solidarity: division of labor, exchange, and competition. Gide argued that all three were, at best, insufficient and, at worst, dangerous. He offered an alternative organizing principle for modern society—consumption. The first model, the division of labor, could be seen, as Durkheim argued, as one of the best examples of social solidarity. But, Gide cautioned, despite Durkheim's elevation of the division of labor to a high moral plane, such division separated men as much as it tied them together. He mocked Durkheim's view that by differentiating men, one avoided conflict; that, Gide said, was a vision of society worthy of "un chef de gare" (a stationmaster). The example of the Saint-Simonians at Menilmontant, who wore vests that could only be buttoned from behind, so that no one could dress without being reminded that he was dependent on his brothers, showed that negative dependency created a solidarity of imbeciles.

According to Gide, the organicist metaphor had also been a source of confused analogies. He commented that the solidarity between a senator and a worker was hardly identical to that between the arms and the stomach. Models taken from economics were more destructive than constructive to peaceful and just social solidarity. Exchange presented another example of sloppy and dangerous analogizing. Economists held that exchange was voluntary and mutually beneficial. While it was true that exchange enriched both sides, it was not disinterested. Hence, defining it as a reciprocal gift, as was frequently done by partisans of solidarism, was nonsense. Exchange arose out of a cease-fire in war and maintained the spirit of its origins. Economists had a third model to offer: competition. Competition had its positive side: it produced the best for consumers. The better a manufacturer satisfied consumers' needs, the larger the profit the producer made. Society's general interest, however, was not enriched by competition; only individual interests were. As the American case demonstrated, free competition led to fraud, trusts, and inferior working conditions. Gide concluded that none of the economic models—division of labor, exchange, or competition—provided a satisfactory set of principles for social solidarity.

The reason these models failed was that they were based on natural relations. It was only when solidarity became artificial—voluntary and reflective—that it became just. True solidarist organization fulfilled the following conditions: its object was as general as possible, common to all men, so as not to serve as the source of division and conflict but rather of unity; and it applied not to accidental occurrences but to the most general and regular social activity. Attempts had been made to approximate these principles. Professional organizations had been put forward as models by such diverse figures as Durkheim, the Social Catholics, and many socialists. Gide reasserted his contention that the division of labor separated men, replacing individual egotism with its corporate equivalent. Professional corporatism forced a kind of armed solidarity, which more often than not opposed progress and general well-being. Furthermore, defining people entirely by their work was degrading. From the gentleman who wore no sign of his profession after leaving the office, to the worker who showered after work, the common goal was merely to be men.

In a democracy, men were equals. This principle was accepted politically; the task was to institute it socially. Perhaps the mutual-aid associations provided a model? They could not be accused of dividing and arousing antagonism among men. Although Gide acknowledged this, he argued that such organizations only reacted to the pathological state of society—illness and death. Although they did embrace a generous solidarity, they remained partial and limited. Normal social life could not be encompassed by a mode of organization designed for the pathological. What about cooperative associations? The main strength of the cooperative movement, according to Gide, was its isolation of a truly universal social characteristic: consumption. Everyman was not a producer, but everyman was a consumer. In modern France, three-quarters of the population produced nothing. Production divided people, underscoring social differences, while consumption promoted uniformity. Differences of income were quantitative, not qualitative. Finally, consumer cooperatives operated on the level of everyday needs; consumption brought different people into frequent social contact. The term communion came from the sharing together in abundance. Consumption was not an accidental or pathological state: "It is the normal, continuous activity in life. The association for consumption could take as its motto: Pro vita!"[40] Solidarity would be achieved only when consumers came together to provide collectively for all their material, intellectual, aesthetic, moral, and religious needs. In such a Cooperative Republic there would be true solidarity, or the richer an individual became, the more everyone benefited.

French Social Law

The history of the concept of solidarity had a legal origin. Roman law had a developed concept of the solidarity between debtor and creditor, rooted in social links recognized in the extended family and enlarged to include mutual aid in professional corporations. The French Revolution and the Napoleonic codification of French law modified and undermined the importance of these links. Under Napoleonic law, an equally dominant strand of Roman law—which viewed the State and the individual as the purely legal subjects—returned with renewed force. The remnants of a larger solidarity were restricted to cases for which it was explicitly stipulated. Article 1202 of the Code Civil states: "Solidarity is not to be presumed; it must be expressly stipulated. This rule remains in effect except in the case where solidarity becomes a full right by virtue of a disposition of law."[41] The problem for jurists sympathetic to the movement was one of overcoming these limitations, of reintroducing the social into legal considerations.

Following the famous Loi le Chapelier of 1791, which abolished the legal status of professional corporations, the individual was supreme in French law. Revolutionary individualism, carried forward by the bourgeoisie and industrialists, was countered during the nineteenth century by a current of utopian socialist and conservative Catholic social thought, and by a thin stream of legal interpretation. The goal of this school of legal interpretation was to define a place for that object which existed prior to both the individual and the State and which was the ground on which they both arose—society. "Legal objectivism," whose leading exponent was Léon Duguit (1859–1928), sought to construct a legal doctrine out of social norms considered as sources of constraint and legitimacy. The problem Duguit and other jurists attempted to solve was: How could one legislate for the social sphere? How could one create and justify legislation which was not based on natural law, sovereign rights, or individual responsibility? How could one formulate a historical administrative law? Thinkers like Duguit, who was labeled an "anarchist of the chair," were keenly aware of the dangers of the growth of the state. How could one formulate a doctrine of increasing responsibility for the social, without also including some principle of limitation of state activity? The counter danger to liberalism's enshrinement of individualism was the danger of a state with unlimited power.[42]

Duguit, Professor of Law in Bordeaux from 1886 to 1928, placed great emphasis on the role of the social sciences in renewing and extending the law. As he said in 1899: "The true name of the faculties of law should be faculties of social science."[43] Duguit saw sociology as a tool to purge French law of its metaphysical assumptions. The originality of his position stemmed from his radical sociological derivation of norms. As François Ewald has shown, this meant an attempt to construct a legal system devoid of any stable concept of justice, one based only on norms. In his "Le Droit Constitutionnel et la Sociologie" of 1889 and "Des Fonctions juridiques de l'Etat Moderne" of 1894, Duguit argued that the law was a branch of sociology and the state an objective fact.[44] Duguit could well have adopted Fouillée's formula "Cogito, ergo sumus" (I think, therefore we are) or Rimbaud's "Je suis un autre" (I am an other).

Duguit opened his public lectures in 1911 by identifying his two opponents: revolutionary socialists and orthodox jurists.[45]

The doctrines of class struggle and of subjective law were both wrong: neither classes nor society nor individuals had rights. The idea of subjective law—either for individuals or the state— was a totally unfounded, metaphysical residue. There was no natural law, nor did universal precepts or absolute right of any sort exist. Law was only the expression of historical sets of social relationships. Napoleonic doctrine may have served a useful function at a certain point of historical development, but in the modern world it was outmoded and impeded society's health. This view of things did not suggest that law operated without constraints, but only that the constraints were social. Individuals were social beings and hence constrained by social rules; violation of these rules provoked social reactions which varied from place to place and country to country, while conformity received social approbation. Duguit acknowledged the insights of the solidarists; for him, solidarity was functional interdependence operating in a particular society at a particular time. However, Bourgeois' quasi-contract was an unnecessary, metaphysical notion. Solidarity was a fact, not a moral imperative. It was not an ideal, but changed throughout history; in this sense solidarity was the opposite of natural law. Law was a question of force, the product of an objective situation.

Duguit argued that the older Roman law based on the idea of subjective rights was drastically altered by his reformulation. The task of French law was to elaborate a political regime lacking any notion of public power, and an economic regime in which the notion of *dominium* was completely eliminated; both would be transformed into social functions. Just as prescientific psychology had invented the idea of a soul as the invisible unifier and ground of psychological phenomena, so too jurists had used the state and its sovereignty as a metaphysical justification of a simple condition of fact. Law was made by the legislative body, and hence was created according to the whim of an empirical group of men. There was no legitimate distinction between administration and *la puissance publique;* both were acts of the government's agents. The distinction between those who ruled and those who were ruled rested on force. "Judicial action is purely material; it is a force which breaks down another force; it is not one will pitted against another will by

virtue of a judicial power."[46] Duguit warned against those col-
lectivists who naively thought the increase of state power would
benefit the working class. This doctrine led to Hobbes's
Leviathan: in the name of mutual protection, an all-powerful
state was devised to oversee a heap of atomized individuals.

The idea of individual rights was usually put forward as a
remedy to this danger. Duguit argued that these rights too
were fictional. They were also ineffective safeguards: they had
never been successfully organized to resist the state's power.
The Declaration of the Rights of Man did not stop the Convention of 1792–95, Napoleon, the Coup d'Etat of 1851, or the
laws of the Second and Third empires. The basis of social reorganization did not lie in class confrontation: neither bourgeois
nor proletarian domination was desirable. To what kind of
state and what kind of society would this insight lead? To those
that were decentralized and constituted as syndicalist federa-
tions. Duguit quickly added that this was not revolutionary syndicalism. Marx's call for class warfare was destructive and
empirically wrong. France was composed of many classes, not
just two; peasant proprietors and small shopkeepers belonged
to both the capitalist and working classes. Whether or not they
would one day disappear, they constituted a potent political
and sociological force in contemporary France. In the future,
Duguit prophesied, the most important group would be the
"classe des salariées," paid functionaries working for the state or
for private business.

According to Duguit, people who were doing the same kind
of work had the same interests, habits, and sentiments. It was
natural that they should feel solidarity with each other. Capitalists had the social responsibility to use their capital produc-
tively. This contribution, and nothing else, established their
rights. As soon as they ceased to exercise their assigned function, the capitalists would disappear. Through a division of
labor, the individual would receive maximum protection
against the state. The mutual interest of different occupational
groups in achieving social harmony and productivity ensured
cooperation. The new man was not Nietzsche's willful individual but a socially embedded one linked to the only modern
anchor, an occupational group. In this decentralized and syn-

dicalized state, public services would be spread throughout society by professional corporations. Otherwise, a state more monstrous than any mankind had known would come into being. The only legitimate function of the state was to sanction, control, and oversee these social laws.[47]

The Social-Spatial Turn

German geographers dominated the field of geography in Europe during the middle of the nineteenth century. Carl Ritter and Alexander von Humboldt (both of whom died in 1859) constructed a totalizing theory of the cosmos, demonstrating the interconnections of all living beings with the earth. For von Humboldt, geography embodied the earth's history, and history therefore consisted of map-reading—that is to say, of the figuration of mathematical, geodesic, climatological, and bio-geographical data.[48] As the century wore on, the French found the German school increasingly mechanist. French Third Republic reaction against German geography is captured by the quip: "Où est le vivant?" (Where are living beings?) The reaction coincided with anti-Darwinism in biology: both were in search of a more humanistic, historically mediated conception of spatial and social forms. They sought to identify forms guided, at least in part, by norms—norms articulated by modern science and applied by disinterested public servants.

French geographers associated with the work of Paul Vidal de la Blache (1845–1918) resisted German determinism and downplayed the inalterability of physical milieu and race, emphasizing instead the mediating role of social factors. A distinctive school of French geography emerging at the end of the nineteenth century emphasized the milieu as an active variable linking society, nature, and history. Paul Vidal de la Blache introduced the concept of *genres de vie* (modes of life), which he traced to Buffon, whom he viewed as the precursor of human geography.[49] Following Buffon, Vidal saw in animal domestication the basic model of variation; artificial breeding of plants and animals combined a rational choice of traits and spatial segregation. Civilization produced the order nature lacked. Once segregation was achieved (whether artificially or through successful colonization), regulatory demographic mechanisms took over. Although based on a pathos of broken harmony, this doctrine entailed pragmatic and hopeful consequences: living beings could be improved by ameliorating milieux, and this constituted the purest civilizing activity. French geography and regionalist reformers aimed at precisely this form of social amelioration.

The task of social geography was to understand how physical and biotic conditions were reflected in mankind's social life. Vidal's scientific goal was to analyze *genres de vie,* a term designed to include both social and spatial identity. *Genres de vie* served, in a functionalist and quasi-organicist manner, to establish a middle ground between the more place-oriented determinism of Ratzel and placeless evolutionary theories. The geographer was counseled to study the fundamental lines of material production in their relations with local natural resources, dietary patterns in relation to local conditions, the blend of agricultural and nonagricultural activities, and the dynamics of circulation systems (transportation, migration, and exchange). Vidal emphasized the contraints on human choices. Although Vidal's approach sought originally to account for rural development, by the end of his life Vidal and his students were applying it to urban and political processes as well.[50]

Genres de vie formed part of each milieu. Milieux were composite products of historical, geographical, ecological, and demographic elements. The socially-constituted, historical multiplicity was active, "endowed with a power capable of connecting and maintaining groups of heterogeneous beings in cohabitation and reciprocal correlation. This notion appears to be the very law which governs the geography of living beings."[51] For Vidal, neither natural harmonies nor spatial determinisms existed. Contingency was the controlling concept; "contingent," in French thought (following on the work of Cournot), meant probable. Contingency functioned within larger wholes, slowly developing throughout history.[52] History was never finished; each battle was only temporary, even if particular moments lasted centuries. This was the *la longe durée* with a vengeance: a picture of constant change, open to modest modification through wisdom and patient intervention.

Modern geographic thought made its first major institutional inroads at the Ecole Normale Supérieure, where Vidal was appointed in 1877 (at the age of thirty-two) and continued to teach until 1898. Support for his nomination covered the political spectrum from the conservative Fustel de Coulanges to the Republican Paul Bert. The strategic importance of this elite student body was no secret: "If the teaching corps, like the army, requires numerous troops, it could no more do without an elite [than could the army]."[53] In 1898, Vidal moved on to the Sorbonne. Before leaving, he placed one of his own students on the faculty at the Ecole Normale, thereby maintaining control of the key posts of French higher education. Geographers profited from these institutional relations: the number of professors of geography rose from 8 in 1876 to 51 in 1909; chairs in geography increased from 1 before 1870 to 4 in 1890 to 12 by the end of the century.

Modern Regions

The regionalist movement is another example of a discourse that emerged long before its practical effects. Not unlike French municipal movements and their advocacy of urbanism laws (to which we turn in the next section), the implementation of regionalist programs remained limited until Vichy. A variety of regionalisms flourished at the end of the nineteenth century, however, ranging from localist novelists to folklore societies to the Fédération Régionaliste Française, formed in 1900, whose membership spanned the French political and social spectrum from Barrès to Bourgeois and the solidarists to certain socialists and, of course, the geographers.[54]

Napoleonic centralization established the basic contours of French administrative structure, as well as the shape of resistance to it, for the rest of the century. Calls for reform came from many quarters. In 1865 a distinguished group of personalities called for a program to "fortify the *commune*, invigorate the *canton*, do away with the *arrondissement*, extend the *département*. Hand over communal affairs to the commune, regional ones to the region, and national ones to the state."[55] The Emperor was sympathetic; in 1869 he promised sweeping decentralist reforms. Republicans issued a parallel reform program in Nancy; an extra-parliamentary committee on decentralization (including Le Play, Maxime du Camp, and Prévost-Paradol) was named on February 22, 1870. Then came the war and the Commune.[56] The Third Republic allowed a certain amount of interdepartmental cooperation; various other minor extensions of departmental and communal initiative were enacted between 1884 and 1914, without any appreciable lessening of administrative centralization. Control (*tutelle*) of the prefects remained in place. Opponents on both the right and the left railed against the denial of individual and social liberty in France. De Lanessan proclaimed that the Republic could not survive with structures that produced only two types of Frenchmen: functionaries and materialistic individualists.[57]

Two of the most famous critics of French administration were Proudhon and Le Play. Although Proudhon did not use the word "region," he did formulate a plan for the French nation to be divided into some twenty self-administering provinces, each representing the local character of its people. "The Frenchman is a convention; he does not exist." Proudhon proposed treating each population according to the structure best suited to its temperament and customs. This was not a project of complete decentralization, as it involved the voluntary ceding of important powers to the state. It is more accurate, using Proudhon's own vocabulary, to talk of mutualism. Local units, from the family to the canton, would give up certain rights (e.g., legal or foreign affairs) in return for certain others (local or economic). Mutualism aimed at dialectically combining social differences at the local level and strongly unifying the state at the national level.[58]

Le Play isolated the commune as the elementary socio-administrative unit. With the establishment of communes as moral and electoral bases, France would exhibit the necessary conditions for the moral regeneration of the race. The communes would be grouped into thirteen provinces. Le Play based his provinces on ethnic and historical elements, considering nascent affinities among the existing departments, geographical contiguity, geology, climate, agricultural production, industrial activity, and the current deployment of commercial outlets. Each province would be ruled by a governor chosen from among rural proprietors by the sovereign power. Universities, courts, and other such bodies would be administered locally. Above all, the financial affairs of the province and state were to be separated completely.[59] Le Play's ideas proved amenable to many camps. Social Catholics took up the theme of regionalism. In October 1886, the Society of Catholic Jurisconsults met in Lille to discuss the relations between the state and the individual. They criticized state socialism (administrative tutelage, secular education, and civil marriage) as well as the leveling individualism of French liberalism. They repeated the standard conservative call for a society renovated through occupational structures and decentralized regionalism, adopting a plan calling for a return to the Ancien Régime.

If Proudhon was the grandfather of the regionalist movement, Barrès's *La Terre et les morts* made it famous. Raging against social leveling stemming from the nefarious influences of Jacobinism and Kantianism, Barrès identified the province as the basic unit of France. He appealed to the authenticity of the provinces and their peoples: "My aim is not to prove supremacy but to have differences recognized. What my ideas amount to is that the land is a powerful force, a soul accumulated amidst a native population, and that wise administrations, instead of scorning or combatting that force, should utilize it."[60] Barrès called for regionalist reform, citing sources as diverse as Taine, Comte, Le Play, Proudhon, and the Republican Program of Nancy. Reform had to come from the base. "Experimentation—that is what all Frenchmen of good faith should demand: sociological laboratories," declared Barrès.[61] Local government would be communal and regional, with regional assemblies. Regions would be natural circumscriptions determined by a commission of geographers and economists. They would be true laboratories of sociology; each would develop its own economic, social, and political patterns. Learning from each other's experiments and from practical principles, regions would emerge to maintain social vigor and solidarity.

Two very different branches of the regionalist movement forming at the end of the century were influenced by Barrès.

One pole, the regionalists in each region, sought to strengthen each region's "âme accumulée" into a cultural movement. Provincial societies were formed, costumes preserved, regional crafts promoted, local historians resurrected, and regional theater invented. These cultural dimensions were taken up by business and tourist interests. The Syndicat d'Initiative, founded in Grenoble in 1889, became their institutional vehicle. The Société pour la Protection des Paysages de France, formed in 1901, proclaimed in its charter: "all natural beauty can be an object of public utility, as necessary to the honor and wealth of a country as to its pleasure."[62] Barrès's conservative identification of diversity and tradition was transformed by other regionalist groups into a modernizing doctrine which saw these as attainable and as the means through which a new France could be forged. The problem was to identify scientifically the appropriate units and to develop flexible administrative, economic, and social structures through which they could be strengthened.

The Fédération Régionaliste Française was christened and launched in 1900 by J.-Charles Brun (1870–1946), with the support of many of the leading personalities of the Third Republic. In its wake was a diverse group ranging from Barrès to Paul Doumer (Governor General of Indochina and President of France), as well as the leading French geographers Paul Vidal de la Blache and Jean Brunhes. Brun, professor at the College Libre des Sciences Sociales and the Institut de Droit International de Paris, and Secretary General of the Société Proudhon, was the central animator of the movement. The FRF provided a link between Republican regionalism and Barrès's nationalism. Its 1901 manifesto remained the charter of French regionalism for the next fifty years.[63]

The movement's rhetoric retained Barrèssian attachment to the *pays*, but these regionalists were equally aware of the necessity of reconciling tradition and industrialization. Brun claimed that Le Play and Proudhon were the forefathers of the movement.[64] The FRF presented an apolitical electoral program calling for economic, administrative, and intellectual decentralization along regional lines. These modern regionalists were for more natural administrative groupings, modernizing economic development, and a more flexible and efficient formula of authority and power; strengthening social bonds; emphasizing neutral social sciences; and balancing the needs of local liberties at the commune level and regional economic development within a unified nation. They opposed "Jacobins of all parties." The regionalist program was based on a rejection of the *département* and of provincialism. The FRF held that Napoleonic departments were arbitrary and irrational and led to obvious absurdities: Lozère and the Nord had same number of administrators, while the population of the latter was fourteen times as great, and its economic production fifty-four times that of the Nord. However, the changes that had occurred during the nineteenth century precluded a return to the old provinces of the Ancien Régime. To alleviate the sickness from which the country was suffering, the regionalists proposed scientific hygiene. They advocated an experimental method: new social sciences, particularly geography, would provide the knowledge necessary for rational reform.

The French left generally distrusted decentralization, fearing its potential for strengthening local reactionary forces and for weakening the nation. Social differences were not part of Republican discourse. Still, some sort of reform was clearly required. While conservative decentralizers focused on rural life, modern regionalists envisioned instead strong modern regions. New transportation methods and new sources of power, such as electricity, were embraced as aids to decentralization. Social liberals like Cheysson advocated a social regionalism: cooperatives, pensions for workers, and other forms of social relief without state aid would lead to regional solidarity, liberty, and responsibility. Many plans were proposed; of particular importance was that of Charles Beauquier, radical-socialist Deputy of Besançon (Doubs) in 1890. Beauquier, who was active in the Musée Social, became the leading protagonist of regionalism in the Third Republic, forming the link between parliamentary efforts toward decentralization and Brun's Federation, of which he became honorary president soon after its founding in 1900. As Beauquier put it in 1912, citing Proudhon: "It is spontaneously, by a process of agglutinization of ethnic, climatic, geographic, commercial, agricultural, artistic, literary, and still other elements—that the region gradually constitutes itself. The administrative division will then be imposed quite simply as the consecration of this fait accompli."[65] Beauquier called for a study of geographic and economic factors in which historic cities would be chosen to serve as poles of attraction for growth. Reducing the eighty-six departments to twenty or twenty-five units would reduce expense and increase efficiency.

Leftist regionalists preferred the term "deconcentration" to "decentralization." They wanted the security of national unity but saw the deconcentration of power as rational, efficient, and healthy. As one spokesman said, this regionalism was both more and less than a decentralist movement: more in that it called for a total administrative reorganization of France (decentralists often accepted the existing administrative organization but called for a transfer of power to the local level), less in that regionalists were not against the state per se but favored better organization of public services. The only scheme the regionalists would accept was that of systematic, but supervised, diversity. In Brun's distinction, traditionalism was passive, whereas regionalism was active. The regionalists were modernizers seeking a more rational and efficient state that would draw on and administer a more scientifically individualized and organized set of regions. Individualization of the parts increased the coherence and strength of the whole.

Vidal wrote a report called "Régions françaises" which became the regionalists' bench mark.[66] In it he stated that France was composed of natural regions within which economic regions had slowly developed. Underlying the artificial departmental map of France was that of another, truer France representing population movements, cultural centers, industrial complexes, railway networks, navigable waters, concentrations of capital, markets, speculations, and intellectual development. The true France would emerge if maps of each of these vital factors, in different colors, were superimposed one upon the other. Vidal argued that modern cities had a particularly important role to play in this restructuring, as they were the centers of France's next stage of development.[67]

During the Third Republic the regionalist movement suffered an almost complete legislative failure, even though most of the important political figures of the Third Republic supported the broad outlines of regional reform. There were several reasons for this failure. The movement proclaimed itself rigorously apolitical. Sticking to this principle—they limited themselves to handing out a questionnaire on regional issues to candidates in 1951—regionalism succeeded all too well. Its program remained at a level of generality at which a broad spectrum of French political opinion could agree, but upon which no one would act. The regionalists never succeeded in organizing an effective lobby. Their main success was a regional reorganization of chambers of commerce in 1919. Finally, regionalism's association was the increasingly shrill and highly sectarian rhetoric of Barrès, Maurras, and Mistral was never overcome by its technically minded proponents.

Socialist Municipalities

Throughout Europe during the later decades of the nineteenth century, an important movement for municipal control over public services gained wide acceptance. England and Germany led the way; France brought up the rear. The success of the public health movement throughout Europe was instrumental in bringing about change. Although the first municipal gasworks had been established in Manchester in 1817 and in Leipzig in 1838, large-scale changes really began in Germany during the 1860s and 1870s. The Paris Electric Exposition of 1881 provoked curiosity throughout Europe, and by 1912 over half of the central electrical stations in England were municipally owned. But by the outbreak of the First World War, France still had none. While in Germany delivery of these new public services had been instituted by Bismarck and businessmen, in France the impetus for their implementation came from the so-called municipal socialists.[68]

Modern French socialism began to take hold as an electoral political force only in the last decade of the century. In the general elections of 1881 the socialists received some 63,000 votes; by 1914 they received approximately 1,400,000. It was really after the elections of 1892 that socialists began to be elected to local political positions and to formulate a set of municipal policies. Despite impressive electoral successes in a large number of French cities, most of the policies developed by municipal socialists were blocked either by the prefects, the Minister of the Interior, or the Conseil d'Etat (the highest administrative court in France), where all cases involving litigation between citizens and the government were heard.[69] Laissez-faire doctrines prospered in France to a larger degree and with a greater degree of inflexibility than in Germany or England. Opposition to municipal socialism also came from the revolutionary, Marxist left, which first opposed it as bourgeois reformism, later joined its campaigns when it rode the electoral crest during the 1890s, and then turned against it again, splitting into warring camps.[70] The policies, debates, and electoral fortunes of the municipal socialists form the background to urban planning projects such as Tony Garnier's famous Industrial City—the charter document of modern French attempts to plan a new society of work, health, and leisure—to which we turn in the next chapter.

Paul Brousse: Socialist Possibilists
The initial framework for the French socialist municipal movement was borrowed from Belgium, where municipal reform ranked high on the political agenda. In 1874 César de Paepe, a leading Belgian socialist, presented a party platform calling for communal public services.[71] Socialists like de Paepe accepted the fact that the road to revolution was (at least temporarily) blocked. They argued for socialization of municipal services to provide necessary, concrete improvements in workers' lives. De Paepe drew a distinction between the control of services by society and by state administration. He called for public control of essential programs such as medicine, communication, education, and security.

In France, it was Paul Brousse (1844–1912) whose name was most closely associated with the politics of municipal services.[72] Brousse first attracted attention by publicly opposing Marx, an action that resulted in his expulsion from the First International in September 1872. Under Bakuninist influences, Brousse became an anarchist, living and working first in Spain, then in Switzerland. During the 1870s, Brousse and other anarchists formulated a doctrine that downplayed the importance of both the state and the unions. By the end of the decade, Brousse was becoming increasingly pragmatic and even considered the possibility of an intermediary political state, which might occur after the end of current society and before the society that would result from the revolution. His expulsion from Switzerland and exile in Brussels and London from 1879 to 1880 confirmed Brousse's reformist tendencies. He returned to France, having shifted from anarchism back to socialism. From anarchism, however, Brousse preserved elements of strong decentralism and antiauthoritarianism. By 1880, he was ready to compromise an anarchist refusal to participate in electoral politics. Firmly socialist, Brousse continued to be strongly anti-Marxist.

Municipal Socialism, 1890–99
Starting with the elections of 1892, and continuing to the end of the century, the momentum of socialist municipalism was strong. It seemed that important reforms could be carried out and a power base solidly established at the municipal level. By the end of the century, however, the limits of municipal power in bringing about reform had been demonstrated, and the splits in the party reemerged. In the 1892 municipal elections, French socialists gained control of the councils of Marseilles, Roubaix, Toulon, Narbonne, and Montlucon, and had won seats in many other councils throughout France (some 800 in all). Coalition politics played an important role in these victories. In Lyons, for example, radicals joined socialists in formal alliances. By the mid-1890s each of the major socialist parties in France had acknowledged the importance of municipalities as theaters of operations and had adopted some municipal programs. Broadly speaking, the Alemannists and the Guesdists adopted the vast majority of the planks of the possibilists' platform, although the Guesdists were consistent in holding that political reform could not come from the control of municipalities but only from national action aimed at seizing

state power. Following this guiding principle, they continued to oppose the socialization of municipal services.

Municipal socialists chose "the socialization of the commune as the best road to the socialization of the state."[73] To this end a series of socialist congresses were held between 1892 and 1899 to forge a common program. The Guesdists refused to participate, thus shattering hopes of unity. Edouard Vaillant remained somewhere in between, working hard for municipal reform, including municipal industries and public services but resisting the federalist or localist tendencies of the Brousse faction. Under Vaillant's leadership a common program was adopted; its most concrete achievement was the creation of a federation of municipal councillors who would share information, expertise, and legal defenses.[74]

The Commune

Socialists placed the highest political priority on achieving some degree of local autonomy for the commune. Although often coupled with larger political demands (including linking the communes at the federal level, a plan that dissociated them from the anarchists), their minimum requirement was some degree of decentralization and autonomy of decision-making. French communes at the time had little such autonomy. A decree of December 14, 1789 organized France into 44,000 communes, each having a mayor and municipal council. Although these officials were at first elected, in 1800 Napoleon dictated that they be appointed. After 1831, city councils were again elected, albeit with highly restrictive eligibility procedures for voters. After 1848 the electoral base was greatly enlarged, but it did not include women until 1945. Elections for mayors (except in Paris) were reinstated in 1882. A comprehensive Municipal Law was adopted in 1884, stating that the municipal council was to be elected every four years, and that the elected councillors would choose the mayor. Although the 1884 law provided the communes with the power to manage their own affairs, this power was never formally defined and was frequently limited by administrative and judicial action. The Conseil d'Etat interpreted the clause as meaning that powers not expressly granted to the municipality were to be denied it. Prefects maintained significant budgetary control over municipal councils, no major taxes or loans were possible without their approval, and they had the right to dissolve councils.

The core of the municipal socialist program was control over the local budget, police, and administration, and freedom to form associations. Other important demands included salaries for municipal councillors, parliamentary immunity, and the right to municipal referendums. Crucial local fiscal demands included local control over budgets, the repeal of municipal taxes, freedom to specify which taxes to impose, and strongly progressive income tax programs. Additional demands included local administration of a range of more generous services: unemployment and workmen's compensation, public health service, free medical and pharmaceutical care, inspections of the water supply, housing, schools, mines, and factories. High on the municipal-socialist list were programs for new, inexpensive housing and stricter construction standards. Vaillant, for example, as part of a plan to create mixed-class neighborhoods, proposed that a percentage of low-income units be required in all new housing built on municipal land. Others called for housing constructed and supported by the commune; units would have sixty-year leases, and tenants would eventually become owners. There were demands to eliminate all private monopolies of public services: transportation, lighting, water, insurance, health care, sanitation, medicine, funerals, assistance, food, and lodging. Calls were made for large-scale public works programs, minimum wages, insurance plans, safety and health standards, free public education, control over textbooks (substituting those teaching science and progress for those presenting reactionary values), and public universities.

In the 1896 elections, socialists received some 1,400,000 votes, winning control over 150 municipal councils, in addition to entering into coalitions with other parties in cities like Lyons, Toulon, and Nice. By 1896 the Guesdists had come out in open opposition to the socialists and set up a rival federation of councillors. This move caused other factions, who now realized that unity was impossible, to shift their interests elsewhere. At the turn of the century a series of attempts was made to unify the socialists. These efforts collapsed around the issue of whether socialists should serve as ministers in non-socialist governments. In June 1899, Alexander Millerand accepted the post of Minister of Commerce and Industry in the cabinet of René Waldeck-Rousseau. The Guesdist and Blanquist factions bitterly denounced him, and hopes for socialist unity were again shattered. Between 1899 and 1901 two distinct socialist parties formed: the Parti Socialiste Français (composed of possibilists, Allemandists, and independent socialists) and the Parti Socialiste de France, (a Guesdist, Blanquist, and Allemanist splinter group). The latter group came out against coalition politics in the 1900 elections. The results were split: Guesdists won in Lille; independent socialists won in Lyons, Marseilles, and a few other large cities.

Shortly after the elections, Guesdist attacks on municipal socialism began again. The Guesdists hoped, at the meeting of the Second International in Paris in September 1900, to turn the issue into a general condemnation. The International made it clear that the advances made did not constitute socialism but were valuable nonetheless. Vaillant drafted a proposal which read

The commune can become an excellent laboratory of decentralized economic life and, at the same time, a formidable political fortress for use by local socialist majorities against the bourgeois dominated central power, once a serious autonomy has been realized. That socialists have a duty, without losing sight of the importance of general politics, to foster an understanding of and appreciation for municipal activity, to accord to communal reforms the importance due them by their roles as embryos of collectivist society and to strive to create the following communal services: urban transport, lighting, water, distribution of electricity, baths, laboratories, department stores, bakeries, teaching, medical care, hospitals, low-rent housing, central heating, clothing, police, municipal workshops, etc.; to create through these services, model institutions.[75]

Between 1892 and 1914 French socialists at one time or another controlled 7 of the 15 cities with over 100,000 people and another 7 of the 23 centers having between 50,000 and 100,000. There were in France some 427,000 municipal councillors and 36,400 municipal councils; the socialists controlled only a tiny minority of these.

Municipalism's Opponents

The municipal movement in France had strong and powerfully organized opponents on both the right and the left. French Marxian socialists, echoing Marx's oft-expressed contempt for utopian socialism, were generally hostile to municipal socialism. Although by the turn of the century, the electoral successes of the municipal socialists were instrumental in softening this attitude at least tactically, deeper suspicion of reformism remained. Emphasis not only on revolution but on the workplace as the key site of struggle resulted in mistrust of doctrines and movements whose emphases lay elsewhere.[76]

The institutional blockage of municipalism came from the liberal right. By the turn of the century an active campaign emerged in France confronting what Pierre Mimin characterized as "a leprosy which spreads everywhere, with a frightening rapidity."[77] Any compromises, he warned, would mean disaster for liberalism. What was acceptable to Bismarck was dangerous collectivism to French liberals. The main instrument of obstruction was the Conseil d'Etat. By 1900 it was clear that its members would block almost all municipal initiatives. They had first addressed municipalism in 1877, ruling against Tourcoing's running its own gasworks, on the grounds that the city lacked technical competence. In 1887 they ruled that Belleville could not run its funicular. Four major decisions between 1894 and 1901 reaffirmed the denial of virtually any industrial or commercial enterprise or services to municipalities. The Conseil d'Etat enlarged the body of those who could sue to include all taxpayers, opening the floodgates of legal action to small property holders. It specified that any power not explicitly granted to a city should be denied it. The right of French citizens to engage in free commerce, voted in on March 17, 1791, was invoked against municipal participation in business.[78] The Chamber of Deputies proved equally recalcitrant; bills extending the right to *régies directes* (direct management) to important municipal services were introduced but defeated. Some partial reforms were achieved, e.g., the 1904 authorization to create free municipal employment agencies. Advances were made in granting more funds and allowing more generous interpretations of certain welfare provisions, working conditions for municipal workers, alleviation of unemployment, and legal service.[79]

Although the reform movements were stifled politically, the forces that had brought them into being hardly disappeared. The underlying consensus on the primacy of the social and the welfare of the population as its guiding norm had not yet been articulated as a paradigm uniting all its disparate elements. The metaphoric use of the symbols and rhetorical tropes of organicism loosely united social solidarity, health, and efficiency into the broadest of family resemblances, but organicisms vary. It is worth remembering that French biologists from Buffon through de Lanessan had stressed domestication as the highest form of natural development. What nature and history had produced, man could bring to perfection. It is also worth remembering that in classical doctrine not only could such processes be represented but finding correct representations was essential to bringing the process to perfection. Both dimensions of a lingering classicism—the world as will and representation—while obviously deprived of the coherence they once had, directed energy toward finding a visible, palpable, bounded form. That form was urbanism.

Modern French Urbanism

At the end of the nineteenth century, spatial, social, and scientific elements were finally combined in a comprehensive model. In one of those moments of conjunctural creativity, between 1899 and 1909 a group of prize-winning architects came together at the Institut de France's Villa Medici in Rome, where they produced a series of models of urban form.[1] The members of the group—including Tony Garnier, Ernest Hébrard, and Henri Prost—had been trained in the architectural traditions of the Ecole des Beaux-Arts, which stressed individual buildings and a grand, axial-symmetrical approach to design. Moving beyond the individual building to the city as an object to be harmoniously ordered, and moving beyond the primacy of aesthetically dictated principles of order, this cohort rethought the urban past while opening the way for urban models for the future.

Their projects ranged from Garnier's integration of industry, zoning, and regional planning in his Cité Industrielle, to Prost's reconstruction of the historical and cultural complexity of Constantinople, to Hébrard's proposal for a universal world capital, a center of science, art, sports, and communication. Despite the modernity of their urban conceptions, these architects did not directly challenge the reigning neoclassical eclecticism of the Ecole. Hence, Garnier and the others can be labeled socially and spatially modern—in their operationalization of society—but not aesthetically or sociologically modernist in their insistence on the importance of history and nature as materials to be manipulated. It is precisely in this sense that they played an important role in the process of modernization before modernism, what I have been calling, despite the clumsiness of the term, techno-cosmopolitanism.

The secondary literature has stressed Garnier's relation to the utopian socialist tradition of Cabet and Fourier. I see Garnier's plan rather as an urban parallel to Bentham's *Panopticon*. Foucault did not read the *Panopticon* as a Weberian ideal type, i.e., as the sociologist's generalized abstraction of the various currents of empirical activity of an age; rather he proposed an alternative use of such plans as strategic exemplars. Foucault suggested finding real schemas and tracing their strategic uses and transformations, as well as the resistances they provoked, as a means of illuminating not an entire age but particular nuclei of knowledge and power. In a like manner, Garnier's plan for an Industrial City, in which he attempted to encapsulate the urban principles of the industrial age in "le cas le plus général" (the most general case), will serve us here (complemented by variants by Hébrard and Prost) as a grid of intelligibility for later developments in modern society. The aim of Garnier's Cité was not to discipline individuals efficiently but to transform the historical-natural milieu into a productive, healthy, and peaceful social environment.

Elements of Modern Urbanism

The sources of modern urbanism in France were diverse. Before we turn to the schema for the modern city developed by this group of architects, several of the sources they drew on and transformed should be mentioned. In addition to those already discussed (philanthropic reform, geography, and socialist municipalists), these included German planning and its emphasis on historicity and infrastructural technical advances, particularly as it entered the French-speaking world through Brussels' burgomaster Charles Buls; and the teachings of two professors of history and technique at the Ecole des Beaux-Arts, Julien Gaudet and Auguste Choisy. The influence of Ebenezer Howard's comprehensive garden city, designed to solve urban problems in England by creating new spatial and social ar-

rangements, its entry into France via the Musée Social, and
Eugène Hénard's comprehensive attention to linking the statistics and sociology of the city to innovative spatial solutions (developed within the framework of a Musée Social campaign for
urbanism laws in France) will be discussed in the next chapter.

Camillo Sitte (1843–1903) is frequently cited as the founder
of modern city planning. Although the importance of Sitte and
his fellow German planners is unquestionable in the world history of urban planning, their impact on France was limited.[2]
Sitte's work suffered a strange distortion in its French-language
translation. His main book, *Der Stadtbau*, appeared in Germany
in 1889 and by 1901 had gone through three rapid printings.
Sitte's work was most widely read in the French translation.
However, "the French edition is a completely different book,
not only poorly translated, but actually enunciating ideas that
are diametrically opposed to Sitte's principles."[3] Translator
Camille Martin, an architectural collaborator of Sitte's in
Vienna, reduced Sitte's rambling personal treatise to a set of
concise methodological considerations. Martin deleted the majority of Sitte's German and Viennese examples, substituting
French and Belgian ones. He even substituted Paris for Vienna
as the center of nineteenth-century urban planning. Martin,
himself a medievalist, drastically downplayed Sitte's interest in
the Baroque and drew almost exclusively on medieval examples. Chapter VII, on streets, was "a complete fabrication,"
which appeared in the 1902 French translation but in no German editions.[4]

Charles Buls: History and Aesthetics

For the founders of modern urban planning in France, the
most influential figure of the urban planning discourse that
flourished during the last decade of the nineteenth century and
the first of the twentieth was Charles Buls (1837–1914). Buls,
mayor of Brussels from 1881 to 1899, was a practical man; his
major treatise, *Esthétique des villes*, was little more than a pamphlet. However, it had the major advantage of being written in
French. Buls claimed he wrote his book without knowing of any
foreign work on the subject, and he does not mention Sitte.

However, attending international congresses on urban problems, Buls could hardly have failed to integrate technical information about zoning and traffic borrowed from his German
neighbors.[5]

Esthétique des villes was mainly concerned with the practical
issue of how to preserve older quarters of Brussels. Adorning
these very local questions were a series of general maxims indi-
cating no sense of a social crisis. Planning was not a response to
political tensions, but a matter of resolving aesthetic and technical problems arising from historical evolution. Buls saw the
expansion problem faced by older cities as one of rapid growth.
Older cities had an unplanned charm, derived from the slow
accretion of historical change and reflecting local character.
New solutions, such as the geometrical schemes created in
America, where spiritual and aesthetic disasters, even if they
were hygienic and facilitated circulation. Buls' maxims covered
the following elements: respect for the historical quality of
cities; acceptance of new exigencies of hygiene and circulation,
with an eye to preserving a city's historical distinctiveness; the
inevitability of modern towns and suburbs, which were to be
made as picturesque and attractive as possible and kept apart
from the old urban framework; and finally, the rejection of
any new domestic or imported architectural style aimed at
homogenizing the built environment.

Julien Gaudet: The Synthesis

From 1894 to 1908 Julien Gaudet (1834–1908) occupied the
influential chair of the theory of architecture at the Ecole des
Beaux-Arts. Prost, Garnier, Hébrard, and Jaussely all attended
Gaudet's lectures. He is well known for having codified the
elements of what is now known as Beaux-Arts architecture in
his massive and systematic *Eléments et théories de l'architecture*,
published in 1902.[6] The ideas presented were the content of his
teaching since 1872, when he had first opened his studio. The
encyclopedic dimensions of the treatise and its untroubled and
thoroughly complacent tone are striking. This was high Third
Republic pedagogy of the first order; the ardent passions that
had led students to jeer Viollet-Le-Duc from the podium, carry

Labrouste through the Latin Quarter, or argue late into the night in innumerable ateliers about the correct style for modern French architecture were absent from Gaudet's pages.[7]

The first and introductory volume of Gaudet's treatise dealt with the elements of architecture: over one hundred pages were devoted to the orders and their uses; almost as many pages given to vaulting; a chapter on staircases; and another on the decoration of windows. Gaudet serenely cited examples from the traditional Beaux-Arts periods: antiquity, the Renaissance, and the classical age. Although he urged young architects to look to other cultures for inspiration, his own choice of plates revealed only the most common examples. For Gaudet, the true task confronting the young student of architecture was to learn to draw well and to master technical details so as to fulfill the architect's true vocation: construction. Presenting a warmed-over Taine, he instructed the students: "The technician is a realizer, beyond whose specific works, special programs, there is the program of programs, which is each century's civilization. Today we are simultaneously democratic and refined, utilitarian and luxurious. Be the artists of your time—always a noble mission."[8]

Detailed considerations of the social and historical dimensions of architecture were almost entirely absent from Gaudet's treatise: he devoted a mere two pages to social forces. As for the introduction of modern materials, Gaudet was hardly more loquacious; he merely cautioned his young architects that they must first be thoroughly conversant with traditional construction methods and have an informed taste before experimenting with new materials. For Gaudet, new materials signaled a technical innovation, not an architectural revolution. In the paragraph following a discussion of iron in gates and locks, he raised the question of exposed iron vaulting, recommending its use in utilitarian buildings such as hospitals and schools, when appropriate, and praising its use in the Bibliothèque Nationale. Gaudet cautioned his students against creating cities *ex nihilo,* as this could lead to excesses. European cities were historical; architects might intervene to correct specific problems, but that was all. Gaudet was appalled by the scale of the schemes proposed by Garnier and his renegade group.

Gaudet has been seen as the culmination of the Beaux-Arts tradition, its encyclopedic synthesizer. Reyner Banham argues that Gaudet embodied in an uncritical manner the deepest guiding principles of Beaux-Arts training, particularly the heart of the Ecole's architectural program: composition. Banham credits Gaudet with no originality, seeing his thoughts as echoing those of J.-N.-L. Durand.[9] At the end of the century, these compositional principles—symmetrical disposition of the parts of a building about one or more axes—were taken for granted, or, following Thomas Kuhn's famous phrase, were taught through the use of "perspicuous examples" in the ateliers by masters to students. However, given new standards of functionality, these uncontested forms would soon be employed in new ways. Gaudet, having emptied the Beaux-Arts doctrines of the last remnants of fixed representational and social content—making architecture a purely technical matter—was to that extent quite modern.

Choisy: Technique and History

The other major influence at the Ecole was Auguste Choisy (1841–1904). His *Histoire de l'architecture* had as its theme the overriding imperative of technique.[10] The constancy of technical problems of construction gave unity to architectural history. Choisy's history was written to demonstrate this technical synthesis: concise and didactic, it overflowed with 1,700 illustrations drawn by his own hand to an invariable formula. Choisy boasted of these drawings: "There is no attempt at artistic effect in them; they are the careful and learnedly drawn representations of fact."[11] For this engineer, structure posed itself as the solution to functional problems. However, Choisy stopped short of embracing the new industrial techniques available at the end of the century. Among the cohort of Prix-de-Rome winners, Prost's work on Byzantine architecture (a style emphasized in Choisy's course) and Garnier's on new functional forms were clearly informed by Choisy's teaching.

By the turn of the century, some students—winners of the Prix de Rome—were deeply dissatisfied with the scale at which they had been taught to work. They sought more than symmetrical compositional principles for spas and museums. These students have been largely ignored in the modernist textbooks of architectural history, because they did not question the Beaux-Arts compositional principles or neoclassical style but only their scale of application and the ends to which they were put. In so doing, however, they opened the way for a major reinterpretation of spaces and societies.

Socialist Reform: Tony Garnier

Tony Garnier (1869–1948) was, and still is, the most famous of the group of Prix-de-Rome winners who were brought together at the Villa Medici at the turn of the century. Of the entire group, only Garnier is commonly mentioned in architectural history textbooks.[12] The modernist canonization was reinforced by the hostile reaction accorded Garnier's project by the academy. His series of drawings of the Cité Industrielle (from the initial sketches of 1901 to the first complete version of 1904) was met by the architectural authorities at the Institut de France with quiet disapproval, open hostility, and then—perhaps most discouraging of all—a quiet contempt: "Monsieur Tony Garnier's supplementary project drawings are of an industrial city. The academy was not pleased with the subject matter, although it admits that the drawings were well executed."[13] A good deal of painstaking research has been conducted to establish the sequence of the versions of Garnier's Cité Industrielle. The details and refinements that Garnier added are of course important, but what is equally striking is the constancy of his conception of the whole, of its basic principles, from the first version to those he produced over the following decades.[14]

Garnier and the Influence of Lyons

Garnier's concern with the social dimensions of architecture and urbanism can be situated biographically. Born in Lyons in 1869, Garnier spent the first twenty years of his life there, before entering the Ecole des Beaux-Arts in 1889. Garnier lived in Paris for ten years while studying, moved to Rome and the Villa Medici for another five, and then returned to Lyons permanently. Lyons was one of France's oldest and most important industrial centers, with a strong labor tradition. Garnier himself was of working-class origins, born in the famous Croix Rousse quarter and never losing touch with the problems and concerns of Lyons' working class. While a student in Paris, Garnier joined the Société des Amis d'Emile Zola. The identification with Zola and his social concerns and politics remained emblematic for Garnier. In various drawings, the entryway to the public assembly halls clustered at the center of his Cité Industrielle was to be engraved with a quote from Zola's novel *Le Travail*. Garnier's project, after all, was for an industrial city, and he was honored to be known as the "Jaurès of urbanism."

Lyons, in east central France, was distinctive for its large and increasingly complex industrial base and for its long history of left-wing politics, ranging from revolutionary through more moderate reform movements. The Radical Party was officially proclaimed there in 1901; the party, as Edouard Herriot, mayor of Lyons and leader of the party, was fond of saying, was aimed at reaching society's middle categories.[15] Other distinctive aspects of political life in Lyons at the turn of the century were the importance of corporatism and the strong Freemason movement. The cooperative movement was particularly influential in the building industry and health services.

As early as the late eighteenth century, Lyons' architects had produced projects for the expansion of the city and the annexation of neighboring towns. Lyons had also had its Haussmann; from 1853 to 1864, the prefect Vaise played much the same role on a smaller scale.[16] As in Paris, long, straight avenues were opened, vistas created, circulation improved, public buildings highlighted, police and military surveillance and response facilitated, and housing built for the bourgeoisie. Some of these elements (geometrical shapes, axial symmetry, and planted boulevards) had been integrated into the Beaux-Arts cursus and were clearly accepted by Garnier. However, Lyons' mayor from 1881 to 1900, a doctor named Gailleton, was highly attentive to questions of urban hygiene. Although Gailleton was ultimately thwarted, during Garnier's youth local issues of public hygiene were actively debated.[17]

Gailleton's successor was another doctor, a specialist in syphilis, named Augagneur. In 1905, shortly before accepting the post of Governor General of Madagascar, Augagneur brought Garnier back to Lyons, an appointment heartily applauded by the new mayor, Herriot, who was to become president of France and who served as mayor of Lyons for the next fifty years. Although Gailleton and his administration did not formulate a comprehensive plan for Lyons, they did propose many of the concerns that later became central to twentieth-century planning. Garnier integrated and synthesized many of them in his vision of the modern industrial city. In Lyons, as in Paris and other French municipalities, water and sewage treatment were high on the list of hygienic reforms. More original and more social were the plans or goals drawn up in 1883 by the Lyons municipality, and supported by the populace, to place schools in each neighborhood. An ambitious public-works program was outlined (and to some extent carried out) over the next twenty years: public baths were built, a hydrotherapy building, a post office, slaughterhouses, modern hospitals, and other civic buildings were discussed both in Lyons' political circles and in its architectural press. On the plan for the city drawn up in 1895, officials included a "Quartier de l'Industrie," located on the Rhône, implying some sense of zoning—one of the pillars of modern urban planning. Whatever its epistemological status, the presence of such an idea was thoroughly coherent in the Lyonnaise context at the end of the century. A tramway system for the center city was instituted in 1879, and by 1897 it had been electrified and extended to the suburbs. There were even plans for regional inter-urban transportation systems. Lyons was one of the most eager recipients of electricity and supported plans for hydroelectric power. The first French automobile factories, those of Berliet, were located in Lyons; French aviation was founded there; and it was there that the Lumière brothers began their experiments in photography in 1882 and completed the first successful French cinema in 1895.

The World Expositions in Paris, particularly those of 1889 and 1900, exercised great influence on the development of new methods of architectural construction and on the imagination of young architects, designers, and future urbanists. Garnier, perhaps more than the other young architects in his group, was struck by their powerful functionality. Rarely mentioned but worthy of note in this respect is the fact that Lyons held the first provincial international exposition in 1872, in the sumptuous 104 hectares of the Parc de la Tête d'Or acquired by the city and designed in imitation of the Bois de Boulogne. The colonial exposition of 1894 was set around the park's lake. The exposition was organized by a Lyonnaise photographer, Johannes Barbier, who had previously organized photographic and ethnographic expositions in Lyons, Paris, and Rouen. Several African villages—*villages types*—and a mosque were reproduced and peopled with 160 natives. The exposition was a great local success, although it is not known whether the young Garnier saw it and, if so, what effect it might have had on him.[18]

In part because of the heavy concentration of industry, both of traditional and more modern metal and textile industries, the architectural world of Lyons was chiefly concerned with utility and functionality, and enthusiastic about technical advances. Consequently, it is not surprising that Garnier was sensitive to the relationship of architecture to social questions. Garnier adopted Viollet-Le-Duc's maxim that "construction was the means, architecture the result." He differed from Viollet-Le-Duc and other architects, however, in that social concerns—not the truths of structure (linked, it is true, to culture by Viollet-Le-Duc), nor the Beaux-Arts search for harmonious monumentality, nor the modernist attention to materials and form—guided him in both construction and architecture. Garnier, in one of his rare pronouncements, wrote in 1900: "Since all architecture rests on false principles, the architecture of antiquity was an error. TRUTH ALONE IS BEAUTIFUL. In architecture truth is the product of the calculations made to satisfy known needs with known means."[19]

All the preconditions for Garnier's comprehensive urban plan were found in Lyons. The city's reformist political atmosphere, its contemporary attention to social problems, its mix of archaic and modern industrial bases, the attention paid by its elected officials to energy and circulation, its regional consciousness, and its attention to health all formed a background for Garnier's studies, plans, and social consciousness. Garnier's contribution lies in integrating, in a comprehensive fashion, new social technologies and industry—spatially distributed and guided by the latest social science norms—into comprehensive urban planning. Both Augagneur and Herriot, his successor, were attentive to the need to devise new solutions to Lyons' social problems. The city thus constituted one of France's premiere laboratory settings.

Garnier at the Ecole des Beaux-Arts, 1889–99

In 1889 Garnier entered the Ecole des Beaux-Arts on a fellowship, the Prix Bellemain. He chose to work in the ateliers of two architects, first that of the orthodox academic Paul Blondel (1847–1897) and later that of Scellier de Gisors (1844–1905), both of whom were known for their interest in technical innovation. Blondel had practiced in Mulhouse around 1890, working on the city's medical hospitals and clinics and on its public library.[20] Opinion differs on whether Garnier was a gifted draftsman; regardless, his heart seems never to have been in the prize competitions. Between 1894 and 1899 he tried and failed to win the major Beaux-Arts prizes. Topics like an "Ecole superièure de marine" in 1896 or a "votive church in a celebrated pilgrimage site" in 1897 were clearly not the kind of projects that would stir the passions of this socially conscious young man. The authorities praised his plans for their simplicity and functionality but consistently criticized their lack of ease and imagination.[21]

During the 1890s, it was Gaudet who decided the competition themes at the Ecole. While many were standard Beaux-Arts competition topics, others, more in line with Gaudet's interest in civic buildings, were of a somewhat more social cast (e.g., in 1894 the prize competition was for an Ecole Centrale des Arts et Manufactures). There was nothing startlingly innovative in this choice; Durand had introduced the study of civic building types into the Beaux-Arts corpus, and they appeared throughout the nineteenth century as subjects of competitions. The age limit of eligibility for the Prix-de-Rome competitions was thirty, and consequently Garnier's last chance was the 1899 competition. The topic that year was "Un Hôtel pour le siège central d'une banque d'état" (a building to house the main branch of the central bank). The complexity of the project lay in the efficient, yet harmonious, linking of a variety of services. Fortunately for Garnier, whose skills lay in solving functional problems, the plan had primacy over the rendering of facades in such a complex building. He met the challenge, winning the first prize. The official commentary, published in *La Construction moderne,* praised Garnier's modern handling of functional complexity: "It is a realistic study of a special spatial organization, a simple plan, highly original and quite modern."[22] The building's style was the purest form of Beaux-Arts neoclassicism.

Garnier at the Villa Medici
By winning the Grand Prix, Garnier was assured five years' support at the Villa Medici in Rome. He arrived in Rome at the end of 1899, during a period of great growth for the city. Between 1870 and 1895, the population had increased from 200,000 to 400,000. Several innovative plans for the city were proposed and discussed, but not put into practice. The Prix-de-Rome winners in architecture already in residence were relatively obscure, if competent, academicians. However, those who immediately followed Garnier and overlapped his tenure in Rome were quite another breed. Many of the founders of modern French urbanism were on the list: Paul Bigot arrived in 1901, Henri Prost in 1902, Léon Jaussely in 1903, and, just after Garnier's departure, Ernest Hébrard in 1904.

Pensioners at the Villa Medici were required to submit to the authorities at the Institut de France a series of drawings of classical monuments. Each of the architects in Garnier's group rebelled at the spirit of the regulations. Garnier's resistance took the form of performing the required tasks according to his own terms, initially complying unenthusiastically, later stretching the guidelines, and finally transgressing them altogether with his submission of a plan for an entire city. The challenge Garnier posed was well understood in Paris. The Institut authorities responded first with critical commentary, "Monsieur Garnier complied with regulations only to the most minimal degree," and then with active disapproval: "Garnier added to his unsatisfactory project two drawing sheets representing, in plan and general view, a city that in no way corresponds to his obligations as a pensioner."[23] To avoid providing a negative example for younger architects, the Academy simply suppressed the presentation of Garnier's drawings.

Nevertheless, Garnier continued on some level to fulfill his obligations to the Institute, while continuing to work on his city plan. He approached the study of ancient sites as a useful auxiliary to his real interests. The Greeks offered examples of both architecture and urbanism, which Garnier admired and felt he could learn from without feeling that their solutions were timeless and perfect. For his major set of drawings in his third year, Garnier chose to study Tusculum, a city on a hillside near Rome, which at the height of its prosperity had had 60,000 inhabitants. The city had a long and complicated history, ending with its destruction by the Romans in 1191. In his studies Garnier emphasized the differences between Tusculum's initial urban core and its subsequent outward expansion. He was intrigued not only by the well-preserved theater in Tusculum (the appropriate object for a Beaux-Arts architect), but by the evidence of clearly demarcated quarters in the city and by remnants of its public buildings.[24] Tusculum served Garnier's needs well, for he found there "enough ruins to get a general idea of that picturesque and marvellously situated city and not enough, fortunately, to be able to do a complete reconstruction."[25] The joys of scholarly reconstruction counted less for him than the search for principles of urbanism. His attention to fitting the general plan in a harmonious way to the site, his spatial distribution of the quarters, and his attention to the details of villas and to the monuments of the city, drew praise even from the Institut members, although the recorder couldn't resist criticizing Garnier's renderings of detail.

Secession at the Villa Medici
Garnier's refusal to bend to the academic program of the Institut initiated a miniature secession movement at the Villa Medici. The other pensionnaires followed suit, stretching the rules: Bigot worked on a reconstruction of Rome; Hulot pre-

sented a project for the reconstruction of Selinote; Prost began to work on his drawings of Constantinople; Jaussely was at work on his "democratic city" and on an entry for the prize competition for Barcelona.[26]

Garnier shared with the rest of this group of architects a distinct lack of loquaciousness. None of its members produced the manifestos so characteristic of other modernist projects in the twentieth century, nor did they spend a great deal of time and energy in publicizing their projects. Hence the exact nature of the discussions that went on in Rome at this period, just how much Garnier's seniority and working-class background were at issue and how he exercised his authority over his younger colleagues, is lost to us. But the plans remain.

Une Cité Industrielle

Before turning to the plan itself, it is useful to situate some of its most general elements in the context of the period. First: regionalism. During this period of conceptual and professional formation in modern French geography, Lyons was an active regional center. In 1894 the 15th Congrès des Sociétés Françaises de Géographie was held in the city and consecrated entirely to the study of Lyons and its region. As its report indicated, "One only really knows a region well when one seizes the ties between its physical nature and its history, its inhabitants, its industrial and commercial development."[27] Vidal de la Blache's emphasis on the necessity of detailed and specific studies to determine the limits of a region was both echoed in and ignored by Garnier's plans. In this sense, Garnier was on the cusp of the utopian line in French city planning—which stretched back through Cabet, Fourier, and Saint-Simon to Ledoux, and in which the plan was its own perfection—and the emergent regionalist-geographical approach, in which local specificity and attention to culture and history were preliminary to and provided the basis for planning.[28]

A second factor deserves attention: Garnier's linking the old and the new. His plan included the existent, historical milieu as well as a solution for relating older and modern sites; up the river (toward the mountains and adjacent to the main rail station) was a small, older city. Not only did utopian plans and Beaux-Arts schemes proceed from blank slates but many later urbanistic projects did as well. For example, when Hébrard, the youngest member of this Prix-de-Rome cohort, elaborated his plan for a world center of communication, he stressed that one of the plan's virtues was that it could work in a number of geographical and national settings. However, Hébrard explicitly drew up site plans for specific locations to demonstrate that his plan could be built and was not merely utopian. When Prost was called upon to serve as chief urbanist in Morocco, one of the centerpieces of his conception of city and regional planning was the juxtaposition of old and new cities. This principle of juxtaposition, at least in a shadow form, was present in Garnier's plan. Garnier even included in his drawings the ruins of a chateau adjacent to the old city, perhaps bowing to the preservationists. However, no historical detail of the old city or the chateau was given, and its functional relations with the new industrial city were presented in a cursory manner. Garnier indicated the coexistence of old and new societies, their centers of power and their social and spatial arrangements, but it was the new sections that drew his energies.

The third element of Garnier's scheme worth considering is its scale. The regionalist movement at the end of the nineteenth century had sought autonomy for middle-sized cities (each of which was to include a full panoply of museums, theaters, and libraries, as well as administrative buildings). Garnier's city, planned for a population of 35,000, fell within this category. However, the city was planned for possible expansion, thus distinguishing it from Howard's garden city schemes. Howard's optimum size was 32,000, but growth was neither expected nor desired. His garden cities—as adopted in France by the Musée Social—were still distinctly disciplinary and moralizing; Garnier's industrial city was more exemplary of the already normalized, welfare-oriented social city. In fact, with the exception of its schools, his city entirely lacked the standard disciplinary institutions.

Garnier's Cité Industrielle was composed of four main sectors: an industrial complex, living quarters, an administrative quarter, and a quarter devoted to health establishments. Each

quarter and each function was independently situated but interconnected with the others. Garnier vividly and coherently
demonstrated zoning, which was soon to become one of the
hallmarks of modern planning. As opposed to Howard, Garnier established a separation of quarters and functions not only
for reasons of salubrity and harmony but also as a way of ac-
commodating growth. Garnier's plan provides an excellent illustration of Canguilhem's social organism in search of its
spatialized organs. In each sector, as in the whole scheme, form
was guided by the latest scientific norms; these norms were
given forms appropriate to their functions.

Industry
Garnier, in a brief preface to a later edition of the plans, wrote
that the determining factor in locating the city was the tributary
river that served as the city's power source. In Garnier's
scheme, this tributary was dammed; a hydroelectric plant distributed power, light, and heat to factories and to the entire
city. The first successful, operating hydroelectric plant had
been opened in Geneva in 1895. Hailed as the solution to the
energy and manufacturing needs of cities, the plant was widely
publicized at the time. Electricity was also much in vogue: the
first international exhibition of electricity had been held in
Paris in 1881, and the Electrical Building and illuminated
waterfall at the Paris Exposition of 1900 drew large crowds and
provoked considerable commentary.

Garnier stipulated that there be primary materials close at
hand for his city's metallurgy factories; hence, he specified that
mines existed in the mountainous region near the Cité Industrielle but also noted that other mineral resources from farther
away could be brought to the city by means of transport organized on a regional scale.[29] The region Garnier described bore
a striking resemblance to the area around Lyons. Garnier remarked that he had had the neighboring industrial cities of
Givors, Rive de Gier, St. Chamond, and St. Etienne in mind as
the general background. The overall topography of the plan
was also reminiscent of the Lyonnaise region. Garnier specified
that the city was located on a high plain traversed by a powerful
river that came out of the nearby mountains and spilled onto
the plain.

Adjacent to the railway station, but separated from it by a large, landscaped square, lay the industrial quarter. Its centerpiece was a vast metallurgy factory. Garnier proposed a set of monstrous furnaces, steel-processing works, work and repair spaces, a special train depot, and a port facility located on the river. The smokestacks of the factory formed yet another symbolic marker. The design was almost Futurist: pure, clean, and surging with strength. Although the Cité Industrielle drew its *raison d'être* from these factories, Garnier provided little technical elaboration. He limited his role to defining the zoning, surrounding them with green, providing transportation facilities, and making them central symbolically. Industry defined the context. However, it was the social and welfare dimensions of modern life—housing, health, and administration—that drew most of Garnier's attention.

Housing

The industrial city was laid out in a flexible checkerboard pattern. To accommodate the unevenness of the site, a certain amount of irregularity was allowed. Within the residential quarter, a further functional division of space occurred. A main thoroughfare traversed the quarter, providing space for a tramway and for commercial traffic. Smaller streets served the interior of the quarter. The pedestrian zones (providing safety and commodity) that ran between the individual houses were an advanced feature. The plan provided for free-standing structures accessible from all sides. Even Garnier's socialist city accepted the single-family house as its basic unit, although later versions of the plan did experiment with duplexes and multiple, low-density units. Garnier's detailed attention to the housing problem was unique among this group of Prix-de-Rome architects. His experimentation with new materials and with a variety of solutions and architectural devices is noteworthy, although failing to influence subsequent housing developments in France or the colonies.

Garnier placed a large number of schools throughout the residential quarters, using them as organizing nuclei and situating them such that no house was more than 100 meters from a school. The schools themselves were divided by level and set in ample green space to be used for recreation and to ensure health and safety. The pavilion solution Garnier used for housing and hospitals was also applied to schools. He included plans for secondary and specialized technical schools but none for institutions of higher learning. Given the extremely generous equipment of the city in other respects—and its relative autonomy—this lack of any institutional means by which inhabitants could escape their class is worth underlining. Here, as in different ways in the colonies, these architects were best at finding architectural solutions for the *aménagement* and amelioration of life and for the accommodation—in a quantitative sense—of growth, but they displayed a total reluctance to consider the possibility of fundamental social or structural change. Their social vision was reformist, not revolutionary, and this separated them from the high modernists who followed.

The center of the city was reserved for a mix of administrative spaces and public functions. Garnier broke these down into three categories: administrative services and meeting halls, collections and archives, and sports and entertainment facilities. These modern, welfare functions were grouped in a large park adjoining the town's central avenue. The archives were placed on an adjacent terrace with plantings that looked out on the river and distant mountains. The focus of the downtown area was a grandiose grouping of assembly halls (with seating capacities of only 3000, 1000, 500, and 100, in a city of 35,000) linked by a sort of covered mall. The entryway to the complex was emblazoned with a text from Zola's *Le Travail* glorifying the dignity of work and the worker.[30] Completing this symbolic grouping were the administrative facilities of the city, including a center for the organization of labor, a building for medical consultation, a post office, and restaurants.[31]

Finally, again using a system of pavilions, choice space was provided for the city's libraries, museums, and archives. The importance given to history and learning was underlined by the central placement of archives in this new town. History and social memory constituted forces countervailing and complementary to science, the other pole of modern authority. The importance given to future developments destined to become history is a striking but consistent part of Garnier's plan.[32] Later socialist urban schemes added the category of "collective memory," that local, unofficial, collective—but simultaneously highly individualized—social glue theorized by Maurice Halbwachs as a guarantee of social solidarity and health.

An extremely generous area adjacent to the administrative complex was allotted for sports and entertainment; it included a huge stadium on the antique model as well as a gym, baths, and playing fields. There was also a theater and a carefully planned park designed for use by picnickers. Garnier's city was located next to an existing city; the street system and main avenue linked the two. Garnier's railway station was located next to the old city. This device was later imitated in a number of the cities built in Morocco under the direction of Garnier's co-pensioner Prost. The railway station was constructed on two levels: one for arrivals and one for departures. Whenever possible, functionally differentiated spaces were indicated architecturally. The station presented a good example of Garnier's intertwining of aesthetic and social concerns.

The station, made of reinforced concrete and glass, was capped by a large tower with a clock visible throughout the city. The tower is a symbolic motif in French architecture: from Quatremère forward, the civic belltower (*beffroi*) was contrasted to the church belltower (*clocher*) as a symbol of civic liberty. Viollet-Le-Duc, for example, used the *beffroi* as a democratic and communal symbol in his work;[33] its central location in Garnier's plan, and later in Hébrard's, was no accident.

The city's extensive health facilities included a general hospital, a modern sanitorium, and a large rest home and hospital complex for victims of industrial accidents. Garnier accepted the fact that industry would produce victims; rather than concentrating on improved factory design, or assigning the problem directly to the political realm, Garnier provided the most comprehensive care available. The integration of the inevitability of work accidents into his plan reveals Garnier's highly representative schematization of a reformist welfare vision of society. The complex of health-care facilities was sited in the city's choicest area, adjacent to the flanking hills and receiving the most sunlight. Because of its advanced design, Garnier's sanitorium has received much architectural attention. The hospital for work victims followed the pavilion plan and was, once again, divided according to function and provided with ample green space. However, its true innovation is its definition of accidents as a social reality, and not merely as the result of the irresponsibility of either the worker or his boss. An essential threshold in the creation of modern society dates from the passage (after eighteen years of debate) of the French law of April 9, 1898 establishing social insurance against work accidents.

As François Ewald has shown at length, European societies at the end of the nineteenth century looked to a massive, social-insurance technology to solve the social, political and economic problems they were facing.[34] With the introduction of new social legislation attention shifted from individual responsibility to assigning risk to socially objective causes. Previously, blame fell either on individual weakness or on chance. Only the former could be indemnified. Now people began to reconsider this position; fault was reinterpreted as an essential dimension of the working conditions themselves. It followed that accidents resulting from the conditions of industrial production should be accounted for in advance and included in production costs. With social insurance, the employer and employee were no longer bound by any mutual moral obligations stemming from or arising out of their interpersonal relations or shared milieux; social insurance freed workers and patrons to be more rational and efficient, eliminating the animosity caused by political differences.

The issue of insurance received attention from the entire political spectrum, though with different motives and different interpretations of its import and targets. Bourgeois, the leader of the solidarist movement, called for universalized insurance against all social risks—sickness, accidents, unemployment, disability, old age—as the only road to social peace.[35] Vaillant, one of the few socialists able to bridge the gap between the reformist and revolutionary wings of French socialism, called for "social insurance against all of life's risks."[36] Finally, in Cheysson's view, "It is the only science to have mathematics as its foundation and morality as its crown."[37]

Garnier's concern with production, living, and hygiene and his provision of extensive facilities for leisure and transportation predate by two decades the main elements of the famous C.I.A.M. charter. Garnier was bolder than Howard, the other titular figure of modern urbanism, in identifying industrialism as the defining characteristic of modern society and consequently choosing an urban site with a generous housing scheme as well as education, administrative, and comprehensive health-care facilities. But, like Howard, Garnier—at least in his initial conception of the project—seems to have downplayed such infrastructural factors as the cost of land. In his later versions he allowed for higher density and explored means of standardizing and mass-producing necessary elements. Among other oversights in the early versions of the plan, but later corrected, is the lack of adequate provision for shops and stores. Garnier had one massive, centrally located market in the original scheme. All small businesses were eliminated.

Another striking feature of Garnier's plan was the lack of churches, barracks, jails, police stations, and law courts. The absence of churches was typical of anticlerical Republican attitudes at the end of the century. Garnier believed that future cities, fully endowed with cultural and social resources for the people, would have no need of churches. The lack of any military or police presence was more striking. Pawlowski's suggestion that Garnier's neglect of these features stems from his exemption from military service (because of his short stature) is amusing. Wiebenson is more to the point in stating that "Garnier, like Fourier, believed in the basic goodness of man: when asked why his city contained no law court, police force, jail or church, he is said to have replied that the new society, governed by socialist law, would have no need of churches, and that, as capitalism would be suppressed, there would be no swindlers, robbers or murderers. It can be assumed that, having omitted a church, he substituted a more 'natural' form of worship, similar to the worship of nature Zola established in his *Travail*."[38] Implicit here is the assumption, made explicit by Lyautey and others in the colonial context, that an inverse ratio existed between the welfare of a society and its dependency on overt forces of order. Order achieved by force was less desirable and more costly than a well-tempered social regulation. Implicit in the technologies of governmentality was the notion that it was possible to transform society so that both force and politics would become unnecessary. Conversely, the degree to which politics or military force was necessary precisely indicated the shortcomings of the technology. Garnier's Cité Industrielle provides an illustration of how such social self-regulation could be achieved spatially.

Garnier presented no plans for financing. In this sense his plan was distinctly utopian and not at all like Bentham's *Panopticon*. Bentham detailed how his Panopticon might be used, exactly how much it would cost, and how it could be marketed. Even though Garnier spent the rest of his life working in Lyons, learning from concrete experience exactly how important financing and political considerations were to the actualization of a project, he never specified such matters in subsequent versions of the plan. Whether Garnier's city is the first manifestation of twentieth-century urbanism or the last gasp of socialist utopianism is more an issue of definitions than of substance, although Garnier's sophistication and his specification of local conditions did point to the future. Garnier and his friends articulated a coherent set of urban planning principles, ones that constitute an important new schema of power/ knowledge; they were, to use Lyautey's phrase, technicians of general ideas.[39]

Neo-Conservative Order: Henri Prost

Garnier has received the most attention and acclaim in architectural history books, but Henri Prost (1874–1959) is of equal or even greater importance in terms of accomplishment. After winning the Prix de Rome, Prost produced sophisticated drawings of Constantinople; won a prize competition for the renovation and extension of the Belgian city of Anvers; headed urban planning in Morocco under Lyautey, directing the largest planning project in the French-speaking world up to the postwar boom; produced regional plans for the Côte d'Azur and the first regional plan adopted for Paris; and headed urban planning in Istanbul. Working under the mantle of powerful and flamboyant figures like Lyautey, Prost himself produced no manifestos. Modernist textbooks continue to ignore him.

Prost at the Villa Medici, 1902–07

Prost won the Prix de Rome in 1902 in a competition for a national printing office.[40] Unlike Garnier, Prost not only won the Prix de Rome at a relatively young age but seems to have received the general esteem of the academy with relative ease. His first *envois*—on safe topics such as a fountain in a Roman patio—were very well received in Paris. The main criticism, if it can be called such, was that Prost's choice of Pompeian mosaics was slightly unorthodox; it was suggested that it would have been preferable to include them in a more fully developed architectural context. It was not until his third year in Rome that Prost gave any indication of unorthodoxy. The third year was reserved for a trip, almost a pilgrimage, to Greece in order (finally) to visit the actual monuments from which so much of the Beaux-Arts ethos was drawn. Provocatively, Prost made a side tour of Constantinople. He had a passion for Byzantine architecture and had arrived in Rome with a photograph of Sainte-Sophia tucked in his baggage. Upon visiting this mosque-cathedral-palace, Prost was taken with its beauty as well as with its deplorable state of repair. He wrote to officials in Paris informing them of the need to restore this important monument, asking for permission to work on it and for aid in seeking funds for the restoration.

The Parisian officials were hesitant and demanded a detailed report. In a report submitted to the Institut at the end of 1905, Prost proposed as complete a rendering as was possible of the edifice's current existence as a mosque.[41] Not only was Prost audaciously enlarging the orthodox terrain of the young pensioners to include Asia Minor but, even more shockingly, he was proposing to draw Sainte-Sophia as a Muslim building. The archaeological and architectural complexity of this great mosque, church, and imperial palace intrigued and moved him. He completed his preliminary drawings and returned to Rome.

The Academy in Paris was uneasy: they wrote Prost, officially discouraging him from continuing the project. Not only the subject matter but the scale were causes for concern. Paul Bigot had already in 1900 placed a classic *envoi*—the Great Roman

Circus—within an urban context, drawing in its neighborhood and proposing a plan for all of ancient Rome. Even though the Academy had rejected it, Bigot's project was an inspiration to Prost.[42] From his earliest days in Rome Prost saw urban scale as the key to understanding the architecture itself. Prost was interested neither in quasi-utopian projects nor in pure archaeology; rather, he was drawn to the historical and cultural richness emerging from reconstruction. He valued the mixture of civilizations found in Rome and Constantinople. Another pensionnaire, Hulot, whom Prost accompanied on the required trip to Greece and Sicily, was also drawn to the urban scale. Hulot looked beyond the required depiction of the temple at Selinote to its urban context: an orthogonal, checkerboard grid. These projects, considered alongside those of Garnier and Jaussely (as well as those of Hébrard, who followed Prost), reveal that a radical redefinition of the calling of these pensionnaires was occurring.[43]

The Academy members were justifiably nervous. Still, they appealed to the Académie des Inscriptions et Belles-Letters for a subvention for Prost's project in Sainte-Sophia. Overjoyed, Prost returned to Constantinople. His magnificently rendered drawings demonstrated the importance of the structure behind the ornamentation at Sainte-Sophia, buttressing, as it were, the theories of Viollet-Le-Duc, Choisy, and earlier Beaux-Arts rationalists. Prost praised Choisy's *L'Art de bâtir chez les Byzantines* (The Byzantine Art of Building) as an invaluable guide, remarking only its lack of illustrations, a lacuna Prost set out to fill.[44] In his report to the Academy, Prost explained that he was able to work in Sainte-Sophia, a functioning mosque, because he had established a connection with a certain Turkan Pacha (the former ambassador of Turkey to Rome), Minister of Pious Foundations at that time. The Minister served as an enlightened protector of Prost, shielding him from the *fanatiques* who might bother him and especially from the police whose "stupid zeal is often a great bother."[45] In Morocco, and later in Istanbul, Prost followed this same pattern, pursuing his work under the protection of powerful figures who had full confidence in his abilities. Since neither Prost, nor Garnier, nor any of their cohorts ever focused on politics, they all found their major opportunities provided by minor autocrats (Lyautey in Prost's case and Herriot in Garnier's). The role of architect/urbanist, technocrat as well as artist of the social, was only possible once political matters were eliminated.

Inherent in this role was a conception of the necessity of Power at the inception of a plan. However, the object attended to was not the Sovereign but the welfare of the population. Given a visionary authority figure, a joint plan, a general *ordonnance,* was possible. However, the order that Prost or Garnier wished to facilitate was not, of course, baroque, but rather an early twentieth-century one. That Garnier called it socialist and Prost did not, while not irrelevant, masks other similarities. They both agreed that the object to be ordered was society. The form of power they sought to activate stemmed from a healthy and well-ordered society. The means to that end were primarily scientific and technical, not representational or political; these factors were obviously present but played only a subordinate role.

Prost's Urbanism

Prost left only a few bits and pieces of prose. Among them is an undated speech found among his papers at the Académie d'Architecture. It was probably written in the early 1930s, but, as with Garnier, Prost's basic ideas seem to have changed little since his student days in Rome. In this speech Prost claims to have invented the word "urbanism."[46] This is interesting on a number of levels. First, it is simply false. The term "urbanism" was first used by Cerda in 1867.[47] It is surprising that Prost was unaware of this, since Cerda used the word and the concept in his plans for Barcelona, a city whose history and planning problems were familiar to Prost through the work of his friend and colleague, Jaussely. Second, the interpretation Prost gave to the term was simultaneously casual and rigorous, modest and arrogant.

What then was urbanism for Prost? He took two different tacks in answering the question, one more or less aesthetic, and one historical and technical. Urbanism was: "a visual art which directs itself to our senses; a beautiful city which we love is one where the edifices have a noble beauty, the promenades are agreeable, and where our everyday life is surrounded by an agreeable decor producing in us a sentiment of profound harmony."[48] The architect was like the painter, except that he worked in more dimensions; his goal was to make us forget the miseries of everyday life. As in the classical age, *commoditas* and agreeableness were the architect's guiding principles. The modern architect should produce a compositional harmony in which social life could unfold with the utmost ease. The basic material of this new art form, like that of the old, was nature, but nature in three dimensions and reproduced artificially, limited only by the architect's imagination. The progression was from canvas, to garden, to palace, to city, to region, to nation. Prost then switched registers: "the *aménagement* of cities has been for the last few years one of the gravest governmental preoccupations; it has become one of the dominant objects of contemporary civilization."[49]

However, Prost went on, a good deal more than pleasure and the harmony of the senses underlay the *commoditas* of landscaped belvederes. Engineers, architects, and sociologists had to join forces to produce a fabric in which housing, circulation, work, hygiene, and aesthetics functioned together. These disciplines all had to contribute, if the vast agglomerations of the modern world were to operate successfully. A major change had taken place in the world: the rise of modern transportation systems in the nineteenth century. Concurrently, vast movements of population had changed the nature of society, particularly of cities, altering their size, their rate of change, and their relations to the countryside, and overwhelming the traditional mode of building cities. Industry in particular had not planned for the larger social needs it had engendered. Renault, for example, employed 30,000 workers at its Parisian plant, but these workers lived throughout the region, traveling great distances to the plants. New means of transportation, the explosion of industry, and new building methods had put 2000 years of civilization in danger. The ultimate consideration for the urbanist was the protection of Western civilization.

Having posed the problem in such dramatic terms, Prost reassuringly shifted his rhetoric. If the word urbanism was

new, the art of building cities was not. To understand the
genesis of current problems, as well as the sources of solutions
to those problems, it was necessary to understand history. Modern French urbanism stretched back to the fifteenth century,
when the urbanism of the ancients was rediscovered. Although
not scientific, these ancient texts provided rich material for the
imagination of Parisian architects. Since everyone in France
imitated Paris, it was to Parisian history that the attentive urbanist must turn. The decisive turning point in that history
occurred when Catherine de Medici decided to leave her lodgings in the Louvre, with the adjacent malodorous streets, and
build the magnificent Tuileries at the edge of Paris. Catherine
drew a long *allée* (now the Champs Elysées) extending out to
the woods and capped by the Place de l'Etoile. Paris's form was
set. Against this background, the real genius of French urbanism
made his appearance: Louis XIV. Louis created Versailles to
pacify France, choosing to conquer the aristocracy through the
pleasures and amusements that Versailles offered rather than
through arms. Louis and his successors did not totally neglect
Paris. They completed its grand avenues and provided great
monumental buildings and places. The *ordonnance* of great perspectives and monuments was carried forward until the time of
Napoleon III and Haussmann, who opened up perspectives
around the old monuments and provided new monuments as
well—stations, markets, and the opera. Provincial cities followed suit. The Republic received good marks: the metro and
the opening of the Bridge and Avenue Alexandre III, built
for a world exposition, were worthy additions.

However, by 1900 French cities faced a thorny problem
whose roots were not so much architectural as administrative:
the uncontrolled and unplanned growth occurring beyond the
old fortifications of Paris and other French cities. Prost saw the
cause of the problem in the introduction of politics into administration. The Republic had replaced the career administrators of cities (outside of Paris) with elected mayors. Many of
these were public-spirited, intelligent, generous, and well-
intentioned. However, even with the best intentions, it was impossible for them to perform their tasks adequately. First, they
lacked the technical competence necessary to run modern

cities. Second, they were forced to run for reelection too frequently to be concerned with long-range public interest. The exception that proved the rule was Paris, under the jurisdiction of the Prefect of the Seine. Internally, urban *aménagement* had controlled growth, but externally, outside the fortification walls, chaos had ensued. Prost believed that a minister of urbanism was needed; state direction was an essential condition of coherent urbanism. The lack of such direction explained why French urbanism had come to a dead halt between 1870 and 1900. The contemporary situation could be summarized: central power controlled but no longer provided a rational ordering.

Anvers: Integrating Difference

By the end of his stay at the Villa Medici, Prost had become a successful and sophisticated analyst of urban and cultural problems. In 1910 he won an international competition for the expansion of the Belgian city of Anvers.[50] The central problem in Anvers was how to treat the old fortifications surrounding the city; exactly the same problem was being posed in Paris, on a grander scale. A successful and comprehensive solution would conceive of the entire city and its future expansion. The specifications of the competition were quite detailed and displayed an educated awareness, on the part of the city fathers, of recent trends in European urban planning, particularly the ideas of the German *Stadtbau*. The city had experienced many changes throughout its history. Normans had destroyed Anvers in the tenth century, necessitating its first reconstruction. By the sixteenth century, the city had become the European center for the spice trade, ensuring its commercial importance for centuries. Prosperity brought growth. During the nineteenth century, elaborate fortifications were constructed to protect the city, but by 1910 they were militarily outmoded and considered stifling to new growth. The old city was situated in an arc in the river Escaut. Fifteen kilometers of fortified embankments stretched around it; beyond them were 33 kilometers of newer fortifications. Between these two sets of fortifications lay some 6,000 hectares of land. Expansion was aimed at this area.

The main technical planning problem was what to do with the old walls: demolish them completely and open the space to new development or reuse them by turning them into a landscaped green space, a buffer between old and new? Given the fact that financial considerations were not specified as part of the competition, it was evident that the second choice was more elegant. However, it presented more technical complications than the first. The complexity as well as the interest of the problem consisted in preserving the older part of the city, nestled around the curve of the river, without cutting it off from new transportation connections. Expansion both directly along the walls and out from the old city along the river had to be carefully thought through. Where would new satellite cities be placed, and how would they be connected to the older core? Prost seems to have spent some time in Anvers preparing his entry, apparently consulting military experts, local civic authorities, and, most innovatively of all, the "petits gens qu'on ne consulte guère" (the ordinary people who are never consulted). Prost argued that the modern urbanist had to understand that the wishes and needs of the people who were to live in the newly reconstructed cities counted more than pure conceptions of the future which despised the population's attachment to the past.

The city's authorities highly praised Prost's refusal to place the citizens of Anvers into a "framework in which they are asked only to function."[51] The principle of separating cultures—in the name of respect for difference—was a cornerstone of Prost's plans. His integration of this principle into the plan was one of the reasons Lyautey chose him to be head of urbanism in Morocco a few years later. In Anvers, the separation was double: between the old and the new quarters, and between classes. Prost had been attentive to difference from the start. He was fascinated, in his drawings for the reconstruction of Sainte-Sophia, by the archaeological layering of different cultural, social, and architectural dimensions. While Garnier, like Prost, was attentive to hygiene, circulation, and zoning he paid little attention to social differences, either of class or culture. Socialism, Garnier assumed, would overcome differences (although his Cité was based on a static class structure).

Prost's planning principles for Anvers were precursors of those he employed throughout his career. First among these was his combining of infrastructural and aesthetic elements: the port area was modernized as well as beautified through sumptuous landscaping. Although the port's location remained the same, its functions were enhanced through structural improvements. Commerce and its infrastructure were the centerpieces of Prost's city plan, as they had been in previous schemes. Circulation was highlighted; a railway station was located adjacent to the port, and was to be constructed in multiple levels so as to facilitate the transfer of cargoes from arriving ships directly to trains on the lower level. The upper level was a long, landscaped terrace open to the sun and to favorable, warming winds; Prost's drawings depict the terrace full of strolling citizens—a kind of urbanist's industrial pastoral.

A second characteristic of Prost's work was the dovetailing of hygienic concerns and decoration: green space provided fresh air for the city as well as serving as the urbanist's basic decorative element. A large, open boulevard—"un grand réservoir d'air"—led away from the terraced belvedere to connect a series of reworked zones—old fort sites situated along the large, circular canal which defined the limits of the old city. Although not specified in the terms of the competition, Prost added a section to his proposal arguing that maintaining the canals would neither pose a problem for public hygiene (he had checked the military records and there had been no major epidemics in Anvers), nor cause financial losses. Even though a certain amount of building space would be sacrificed, filling the canals would be more expensive. Moreover, once landscaped properly, the old canals would contribute to the beauty of the entire scheme. Unlike Garnier, Prost early on revealed marked attention to cost and practicality.

One of the old forts, located not far from the docks and train station, was to be transformed into a "cité jardin populaire" or "ouvrière" (garden city for workers) containing a church, schools, municipal buildings, and an adjacent park. Class segregation was explicit: "It seemed impossible to us to dream of a single park for aristocrats and commoners."[52] Prost proposed to give the workers a full set of services: gardens for children, workers' clubs, schools, libraries, public baths, and swimming pools. The details of housing were sketchy—Prost hoped that the forthcoming Congrès de Londres (set for October 1910) would provide aid in this domain—but he did state that he approved of recent English housing efforts like those of Hampstead. Another fort site, slightly farther east, contained a Palais des Beaux-Arts and a music conservatory. To the west of these monumental structures Prost proposed a small, artificial lake to be surrounded by luxury hotels. This area was to be the quarter for the rich. Between this quarter and that for the working class was an area designated for the bourgeoisie. Plot size and house dimensions, as well as amenities, varied according to status and wealth. Farther down the main boulevard was a large, public square with a vast exposition hall—analogous to the Grand Palais in Paris and the Crystal Palace in London—surrounded by ample gardens and monumental, Beaux-Arts public buildings. Adjacent to this public square, a former military parade ground was converted into a combination sports terrain and landing field for helicopters. A special hotel for air travelers and a signal tower for aviators completed the square's composition. More public buildings, massive churches, and concert halls, each set in large, open areas planted with regular rows of trees (using the existing but embellished canal system whenever possible) formed the city's infrastructure. Park space was amply provided throughout the city. Prost carefully designed a system of avenues within the city that facilitated the siting of monumental buildings and circulation but were also linked to highways coming into and leading away from the city in the direction of both adjacent and distant towns; this system reappears in his plans for Morocco.

Technically Modern

Prost's plan sought to integrate an existing city and its complex history into a flexible plan that allowed for change and continued economic prosperity. Regional economic and transportation planning required careful attention to the infrastructure of ports, stations, and roads necessary to prosperity. In Prost's scheme, this infrastructure was beautified. A basic zoning system for industrial, commercial, and public residential sectors was clearly articulated in the plan, incorporating both social and functional differences. A generous cultural infrastructure was provided, as were ample facilities for sports, leisure, administration, and education. The principles of social hygiene were accommodated through attention to green space, well-sited facilities, and broad thoroughfares. There were two hospitals: one placed next to the railway station (because of the site's healthier air); another placed behind the aviation field, where it would receive light and air. Prost stressed the humane quality of the pavilion solution employed for the hospitals. Churches in Prost's scheme stood forth as visible, public monuments fronting the imposing monumentality of Beaux-Arts public squares. The city's major military barracks was to be transformed into a *Maison du Peuple*. Although a necessity, the prison was located away from the workers' quarters, so as not to cause sadness. If, following Jurgen Habermas, we define modern neo-conservatism as an uncritical embracing of economic and technological change combined with a longing for social stability and a legitimated social hierarchy, then Prost's plans are a prime example of this tendency.

Scientific Humanism: Hébrard and Andersen

Garnier's socialism had implicitly included a view of history as the ground of communication for social life; the centrality of his complex of buildings for archives, libraries, and collections indicated the future social importance he attributed to historical memory. In that sense Garnier was quite modern. Prost, partly by temperament, partly because his political model depended on authority, was more attentive to specific details of local and civilizational history. His passion for and attentiveness to the artistic and cultural layerings in Sainte-Sophia and his admiration for the French traditions in gardens and painting, made him perhaps the most typically Beaux-Arts of his group. In making these differences an essential component of his urbanism in Morocco—by operationalizing difference—Prost was, in an important sense, even more modern than Garnier.

The last of the group of Prix-de-Rome winners, Ernest Hébrard (1866–1933), had the most systematic, if superficial, view of history, form, and society. Hébrard and his associate, Henrik Christian Andersen, a wealthy American sculptor living in Rome, developed an elaborate, theoretical evolutionary scheme for all of humanity, a sort of neo-Hegelian march forward of architectural typology and social form culminating in their World Center of Communication. Their scheme, which included a center for the administration of the world's science, religion, and arts, as well as a comprehensively planned model city, was meant to embody and facilitate humanity's progress—to provide both the forms and the norms for humanity. The city was not utopian; it was tailored to fit a number of specific sites from New Jersey to Istanbul.[53]

Forms and Norms

For Hébrard and Andersen, architectural and human history formed an interconnected, mutually intelligible pair. Proper deciphering of their historical relations provided the key to understanding humanity's future. All past architectural constructions had met definite mental, social, and political needs and corresponded to phases of moral or spiritual development. In the first decade of the twentieth century, the world's nations had become increasingly interdependent; economically this interdependence provided the possibility of universalizing human progress. Nations were no longer isolated units; religion and war, the pre-modern twin motors of history, had overcome national barriers: "War has brought groups of people together, uniting their achievements, setting up ideals, blending nationalities, but the future must find a means other than destruction."[54] As man's higher nature asserted itself, international disputes would not involve the sacrifice of human life. The norms of reason in the twentieth century turned on universal welfare, prosperity, and science. Universal history was open-ended; the instruments for ensuring a harmonious future were at hand. In order for science, religion, and the arts to play the regulative role they deserved, a space—both literal and figurative—had to be created for them. Hébrard and Andersen accepted the task of creating an urban context in which the transition to a world of peace and true communication could unfold.

The Universal Elements and Their History

For Garnier the contemporary industrial situation dictated a socialist welfare response; Prost, in a more conservative fashion, looked to history and culture as reservoirs on which to draw to achieve a healthy social order; for Hébrard and Andersen, history traced a trajectory toward centralization, peace, interdependence, and the triumph of universal norms for humanity. Architecture provided a privileged code for deciphering humanity's development. The history of architecture could be read as the history of human progress. Three universal human needs—shelter, boundaries, and signaling—provided the grid of intelligibility. The contents, interrelations, and relative weight of each need, as well as the architectural solutions devised to meet them, varied from epoch to epoch.

As was common among architects, Hébrard and Andersen identified the circular hut as the primitive form of all shelter.[55] The hut was a true universal; the beaver constructed circular forms with as much skill and in the same manner as paleolithic man. The passage from the round to the rectangular plan marked the end of the primitive epoch: mankind had separated itself from the animal kingdom. Groupings of huts indicated the first seeds of rational planning, necessitating forethought and the rudiments of geometry, as well as social cooperation. Man's spiritual development began with the appearance of the third human universal—signaling. Although at first sacred spots were only marked in some way, man soon erected structures having a skyward thrust: domes and spires of cathedrals and minarets of mosques springing upward with increasing audacity.

Forms and Societies

Humanity's first great architectural achievement was a vast, monumental, and planned geometric "city," the Assyrian despot's palace. The structure was topped by a seven-story tower—an observatory—reaching for the stars. The social cost of the palace's construction, however, was horrendous. This disjunction between architectural achievement and social suffering provided the grid for decoding history, for bringing together forms and norms. The Egyptians, though also ruled by despots, contributed the use of stone, thus achieving a permanence lacking in Assyrian architecture, and the column, which permitted spaces of greater monumentality. Together these advances made possible a new form: the temple, the home of a god. The Hebrews exploited and transformed the Egyptian discoveries in the Temple at Jerusalem. For the first time, a nation, not an individual king, was the subject of representation.

The Greeks made three major contributions to progress: a new aspiration (the perfection of human life); a new moral unity (consciousness of the Greek race); and a new architecture (characterized by a pleasing monumentality based on harmonious groupings of buildings). Once the gods came down to earth, perfection, control, and harmony of life became possible. Moral unity transcended political dissension. This centralization of spirit meant that the contribution of one was the gain of all. In the Orient, cities were built for despots and gods; in Greece, for everyone. This new social advance required a new set of architectural forms. Delphi was the pinnacle of this period, grouping the arts, religion, and sports in a single, harmonious space. Alexander the Great, with his architect Dinocrates, drew up plans for a new world capital. The combination of an enlightened despot and a great architect produced the first universal space: the administrative center of an empire. Because of its corruption, Rome failed as a world capital. Diocletian's Palace at Spalato (Hébrard's Villa Medici project), with its fortified enclosure and thick, inward-turning walls, foreshadowed the coming dark ages but displayed virtuosity in grouping administrative functions into a harmonious plan. While Rome sank into decadence, Christ's universal message arose, finding an architectural setting in Justinian's Constantinople. The basilica form, which achieved perfection in Sainte-Sophia, combined Oriental influences with a meeting space and a spiritual presence.

For Hébrard and Andersen, the essential element of modernity was centralization. Nation-states—particularly France—embodied a movement toward unity that culminated in one king and one capital. In the nineteenth century, centralization moved beyond national boundaries: the international expositions provided the opportunity for scholars, artists, and technicians of all nations to meet, exchange ideas, and demonstrate new techniques. Although temporary, these expositions were the first steps toward truly comprehensive, international cooperation. The Exposition of 1867 was the first modern effort to arrange a universe of nations in a single spatial scheme. Hébrard and Andersen devoted three pages of exuberant praise to the Eiffel Tower—more space than they used to discuss Rome, or Haussmann, whom they dismiss in one line. Clearly, the next logical step was to establish a permanent site for international cooperation: "Nations will have to build a city in common, especially planned to unite their representatives. The creation of this international center will no doubt be the most original work of the twentieth century."[56]

Hébrard and Andersen's history of world architecture rarely mentioned geniuses; architects and engineers were celebrated for their roles in a larger story. But neither did their history celebrate the efforts of the common man or laboring masses. Although the motors of historical change—war and religion—were identified, they did not analyze the processes of social and cultural change. There were few real actors (collective or individual) in this drama, and causes were absent. The hero of the story was the universalization of culture and technology; its villains, those factors blocking the actualization of health, science, and communication—technical backwardness, the spirit of parochialism, and blind political passions.

A Center of World Communication

Science and health concerns mandated that all future cities be planned. The real enemies facing mankind, said Hébrard and Andersen, were no longer invading armies but unhealthy social conditions resulting from the lack of scientific planning. Zoning was the first principle: the city of the future needed residential, business, and industrial quarters furnished generously with park space and connected by broad, tree-lined avenues to a central administrative and cultural core. Ideally, the city would be traversed and demarcated by a system of navigable canals, providing not only access to the sea but a picturesque and healthy setting. In the residential quarters, scientifically established amounts of cubic space (both within and around each house) were normative. City planners would mandate the construction of a system of public baths, laundries, hospitals, churches, theaters, lecture halls, and markets. The right to light, recreation, and culture were essential to the peace and health of humanity.[57]

Hébrard and Andersen drew detailed plans for a modern and comprehensive underground transportation system linking the city's quarters with each other and the world beyond. Similar care was devoted to planning municipal heating and electrical systems. The city would be both a center of world communication and a sizable metropolis in its own right. Six residential districts, each containing between 100,000 and 120,000 inhabitants, were included. Details of housing were not provided; there was a sketch of peripherally located industrial quarters, and beyond these industrial zones provision was made for garden suburbs. Each suburb would form a semi-autonomous unit with its own administrative and cultural core; modular growth based on this unit was contemplated. Although Hébrard and Andersen shared many assumptions and principles with Garnier and Prost, each of these projects emphasized a different dimension. Whereas Garnier paid careful attention to housing, and Prost to commerce, class segregation, and circulation, the interests of Hébrard and Andersen were clearly elsewhere. Aside from detailed studies of the transportation and heating systems necessary for a city of this magnitude (commissioned from an outside team of experts), the technical and, strictly speaking, urban dimensions of daily life were barely touched upon. The real energy went into conceiving and planning the administrative and cultural core.

Hébrard and Andersen placed their city on the coast. Arriving travelers would encounter a harbor topped by Andersen's fleshy and thoroughly academic Beaux-Arts statuary. The centerpiece of his sculpture was a fountain of life embodying the seasons, fellowship, and love, with chubby babies held aloft by muscular men and women. A boat basin separated the port from the first major complex, a center for physical culture (or Olympic center) to further the development of the human body and to facilitate, through comparison, the attainment of ideal standards of strength, endurance, and physical beauty. The stadium was flanked by playing fields; the only surprise was the inclusion of a baseball diamond. An institute for the scientific study of physical activity was located adjacent to the fields. Its aim was to furnish scientific norms for the improvement of the race. The proto-fascist ring of these phrases is misleading; the only "race" being strengthened was the human race. The message was: utility, hygiene, and vigor through knowledge, not mass mobilization or defense of the nation.

Flanking the Olympic center was the art center, which contained a temple of art, a conservatory of music and drama, a school of art, a museum of casts of world masterpieces, an art library, and an open air theater, all in impeccable, neoclassical, Beaux-Arts style. Not only Andersen's sculptures, but the makeup of the artistic programs and even some of the buildings—such as the Museum of Casts—were direct replicas of the Parisian Ecole des Beaux-Arts. The port and the Olympic and art centers were clustered at one end of the city's main axis. At its other end lay the administrative, scientific, and religious centers, set around a large, circular place. Hébrard and Andersen envisioned this public square and its associated buildings as the communicative center of the world. The city would host an endless succession of world scientific congresses, provide an archive of advances in all scientific domains, and facilitate the greater good of humanity through the centralization and rapid dissemination of information. "It is in the power of science to purify the world, to exterminate destructive germs from every fibre and nerve, to give strength and precision to all mental and physical efforts. Science in the near future will provide for all man's essential requirements."[58]

Although the pure sciences would have their place of honor in the city, Hébrard and Andersen gave highest priority to disciplines concerned with health. As the world became increasingly interconnected, contagion posed a greater threat. Thus a central bureau of world hygiene, hard at work to fight fraudulent medicines and coordinate research, was of the highest necessity. Adjacent to the hygiene center in the scheme was a permanent world center for the study of law and criminology. Crime and degeneracy posed a worldwide threat: "Modern criminal jurisprudence regards punishment as among its lesser tasks; it concentrates its efforts upon the means for preventing crime. Crime is organized internationally; the prevention of crime must therefore be similarly organized."[59] One hesitates to think what exactly these high-minded reformers had in mind. Whatever it was, it would be housed in an immaculate Beaux-Arts building. Beyond the temples of science and criminology was the temple of religions. Like art, science, and hygiene, religion had entered a universal stage. God spoke with different voices in different places, but the message was the same. Yet another splendid Beaux-Arts temple housed God's message of eternal life and comfort.

Undistorted Communication

Finally, in the center of their monumental place, Hébrard and Andersen proposed a world press center, topped by a truly gigantic Tower of Progress. The world's best reporters would gather in the press building to keep pace with the latest breakthroughs in science, art, and religion, as these were achieved in the adjacent buildings. Breakthroughs would be immediately broadcast to the world from the Tower of Progress. The tower was an appropriate symbol of the whole city, indeed of the future of mankind: "This Tower of Progress was conceived to be of practical utility to men of all nations: to record their requirements and to plead their causes, to protect the inventor and the worker and to look after their essential economic needs, to be the intermediary between the capitalist and the laborer, to protect their rights and to plead their case before the world, to increase the development of hygiene, to make possible more elevated social conditions, and above all, to uplift the oppressed and to harmonize all human efforts."[60] Not only would undistorted communication overcome all strife in the world, making it healthier and more just, but, as the tower represented the spiritual pole of man's being, man's deepest, universal spiritual needs would finally be met.

As war was one of history's motor forces, neither piety nor politics had sufficient power to prevent it. Hébrard and Andersen denied holding any political position; the center for world communication may not have been a critique but it certainly embodied a strategy. In modern times, social strife consisted of class conflict. Modern captains of industry, understanding the dangers posed by class warfare, agreed to the need for a more just administration of industrial expansion. Enlightened workers and capitalists saw that science provided a neutral authority: science in the service of human welfare. Hébrard and Andersen intended their city to be built. Its compactness and self-contained basilica form allowed it to be suitably placed in numerous locations. After careful consideration, they proposed a series of sites along the Atlantic coast in America, others on the shores of the Mediterranean, and still others in Belgium, Holland, and Switzerland. They were on the verge of achieving their objective at a site outside Brussels when the First World War broke out.

8
Specific Intellectuals:
Perfecting the Instruments

This chapter introduces dimensions of the technical elaboration of the urban scheme developed in Rome by the Beaux-Arts cohort. These include Eugène Hénard's detailed proposals for alleviating Paris's circulation and open-space dilemmas and Ebenezer Howard's garden city projects and their French reception. Both Hénard and Howard's ideas, suitably adapted to the Musée Social's conceptions of society, change, and politics, were combined with principles of planning derived from Garnier and Prost's work into a campaign for planning laws in France.

During the period between 1905 and 1914, French reformist socialism was renewed on several fronts. During this decade many of the topics treated by reformist socialists ran parallel to those of the neo-conservatives of the Musée Social: cooperative movements, consumer issues, housing, and, of course, urban planning. Although it is a commonplace that the Dreyfus affair was the crucible for the forging of the modern intellectual as a type, in the decade following the affair another type of intellectual emerged as well. Contrary to the methods of Zola, these intellectuals adopted a strategy that avoided major ideological polemics and concentrated on sectorial questions, which they approached in detail. Among the most interesting of this type was the Groupe d'Etudes Socialistes, dominated by young and brilliant normalians including the anthropologist Robert Hertz and the sociologist Maurice Halbwachs. Like the group of Prix-de-Rome winners, these elite normalians represented a social type: the specific intellectual.[1]

All of the major European urban planning movements of the early twentieth century, and especially that of France, sought a course between laissez-faire liberalism and major state intervention. The typical strategy was to attempt to influence the real estate market by means of public intervention for roads, public transport, and parks. The Germans led the way. The flourishing international congresses made the French well aware of these developments and of the lag between their efforts and those of Germany and England. Although housing and social hygiene laws were passed in France, representing an important, first institutional step away from philanthropy, the consistent inflexibility of the Conseil d'Etat combined with the political resistance of large blocs of the French electorate to stymie effective action. For example, the 1902 public health law permitting some public intervention in combating hygienic abuses was finally being timidly implemented. It met with opposition from the press as well as with the scholarly production of dissertations with such titles as "Abuses committed in the name of public hygiene against the rights and liberty of individuals." The example of Haussmann's expropriation procedures and the resulting banishment of large numbers of the poor from central Paris, as well as the vast profits made by many of his supporters, were recent enough to occasion a certain caution on the left. Fundamental divisions in French society were mirrored in the Parliament, which often voted for laws without sanctions or application procedures, ensuring that these would not be put into effect. A reactionary faction of Parliament within the small farm bloc (shielded by protectionist tariffs) allied with large industrialists to oppose expropriation of land, and managed to keep France from passing the sort of urban planning legislation that Germany, England, and Switzerland (hardly revolutionary regimes) had enacted at the turn of the century.[2] This did not mean that French efforts were a failure in any simple sense of the term. They did succeed in establishing a discourse which, later, as transformed and implemented in different contexts, had major effects on social and environmental planning.[3]

Paris: Industrialization and Suburban Growth

The demographic history of the Parisian region's late nineteenth-century growth has been well studied. Between 1851
and 1901, the population of the Department of the Seine (including Paris) had risen from 1,422,065 to 3,669,930. The suburbs exploded from 257,510 in 1861, to 955,862 in 1901, a
growth rate three times that of Paris itself. The increase was
due in large part to the immigration of unskilled labor drawn to
Paris during Haussmann's construction boom, and to peasants
forced off the land in a series of depressions occurring between
1870 and 1890.[4] Paris and its suburbs were becoming industrialized. Suburban industries tended to be large; by 1906, for
example, the percentage of factories employing over 500 workers was almost three times as great in the suburbs as in Paris.
Suburban factories were mechanized, further differentiating
the economic and social composition of the suburbs and city.[5]

After the turn of the century the growing transportation
system played an increasingly important role in linking Paris
and its suburbs: one could argue that transportation turned the
latter into true suburbs.[6] The appearance of the first train lines
in 1837, the omnibus in 1856, tramways after 1885, the Métro
in 1900 (spurred by the Universal Exposition), and the suburban autobus in 1910 provided the necessary infrastructure linking Paris and its immediate hinterlands. The years between
1895 and 1914 were the boom period in modernizing public
transport: 92 kilometers of Métro tracks, three railroad termi-
nals in Paris, and double tracks for several rail lines serving the
suburbs were constructed, and transport began to be run on
electricity. Use of the Métro increased from 16 million rides per
year in 1900 to 312 million in 1909.[7] Transportation brought
speculation; land values of suburban areas linked to Paris were
as much as twenty times higher than those without transit services. Agriculture was chased away by industry and housing.

Housing for the upper and middle classes was being built at
record rates but not for the poor, and the housing and health
crisis of the end of the century was the result. The 1896 census
indicated that 14.9 percent of the population lived in over-

crowded conditions, with the percentages in more proletariat areas rising to over 60 percent. Government policies actually discriminated against building lower-cost housing by levying proportionally higher taxes on it. Although reformers of the Musée Social, as well as government officials and social scientists, had actively studied and made public the basic statistics, social problems, and hygienic threats, very little had been done to ameliorate the situation.[8]

Eugène Hénard: Traffic and Parks

The Musée Social established its Section d'Hygiène Urbaine et Rurale in January 1908. Present at the first session were Jules Siegfried, Georges Benoit-Lévy, Georges Risler, Robert de Souza, and Eugène Hénard. The work of this group was formally divided into two teams. One group, headed by Hénard, was charged with investigating problems and proposing planning solutions. The other group was charged with drafting legislation and discovering legal mechanisms for implementing the proposals made in the first section. The proposals made by Hénard between 1903 and 1909, and put forward in his *Etudes sur les transformations de Paris*, shaped the agenda of the urban and rural hygiene section: he called for a campaign for open spaces centering on the issue of Parisian fortifications and for a law requiring planning for all French cities over 10,000.[9]

Eugène Hénard (1849–1923), the son of a professor of architecture at the Ecole des Beaux-Arts, completed his studies in 1880 without winning the Grand Prix. In 1882, he was appointed to the Travaux de Paris, the office in charge of municipal architecture, where he remained throughout his career, working primarily on school buildings and acquiring a detailed historical and technical familiarity with Paris. Hénard directed the construction of the famous Palais des Machines at the 1889 fair, arguing (unsuccessfully) after the fair for its preservation as an architectural monument. At the 1900 Exposition, he designed a Palais de l'Electricité, a grandiose celebration of the new world, and a Hall of Illusions, a Moorish, hexagonal structure with interior walls composed of mirrors.[10]

Hénard began what may have been among the first statistical and sociological studies of traffic. He contrasted de la Mare's 1738 *Traité de Police* observation that in the middle of the sixteenth century there were only two carriages in the city—those of the queen and the Princess Diane—with the estimated 65,543 vehicles on the city's streets in 1906. His work was more than merely quantitative: Hénard developed a classification of Parisian traffic (household, professional, economic, *mondaine*, holiday, and popular), plotting the patterns and densities of each period of the day. Hénard was resolutely comparative and historical, believing that although each city had its own particular past which had to be understood and respected, there were also general, structural regularities. Comparing London, Moscow, Berlin, and Paris in order to ascertain why these metropolises suffered less from congestion, Hénard concluded that Paris lacked a network of roads connecting the center to its extended system of peripheral highways. Hénard produced detailed studies of circulation patterns and proposed numerous alternatives and improvements, including linking the major road networks in, around, and through Paris, with careful attention to preserving the city's monuments.[11]

Combining his statistical analysis of types of urban circulation with aesthetic considerations, Hénard designed a split-level intersection (separating pedestrians from traffic) to facilitate traffic flow. He also addressed the problem of how to direct traffic around major intersections. In 1905, busy intersections, like that of the famous Place de l'Etoile, lacked common traffic regulations. Hénard devised the rule that drivers on the right have the right of way, which still stands today. His idea was first experimented with in 1907, and was incorporated into the first official French traffic regulations in 1912. Hénard made a series of specific, technical contributions: the *carrefour à girations*, separation of pedestrian and vehicular traffic; alerting others to the necessity of planning for automobile traffic in cities; and the statistical and analytic study of traffic patterns in particular cities and their surrounding regions.

Concurrent with his passion for traffic problems, Hénard concerned himself with equally detailed statistical, historical, and comparative analyses of open space and parks in Paris. More than frivolous luxuries, parks to him were indispensable to urban hygiene. Hénard dramatically demonstrated how a lack of central planning, combined with uncontrolled speculation, had resulted in a 64 percent decrease in the city's open spaces during the nineteenth century, while the city's size and population had tripled. Comparatively speaking, Paris was a disaster; it had one-third the park space of London with half its population. Paris in 1903 had only ten parks of at least ten hectares, and thirty-six planted squares, for the whole metropolis. Making the public aware of the need for open space became an important part of Hénard's work after 1903. His efforts focused on the Champ de Mars area (where the International Expositions of 1867, 1889, and 1900 had been held) and the much larger fortifications around Paris. Hénard advocated creating the first in-city airport on the Champs de Mars, proposing the use of the Eiffel Tower as its signal post, and surrounding the landing site with cafes and planted zones. He argued that a great city needed a civic center; the Champ de Mars had served this function during the great civic rites of the Revolution and throughout the nineteenth century with the Expositions.[12] Hénard's plan was vigorously opposed and eventually defeated by the Parisian Municipal Council, which proceeded to sell a large parcel of the land to developers for a railway station.

By the turn of the century, it was clear that the vast fortifications built around Paris in the 1840s and taken over by the city in 1859 and 1883 were militarily outmoded.[13] When it was decided that they should be razed, Hénard proposed an ambitious project creating nine regional parks around the periphery, replacing the old fortifications. Criticizing other proposals as insufficiently urban, he advocated using roughly 10 percent of the 800-hectare area for park space (thus increasing Parisian park space by over 60 percent) and the rest for housing and a large ring road connected to regional road networks. Hénard's parks were meant to be centerpieces of the neighborhoods surrounding them. His plan for housing called for a mix of social classes. Arguing that innovative planning could make aesthetic and utilitarian considerations work together harmoniously,

Hénard proposed a system of apartment buildings innovatively sited along the ring road. These were his famous *boulevards à redans*, or "stepped boulevards." Hénard thought of placing buildings in "steps," so that smaller parks could be situated between the road and buildings, increasing green space without sacrificing overall density. By placing his apartment buildings at sharp angles to each other, he increased the amount of light available for the greatest number of apartments. The additional open areas were reserved for gardens, shops, cafes, and other explicitly social purposes. Various reform organizations, including the Musée Social, strongly backed Hénard's project, and his ideas were widely discussed by other urbanists. But Hénard's plan to build 75,000 apartment units was an anathema to real estate interests, and no general plan was implemented. Most of the fortifications area was sold piecemeal after the First World War.[14]

The Garden City

Ebenezer Howard's *To-morrow: a Peaceful Path to Real Reform*, published in 1898, is often referred to as founding modern city planning.[15] Howard's ideas and the eventual construction of two English garden cities, Letchworth in 1903 and Welwyn in 1920, have had an undeniable impact on the discourse of urban planning. Howard (1850–1928), a self-proclaimed pragmatist, explicitly distanced himself from utopian schemes. His achievement lay in bringing together a number of diverse elements, drawn from other plans, and combining them in one unified, successful scheme. Howard saw rural migration and the decline of cities as the central social problems facing England. Howard thematized the issue of scale. Cities of around 30,000 people, set in the countryside, were the answer; business, agriculture, sociality, and a healthy environment would surely produce a friendlier and more cooperative social life. Social peace lay in a harmoniously planned environment, one which combined social concerns with individual freedom, nature, and culture. Howard conceived of the garden city as a model reproducible in series across the landscape, with large areas of agricultural land and green space separating these new towns. Gradually the great metropolises would disappear, replaced by hundreds of functionally differentiated garden cities. This decentralist strategy was part of a radical belief in the liberating potential inherent in new technologies, such as electricity.

Howard drew up a plan for a symmetrically organized city set within a circle. Drawing on Dr. Benjamin Richardson's *Hygeia, A City of Health* of 1876, Howard planned for low-density housing set in ample greenery and divided by wide avenues; Howard's garden cities were to be small-scale manufacturing centers. The combination of industry and hygiene introduced zoning. Factories would lie on the periphery of the circular city, serviced by a rail system and yet within walking distance of the residences. The center of the city was to be devoted to leisure and civic activity, providing a common focus for each of the five wards into which the city was divided. Each ward was composed of single-family houses surrounded by gardens. Howard planned for class differences. Drawing on Wakefield's *Art of Colonisation* of 1849, Howard argued that one of the mistakes of many colonization schemes was to have representatives of only one class.[16] Each ward would have a centrally located school building which would also serve as a library, meeting hall, and possible church.

Howard was emphatic that expressions of individuality were to be encouraged whenever they did not conflict with the general good. He felt strongly that the strength of his system was the flexible combination of a rational common plan (for the essential infrastructural matters) combined with a nonprescriptive approach to details. While encouraging private enterprise, the town would limit the number of franchises for each service and control the quality of goods presented to its inhabitants. The town center was to be filled with large, public buildings: a town hall, library, museum, concert and lecture hall, and hospital. Here the highest values of the community would be brought together—culture, philanthropy, health, and mutual cooperation. In addition to the manufacturing establishments (boot factories, cycle works, jam factory, engineering firms, furniture factory, clothing factory, and printing plants) located at the city's edge, generous amounts of farmland provided efficient and economical sources of employment and fresh, inexpensive produce for the city. Their proximity would reduce transportation costs, as well as ensure that no urban sprawl would ensue beyond the perimeter of the circle. Howard was a firm believer in "gas-and-water socialism," and he stipulated that the town's board of management should provide all utilities on a nonprofit basis. Engineering systems constituted the largest set of municipal services. Howard also thought the town might establish municipal bakeries and laundries. The private industry of the town would be civic-minded and contribute to municipal services and general well-being. Cooperative building and pension societies might also be encouraged.

As Howard meant his scheme to be practical, he devoted a good deal of thought to its financing. He devised a scheme of joint ownership, with guaranteed interest on loans. Eventually, through a mutual fund for investors and residents, the original investors would be bought out—ownership of the town passing to its inhabitants—but with continued payments by the residents substituting for taxes and providing the necessary funds for civic and municipal services. Howard felt he had discovered a rational means, based on self-interest, to overcome the social antagonisms inherent in landlord/tenant relationships. He advertised the "absence of plan" as one of the scheme's innovations. Howard repeatedly argued that a successful scheme had to retain flexibility, remaining open to the specifics of the situation in which it would operate and to the will of the inhabitants.

Although the Musée Social never adopted the garden city as an officially designated goal of a legislative campaign, its members opened their conference doors to its chief French advocates, Georges Risler and Georges Benoist-Lévy. Benoist-Lévy had followed the movement's early stages in England and the United States and lobbied vigorously for its acceptance in France. Risler presented garden cities as effective means for furthering a combination of social-economist and philanthropic goals: garden cities would provide the environment for disciplined, family-oriented, hygienic, and *prévoyant* workers. Risler articulated the French transformations of the English garden city doctrine in a conference at the Musée Social in December 1909. After a brief pastoral about the timeless need for greenery and fresh air, in contrast to the misery of popular

housing, Risler sounded a familiar Musée Social refrain:
France was falling behind, even though the idea of garden
cities had originated in France, at Mulhouse.[17] Risler praised
the mining city of Dourges, where the company had built 374
pittoresque cottages with individual gardens, increasing the so-
lidity and health of the nuclear family by anchoring it in the
"home." He neglected to mention the contrast between the
moralizing and disciplinary emphasis on the individual house
at Dourges (each separated from its neighbors by twenty meters) and the cooperative ethos of Howard and his architects.
He also neglected to mention the difficulty Howard faced in
financing, the consequent modification of the ownership
scheme, and their essentially middle-class and skilled-artisan
(rather than working class) populations. Howard's cooperative,
small-scale, and innovative scheme became, in Risler's rendi-
tion, little more than an updated disciplinary technology. However, after the First World War, socialist municipalities adopted
and modernized the garden-city idea, emphasizing its urban
and social components. To understand these developments, we
will now examine socialist urban discourses before the First
World War.

Sociological Socialism

Beginning in 1908, the Groupe d'Etudes Socialistes met each
month to reflect on the future of socialism. This did not mean
discussing Marx; rather, their approach has been nicely characterized as one of *bons dossiers* (exemplary position papers).
Charles Andler, a key link to the Ecole Normale, summed up
the group's ethos by saying, "We tried to be irreproachable
technicians."[18] The published fruits of their labors are found in
the sixteen issues of *Les Cahiers du socialiste* covering themes
such as foreign models for municipal socialism (Louis Garnier),
assistance and the communes (A. Bianconi), municipal land
policies (Maurice Halbwachs), free space and fortifications
(Albert Thomas), the suppression of city tolls (Henri Senan),
direct administration (Albert Tanger), and economic organization of the commune (H. Lévy-Bruhl and A. Prudhomme).
The Group's themes—cooperation and municipalism as the

route to socialism rather than class conflict—demonstrate a direct affiliation with Paul Brousse's "possibilists." The new targets for socialist action included a rejuvenated commune as the basic social unit. A socialist commune would arise from citizens directing their own affairs without the interference of corporatist or bureaucratic intermediaries. In this transformed city, not only would citizens (as opposed to "workers") be in a position to run their own lives, they would have new rights— rights to housing and to health. Optimism ran high.

Among this group of reform socialists, the three most relevant to this narrative are Henri Sellier (1883–1943), a socialist politician and administrator and arguably the major figure in French urbanism during this period; Albert Thomas (1878–1932), a normalian and Minister of Armaments during the First World War; and Maurice Halbwachs (1877–1945), also a normalian and one of the leading Durkheimians. Halbwachs' work was fundamental to the new problematizing of the relation of social life to space, history, and sociology. His analysis of land values, tax policies, and social-class dynamics (and their spatial arrangement) offered these reform socialists the most comprehensive sociological basis for analysis and action. His *La Politique foncière des municipalités* (Municipal Land Policy) became a handbook for Sellier. Lyautey would put its essential principles into effect in Morocco.

Halbwachs was from a family of Alsatian academics. His father moved to France in 1871, and Halbwachs arrived at the Ecole Normale Supérieure during the Dreyfus affair, to find the once apolitical school enmeshed in politics. Like many others, Halbwachs chose the humanist socialism characteristic of the Ecole and its librarian Lucien Herr. More surprising was Halbwachs' abandonment of philosophy, despite his admiration for Bergson (who was then teaching at the Ecole), and subsequent lifelong commitment to sociology as an empirical discipline. Halbwachs' law thesis, *L'Expropriation et le prix des terrains à Paris, 1880–1900,* was politicized, applied sociology. Jaurès admired it, and the socialist party published a popular version. Halbwachs' was the first thesis to be based on "direct observation of the facts under study" in any faculty of letters in France, in any of the human sciences.[19]

In the thesis, Halbwachs argued that a double inequality had arisen in Paris during the nineteenth century. First, access to health-giving green space and light, which had been previously distributed evenly throughout Paris, had become increasingly restricted to richer neighborhoods. Second—and this was the crux of urban problems as well as the fulcrum of their solution—urban land values had increased rapidly. Those profiting from these spiraling increases had done nothing to deserve such gains. Just as municipalities could not leave bread prices unregulated, Halbwachs argued, rent and housing could not be left to speculators. The increase of urban land values was due to social, not individual, causes. Haussmann's improvements, the railway stations, the new streets, and the parks were social ventures. Social solidarity was present in a city, even if individuals did not realize it, even if neighbors did not know each other. It was only just, Halbwachs reasoned, that this social reality be recognized for what it was and a return compensation made to society.

Socialist municipalities should not destroy this surplus value but use it for the common good. Once socialists understood these sociological laws, they would be in a position to plan for everyone's benefit. The key was to take hold of these riches while they were in the process of forming, not afterward. Not only should cities buy up as much open space as possible, in anticipation of future growth, but in the name of the public interest (as in England and Germany) they should not sell land but only lease building space. Once this principle of justice was established, and once the sociological evolution was understood, the course of action was clear: planning. The opportunity for total planning was particularly attractive in the suburban areas surrounding the great cities. For Halbwachs, planning should extend not only to broad patterns of land use but to specifics like style; socialist planners, reinventing Fourier, should take account of the diversity and variability of tastes. Sociological insight and technical, legal tools would make possible a rejuvenated, healthy, and more just society.

Sellier, the socialist mayor of Suresnes, head of the Office Départemental des Habitations à Bon Marché, Deputy of the Seine and Minister of Public Health under Léon Blum, must figure among the exemplary carriers of French urbanism between the wars. Sellier developed new definitions of and responses to what was generally agreed to be a new type of society; he considered politics, administrative strategies, engineering, and aesthetic and architectural factors in approaching a society increasingly characterized by the importance of employees and the middle classes. He saw clearly that even if the planning fight were won, new social problems would have to be confronted, requiring new social forms to embody the new norms of modern life: "The city should not be only an immense collection of families grouped together by a methodical plan. It constitutes also a fecund laboratory of social solidarity."[20]

.Just as Lyautey's aristocratic origins played a central role in shaping both his political and social views and his self-invention, so too Sellier's working-class origins were important in determining his persona and career. Sellier's father was a cannon maker, qualifying him as an elite within the working class (later in life Sellier's parents opened a small watch and jewlery shop). Although Sellier soon rose in society and was never himself a manual laborer, he played on his background skillfully.[21] His interests and affiliations were formed at a young age and remained extremely stable; he first joined the Parti Socialiste Révolutionnaire du Berry in 1898, manifesting a strong interest in the cooperative movement. It was the cooperatist dimension of French socialism which drew his passion and in which his administrative and political career took shape.

Sellier won a government scholarship for secondary school studies in Bourges. It is at this moment that he came under the quasi-paternal influence of Edouard Vaillant, a leading proponent of socialist municipalism, and one of the few major figures in French socialism capable of straddling the fence between the revolutionary wing represented by Jules Guesde and the pragmatic republicanism of Jaurès.[22] Although for a period they quarreled (over socialist participation in a right-wing government), Sellier never reneged on his allegiance to Vaillant, and consistently underlined his intellectual and political loyalty to Vaillant's brand of socialism.[23] On a trip to Germany with Vaillant, Sellier met the other major person who would influence his ideas and practice, the brilliant, young normalian, Albert Thomas. Sellier and Thomas shared an admiration for the social-democratic wing of German socialism and its leader Edouard Bernstein. Both embraced Alfred Fouillée's famous challenge that "socialism will be sociological or it will not be," and both were more interested in practice, in administrative reform and technical detail, than in theory (or socialist purity) for its own sake. Sellier was a pragmatist, believing, as did many others of his generation, in the importance of positivist social science in understanding the evolution of social forms and in constructing a more just society. The pragmatics of social problems interested Sellier more than doctrines; a socialist reformer, he was a member of the Communist party from 1921 to 1922, while associating with members of the Musée Social.

Sellier's thought, his objectives, and his methods were formed in the matrix of renewed reflection on the objectives and principles of socialism. He focused particularly on union activities targeting an important new group of workers— salaried employees—who, to cite one example, constituted close to one-third of all union members in Lyons before the First World War.[24] This growing sector of government employees, department store employees, office workers, and the like, required a different organizational approach and a different set of goals from the traditional unions for industrial workers.[25]

Sellier came to Paris under the aegis of a scholarship from the Chambre de Commerce de Paris, which enabled him to earn his *licence de droit* in 1901 and a diploma from the Ecole des Hautes Etudes Commerciales. He worked in a bank, then served as a functionary in the Ministry of Commerce, before winning a competition for a post in the newly-founded Ministry of Work, where he implemented social legislation dealing with such issues as the length of the work day, hygiene, and physical safety in the work place. In 1906 Sellier quit the ministry and was elected Conseiller Général of the canton of Puteaux-Suresnes, on the opposite side of the Bois du Boulougne from Paris. By this time Sellier was rising in the socialist ranks; he was nominated as the socialist representative of the Conseil Générale de la Seine in 1910. Reelected in 1912, he remained a member until 1941, when Vichy officials removed him from office. In 1915 Sellier became chief administrator of the Seine's Office Départemental des Habitations à Bon Marché, whose creation he had advocated. The post provided Sellier an important forum for propagating his ideas. Running on a socialist ticket, Sellier was elected mayor of Suresnes in 1919. In the 1925 elections he headed an electoral list entitled: "Bloc des ouvriers et des employés pour la défense des intérêts communaux" (list of workers and employees for the defense of common interests). Sellier was a member of innumerable national and international committees, was extremely active in parliament, served as a professor at the Institut d'Urbanisme, and cofounded the Fédération Internationale de l'Habitation et de l'Urbanisme. The capstone of his career came when he was named Minister of Public Health in Blum's first government in 1936; he was offered the post of Minister of Work in the second but refused it, interpreting the offer as a repudiation of his achievements in public health. Forced to retire in 1941, Sellier died in 1943.

Sellier joined the Groupe d'Etudes Socialistes in 1908, at the height of the debate over the Parisian fortifications. Although Sellier was a relatively prolific writer—or at least editor—of reports, he shared with such members of the Musée Social as Georges Risler the habit of a relentless repetition of themes combined with a large quantity of comparative data. Neither man was a theorist nor an intellectual with universalist ambitions. Like Risler, or Prost, Sellier's energies were drawn to specific issues and problems. His general concerns were established during his early contacts with Vaillant and the Groupe d'Etudes Socialistes, and varied little over the next two decades. A particularly clear presentation of Sellier's position is found in a small book, published in 1920 and aimed at a relatively broad audience, which he wrote in a series edited by Albert Thomas entitled *Les Documents du Socialisme*.[26] This was essentially the same text Sellier had presented to the Groupe d'Etudes Socialistes in 1912.

While the changing population distribution in the Paris area presented its own intrinsic social and economic problems, the massive, unplanned growth also posed problems for an administrative structure constructed for an entirely different society.

For Sellier and his allies, the Parisian agglomeration was a single socio-economic unit. The older administrative grid was outmoded and detrimental to healthy, regulated growth. The lack of any effective land policy meant that the suburbs of Paris were cheap locations for industry. This development, however, was occurring at the expense of what Sellier (extending the analyses of the possibilists) described as "social cost" and "urban cost."

Social problems in cities, Sellier argued, were not new; Thebes, Memphis, Athens, and Rome had had urban problems. What was new, what characterized urban development in modern times, was the explosive, outward extension of major cities. In Paris, the king (for political reasons) had vainly sought to prevent expansion beyond the city's limits; despite these efforts some industries had moved outside Paris's gates, as had aristocrats following Louis XIV's own example. These were the first manifestations of modern functionalization and specialization of spaces. The trend continued; the modern city seemed destined to sprawl outward indefinitely. Sellier was not nostalgic about the walled premodern city, where no functional spatialization could emerge, historical styles were jumbled together, and social classes intermingled. Modern cities throughout Europe were characterized by centrifugal extension and specialization of quarters. Responses to this process varied, however. Cities like London and Berlin had addressed the problem directly and rationally. Sellier argued that the modern distinction between "home" and "business," central to the healthy development of modern society (and recognized in English planning legislation) was not acknowledged in France, creating great hardships. London and Berlin used transportation as a planning instrument, while in Paris the spread of transportation systems and housing remained irrational, benefiting speculation and development only in areas already wealthy, while ignoring real social needs. Maurice Halbwachs had demonstrated how the wealthy classes had captured the central city, chasing the poor to Paris's chaotic periphery.

French administration was poorly structured to meet changing situations. Submitting the diverse communes of France to a single set of administrative regulations violated any conception of rational administration in which "rules are conceived in accord with the nature of the agents they are meant to administer."[27] The answer was not to annex the suburbs to Paris; this would only exacerbate the bureaucratic nightmares. The eighty-nine departments of France were the proper units of administration. They were large enough that rational planning for health, transportation, industry, and housing was conceivable, and not so large as to lose touch with the political and social realities of the communes. It made no sense for one commune to set up water purification plants if the water in neighboring communes remained untreated. Halbwachs' principle of taxing the surplus value of urban housing should be extended to the departmental level as an equitable means of paying for these new services. The social and technical means were at hand to generate collective wealth, to distribute it equitably among the members of the collectivity, to take hold of society's basic institutions, and to install a rational administration that would assure each individual's biological needs while improving general welfare. In sum, Sellier advocated totalization and individualization through science and rational planning.

The Campaign for Planning

Coordinated with the Musée Social's drive for open-space legislation for the Paris fortifications area was a campaign for urban planning. The passage of the Town Planning Act in England in 1909 contributed to the Musée Social's sense that France was falling dangerously behind other European countries. Jules Siegfried championed the idea of mandatory planning in France and drew up proposed legislation for a commission to be housed in the Ministry of the Interior. A version was presented to the Municipal Council in Paris in April 1909, the first attempt to ensure systematic planning. The same year Charles Beauquier, a deputy from Doubs, regionalist, amateur historian, sociologist of Paris, and president of the Société pour la Protection des Paysages de France, introduced a similar law requiring long-range plans. Neither bill got very far in the Parliament.[28]

The leader of the planning battle for the Musée Social was Georges Risler. In 1910, he produced a document urging long-range planning for services as well as open spaces. Planning was the first principle of social hygiene; prevention was the most valuable of cures. But France had fallen sadly behind in all planning areas, and since 1870 had displayed timidity, disdain for public beauty, and a general lack of vision. If, Risler asked, it was rational to plan for one's home, one's garden, and the education of one's children, wasn't it irrational to ignore the future of French cities? Two related but separate tactics were outlined. First, Risler advocated requiring public officials to have some familiarity with planning principles; second, the public had to be educated "to the fact that questions of hygiene, art, and comfort were of primordial importance to the physical development of our race and its moral and intellectual elevation."[29] The French political system, Risler argued, was ill equipped to cope with issues of general import. It was constituted to favor only local, narrow interests that paralyzed parliamentary action. In the view of the Musée Social, other forms of action had to be invented to save France; a combination of public opinion and technical expertise, embodied in a planning law, was the most promising solution.

After arguing that planning was a traditional French activity, Risler shifted ground and sounded the danger call: Germany had the most advanced conception of general planning, and England had the lead in actual housing. Risler also acknowledged the accomplishments of Buls in Belgium. Hénard, Stubben, and Sitte were noteworthy contributors, but it was Buls who had succeeded in combining the German sense of planning with a French feeling for beauty. Buls had tackled the most difficult task, the renovation of old quarters, which demanded the most subtle combination of art and utility. If the most integrated and harmonious urban art was in Belgium, the most comprehensive planning was taking place in Germany, where advanced theories were applied rationally. Well-conceived road systems and ample park land were carefully laid out and their contribution to hygiene and beauty appreciated. Hygiene and construction regulations for residential interiors, as well as rules concerning the density, placement, and inspection of houses were exemplary. The main German advance lay in the treatment of centers and peripheries. The English concentrated on new suburban building, whereas the Germans sought to preserve the old center cities while providing new housing at the outskirts.

The major threat to planning was speculation. Risler found the German goal of controlling speculation utopian. He preferred the English tactic of using transportation planning to guide zoning and limit speculation; land was secured for these purposes, and lots were systematically laid out around the public spaces. Risler reluctantly acknowledged the success of German municipal control of land and services in cities like Cologne, Frankfurt, Stuttgart, and Wiesbaden; the last was a resort city, "La Mecque sanitaire," whose population had doubled in twenty-five years, but which had the lowest mortality rate in Germany. Finally, the 1902 Frankfurt law allowed for expropriation if the property was declared in the public interest by the municipal authorities and at least half of the property holders. The city was obligated to compensate each proprietor through proportional shares, minus a share deducted for public space. Benefiting all concerned parties, the procedure avoided both the courts and direct political action. The British Town Planning Bill of 1909 stipulated that planning in all British towns was to be transferred to local government boards. France would have to change her ways if she was to survive in the modern world.

The Musée Social urged the passage of new laws; France needed a planning law, equipped with legal machinery, to make expropriation work. In 1911 the Musée under Siegfried's initiative proposed the first detailed planning scheme for Paris and its region. The plan included elaborate roadworks extending into the region, a major increase in park space, reserve land for future parks, and two large airfields.[30] Hénard was ailing; his two chief assistants, Alfred Agache (1875–1959) and Henri Prost, would henceforth carry the banner for French urban planning.[31]

For the Musée Social urbanists, then, the basic, universal principles of urban planning were identifiable. The art lay in applying them to specific situations. Local specialists had to study local conditions before drawing up an initial plan. These studies would include the collection of available data on the physical geography of the region and city; the city's evolution; general hygiene; social and economic characteristics; technical mapping; land values; labor and material locally available; and traffic conditions and future needs. Once a synthesis was achieved (timing was not specified), a preliminary plan would be presented to a municipal commission for inspection. The Musée Social urged that this commission be composed not only of political representatives but of specialists familiar with the history, archaeology, commerce, and industry of the region. After consultation, detailed maps and plans could be drawn.

The urbanist had to decide first on the distribution of quarters or zones. He would be aware of the historical tendency to differentiate quarters according to occupational specialization, and be attentive to its local application. Industrial quarters should be placed near the means of transport and with due attention to the prevailing winds. Overly rigid differentiation of functions was pointed to as one of the few flaws in German planning; absolute interdiction of light industry in the central city was not necessarily correct for all cities. Workers' quarters should be near the outlying industrial quarters for reasons of hygiene and convenience, but also because land for fully equipped garden cities would be less expensive there. Commercial quarters should generally be in the center and carefully planned for easy access. The most difficult element to generalize was the placement of residential quarters, which depended greatly on the history of local conditions. The backbone of the city was circulation: the road system, including squares, crossroads, monuments, and public transportation, should follow Hénard's guidelines.

Every French commune needed a carefully grouped central administrative center, a church, and a primary school. Public meeting houses with library and recreation facilities, common in America, were recommended for larger communes, which should also include hospitals. Hygiene was given highest priority and was the guiding principle of all aspects of the plan: for roads, air, houses, and municipal services for water, garbage, and fire protection. The Musée Social remained silent on the municipalization of services. With great reluctance the Musée Social planners proposed a state organization to run the reconstruction planning efforts, but they repeatedly underlined the temporary nature of such an office. The details of a hierarchical organization were laid out. Speed and efficiency were the reward; state control was the price to be paid.

Tools: Expropriation, Plans

Implementing the Musée Social schema for the modern city remained problematic. Attempting to find a middle ground between liberalism (with which Musée Social activists shared a strong anti-state position) and more statist doctrines (with which they shared a sense of social crisis) was extremely difficult both discursively and politically. Almost all aspects of the Musée Social's proposals for urban planning entailed the expropriation of land. Planning required three major steps: stabilizing land prices, simplifying acquisition, and facilitating recovery of outlays for the communes through sharing of the surplus generated by the improvements. Stable land prices were absolutely essential. However, the announcement of a plan to improve undeveloped suburban land could well become the occasion for speculation. Consequently, the law had to ensure that land prices were determined in advance of any speculation. The model proposed was the 1897 legislation of the Swiss city of Lausanne, in which, following German precedent, the commune was given the right to expropriate land within new street alignments, land within twenty meters of such new alignments, and land within newly created parcels which would create health hazards. French public opinion was not yet ready for such steps, even though stable countries (England, Holland, Denmark, and Switzerland) had already instituted these regulations.

A certain amount of legislation existed in France for road alignments (a royal edict of 1607) but none for plans of extension and *aménagement*. Under the Ancien Régime, the king had a legal right to withdraw use of land through the power of eminent domain. Following laws of 1810 and 1833, and culminating in the law of May 3, 1841, any expropriation of property became subject to controlled, costly, and complicated procedures.[32] Haussmann introduced major changes in these laws on March 26, 1852 and September 27, 1858, opening the way for eventual state intervention in the urban fabric. Expropriation for public use was now extended to whole buildings, in the name of the traditional alignment criteria as well as new hygienic considerations. However, the Conseil d'Etat had severely restricted its scope by consistently denying the public-utility classification to most proposed projects. One way around these costly and slow procedures was one of the oldest accepted principles of intervention: alignment. The right to prevent any form of building along a road without indemnization secured some land for municipalities. Military defense provided another point of entry; the Musée Social was reduced to arguing that the old fortifications areas should be considered as part of a hygienic defense of Paris.

Two documents which synthesize the Musée Social's urban planning program are Robert de Souza's *Nice: capital d'hiver* [Nice: Winter Capital] and Agache, Aubertin, and Redont's *Comment reconstruire nos cités détruites* [How to reconstruct our destroyed cities].[33] Both books are misnamed. The latter, written in 1915, while certainly anticipating the end of the war, closely followed the lines of thinking proposed by the Musée Social during the previous decade. De Souza's book was more than a local document, intertwining a coherent synopsis of the major tenets of planning along with local proposals for Nice. It stands as one of the most detailed regionally-oriented proposals within the Musée Social corpus.

Robert de Souza was one of the charter members of the Musée Social's Section d'Hygiene Urbaine et Rurale. Other members of this movement, like Risler, had not been sharply critical of previous planning efforts, but de Souza presented a categorical attack on French planning. His summary of the 1910 London Town Planning Conference was typically alarmist. Neither the loss of French artistic genius nor public ignorance could be blamed for French backwardness. The root cause lay with the hidebound mediocrity of France's administrators and engineers: "Our conceited state engineers produce incredible stupidities in all our Departments, not to mention that any sign of aesthetic good will is almost always fought by them."[34] This dreadful state of affairs was the prolongation of Haussmann's nefarious legacy. His work in Paris was not really a modern, organic plan, but the work of bureaucratic and police administration guided by engineers and petty politicians. A map of public works accomplished in Paris from 1870 to 1900 revealed no master plan but only a scattering of small projects evenly distributed by electoral district. There was no concern for the expanding suburbs and no thought for the region. Paris was heading for disaster, and in the rest of France the situation was worse.

De Souza painted a rosy picture of matters abroad. Cities were being built with general plans combining the latest advances in hygiene and art. Architects and planners, disdainfully referred to by French engineers as poets, operated with a comprehensive set of planning concerns; hygiene, commerce, history, and traffic were methodically combined into a single framework. The problem was not talent; French architects and planners had many successes to their credit, though unfortunately not in France. Most notable among these men of vision were Prost, Jaussely, and Benard. Prost's plan for Anvers included considerations of zoning, hygiene, and circulation planning. Prost surpassed the Germans in his typically French sensitivity to local subtleties. His plan for Anvers was remarkable in its skillful combination of the city's older urban fabric with new suburban growth. Other examples of French successes abroad were the plans for Adelaide, Buenos Aires, Guayaquil, and Berkeley.[35] De Souza looked to the colonies as offering the greatest field for experimentation and embodying hope for planning: "In the colonial lands especially, the very old and the very new, outside of all civilization, or in conflict with our own by reason of its overly archaic and inassimilable civilization, it is the only solution that will satisfy both modern progress and the picturesque."[36] This grouping of the picturesque, progress, and civilization as the constituent elements of modernity was characteristic of these Beaux-Arts reformers.

The term "plan" remained a catch-all. Until 1918, in the legislative debates "plan" and "program" were used interchangeably. Augustin Rey proposed a distinction between the "program," restricted to preliminary study of the empirical variables (physical site, climate, and social and economic variables), and the "plan" which incorporated them.[37] Agache, Aubertin, and Redont described the program as a guide which introduced the directing principles of the plan, setting forth certain broad parameters and options. Although the idea of the plan paid lip service to change, the conception of change was essentially quantitative, i.e., more of the same. Planning amounted to increased efficiency and a more rational distribution of elements; planning remained basically a symbol of a new social order.

Not a Style but a Social Art

While later modernists valorized style (the distinctive mark of architectural genius) per se, for these reformers style was a tool useful in attaining other ends. Style was an element of the environment in two senses: it was the product of the historical and natural milieu, and it was a tool to be used in modifying that milieu. Although in the Musée Social catechism science and art were always paired, the aesthetic problem had been posed in basically architectural terms, as the distribution of elements within a plan. Questions of architectural style were rarely addressed directly.[38] During the campaign for planning laws, the Musée Social endorsed regional styles, for public as well as for individual buildings: "Out of respect for the traditional physiognomy of our cities and villages, we propose that municipal edifices be conceived with a character appropriate to the region."[39] Cities had to be agreeable for all: aesthetic harmony was not a luxury but a public right.

Léon Rosenthal, a socialist associated with the Musée Social and art critic of L'Humanité, offered one of the most comprehensive presentations of this aesthetic position.[40] Rosenthal dedicated his book to Roger Marx, the author of L'Art social and champion of the renewal of French minor and decorative arts.[41] Rosenthal's book was a kind of primer, methodically rehearsing Musée Social doctrine in each chapter and supplemented with a concise bibliography. The first reference was to Buls' Esthétique des villes, followed by references to the work of

Vidal de la Blache, Jean Brunhes, Louis Bonnier, and Marcel Poëte (the latter being associated with the creation of the Institut d'Histoire, de Géographie et d'Economie Urbaines).[42] Rosenthal criticized the plan/decor which sought to "compose or disengage decors, to view cities as abstractions, indifferent milieus'upon which one can act according to whim."[43] For Rosenthal, modern city planning was "un instrument de vie totale" (an instrument for the whole of life), originating with and returning to historical and social elements. Style could not be isolated from the geographical, historical, and social milieux in which it was meant to function. Although he repeatedly criticized the sterile repetition of older forms, Rosenthal was not calling for a modernist break with the past but only for a more judicious balancing of style and setting.

Rosenthal was optimistic that the postwar reconstruction effort would provide the opportunity for a renewal of French architecture. Necessary economizing would reduce the French tendency toward grandiosity and pomp and instill a new functionalism. Architects would be forced to think first of local materials and modern innovations such as reinforced concrete before importing marble. The same balance should apply to preservation; buildings should not be preserved merely because they were old. If they were unhealthy, dangerous, or ugly, there was no reason not to destroy them. Drawing on Vidal, Rosenthal identified the region as a source of style, reminding his audience that regions were living unities, changing through time. While favoring the diversity and specificity of regional styles, Rosenthal underlined that such styles were products of complex historical interactions of milieu and form. Blind loyalty to regional types only propagated pastiche. Styles emerged from intelligent use of local materials and skills; because of the historical sedimentation they embodied, they remained generally preferable to foreign styles. True regionalism was not backward-looking nostalgia; it was based on a rational appreciation and contemporary evaluation of the historical and social elements of the milieu.

Modern life posed new challenges. Democracy demanded new social spaces to encourage athletic, educational, musical, and scientific associations. The architect had to learn to create new types—hospitals, museums, public meeting halls, and train stations—to meet scientific advances and new social needs. The department store offered a great challenge to architects, as did the factory; modern life also called for a redesign of boutiques, bakeries, and butcher shops. Types had to be reintegrated into the local milieu as well as modernized. Rosenthal criticized the design of post offices and schools by Parisian architects who had never visited the towns in which these structures would be placed. Before intervening, a good architect ought to live in the city, walk its streets, use its services, and talk to its people. Modern times had special needs: "A renewed action, a virile will, and a reflective spirit will be necessary everywhere. Resuscitated cities must become perfect instruments, adapted to all of life's needs."[44]

Techno-Cosmopolitanism:
Governing Morocco

In Morocco, Lyautey and his team sought and partially achieved the latitude to expropriate property, levy taxes, and coordinate land-use policies which proponents of "enlightened, neo-conservative" Musée-Social urbanism were vainly advocating in France. It was in Morocco, under Lyautey's leadership, that France's first comprehensive experiments in urban planning took place. While sharing the Musée Social's social paternalism, Lyautey looked to a complex juxtaposition of modern city planning with traditional Moroccan cities and their inherent social hierarchies (both encompassed by a national strategy of development) as the social field within which a controlled diversity might be constructed and regulated. With the socialists, Lyautey was outraged by uncontrolled speculation and felt the need for regional coordination of services; he also concurred that local communities should serve as social anchors for national policies concerning social needs. He also adopted such innovative technical proposals as the expropriation scheme Maurice Halbwachs prepared for the socialist party. The rest of Lyautey's politics and outlook differed dramatically from those of the socialists.

The protectorate form (like paternalism) employs a rhetoric of cooperation, progress, and mutual accommodation. Lyautey pushed this form further than most. But he was not ready to face the question posed about his policies by a professor at the University of California at Berkeley in 1933: "What does happen when superiority is not sufficiently recognized, and what would happen should it disappear through the success of European tutelage?"[1] The colonial situation was characterized by a false *fraternité*, the denial of *egalité* (in the sense of advancement through merit) due to French defense of national interests as well as to Moroccan elites who made no pretense to equality with their countrymen, and the absence of *liberté*, when neither French nor Moroccans had a right to any real political participation in deciding their fates. Under such conditions (and these were the ones that existed), a protectorate shifts from being an idea of government and becomes a device appropriately analyzed as a social technology.

Nonetheless, Lyautey did prose the problem of what norms and what forms of difference could coexist in the modern world. His search for a form within which the "spectacle of a congregation of humanity where men, so unalike in origins, dress, occupations, and race, continue, without abdicating any of their individual conceptions, their search for a common ideal, a common reason to live" is still valid.[2] Which social, aesthetic, ethical, and political forms could bring modernity and difference into a common frame is a problem, it is worth underlining, which persists today in Morocco, France and elsewhere.

Invasion and Protectorate

After Madagascar, Lyautey had returned (with a promotion) to the boredom of French garrison life. Again frustrated and restless, he activated his Parisian contacts and had Charles Jonnart, Governor General of Algeria, appoint him in 1903 to a delicate command in Ain Sefra, the southern region of Algeria bordering on Morocco. The border skirmishes and mobile tribal factions moving back and forth across the disputed frontiers enmeshed Lyautey and the French in larger contemporary European colonial politics. Without discussing in detail the extraordinarily complex diplomatic and political maneuvers that led to the French conquest of Morocco, suffice it to say that cat-and-mouse games continued throughout the period. Lyautey led his troops in and out of Morocco several times, in clear and conscious violation of international treaties. A series of incidents probably provoked by the French in Casablanca and Marrakech in 1907 were used as excuses to bombard Casablanca. Following these clashes, Lyautey made his first official visit to Morocco in December 1907, when he was sent to inspect the French troops who had landed in Casablanca. With Jonnart he formulated a plan to establish a protectorate in Morocco, thereby settling the Algerian border questions and "completing" the work of French imperialism in North Africa.[3]

During this period Lyautey was consulted on Moroccan policy with some regularity by the reformist-socialist Minister of War, Alexandre Millerand, whose admission to the cabinet had sparked debate and caused division over the relationship of socialism to electoral politics.[4] Poincaré, replacing Caillaux, forced the Moroccan sultan Moulay Hafid to sign a protectorate treaty on March 30, 1912. Under the treaty, France was obliged to appoint not just the head of a military mission but also a resident-general. The majority of the cabinet preferred a civilian appointment. However, with an uprising in Fez, the balance tipped the other way. A meeting of the cabinet was held on April 27. None other than Léon Bourgeois made the crucial arguments for a military appointment. The question was who should fill the position. Millerand succeeded in promoting Lyautey who, at the age of fifty-seven, became the first resident-general of Morocco. He succeeded in driving a column of troops from Algeria to Fez and then into the city itself. Although the military pacification of the tribes would not be completed for another twenty years, the protectorate was in place.

The First World War was an extremely trying period for Lyautey. The Germans (apparently with explicit orders) burned his family chateau in Lorraine, destroying his personal archives as well as the material traces of his "ancestral" ties to Lorraine. His sister's husband was killed early in the war; shortly thereafter, Antonin de Margerie, his closest childhood friend, died prematurely, as did Albert de Mun, with whom Lyautey had reestablished cordial relations. Lyautey was divided in his loyalties and ambitions between assuring the success of the protectorate and returning to France to play a major role in the war. Several of his close colleagues in Morocco had been recalled to France and appointed to high posts. Lyautey knew the protectorate was extremely fragile: the entire central area of Morocco was in rebellion, and the cities could easily join in. While the protectorate offered Lyautey the possibility of a major accomplishment at the end of his career, the real center of military and political action and reward was in Europe. Lyautey was not without his enemies, and Parisian wisdom in the early stages of the war saw that he was kept at a distance, in Morocco. Having no other option, and hoping his time would come, Lyautey assumed a stoic profile.

In Morocco, military pacification of the tribes took center stage. Lyautey's pacification doctrine bore early fruit: from 1912 to 1914 the pacified areas were contained. Large numbers of Moroccan and other colonial troops fought valiantly for the French in Europe. While colonialism had never enjoyed wide public support in France, the troops' loyalty played a significant role in improving the image of the colonies after the war. Lyautey organized a series of expositions in Morocco to stimulate the economy as well as to promote confidence in French Morocco's future. Biographers like Le Révérend breathlessly recount the effect these fairs supposedly had on the Moroccans; in June 1915, a rebel chief in the north agreed to surrender if he was authorized to visit the fair in Casablanca. Lyautey, as was his practice, received him publicly with full honors. This honorable surrender (Lyautey had learned from Gallieni how to stage such surrenders) no doubt explained the incident more than the chief's purported fascination with modern tractors. It is worth noting the increasing skill with which Lyautey used modern publicity techniques as political tools to mold French opinion.

From the beginning, Lyautey's relationship with the colon community in Morocco was strained. The French press in Algeria, judging him too sympathetic to the Muslims, had vigorously campaigned against him. Newspaper charges of his homosexuality corresponded with his marriage to the wife of a colonel killed in the war, who played an active and visible role in assisting him in social welfare affairs. From the outset, Lyautey alienated the local French press in Morocco by opposing the entry of large numbers of agricultural colons, fearing their effect on racial relations: "As much as I can rely on certain industrialists and merchants, certain of my agricultural colonists have the mentality of wild beasts."[5] His views of the former, however, were significantly less glowing when it came to land speculation in Casablanca. Lyautey's choice of Rabat over Casablanca as the French capital was directly related to the strength of these same industrial and commercial interests in Casablanca. Lyautey wanted a colony he could run on his own terms.

Throughout his career Lyautey was certain that the arts of government he deployed in the colonies were also applicable in France. He dreamt of leading a centralized, rationalized, and authoritarian war government, engaging all three estates, of "all of the vital forces of the nation for the war effort: infrastructures, materials, factories, harvests, new army recruits, finances, foreign propaganda, all forward looking."[6] Lyautey repeatedly contrasted his vision of a self-sacrificing, elite, team effort with the bickering, indecision, and pettiness which he and many of his generation, on the left as well as the right, saw as the essence of the parliamentary regime.

On December 10, 1916 Lyautey received the telegram for which he had been restlessly waiting, offering him the post of Minister of War. If he accepted, what would be the consequences for Morocco? The message came from Aristide Briand. Overjoyed, Lyautey telegraphed back a conditional acceptance, learning immediately via the press that his appointment had already been announced. He also learned that the Ministry of War had been divided into three parts—war, transport and supplies, and arms production—without his consultation. Lyautey was assured that the three sections would remain under his authority. Lyautey maintained untroubled relations with Albert Thomas and his team of socialists in the arms production section; his major disagreements were with the military. Lyautey arrived in Paris on December 22 to find Joffre dismissed as head of the general staff and replaced by General Nivelle, who had already drawn up an ambitious (and catastrophic) plan for a renewed offensive strategy. The trap was clear; Lyautey was merely to mask the plans of others. On March 14, 1917 he fell into another ambush, clumsily and indignantly refusing to answer parliamentary questions on his plans for aviation on the grounds that information had consistently leaked to the Germans. In a stormy parliamentary session he was accused of preparing a dictatorship. After eleven weeks of his ministry, lacking support as well as the skills necessary for Parisian struggles, Lyautey resigned. When Nivelle's plans proved disastrous, Clemenceau was called to head a government instituting the coordination of powers Lyautey had proposed. After two months of recuperation in Vichy, Lyautey returned in May 1917 to his post in Morocco, which he held for eight years before being deposed by none other than Marshal Pétain.

From the Classical Self to the Modern Subject

Lyautey returned to the question of social hierarchy time and time again during his life. The problem had three aspects for him: the identification of an elite, the problem of form, and the valorization of social difference. Although Lyautey had identified the problem of modern elites as early as 1891 in his article on the "Rôle Social de l'Officier," it was only during the Moroccan period that he began to employ the term "aristocracy" with any consistency. During periods of stagnancy and personal doubt, he indulged in fabricating an aristocratic genealogy for himself. To prove his royal blood, he traced his maternal line back twenty-two generations to Saint Louis. This attachment to the symbolism of bloodlines was deep in him. At other times, Lyautey knew that blood as a principle of legitimation for a modern elite was, at the very best, a dubious fiction which he manipulated to serve his own ends. His criticism of the aristocratic officer corps and its bourgeois imitators was too merciless to permit lapsing permanently into these reveries.

Lyautey knew that merit was the only source of legitimacy for an elite in the modern world. But how could one identify this elite, and how could it be reconciled with modern democracy? Speaking to an association of students, Lyautey struggled to define the modern elite so as to correspond with an aristocracy: "*Aristocrat* comes from the word *aristoi-krates,* which doesn't mean the 'nobles' in the sense of a caste, but the best, the elite.

Krates means power. Therefore, *aristoi-krates* means power exercised by the best, from above."[7] Written in 1930, the almost parenthetical "from above" revealed his abandonment of even the vestiges of democratic political participation. Rejecting equality, Lyautey substituted a paternalistic *démo-philie:* "I love the people, among whom I live. But if I love with all my heart, it is as a protector (*patron*) and not a democrat."[8] In 1920, at the height of his Moroccan experience, but following his disastrous experiences in the French Ministry, Lyautey wrote to his friend Paul Desjardins, "I have the dogma of social hierarchies in my blood, and all of my life, all of the practices of government have duly strengthened these sentiments in me."[9] Such common goals of health, vitality, justice, and beauty could only be actualized through a social hierarchy guided by an elite.

Le Révérend presents an anecdotal explanation of Lyautey's stubborn opposition to representative democracy: Lyautey's long absences from France. A stronger case lies in the problem of norms and forms. Lyautey's principle of legitimacy was still based on connecting virtuous character with social forms through which this virtue could be actualized. Lyautey was still playing on the registers of representation and character, attempting to provide an anchor for modern society. One of Lyautey's close collaborators in Morocco, George Hardy (a geographer and head of the protectorate's educational services), was at pains to distinguish Lyautey from Barrès. Hardy maintained that although their language at times sounded familiar, their attitudes were profoundly different. Barrès's traditionalism concealed resignation; Lyautey respected tradition but was totally opposed to such backward-looking, nostalgic resignation. Conservatism for Lyautey required incessant action.[10] Lyautey was not ready to take the next step, to cross the threshold into full-blown modernism: from an elite legitimated by character (ethical superiority, service, and discipline) to one based on purely technical qualifications. Lyautey's team, motivated by a dynamic *esprit de corps,* was not yet a technocracy.[11]

Lyautey was generally lucid about the fictional and rhetorical character of genealogical exercises. During the latter part of his life he understood the symbolic importance of his aristocratic fiction and its function in modern society, hence the importance this aristocratic discourse assumed in the biographies he commissioned. When he told his most important biographer—André Maurois—"you have invented me," he neglected to add (though certainly understood) that he had long since mastered the task. Throughout the course of his life Lyautey was self-conscious about his style, holding that "Form is a clear sign of character; appearance reflects intellectual and moral breeding."[12] Lyautey's self-invention was based on rigorous self-discipline and on carefully staged public appearances. Like Baudelaire, Lyautey was a dandy, maintaining a personal and social elegance amid the banalities of modern life. He understood that his persona was more than personal; it was an important component of the social arts of government.

His *mise-en-forme* (fashioning) of all aspects of life—from his dress, to his marriage, to his home, to his team, to the architectural forms of the protectorate—was orchestrated with increasing agility and desperation. Lyautey had integrated a theatricality of self, work, authority, and order into his political strategy. By the time he arrived to take command of Morocco, this modern theater was part of his program. His restless attention to all details of the protectorate, from his own demeanor to the form of the cities, was more than a quirk of personality. The milieu was no neutral backdrop; it was the semantically rich product of history. Giving the protectorate a visible form was a political task of the first rank. The reconstitution of Morocco's architectural patrimony (for example, the preservation of the *décor artistique*) was more than a question of attracting tourists (although the economic and political interest in tourism was considered). Lyautey believed, in a last whisper of the Baroque, that appearance was at least functionally equivalent to being. Reconstruction was thus an essential component of pacification, including the pacification of the French.[13]

Lyautey's vision of political order turned on the perpetual manipulation of appearance before an audience both Moroccan and French. It was, in fact, Lyautey's bulwark against direct political participation on the part of either population. The protectorate form justified prohibiting the hated French parliamentarianism. Writing to Jonnart, the former Governor General of Algeria, Lyautey vented his spleen against the French:

Depraved and blind to the true meaning of the Protectorate, to the legitimate rights of the natives, the colonists claim for themselves all the rights of Frenchmen, behaving as conquerors in a conquered land, disdaining the laws and institutions of a people which exists, owns, keeps accounts, which wants to live and which does not intend to let itself be despoiled or enslaved. This becomes evident in the violence and animal belligerence characteristic of the French electorate; the result is an asphyxiating atmosphere.[14]

Lyautey denied the French political participation by defending the Moroccans; he defended the lack of Moroccan participation by invoking his respect for the hierarchical character of their institutions.

The society Lyautey sought to create, the society he hoped would spring to life in his new cities, was doubly hierarchical. Moroccan society exhibited a viable hierarchy: the requisite social forms existed, as did the range of virtues necessary to activate them. During the course of Moroccan history, an order had gradually defined social and spatial forms. Lyautey's adherence to the protectorate form (rather than to a doctrine of assimilative colonization) derived from this evaluation; the task consisted in identifying and strengthening these existing social forms and practices. He laid down the following imperatives: "Vex not tradition, leave custom be. Never forget that in every society there is a class to be governed, and a natural-born ruling class upon whom all depends. Link their interests to ours."[15] It was time to introduce a technical modernity, with its advantages of hygiene and science, so as to reawaken Morocco's dormant energies without destroying its social forms.

This rhetoric of tradition was part wish-fulfillment, part strategy, and part rhetoric—meant to move an audience—and must not be taken too literally. Lyautey was in no position to adopt a contemplative Orientalism; he was no Pierre Loti in uniform.[16] Lyautey was a conservative and not a reactionary; he knew perfectly well that Morocco was undergoing an inexorable process of change. The challenge was to find forms that would preserve social hierarchy and its associated character structure through the coming turbulence. Lyautey's strategy was to renovate Moroccan society by transforming its elite. The problem lay not in identifying this elite but in finding French agents with sufficient knowledge of the country and the requisite character to orchestrate a direct, but highly formal, modernization of the Moroccan nobility (who would then guide the rest of society): "It is through this agent, in continual contact with the native chief, that the chief's horizons will gradually broaden, and, through him, that of the people; it is through the agent's efforts that we will implant, little by little, our ideas of justice, humanity and progress."[17] For Lyautey the thorny problem was the social practices and the character of the French. He frequently combined a rhetoric of despair with the French with one of indulgence for the Moroccans: "I have come out of this with an unspeakable contempt for my compatriots. I no longer work for any other cause than that of rationality and history, for Morocco in itself—and also for dear Muslim Morocco which has preserved all the traditions which I respect, all of the social ideas I share."[18]

What form could a modern hierarchy take? Lyautey's program of building the *villes nouvelles* adjacent to Morocco's older cities maintained Moroccan cities close to, but separate from, modern French settlements. Neither the norms nor the forms involved in this strategy were universals. As Lyautey's head of education put it, the French task in Morocco "should not in any way be confused with this 'civilizing mission.' "[19] The theatricality of tradition, it was hoped, would present a constant social and moral stage to the French. If there was a civilizing mission, its target was the French. The problem was embodying the norms of science and art while creating an environment in which politics would not destroy the possibility of social hierarchy. At the heart of Lyautey's strategy was the problem of how to govern this doubly hierarchical situation. Precautions had to be taken: "There are two kinds of people from whom I wish at all cost to protect Morocco: the expropriators and the missionaries."[20] If these groups were excluded, a well-tempered modernity would have a chance of success. While the two solutions were different, their association, Lyautey dreamed, would be complementary.

Leaving aside the fictive Moroccan society Lyautey's discourse projected, a question remains: What would a modernized Moroccan society look like? Lyautey has been appropriately criticized for his limited provision of modern public facilities for the Moroccans (schools, adequate health facilities, and representative institutions), and such criticism is valid. Whatever credibility this form of government had under Lyautey, under his successors it was little more than a facade masking non-action, neglect, and inequality. As Jacques Berque has pointed out, the discrepancy between the money spent on the old and new cities was immense.[21] Between 1912 and 1924, 36.5 kilometers of sewers were built in the new cities of Casablanca, Fez, and Rabat, while only 4.3 kilometers were built in the older sections of the same cities.[22] But the most telling flaw was the static conception of the space allotted to the Moroccans. Despite all the rhetoric of modernization, no provisions for growth or change were made.

Lest our anti-colonial hindsight become too sanctimonious, Daniel Rivet, in his monumental thesis on Lyautey in Morocco, documents the strong preference of Moroccan "notables" for a sanctuary away from the impure space of the Christian invaders. Such preferences were transmitted to Lyautey, who was all too eager to comply. He prohibited Europeans from entering mosques, a statute or custom which had not previously existed in either Morocco or Algeria. Further, it should not be forgotten that the spatial segregation of populations by religion was a central component of traditional Moroccan urban space. In addition to the desire of the Muslim elite to live apart from the Christian invaders, and the fact that many rural migrants found recognizable social networks already in place, a revealing bit of data indicates how Moroccans of the period viewed the twin-city ideal. The *Jeunes Marocains*, the sons of the notables toward whom Lyautey directed his policies, penned the first "Plan de Réformes Marocaines," denouncing the favoritism shown to the French but not criticizing the system of dual cities. In fact, the two types of *citadinité* coexisted until the Second

World War.[23] When opposition to the protectorate exploded in the 1950s, its arena was the streets and large avenues of all the cities, old and new.

Social City

French colonial cities, especially in Algeria, were constructed by army engineers trained at the Ecole Polytechnique or the Ecole des Ponts et Chaussées. The design of governmental buildings in these cities was assigned to prize-winning architects from the Ecole des Beaux-Arts, chosen by means of competitions held in France, who usually had never visited the actual cities. To Lyautey, these bureaucratic cities designed by military engineers combined the worst aspects of French administration; at every level, they were petty, ugly, ill-managed, unhygienic, and contributed to the social, aesthetic, and political ills plaguing France. In Morocco, Lyautey would show how things could be done differently.

Lyautey chose Henri Prost to be the head of urbanism in Morocco. According to legend, Lyautey greeted Prost at the port in Casablanca in December 1913 with the broad outlines of a program: (1) preservation, to show respect for the artistic and social integrity of Moroccan cities, and (2) application of modern principles of urbanism in an ambitious program of constructing *villes nouvelles* (new cities), as distinguished from existing unhealthy and chaotic European cities. Lyautey attempted to attract as many architects to Morocco as quickly as he could. Fortunately for his plans, there seem to have been quite a few talented who had been wounded early in the war. Jean Marrast, one of Prost's assistants, has said that in 1918, when the Americans actively entered the war, Lyautey gave orders to speed up public-works projects and to begin others as soon as possible: "It was the counterattack of the construction sites."[24]

Lyautey's strategy emphasized the necessity of reorganizing power relations among social groups. In his view, social transformation could only be achieved through large-scale social planning, in which city planning played a central role. Lyautey later praised Prost in grandiloquent terms: "The art and science of urbanism, so flourishing during the Classical Age, seems to have suffered a total eclipse since the Second Empire. Urbanism: the art and science of developing human agglomerations, under Prost's hand is coming back to life. Prost is the guardian, in this mechanical age, of humanism. Prost worked not only on things but on men, different types of men, to whom *la Cité* owes something more than roads, canals, sewers and a transport system."[25] For Lyautey and his architects, then, the new humanism applied not only to things but to men, and not only to men in the abstract—this was neither high modernism nor Le Corbusier's humanism—but to men in different, specific social circumstances. The problem was to orchestrate this diversity, to conceive of and produce a new, modern social *ordonnance.*

For Lyautey, Algeria was the negative example of how to run a colony. He abhorred—for political, social, and ethical reasons—the values of the European colony, its racism, insularity, and rapaciousness. He saw the roots of these values in the structure of the colonial situation and in French society; both had to be radically altered if either were to survive in the modern world. For Lyautey the enemies were both the revolutionaries on the left and the bourgeoisie on the right, with its interest groups, short-sightedness, and impotent parliamentarianism. A new political, social, and spiritual system had to be found for France. The colonies constituted a laboratory of experimentation for new arts of government capable of bringing a modern and healthy society into being.

The group who would guide these efforts were men of art and science. Lyautey sought a new administrative elite, above politics and concerned only with the long-range public good. As a leading architect, Albert Laprade, put it: "we had the sentiment of belonging to a great century; returning to France we had, like so many others, a certain melancholy. In Morocco we found a lively public passion, a collective faith: in France discouragement, triumphant mediocracy, tyrannical jealousy, a sense of defeat and fatalism, no leaders with a great vision of the collective potential of modern will and technical competence."[26] These men, like so many others in the twentieth century, were trying to escape from politics. This did not mean, however, that they were unconcerned with power relationships.

Lyautey formulated his social mission as follows: "to rip France from its current decomposition and ruin, through a violent reaction to its practices [*moeurs*], its inertias, its complacencies, by forming a more and more numerous group of the strong, unself-interested initiators, those who view things from on high."[27] The agenda called for the invention of new forms of governmentality through which to reshape the fatally decadent and individualistic tendencies of the French. This was why the cities of Morocco were of such importance in Lyautey's eyes; they offered a way to avoid the impasses both of the metropole and of Algeria. Lyautey's famous dictum—"a construction site is worth a battalion"—was meant literally. Lyautey feared that if the French were allowed to continue practicing politics as usual, the results would be catastrophic. A directly political solution, however, was not at hand. What was urgently required was a new scientific and strategic social art; only in this way could politics be sublated—and power truly ordered.

The Most Modern Legislation

In April 1914, the first comprehensive urban-planning legislation in the French world, containing all the basic principles of Musée Social urbanism, was decreed in Morocco. It differed in two distinct ways from the French planning laws eventually passed after the First World War. The first was its principle of separating native cities from new cities (although variants of class and historical separation had been included in Musée Social discussions). The second was its means of implementing the legislation: by decree, not parliamentary legislation (resulting in massive and rapid expropriation); and by combining local responsibility for implementation with a limitation of local rights. The law included a vast number of regulations stipulating the width of streets, alignment of buildings, the height and construction of buildings, and architectural standards concerning color, style, and so on. A second law passed six months later gave the Protectorate extensive rights to install a technical infrastructure ensuring hygiene and services. A third law proposed property-holders' associations in each quarter, with joint responsibility for meeting zoning and architectural requirements. The government retained the right to substitute other land for that which it expropriated for large projects. All Moroccan cities were required to produce a *Plan Directeur*. None of these laws existed in France.

All cities were to be planned, ensuring control over future growth. In order to control speculation, once a plan (for an entire city and its quarters) was established, it was to be made public; during a one month period objections could be registered. After this short delay, a decree would be passed legalizing the plan. The scope and authority of each plan was total; its "public utility" clause was comprehensive. Everything falling within its boundaries was required to meet modern standards, even when these were not detailed in the planning document itself. For example, although the plan only specified the major road system, all the minor roads had to meet the code. Building permits were granted only if plans met the most rigorous water, sewage, and aesthetic standards. Strict regulations concerning architectural style in both the *villes nouvelles* and the medinas were defined. These last considerations were absent from French planning laws even after World War I.

Hubert de la Casinière, head of the Service du Contrôle des Municipalités du Maroc, argued that, lacking any means of implementation, the French urban-planning legislation had remained entirely Platonic; he boasted that in Morocco, where the administration was unconstrained by electoral contingencies, it would be possible to take action. In Morocco the task was not to invent principles but to apply them efficiently and comprehensively. The main obstacle to achieving this goal was private property, which was to be controlled by means of administrative decrees in the name of the public interest. Lyautey was not restrained by a constitution, a parliament, or a Conseil d'Etat. Only in Morocco were the conditions of authority such that private interests could never block a project serving the public good; the Moroccan municipal legislation gave the administration almost total latitude. De la Casinière bluntly, if defensively, asserted that only in such a regime could such dramatic progress have been made in so short a time.

Special expropriation legislation was passed on August 31, 1914, permitting expropriation by zones; not only the buildings

immediately concerned but all those in the zone could be expropriated either to prevent speculation or to ensure health or
aesthetic qualities. Power to expropriate property for the public
good, to control speculation, and to retain for the collectivity
profits from improvements was granted. Zoning by function
was mandated (including extensive powers to establish no-
building zones). Property values were to be fixed previous to
the publication of the plan. Expropriation procedures differed
from those in France; instead of letting a jury of peers decide
on the level of indemnification, this power was given to a judge,
as was the power to declare negative indemnifications if other
profits accrued to the owner from the planning improvements.
De la Casinière cited, as an example of the efficiency of the
Moroccan legislation, the construction in 1922 of the boulevard
of the 4e Zouaves in Casablanca. In Prost's plan, this boulevard
constituted the major axis of downtown Casablanca, linking the
port and a proposed central Place de France by means of a
broad avenue. However, part of the proposed avenue (a symbol
of modernity linking commerce and industry as well as marking entry into Casablanca) was already lined with a variety of
Moroccan buildings. In France, negotiations with individual
owners would have dragged on for years; in Morocco, Lyautey
applied the expropriation powers, and within four months the
boulevard was under construction. The procedures were both
authoritarian and effective.

A royal decree or *Dahir* of August 12, 1913 called for imma-
triculation of land in accordance with the Australian Torrens
Act (a model long advocated by the Musée Social), which required all land to be registered, all deeds established, and the
rights and obligations of both the administration and local
landowners specified. This decree brought all urban land
under the French property system and was the subject of all the
predictable abuses.[28] Provisions were made for land to be expropriated for public purposes, with the profits from the sale of
the land to be used to pay for site improvements (roads, lighting, water, and drains). This was essentially the procedure advocated by Halbwachs and his socialist allies in the *Cahiers du
Socialiste*, which had been consistently opposed in France.

Following an idea proposed by the Musée Social, a law of November 10, 1917 established and assigned broad powers and duties to local property holders' associations. These associations were granted the power to redistribute property to meet the requirements of local plans. In effect, this provision meant that at least temporarily all the property within each jurisdiction was treated legally as if it were communally owned. For example, if the plan called for a road to be cut through its quarter, an association was required to draw up a plan for indemnification of its members. The government provided a technical specialist to assist them. The association did not have the power to block the proposed project; its rights were limited to the discussion of indemnities. Only fully registered properties were protected, forcing compliance with the decree. This provision opened the door to significant abuse, particularly concerning the rights of Moroccan property holders. The first test of these provisions, carried out in Casablanca, revealed some shortcomings, and the first modification was to divide the city into neighborhoods. The initial application seems to have been mechanical, not taking into account the differences in value of different buildings (i.e., that corner buildings were better business locations). A formula was devised to rectify this: more technical aid was recommended and in certain instances more generous indemnification. Political complaints were simply recast as technical problems: changes were made to perfect the technical components so as to undercut the charges of arbitrariness while not deviating from the principles of comprehensive planning and obligatory local participation in the plan.

Hubert de la Casinière defended the separation of quarters on hygienic terms: the habits of the lower classes propagated epidemics.[29] Islamic fatalism, he continued, insured that pre-Protectorate Morocco had no notion of public health. Hence the priority given to the political and humanitarian work of French hygienists. As early as November 1912, Lyautey created municipal hygiene bureaus. In 1915 additional legislation was passed; its comprehensive goals included fighting epidemics and contagious diseases, collecting sanitary and health statistics, enforcing housing and urban-hygiene provisions (particularly for industrial settings), providing medical assistance and food, and surveilling prostitutes. Individuals violating hygienic principles were held legally responsible for the charges necessitated to correct the abuses. To avoid epidemics, further statutes gave the municipality practically unlimited powers of entry into houses, and of prescribing mandatory rectifications. A principle of "public responsibility" was invented and enforced. The goal, de la Casinière insisted, was not segregation for its own sake. He criticized plans—in Fez and Meknes—in which the new city and the medina were spatially separated by too great a distance, requiring expensive transportation networks to link the two populations.

Guillaume de Tarde, another urbanist, attempted to defend Lyautey's policy as one of degree: "Separation, yes, but not radical separation. This is not a kind of contemptuous attitude toward the native city (an attitude which I think is the English approach)."[30] When the main function of separation of populations was surveillance and domination, the principle became nefarious. The English model of separation only reinforced a dangerous paucity of social contacts. Upon reading Kipling, de Tarde realized that British colonialism was essentially a "structure of police intelligence." If the British citizen wanted distance, and therefore required police information, the Frenchman "loved the excitement of social life, thanks to which he knows what's going on."[31] European cities should be built close enough for contact, but not so close as to absorb the native city. Deciding how this should be accomplished required the art of the urbanist, who was called upon to integrate adroitly local social realities in a successful plan.

Islands of Modern Civilization

Lyautey's urbanism set ambitious goals. The proposed responsibilities of municipal administration extended to "the organization of agglomerated social life."[32] The task, reminiscent of that of eighteenth-century police, was particularly challenging in a new city with no history, customs, or social practices. De la Casinière performed a discursive ground-clearing operation. First, he made clear the differences between Moroccan and

French history. Previously Moroccan administration had been bereft of administrative tools for hygiene and other essential municipal services. To the extent that these services had been provided, it had been done by the *habous* or charitable religious foundation. Municipal administration had no control over its own resources; its inability to plan marked its archaism. The egregious "Orientalist" insistence on Morocco's supposedly isolated and static history was shared by all the Moroccan planners from Prost through the Le Corbusian Michel Ecochard.

If the Moroccans had shown themselves incapable of inventing the administrative and scientific tools of modern municipal life, an opposite threat to modernity was posed by Europeans who flocked to Morocco to make their fortune. Casablanca was portrayed by the planners as suffering from the California or Wild-West syndrome: each boat brought "those undesirables down to new countries where everything remains to be done."[33] The "anarchy" produced by these people demanded mobilizing science and art to regularize the situation.

It also apparently demanded the elimination of representative political institutions. The strategy was control from above, legitimate as a means of ensuring the common good. While de la Casinière juxtaposed the archaism of Moroccan administration with the modernity of French planners, the key distinction in municipal legislation was between truly modern legislation and the sclerotic institutions of France. France's elected municipal councils—in the eyes of de la Casinière a paralyzed and confused mixture of political assemblies and bureaucrats—had too often posed obstacles. Imitating the French model was not the path to efficient, modern rule: "It would be a mistake to try to transplant the organs of an old society into a new country."[34] The goal was to create "isles of modern civilization." For Lyautey and his team, this meant exploiting the latest physical and social technology and avoiding politics. It has been pointed out that the characteristic feature of the protectorate system was the desire to erase the line between executive and legislative (not to mention parliamentary) powers.[35] This temptation, as we shall see, spanned the political spectrum, albeit with differing degrees of regret over the price to be paid.

Rabat: Capital

During the course of 1913, with the military situation still very much in question, Lyautey debated the choice of the capital city, pondering the relative advantages and disadvantages of Fez, Rabat, and Casablanca. Although he chose Rabat, he was adamant that no single city should dominate the country. The royal city of Fez with its cultivated bourgeoisie, merchants, and scholars would continue to play an important economic and cultural role, as would Casablanca, designated Morocco's economic capital. Lyautey intended to link these cities in a functional, national network. Rabat would be "the factory headquarters. The first condition of operation for any enterprise is that its nerve centers function freely, that management [*la direction*], whether it be of a factory, a trading company, or an army headquarters, be installed under the best possible conditions and that all the elements be organized in close proximity."[36]

In October 1912 a state architect named Petit was sent out from Algiers to sketch a plan for Rabat. Lyautey was furious: Petit's circulation plan was thoroughly inadequate; his scheme provided no control over speculation or building styles. By the end of 1913 the military situation was sufficiently under control (at least on the coast) for Lyautey to turn his attention to planning matters. Urging "a well-ordered, logical city plan, adapted to local conditions," Lyautey turned to Prost.[37] Prost recounts how the discussions of the plans became "political and technical councils, gathered together under the chairmanship of the Résident Général, engaging central and local civil services, engineers, architects and doctors, and anyone whose personal experiences were liable to shed light on the many issues at hand."[38] The social ambience of the plan's production, although mentioned in almost every participant's memoirs, has not been commented on by historians. Lyautey was highly conscious of orchestrating pressure and sociality. Anyone who doubted the value of the effort would not last long under these circumstances. A group élan and mutual investment in the overall result were Lyautey's means of avoiding the despised bureaucratic mentality of France.[39]

Distribution of Functions, Theater of Limits

The sense of urgency was counterbalanced by an awareness of the need for technically proficient preparation. It was essential to remap the terrain topographically before preparing alignment plans for each quarter and the decrees implementing those plans. The recruitment and training of specialized personnel to implement the plans caused delays, as did fiscal constraints. The basic plan was not implemented until 1924 and more or less completed by 1930. This delay encouraged speculation in Rabat and in similar situations elsewhere.[40] The most modern construction standards were imposed; height of buildings was determined by the width of avenues; open space and views from the buildings were fixed; and, above all, zoning was specified in detail. Rabat was to be linked with Casablanca (and other cities) on several levels, one of which was a national network of roads connected to the internal circulation pattern of each city. A modern rail system was planned and embedded in the city's structure.

The main administrative area was located away from the sea, running between the walls of the old medina and the sultan's palace. The European commercial district was set on largely undeveloped land in the triangle between the old medina, the sultan's palace, and the future headquarters of the resident-general. A military quarter was planned but not built; an industrial zone and further residential zones were planned and eventually realized. Circulation between these zones was organized around two perpendicular systems of roads. The first was a continuation of the road linking Casablanca and Fez, which bifurcated as it entered the Western section of the new city, with one part continuing along the outside of the medina and the other leading up to the imperial palace. The second system was composed along a north-south axis linking the old medina to the residence and the palace.

Prost included a system of parks and public gardens absent in Casablanca.[41] Lyautey sought efficiency and beauty: "You will arrange this busy hive in such a way as to avoid making barracks. It should be attractive and cheerful; no enormous constructions, but, as much as possible, pavilions swimming in greenery, conveniently linked by arcades or pergolas."[42] The main avenue of the city was planned to contain all the major services (including an underground railroad station). Prost, perhaps inspired by Garnier, built an underground system of tracks leading to the rail station. This administrative core was to be a center of circulation in all senses of the term. Stylistic control was rigorous but inventive: conceived to facilitate communication among government services and to permit expansion, it included an extensive arcade punctuated by gardens, kiosks, fountains, and pergolas, so as to create a calm and intimate atmosphere for administrative activity. An architectural critic hostile to the political dimensions of Prost's project described the work as enormously refined, saying that Prost's office arrangements could be taken as models for the modern city.[43]

Prost's plan envisioned an eventual population of 50,000 Europeans. The European presence in Rabat grew largely as a function of the Protectorate's administrative services, and hence was easier to regulate than that of Casablanca. The area planned for the European city was ten times that of the medina; European quarters surrounded the medina, prohibiting its expansion. This was one of Prost's major mistakes, as it ensured eventual overcrowding in the medina.[44] Although neglected, the medina was not left unaltered. Its major thoroughfares were paved to facilitate the movement of goods, as well as for hygienic reasons. A certain amount of embellishment (e.g., tiles around fountains) was undertaken as part of Lyautey's economic and social policy of recreating an urban artisanal class. Stylistic controls were put into effect by means of a *Dahir* of February 13, 1914.[45]

An area of 250 meters around the medina was declared a no-building zone. A triangular park and adjacent cemetery extended the open space. This large area has been described as a *cordon sanitaire*. Indeed, as with Haussmann's avenues, the potential military, police, and circulation functions of such an open area are evident; Prost was continuing a tradition with this spatial arrangement. The slow but sustained move toward separating cultures had already begun in other parts of North Africa. The first urbanist operations in Algeria were motivated primarily by military considerations. Restrictions on building and movement followed directly from these concerns. By mid-century, as the conquest solidified, the desire for wide, densely-planted avenues, grand monuments, hospitals, and other European forms led to new interventions in the older urban fabric. The doctrine of two separate and opposed urban forms had not, however, been formulated, and only came into its own in Tunisia in the 1880s. Administrative services were placed on one side of the old city of Tunis, and the European commercial quarters on the other. There was differentiation but not rupture. It was not until the city plans of 1919 that the separation became official. Although Tunis's urbanist, Valensi, devoted more attention and resources to developing a modern infrastructure for the medina than did Prost, the results were the same: the medina's growth was limited, resulting in overcrowding and museumification.

François Béguin, in a striking turn of phrase, referred to the retention of the walls of Moroccan cities and the large open zones adjoining them as a "theatralization of limits."[46] But one wonders what kind of theater was intended. For authors like Janet Abu-Lughod, Prost's plans were a theater of apartheid. One could just as aptly call this space a theatralization of urban diversity. It served not only as a safety zone and segregative space, but as an intercultural meeting ground where many cafes, small shops, and a bus terminal were located. Over the years the supposed *cordon sanitaire* functioned as one of the more socially active areas of the city. As Halbwachs had proven in Paris, the real actors were social groups who improvised on the script planners and emperors had provided for them. In modern theater, the boundary between the stage, the actors, and the spectators is often blurred.

Monuments

In the early days of the protectorate, French scholars busily conducted detailed archaeological, architectural, and topographic surveys of Morocco before the actual invasion and conquest. As Edmund Burke has shown, the period leading up to conquest was characterized by high-quality research and an impressive objectivity and openness toward Morocco and other Muslim countries.[47] Louis Mercier's description of Rabat at the turn of the century offers a particularly rich example of this type of inquiry.[48] Lyautey proceeded on the assumption that the particularities of each case should guide local policy. Anticipating Clifford Geertz and Edward Said, in 1927 Lyautey argued against attributing a trans-historical, trans-cultural essence to the Orient; there were Moslems, but no "general Islamic experience."[49]

Lyautey fought actively for the preservation of notable buildings. The Service des Beaux-Arts et des Monuments Historiques was created in November 1912, directed by the artist Maurice Tranchant de Lunel. The Service sought to preserve not only individual buildings but an "ensemble of construction."[50] In Rabat the choice of sites to be protected included the Casbah des Oudaia, a walled-off quarter where royal troops had been lodged. The Mosque and Hassan Tower complex, vestige of an immense mosque begun by the Almohade sultan, lay in ruins on an open field. It had been parceled out to individual owners, and someone had even built a tennis court close by. The Service acquired the land, commissioned studies, and saw that the essential reconstruction was accomplished. An area of 50 meters around it was declared a no-building zone, and new buildings in a much larger surrounding area were restricted in height to 8 meters. By strict restoration of the individual buildings and of the site itself, the French turned these "artistic vestiges of a shining civilization" into monuments.[51] The groundwork was laid for tourism, the museumification of Moroccan culture, and a new historical consciousness.

A city-wide policy of architectural control over Moroccan construction was instituted, and was applied also to French construction. The goal was to avoid a pastiche of Algerian "moorish" styles, characterized as "world's fair decor," as well as the individualism of suburban kitsch. The service sought to define a French architecture adapted to Moroccan conditions.[52] Even in Rabat the control achieved was not total. Some of the poorer European quarters were characterized by the *banlieue-de-Paris* eclecticism Prost and Lyautey so detested. It is worth noting that Moroccan Jews and Muslims moved out of the medina and

lived alongside the poorer French in these peripheral quarters.[53] As the major lines of Prost's plan became clear, speculative and uncontrolled building occurred. In 1917 Lyautey used
the construction of a commercial and agricultural fair (adjacent
to the palace) and a tramline built to transport visitors as a
means of developing a whole new quarter, as well as of orienting construction along the stylistic lines he valued. He succeeded in creating a large park and university buildings and in
defining the quarter as a choice location for luxurious villas.
Wealthy Moroccans hired Lyautey's architects to erect modern
villas there. Class separation was emerging and ethnic separation was general, but neither amounted to apartheid.

Limits

Even the harshest critics of Lyautey's colonial aims concede that
Rabat's extension was an aesthetic success. Abu-Lughod writes:
"There is no doubt that the master plan drawn up by Henri
Prost was impressive. [E]xisting features of pre-1913 Rabat
were sensitively integrated into the scheme and were used as
the basis for a rational organization of the newer quarters."[54]
Socially, economically, and politically, however, the plan was
inadequate. Planning not only did not stem speculation but
probably encouraged it. Prices in the central administrative
areas rose 500 percent between 1915 and 1921, even though
the main administrative buildings were all built on the sultan's
land.[55] The political aim of control appears to have been
achieved.

Why didn't Prost plan for future growth of the Moroccan
population or provide it with adequate services? At the 1931
International Conference on Colonial Urbanism, Prost lauded
the political objectives of Lyautey's urbanism. He rehearsed the
list of justifications: Europeans and Muslims had different cultural habits; the protectorate was a collaboration; it was not
meant to change Moroccan customs. The introduction of wide
streets and a modern infrastructure of water and sewers would
ruin the medina's charm. Aside from the aesthetic and economic advantages (tourism), there were social reasons for preserving its picturesque character: it conserved Moroccan social

customs and presented an image of social hierarchy to the French. Acknowledging that his initial plans for Morocco had been overrun by events, Prost urged that the main theme of the next colonial urbanism congress be the preparation of new cities to accommodate the rural masses flooding into the cities of North Africa. The conference never took place.[56]

The plan for Rabat itself, with its sharply drawn quarters and clearly defined zones, led over time to a certain rigidity. The first consequence was increased population density in the medina, which had been effectively boxed off (population rose 50 percent between 1912 and 1930). Crowding led to internal subdivision of housing, as more and more families were crammed into the same amount of space. Second, *sauvage* settlements began to appear along the foggy ocean-front areas beyond the limits of Prost's plan. These settlements were often financed by Moroccans who plotted the quarters and named them after themselves—Lazreq, Rifai, etc. But these areas frequently lacked adequate water and sewers. To live in the quarters required some regular income, and so it was that around them even poorer Moroccans began to settle in precursors of the *bidonvilles* (shanty towns). In addition to his colonial arrogance, Prost's shortsightedness was representative of this era of planning. The inability to predict change, to account for new variables such as the lure of the city (still poorly understood), and to find an adequate form to accommodate these processes, were weaknesses Prost shared with his entire cohort of planners on both the right and the left. The same processes of increasing density (resulting from underestimating growth), uncontrolled aesthetics, and hygienically substandard development were also occurring in France. This is not to deny the specificities of the colonial situation, but it does point to the more general limits of authoritarian planning by experts.

Casablanca: City without Citizens

Casablanca has posed problems not only for the urbanists who sought to control its growth but for those who seek to describe it. André Adam, the leading French historian of Casablanca, echoes the urbanists' ambivalence and caution toward the city's heterogeneous history and its less than savory inhabitants. Despite repeated statements from urbanists to the contrary, Casablanca had an incontestable past; in fact, occupation of the site has been traced to neolithic times. However, since it was never a royal city nor a major economic center, it could be said to have been a city without urbanity.

The earliest known name of the city, probably of Berber origin, was Anfa. As early as the fourteenth century Anfa had city walls, schools, and administrative officials. Its inhabitants engaged in trading and piracy. The Portuguese, already established at several sites on the Moroccan coast, sent a punitive expedition to raze the city in 1468 and again in 1469, leaving it in ruins for three centuries. The city was resurrected for strategic reasons during the last third of the eighteenth century. By about 1770, the city had acquired the name of *Dar el-Beid'a* (the white house), perhaps derived from the *caid*'s house, a large construction whitened with chalk which doubled as a lookout tower.[57] What the French called the old medina dated from the late eighteenth century and had been constructed essentially to complement the cannon emplacement and the garrison. The sultan built the city's walls, military installations, and customs buildings. Neither monuments nor even a royal palace were built, and the interior arrangement of the city was left to its inhabitants. The population was initially composed of functionaries, troops, and the flux of rural people attracted by the city's activity. There was no established, educated commercial bourgeoisie as in the major Moroccan cities of Fez and Rabat.[58]

Speculation, Dynamism

The French invasion and colonization radically altered the situation. The first wave of French immigration brought economic activity, but not the kind of order pleasing to urbanists or most historians: "The citizens were Frenchmen who had built, beside the Moroccan city, a city to their own liking [*à leur convenance et selon leur génie*] but of the same disorderly, speculative, and soulless nature as the American boom towns."[59] Comparisons with America were common. French historians continue to talk of a "gold rush," of a chaotic, if energetic, seizing of an open frontier.

Casablanca's dynamic commercial activity, its ethnic mix, its wide disparities of wealth and power, and its particular energy and order were evident from the early years of the century. Casa's population had risen from 700 in 1836 to roughly 20,000 (including some 5,000 Jews) by 1907, including a floating population of 6,000 Moroccans fleeing rural drought and drawn by the city's commercial activity. Its port was the busiest in Morocco. During the period of insecurity and invasion from 1907 to 1912, the European population of Casa exploded: from 1,000 in 1907 to 5,000 in 1909 to 20,000 in 1912 (12,000 of them French). After a 1911 accord with Germany giving the French permission to invade, the Moroccan "gold rush" accelerated; by the beginning of 1914, Casablanca housed some 31,000 Europeans (15,000 French, 6,000 Spanish, 7,000 Italians, etc.). Two-thirds of the Europeans in Morocco lived in Casa. The Jewish population expanded rapidly, reaching 9,000 by 1912, as did the Muslim (30,000 in 1912). On the eve of the Protectorate, *la bourgade misérable* (the miserable market town) was thriving. From its inception, the European colony in Casablanca was particularly diverse, containing a goodly number of Italian, Maltese, and Spanish workers. Like Algiers, it attracted a substantial working-class population. Morocco's first labor union was formed in Casablanca in 1910 by a French socialist militant who, having invested in land in the future industrial quarter, grew rich. His ambition, if not his fate, was representative. But as there was neither oil nor gold in Casa's soil, its sources of easy fortunes were land speculation, commerce, and the port.

All speculation rested on the premise that France would conquer Morocco. Under Moroccan law and the various treaties agreed upon by the European powers and imposed on the sultan, foreigners had no right to own land. Despite this inconvenience, massive investment was made in land. The anticipation of profit was not restricted to the European community: Moroccans joined in the speculation, either alone or in joint ventures with Europeans. Speculation fed on itself, causing a massive inflation. Land prices rose as much as 600 times; certain areas of Casa were more costly than parts of Paris. These speculative forces meant that actual construction in the pre-Protectorate years was relatively slow; available money was invested in land. However, just outside the old medina, in the area between the French military camp and the Muslim cemetery (south, southeast of the port), frantic building was taking place, guided neither by aesthetics nor by hygiene.

Although the French colonial lobby, particularly Le Comité du Maroc, had been urging intervention in Morocco for some time, Casablanca's first factory was built only in 1908. It was only with the establishment of the Protectorate and its state guarantees that major capital began to be invested (by Schneider's Compagnie Marocaine, the Banque de l'Union Parisienne, and other banks). Commerce remained the dominant economic activity in the early years. Although the police functions for Europeans were ceded by the Spanish, from 1907 forward the French sought to establish some form of administration. At the end of August 1907, joint French/Moroccan controls were put in place, and a budget was created. By 1913 a somewhat more elaborate structure was created, having twenty members. As it had very little statutory power, it served mainly as an organ for venting opinion. Nonetheless, it coexisted with a vocal, vigorous (and highly self-interested) press.

From the moment of his arrival in Morocco, Lyautey had been suspicious of Casablanca and its European inhabitants. A sustained and personal press campaign against him did not win him over to Casa's cause: "I am aware that in my hands authority will remain inflexible and that no concessions will be made to demagogic pressures."[60] The circling of the sharks necessitated, he felt, a strong captain to guide the ship. In 1913, after some hesitation between Fez and Rabat and some juggling of political pressures from Paris, Lyautey made it known that Casablanca would not be the official capital of the Protectorate. When he announced his choice of Rabat a small *fronde* (rebellion) broke out in Casablanca. He stressed that the choice of Rabat was part of a larger conception of the Protectorate, i.e., that Fez would continue as the center of Moroccan tradition and that Casablanca was destined to be the economic center of the country (Meknes was the designated agricultural center of the colon population). Lyautey's strategy was to make Casablanca one element of a complex whole; he would do everything possible to ensure that the city prospered, but also that it did not become another Algiers. To underline his points, he had the army begin sanitary operations. Casablanca's role was reinforced by Lyautey's decision to construct a major port in the city. As early as 1912, against the technical advice of certain experts, Lyautey opted for a massive scheme covering 140 hectares. This was a truly spectacular gesture and posed a major technical challenge. Lyautey vigorously defended this project in Paris and was awarded funding to begin construction. Against all odds, the port was functioning by 1921.[61]

In 1907, the walled medina occupied some 60 hectares adjacent to the port. Immediately outside the city walls were a market area (supplementing markets in the city) and a cemetery. Near the port was a small extension of the walled city which the Sultan Moulay Hassan had built to contain the Europeans, but which they had refused to inhabit. This quarter lacked permanent residents; Moroccan troops were lodged there periodically, and a French military hospital was built there in 1907. The city itself was divided into three sections: first was the bourgeois section with the administrative headquarters, port officials, commercial houses, consuls, and Europeans, as well as the major mosque and saint's tomb. Before 1912 this quarter was the center of European activity as well as Moroccan governmental institutions. Second was the *mellah*, or Jewish quarter, atypically not walled off (spatial segregation of religious communities in Morocco was hardly a French innovation; Jews had long been required to live in special sections in many Moroccan cities). In Casablanca, Jews and Muslims lived adjacent to each other on certain streets and even in certain buildings. Violence between the communities was apparently not as frequent as in other cities. The Jewish population was extremely poor; although living within the city walls, some Jews lived in tents or the first *bidonvilles*. This area was one of the first to be destroyed, as it was immediately adjacent to the area designed as the Place de France. The third quarter, the *tnaker* (a rural compound surrounded by cactus), was occupied by the poorest inhabitants and was the point of entry for tribal people moving to the city. But as immigration from the countryside increased, the distinctions between these quarters blurred. An open area flanked the *tnaker* and functioned as a kind of public park. To the west of the medina another quarter began to form, the product of Moroccan speculation. This area was developed by wealthy Moroccans who built houses for themselves and occasional Koranic schools, and then laid out lots in straight lines meeting at right angles. Streets (being unproductive) were kept very narrow. In sum, Casablanca was highly distinctive in its mixing of populations; its peoples constantly refused spatial segregation, whether defined in terms of religion, race, ethnic group, or class.

An Indefinite Suburb in Search of its City

Initially, the European population was located around the military encampments and the market area adjacent to the medina. Speculation was the motor force of the city's birth and growth, as well as the chief characteristic of its inhabitants' ethos—if not that of its administrators, urbanists, and historians. In 1913 a contemporary observer captured this spirit when he compared Casablanca to "an ocean of hovels, a sort of unstructured suburb to an as yet unbuilt metropolis."[62] In the early years, investors drove land prices skyward but built comparatively little. Areas in which building and habitation did take place often reached extremely high densities, with the expected consequences. From the early days of the twentieth century, poorer people (and farsighted investors) were driven continually farther from the city center around the port and Place de France, even though substantial tracts of land remained undeveloped. The result was a spatial extension toward a continually receding periphery. One of the very first acts of the administration was to create a boulevard of four kilometers, considered disproportionately large at the time. An unintended consequence of this speculative, unplanned sprawl was the establishment of a circulation system far in excess of projected requirements; areas located well beyond the urban perimeter were filled in during the building boom that followed the First World War.

The result was the second characteristic of Casablanca's growth: its consistent surpassing of the growth predictions of both urbanists and journalists. This dynamic, speculative sprawl led to a crisis in both the quantity and quality of housing available to the European and Moroccan populations, a crisis that continues today. It is worth mentioning that working-class, Mediterranean proletariat and subproletariat Europeans lived in *bidonvilles* as well as in substandard housing in the old medina. For different reasons, none of the forms of urban growth, from uncontrolled speculation, to Prost's Musée Social urbanism, to Ecochard's "progressive" urbanism, to Moroccan state planning ever proved adequate in planning or providing for Casablanca's highly diverse citizenry. Although the modern city was born and flourished under the sign of speculation and free enterprise, its leading citizens were not above blaming the government for its problems. Typhoid and plague epidemics in the winter and spring of 1913–1914 brought calls for intervention. Profiting from this fear, and the temporary acceptance of planning measures it produced, Lyautey ordered an energetic clean-up by a military team for the littered field area around the *Grand Suq*, just outside the medina's walls.

Prost was given the task of creating order out of what was referred to as an already chaotic situation.[63] Prost's plan turned on articulating the circulation network of the city and its economic functions within a zoning framework. He gave strategic importance to the placement and connections between the port and the railway station; between these poles he situated the commercial and industrial zones. Prost's plan encompassed 1,000 hectares. At a density of 150 inhabitants per hectare, this yielded a plan for 150,000 people, and led to Prost's being accused of megalomania.

Preliminary topographic and geological analysis—carried out under the pressure of speculation and increasing construction—confirmed the zoning choices. The industrial quarter (in the east and running north along the coast toward Rabat) had rocky soil, excellent for foundations and bad for gardens. In the west and southwest, the soil was richer and easier to irrigate. Wind patterns, which would carry future industrial waste away from the rest of the city, dictated the east as industrial and the west as residential. Between the two would lie two points of reference: the Place de France, the point of entry of the world (through the port) as well as the commercial center; and close by, the Place Lyautey, the administrative center. The spacious Place de France provided a focal center for the city's future commercial activity as well as an open and easily secured zone next to the old medina and port. Prost decided to take down the wall of the adjacent medina in order to enhance circulation (by means of a grand avenue leading to the port), scale, and symmetry. The Place was to house banks, commercial headquarters, luxury stores, restaurants, hotels, and concert halls.

Lyautey's decision to make Casablanca the economic pole of the country and his decision to expand the port to international scale required a major road system leading to and from the area, for commercial and industrial use as well as for symbolic grandeur and harmony. Given the existing ring-road system, Prost developed a fan-shaped system of roads centered on the port area but also connecting the major roads out of Casablanca to the rest of the country. A large avenue linked the train station to the Place de France. At the time Prost drew up his plans no tracks had been laid. The boulevard serving the industrial quarters also connected with the central road to Rabat; this road became the main intra-city commercial artery, and its corridor was soon the site of speculation and growth. Three hospitals for three clienteles (civilian, military, and native), grouped around a common set of laboratories and specialized facilities, were proposed. Prost planned a distribution of schools no more than 800 meters from residential areas. The war halted implementation of the plan, which was begun again in 1918. In the interim, the administration classified streets into *voies urbaines* (city streets) and *voies privées* (private streets), according to whether the property holders cooperated with the plan requirements: only the first group received paved streets.

In the eyes of urbanists and historians, the race against speculation and gold-rush immigration was at best tied. The lack of control over land acquisition combined with the plan's designation of areas for future growth actually increased speculation. The circular boulevard—which Prost had conceived as the outer limit of the city—was surpassed by the end of the First World War. A group of small settlements, almost villages, arose in this area, and a second peripheral boulevard and road system were required to provide services for them. After Prost's departure in 1923, pressure from settlers succeeded in abolishing height restrictions, and modest skyscrapers and apartments sprang up along the main arteries. The other consistently mentioned failure in Casablanca's planning was the lack of green space (the contrast with Rabat is striking). The only major park, an area of 30 hectares, was a sports field placed behind the Place Lyautey. Other green squares and open spaces were swallowed up by speculation.

The Style of the Protectorate

In Prost's plan, a large avenue linked the Place de France and the Place Lyautey. The latter site was occupied by the main barracks of the French army. Prost and Lyautey intervened to keep the military from solidifying these barracks in concrete, and succeeded in having the major military emplacements removed from the downtown area. Throughout Morocco, but particularly in Rabat and in Casablanca, Prost and Lyautey attributed a major importance to public buildings. They agreed that in Casablanca the facades should be constructed first and an area for expansion left behind, to be filled in when time and resources permitted. Prost said of the Palais de Justice in Casablanca, "it was morally necessary to build the facade, more so as it occupied the back of the administrative square."[64] The role of the Place Lyautey was to symbolize (and actualize in its administrative functions) the Protectorate as a mediating institution. The two societies would meet there; hence its importance, and hence the need to give appropriate form to this crossing.

Before describing the Place Lyautey, some background concerning public spaces and architecture in colonial North Africa is required. François Béguin makes a distinction between the "Conqueror's Style" and the "Protector's Style."[65] Here, as in so many other domains, Algeria was Lyautey's counter-model. Algiers and its central Place des Armes represented the Conqueror's Style—carved out at the foot of the medina in Haussmannian fashion by army engineers. Mosques were destroyed or converted into barracks and churches. Materials from the most famous monuments were used to rebuild the French city. Travelers in search of the exotic lamented its French character. This was precisely the vision of the city held by many of its citizens; proposals existed to raze the old city entirely. During the course of the nineteenth century, Algerian cities and public buildings closely imitated the succession of Ecole des Beaux-Arts styles. Architects who won prize competitions in France were assigned state contracts in Algeria, much as they might have been in Bordeaux. The first stage of colonial urbanism in North Africa, then, was characterized by destruction of existing urban structures and the creation of urban spaces based on French principles.

Napoleon III's trip to Algiers in 1865, his celebration of the idea of an "Arab Kingdom," marked the end of wanton architectural destruction and the beginning of a politics of conservation of architectural monuments. Aesthetic appreciation of Arab art and urbanism began with the consolidation of the conquest of Algeria and Tunisia, and with the arrival of different groups of French proposing a more associative policy.[66] Governor-General Charles Jonnart, the man who brought Lyautey to Algeria, guided the strategy of associating architectural style and colonial politics. Under Jonnart a systematic search for Arab forms began. In Tunisia the neoclassicism of public buildings gave way to a neo-Moorish style by the first decade of the century. This eclectic style was explicitly meant to symbolize the protectorate politics of association, the style of the protector who had already vanquished. Local French architects began a movement of redefinition, turning away from monumental form. In the early years of the twentieth century a range of texts treated vernacular architecture: V. Valensi's *L'Habitation tunisienne*, or R. Guy's *L'Architecture moderne de style arabe*. This work was important for its valorization of local construction techniques and its appreciation of local colors and geometric shapes. North African architecture, like North African culture, was to be comprehended in its diverse forms of adaptation and beauty.

Lyautey preached a simplicity and sobriety of style. The forms embodied the norms he sought to impose. We are attached, he said, to the best characteristics of Arab architecture which "prides itself on fashioning its exteriors solely with simple contours and façades."[67] The style of association consisted in simplicity of form, minimal decoration, and geometric spaces. Morocco's public buildings would present Morroccan forms in the service of modern norms of technology and administration. Lyautey and Prost brought the neo-Moorish style for individual buildings to its highest point of achievement. The administrative buildings (central post office, central bank, law courts, Hôtel de Ville, records offices, etc.) were formally distributed around the Beaux-Arts, symmetrical space. Prost drew the original plans in 1914–15, and they were executed beginning in 1922 by Joseph Marrast, who was responsible for the widely acclaimed architecture. The law courts offer a striking example of Beaux-Arts composition, geometric spaces, and elegant use of revivified artisanal work. The city hall was especially successful architecturally: three stories of offices surrounded a resplendent interior courtyard filled with fountains, basins, luxurious vegation, and excellent artisanry. "The extension into the interior of the building of these landscaped spaces establishes a sort of marriage of traditions, between the urban European landsape and the Arab, terraced house."[68] It seems fair to say that, however one evaluates the political project of the Protectorate, certain of its formal experiments were highly successful.

Arabisances: The New Medina

Prost has been frequently (and justly) criticized for neglecting Moroccan housing needs. At the very least, the strategy of separate types of cities, whatever its other complexities, reflected a tendency to do less for the Moroccans. The city's administrative and infrastructural needs were given the most immediate attention. More rigid control over European construction produced more and better housing in the European quarters. It is also important to underline the class bias of Prost's urbanism: Casablanca's large population of poor Europeans were given little consideration and mostly lived in substandard housing. The seigneurs of the Protectorate did not welcome their presence. Prost was not unaware of the situation. As early as 1917, following the principles of spatial separation, Prost proposed a new medina for the expanding Moroccan population, some two kilometers away from the old one (now completely surrounded by European constructions, the Place de France, and its associated arteries) and far from the initial European settlement, near the sultan's new palace and along a main circulation axis that would link it to commercial and industrial activity. However, typically speculation-motivated expansion as well as general indifference to the spatial separation of populations meant that Prost's neat compartments were soon obliterated.

In a combination of enlightened self-interest, political maneuvering, and traditional Moroccan largesse, Muslims, Europeans, and Jews all contributed to the birth of the new quarter. Protectorate paternalism was exemplified by the fact that the director of the *habous* was French. Consistent with this paternalism, the director foresaw the need for more housing for Muslims and proposed using lands owned by the *habous* for a new medina which would provide moderately-priced rental housing. The proposed area was extended by the gift from a wealthy Jewish merchant of an adjoining plot. Because of its religious nature the *habous* could not accept gifts from Jews, so the merchant offered the land to Sultan Moulay Youssef, who accepted the offer (keeping one-quarter of the plot for the construction of a palace), thereby rendering the project legitimate. On a second quarter, the sultan constructed housing for the palace staff, and his chamberlain built a small city on the third. Finally, the fourth quarter, enlarged by further purchases of adjacent land, was given over to what the French would refer to as the *habous* quarter.

Social Aesthetic

Prost assigned the task of designing the quarter to Albert Laprade (1885–1978), a Beaux-Arts architect wounded in the war and assigned to Morocco. Upon arriving in Morocco, Laprade enthusiastically filled his notebooks with a large number of drawings of vernacular Moroccan architectural motifs, searching for a vocabulary of social-spatial elements. French architects pursued systematic inquiries into the Moroccan house, quarter, and city as a total social environment which they hoped to reconstitute. The task was to decompose the charm into its architectural and urban elements and to learn how to recompose them into new forms combining modern technology with these socially rich stylistic elements. Laprade and his friends hunted for revealing details—the habit of placing olive trees next to white walls, vines against walls, and wells in the shade. The aim was not only to recreate beauty, but to identify the constituents of the sensibility these forms embodied. Laprade sought "the values of *ambiance*."[69]

This was a self-consciously understated architecture, which explored the interconnections of forms, social practices, and historically sedimented values. For Laprade, architecture was more than style; it was socially mediated nature, urbanity, a whole way of life. Laprade wanted to reconstitute everyday life, but a specific everyday life. From decoration and embellishment to forms, sobriety, minor arts, and ordinary (social rather than symbolic) life, Laprade and his friends sought the morphological meetings through which Moroccan forms endowed nature and culture with a particular unity. Architects of the next generation would seek through similar experiments to distill a pure form, a modern style; they would seek and claim to have found universal forms matching the universal norms of science. This was not Laprade's or Lyautey's project.

Laprade drew initial sketches for a new medina; however, his work on the Residence in Rabat took precedence, and he passed the project to two associates, Cadet and Brion. Building on Laprade's observation of houses, public spaces, and social practices, these two built a whole quarter in which a modern, technical infrastructure was concealed beneath a neo-Moorish facade. House exteriors were anonymous and lacking in any indications of the status of the inhabitants; light, air, and privacy were provided by interior courtyards; the street system included minor streets with no vehicular traffic and major ones designed for automobiles. The medina was conceived as a true quarter or neighborhood. It is worth noting that the thematization of neighborhood, *unité de voisinage,* although already being practiced by American planners, was not yet an element of French urbanism during this period.[70] Planners included a variety of services and Moroccan or Muslim *équipement:* market spaces, neighborhood ovens, public baths, Koranic schools, a modern school, mosques, the administration of the *habous,* courts, and later *pasha*'s administrative offices (only finished in the 1950s). Several *lycées* and major markets also eventually clustered in the area, and an area reserved for prostitution was built nearby by private initiative. A detailed plan for the quarter was developed by a municipal architect: a rectangle of 160 by 150 meters, entirely closed except for one entrance with a police and military post. It contained 175 housing units, 42 boutiques, 8 cafes, and a dispensary. The quarter was closed down in 1954 for political reasons. Its neo-Moorish architectural style and general urban design has been criticized more by subsequent modernists than it was by its Moroccan inhabitants. In the early years, the bourgeois population of Fez—one of the most refined of all urban, Moroccan groups—were most eager to live there. As Casablanca took form, the wealthier Fassis gradually moved into villas and were replaced by state employees and other middle-class groups. Today, the medina is a functioning middle-class neighborhood.

New Medina Sprawl
One of the reasons for choosing the site of the new medina was the existing commerce along the adjacent Marrakech road. The two main Moroccan quarters (the old and new medinas) were linked by this road; the European quarters lay in between. In 1920 the administration acquired 10 hectares adjacent to the new medina through expropriation, and the city rented out parcels of this land for construction. In these new areas, planning was overrun by an influx of populations and insufficient greenspace. Prost's zoning was ignored in other quarters as well: villas were built in the industrial east, and some industry was located in the residential west. Although planners and historians constantly express disappointment with Casablanca, their judgments can be contested. When one compares the his-

tory of Casablanca, with all of its problems and shortcomings, with other great metropolises of the third world (and certain of the first and second) it seems clear that it was fairly successful. Taking into consideration its mixing of different populations in relative peace, the fact that Casablanca was healthier in 1950 than was Paris, the variety of architectural styles and scales contained within a comprehensive circulation pattern, the restless energy of its people, its function as a world port and as the internal port of entry to the industrial world for generations of rural Moroccans, and its political role in resisting colonial as well as royal abuses—one concludes that the picture is far from negative.

New Technologies: Pétain

Lyautey's career in Morocco was ended by a rebellion, led by Abd el-Krim, in the Rif mountains of northern Morocco. Substantial scholarly attention has been devoted to deciding if his movement was the last of the traditional rebellions against foreign intruders, or the first of the modern movements for national independence.[71] While the question is intriguing and important, the confrontation between Lyautey and Pétain over how to fight Abd el-Krim, while less ambiguous, is arguably of equal historical significance.

In the early 1920s Lyautey was increasingly preoccupied with the growing influence of Abd el-Krim in the Spanish-administered zone of Morocco's Rif mountains, and with his calls for an independent Berber nation. In the French zone, the Berber tribes both in the Middle Atlas mountains and in the western areas of Morocco surrounding the city of Taza remained either unpacified or uncertain allies. The danger of the situation was compounded by the gradual reduction of French military forces in Morocco; occupation of the Rhine and Ruhr took precedence. Anticipating an attack by Abd el-Krim in French-controlled territory, Lyautey insistently called for reinforcements from France. The attack came on April 11, 1925, a month before it was expected and before the promised reinforcements had arrived from Algeria. A ministerial crisis in Paris that same week delayed concerted action. Lyautey, in his late sixties and recovering from a major operation, asked Paris to appoint a general to command the northern front, but was refused.

Politically, Lyautey, who had had good relations with Edouard Herriot, encountered opposition from his successor Paul Painlevé.[72] Painlevé sent Pétain, head of the armed forces, to Morocco on an inspection mission. Pétain and Lyautey already knew each other, as Pétain had made a previous inspection visit to Morocco in 1922 and stopped in Casablanca in early 1925. In the course of returning to Paris with Lyautey's plan of battle, Pétain met the Spanish prime minister, Primo de Rivera, in the Spanish zone. Without informing Lyautey, the two drew up a new plan of attack. Pétain returned to Paris and convinced Painlevé of its worth. Pétain boasted at a Parisian dinner, "There is not enough room for both Lyautey and me in Morocco."[73] Pétain returned to Morocco in full command of military operations. Fresh troops (refused to Lyautey) were dispatched from France. Lyautey, recognizing that his era was over and that his pacification approach could not be more foreign to Pétain, resigned on September 25, 1925.

Pétain commanded 100,000 troops and 40 generals. After the winter rains and unsuccessful negotiations, the offensive was unleashed. By the end of May, 1926, Abd el-Krim was beaten. Guided by a radically different conception of power, Pétain totally altered Lyautey's military strategy. Instead of small groups of mobile troops in contact with local tribal groups, Pétain substituted the tactics of modern European war: massive groupings of troops, heavy artillery, and the systematic occupation of territory following a fixed plan of attack. The conquest of territory, not political action with the tribes, dictated Pétain's plan of action. To limit French losses, Pétain relied heavily on massive artillery power to weaken the enemy. He also reinstituted Bugeaud's Algerian strategy of systematically destroying crops, supplies, and the economic infrastructure. Pétain's strategy was "based more upon spatial and temporal rationalization and the use of mass-produced war equipment than upon the manipulation of social structures."[74] Abd el-Krim was to be crushed.

The Rif war was a laboratory of modernity in a number of senses. The Spanish army experimented with techniques it would soon use in Spain's civil war. Pétain's tactics became textbook examples for a French army preparing for the next disaster: "Security, rather than speed, mobility, and efficiency, was responsible for the maintenance in 1939 of a style of mobilization which was total—involving men, resources, and firepower—but still very stationary in space and time."[75] This strategy was challenged only by the young De Gaulle. Although French aviation was used successfully in the Rif, Pétain failed to grasp its true importance; in Morocco Pétain's aviation strategy and the lessons he drew from it were based on the lack of enemy aircraft.

Preparing for the major encounter with Abd el-Krim, Lyautey, in 1924, had assembled the Orientalists at the Institut des Hautes Etudes Marocaines (Lévy-Provençal, Terrasse, Colin, and Basset) to collect all available data on the Rif. On the first day of Abd el-Krim's general offensive, Lyautey held a meeting of his native-affairs council, at which he predicted Morocco's inevitable independence and argued for a politics which would lead to friendship between the two countries. Lyautey's ultimate ability to negotiate Morocco toward independence is debatable, but Pétain certainly expressed no such sentiments. Pétain advocated more direct control by the French government over Moroccan policy, leading to more standard colonial policy throughout the empire. The destruction of rural social structures accelerated the population movement toward Morocco's urban centers, forming a social base for future nationalist political movements. Finally, Abd el-Krim, it seems worth mentioning, dreamed of transforming his tiny capital of Adjir into another Ankara.

A 1931 Conference on Urbanism in the Colonies summed up the state of the art. The mood in Paris was confident, contrasting with a growing pessimism about the possibilities of urban planning in France itself, as well as Lyautey's bitter realization that his colonial dream was over. There was general agreement among the participants, a complacent consensus on the basic principles of Musée Social—or more accurately by 1931, Moroccan—urbanism. There was also general agreement that Lyautey should be considered the greatest urbanist of modern times. The Congress agreed on twenty-one points. It called for the mandatory institution of *plans d'aménagement et d'extension* for all agglomerations, requiring that these plans be approved by those competent to do so, that the designs respect the practices of the "races" involved but not exclude contact between them, that the cities be airy and well planted, that architectural pastiche be avoided, that local arts be used as much as possible in ornamenting these cities, that modern arts be used for modern necessities, that hygiene be the norm in all dimensions of the plan, that historical monuments be preserved, and that aerial photography be used in planning.[76]

The only awkward issue was the segregation of the new cities from the existing, indigenous ones. A central concern of the Congress was conceiving of and building cities where different races (as they were called) with different customs and practices cohabited. Whatever the limitations of the approach—and they were manifold—it is crucial to realize that this congress was the last major occasion at which cultural difference (which tacitly included class difference) was directly thematized for decades. Norms, in the future, would turn on a technocratic universalism potentially (but not inevitably) more democratic and certainly leading to greater homogenization. In such a scheme, difference, quite literally, had no place—except as a relation in a statistical continuum.

10

Middling Modernism:
The Socio-Technical
Environment

Lyautey had invested heavily in the power of forms to reinvigorate sedimented social relations and shape new ones. Henri Sellier, the leading urban reformer of the interwar period, was solidly anchored in French socialist conceptions of justice. Faced with many more practical constraints, Sellier posed the problem of the ordering of space and population in a different fashion. The object of Sellier's attention was the *agglomération*. The *agglomération* was no longer viewed as a territorial unit in the sense of a space defined by long-term, historico-natural processes, neither was it primarily a historico-natural milieu or the public, social-political space which the French refer to as *la cité*. Rather, the term now implied a more abstract space—a socio-technical environment—upon which specialists would regulate operational transformations. The norms guiding Sellier's emerging socialist modernism were the welfare of the population, the maximizing of individual potential, and the linkage of these two engineered by an efficient administration manned by committed specialists dedicated to the public good.

After the First World War, Sellier conceived of the problem in terms of mobilizing political support for this flexible, new administrative structure—based on statistical projections and abstract social unities—while retaining traditional political accountability and social bonds. While explicitly concerned with social justice, Sellier sought to move beyond right/left political distinctions as well as traditional class divisions. Employing a sociological rhetoric of objectivity, Sellier proclaimed: "The tentacular city is a fact. Its advantages and disadvantages may be discussed, but it would be stupid to deny it and reckless to hinder its social role."[1] This statement represents a significant step away from the philanthropic concerns over workers' housing, the hygienist focus on *îlots insalubres* (unhealthy zones) and, obviously, from revolution.[2] For Sellier and his allies, the Parisian *agglomération* formed a single socio-economic unit. The older administrative grid, composed of the city and its surrounding communes, was not simply outmoded, but positively detrimental to healthy development. Coherent policy toward housing, transportation, and social life in general, was totally lacking. The absence of any effective land policy meant that the suburbs of Paris offered inexpensive locations which industry exploited in a socially and hygienically irresponsible manner. Such development was occurring at the expense of what Sellier (extending the analyses of the possibilitists) called "social cost" and "urban cost." The task was to develop techniques to combat the social plagues accompanying unregulated capitalist expansion.

Maurice Halbwachs identified the increasingly tenuous fabric of social relations among workers as the chief danger facing French society. He reasoned that since modern working conditions were producing increasingly desocialized individuals, the answer to social health lay with creating the richest possible social milieu away from work. Following Halbwachs' logic, Sellier called on architects, urbanists, and social scientists to produce and regulate an optimum social environment, which would rehumanize modern life. He proposed a ring of garden cities around Paris, designed according to Beaux-Arts principles of urbanism, employing regional styles, and oriented toward a new type of citizen, the employee.[3]

By the mid 1930s, frustrated by his lack of success, Sellier's ideas evolved, or better, involuted. He reluctantly placed less emphasis on local-level political participation, and more on social-scientific administration and the exigencies of cost analysis. Sellier was a transitional figure. While clinging to an older, socialist symbolism (politically, historically, and socially), during the course of the interwar period he gradually adopted a more modernist sociological and administrative language of self-referential form unmoored from these older referents. While

Sellier clung to history and locale as sources of legitimacy and solidarity, his younger assistants and successors were more relentless, gradually stripping away such architectural, historical, and social references in the name of efficiency, science, progress, and welfare: *middling modernism*. The broad lines of Sellier's project are discussed below: the piecemeal and often reluctant articulation of a middling-modernist discourse, cut off from older forms of sociality and guided by proliferating scientific norms administered by experts. Sellier embodied the tensions inherent in balancing a socialist conception of *la cité*— that public space of politics—with that of the *agglomération*, that anonymous space of regulation and rationalization.

Unbureaucratic Bureaucrats

In the interwar period proposals abounded concerning the need for and advantages of experts exercising more power in overcoming crippling political blockages and bringing France into what was increasingly referred to as the modern world. During the 1930s there was a good deal of discussion about planning in France as in other industrial countries, and after 1935 a number of pro-planning technicians even held government positions. However, as the technical tools and statistical data required for modern planning were largely unavailable, most of the self-proclaimed plans of the interwar period were little more than manifestos. Still, they were important in creating a discursive space which would be filled during and after Vichy in a more substantial and enduring manner.[4]

American and German models of industrial modernization fascinated a sector of the French business community and intelligentsia as early as the Universal Exposition of 1900, but were not widely endorsed until the time of the First World War. The social and political implications of Taylorism were particularly captivating to groups like the Musée Social, which early on advocated introducing it into diverse realms of French life. On the left, Edouard Herriot proposed a technologically inspired Fourth Republic as a means of overcoming the continuing parliamentary blockage of what he perceived to be France's national interest. Henri Fayol and the movement for management reform (which combined Taylorism and Fordism) advocated modeling the state in the image of a new, efficient, industrial apparatus. Fayol's dramatic proposals—such as transferring state bureaucracies to private hands—were not adopted, but new management methods were instituted to some extent in both business and government. It is hard to align the players of this discursive field according to the usual right/left political divisions. The major institutional enthusiasts of planning during the interwar period were the unions, particularly the leftist Confédération Générale du Travail (C.G.T.), who were convinced that experiments during the war demonstrated the compatibility of industrial productivity, higher wages, and improved negotiating power for workers.[5]

Before the First World War, the French public sector, largely inherited from the Ancien Régime except for its railroads, consisted mainly of artistic workshops. The state, consistent with liberal doctrine, had no program for economic management and lacked the data and analytic tools to invent one. This situation changed dramatically during the war. The role of the state expanded at an unprecedented rate: military expenditures literally exploded, such that service on the debt exceeded the entire prewar budget. Disparate conceptions of how to orchestrate and establish more efficient and productive relations between state and industry divided the government during the war. Organizational methods and the information and political strategies necessary to implement them grew in complexity. However, in France many of these "modernized" institutional arrangements were dismantled immediately after the war. The key players, cartels of industrialists, politicians, a small group of bureaucrats who had become specialists in navigating between the conflicting institutional forces of French society, and believers in the new techniques of understanding and regulation coexisted uneasily during the interwar years.[6]

For our purposes, the third group—"unbureaucratic bureaucrats"—is of primary interest and is embodied in the work of three men: Albert Thomas (1878–1932), Etienne Clémentel (1864–1932), and Louis Loucheur (1872–1931). The number of high-level bureaucrats involved in reorganizing French industry and production, and the relation of these to the state, was very small indeed. It has been estimated that in 1913 the corps of leading functionaries numbered around one thousand; only ten men in the Ministry of War had any direct involvement with industrial production, and one inspector was in charge of the entire artillery production section.[7]

The first important test of large-scale state planning came during the First World War. Alexandre Millerand (who had championed Lyautey in Morocco) had appointed Thomas at the outbreak of war to organize the French railroad system, and then, in October 1914, to work in the department of the fabrication of war materiel in the War Ministry. Thomas was no ordinary bureaucrat or standard political appointee. Although Thomas entered first in his class at the Ecole Normale Supérieure in 1898, first in his history class at the University of Paris in 1900, and first in the aggregation of 1902, he chose the active political life over the university career to which such impressive achievements ordinarily led. In May 1915 he became under secretary for artillery and munitions, and in December 1916 Minister of Armaments. His ministry was staffed by Ecole Normale graduates: François Simiand, Mario Rocques, William Oualid, Hubert Bourgin, and Maurice Halbwachs. Thomas remained until September 1917, when the socialists finally left the government. After the war, although reelected to the Chamber, Thomas (with American support) accepted a post as head of the Bureau Internationale du Travail in Geneva, where he remained until his death in 1932.[8]

In contrast to that of its allies, war production in France remained largely private. Hence the main task for Thomas consisted in establishing forms for a contractual relationship between industry and labor. He classified workers as producers sharing certain common goals with industrialists, rather than as a separate and antagonistic class. Thomas was accused of betraying workers' interests and of suspending the gains of the labor movement. He certainly did not see the war or his stint as minister as a means of making revolutionary political changes. Instead, Thomas talked of "the socialism of war" or the "socialism of Le Creusot."[9] Thomas's ministry was in charge of all war production, and consequently involved massive organizing and mediating. He pleaded for more rational production methods and the introduction of Taylorism. He proposed a model armaments factory embodying rationalized production techniques and modernized labor relations, though the factory was never realized. Among other innovations, Thomas introduced mandatory arbitration of labor disputes; establishment of a minimum wage for the Parisian region; major state presence in economic and trade-union affairs; and fixed planning objectives arrived at through joint negotiation.[10] The elements of Thomas's vision of postwar France were drawn directly from his efforts in the armaments ministry. Its essentials were industrial concentration and renovation, industrial democracy, class collaboration, and selective nationalization of industry and services. Thomas lost out to other forces; many of his innovations were dismantled after the war. The result of the war was to strengthen the power of heavy industry and of industrialists, who were successful in concentrating and coordinating their efforts.[11]

Etienne Clémentel, another champion of new structures, survived longer than the socialist Thomas—in part because he was less vulnerable politically but mainly because of the different role played by the Ministry of Commerce, which he headed. A radical, Clémentel had been minister of the colonies from 1905 to 1906, and served as minister of agriculture and finance in the following years. He was a playwright, librettist, and historian as well as a skilled artist and a friend of Monet and Rodin.[12] Clémentel became Minister of Commerce late in 1915 and held the post for five years, largely free of political interference. He developed detailed plans for France's economic modernization through a state-directed economy. Among other reforms, he and Henri Hauser developed a program for economic regionalism based on corporatism and rationalization of bureaucracy as keys to progress. Clémentel envisaged regional bodies with large budgets and technical staffs that could mobilize local energies: each would function as an industrial capital for France—Lyons for silk, Grenoble for hydroelectric power, and so on.[13]

Clémentel was an ardent advocate of increasing the role of bureaucratic technicians in order to rationalize the economy. He planned a considerable expansion of the research and information components of the Ministry and enforced compliance on the part of reluctant industrialists through his control over the allocation of resources. Clémentel "proposed the annual publication of production statistics, the creation of a prices board to determine normal prices through the expert assessment by bureaucrats of production costs, and the establishment of an industrial council, which was to be a state-supervised alliance of industry and science to ensure that French industry would remain in the vanguard of modern technological advance."[14] As with Thomas, Clémentel's ministry, controlling all French imports and (indirectly) all non-military production, was run by a very small group of young men, aptly characterized as "unbureaucratic bureaucrats."

Louis Loucheur, a graduate of the Ecole Polytechnique, architect, head of the Northern section of the French railroad, and self-made millionaire, had the greatest immediate impact on postwar policies. He was a tough-minded business man—Protestant, like so many members of the Musée Social—surrounded by the "technocratic" avant-garde of industry. Loucheur became undersecretary for armaments and war manufactures under Thomas, in charge of directing relations with industry. Through his political connections and manoeuvers, Loucheur succeeded in replacing Thomas in 1917, when the socialists resigned from the government. Under Loucheur, the Ministry of Armaments staff contained more graduates of the Ecole Polytechnique than the Ecole Normale. After the war, Loucheur became Minister of Industrial Reconstruction, and favored the full-scale return to private enterprise (except in the war-devastated northeastern region).[15] Although Loucheur and Thomas were strongly opposed on the role of the state in economic policy, they agreed on the need for a rational urban policy based on collective transport and healthier housing conditions for workers, if the French economy was to be competitive in the postwar years.[16]

It is fair to conclude that the war provided a laboratory situation in which experiments with modern elements were seriously undertaken. To say that the experiments with mass production, planning, and the ideology of *productivisme* were defeated gives only a truncated view. Millions of people were involved in these experiments, and their dismantling did not erase them from history or from contemporary debate. Many of these experiments would be resurrected under German pressure during the Vichy regime, and under American pressure during the reconstruction period following the Second World War. To mention only one example, Jean Monnet, architect of the first French Plan (and later of the Common Market), was a director of Clémentel's cabinet. Finally, a small but significant number of unbureaucratic bureaucrats gained invaluable experience in the inner workings of French society, and they were among France's first technocrats.

The understanding of and institutional setting for social statistics in France was changed by the war. First, the more powerful method of probabilistic statistics, which had flourished for several decades in England, made its entry—transformed in content and applications—into France. Second, the effective use of statistics during the war provided the approach with an institutional base and a new legitimacy.[17] As we have seen, the first great systematizer of social statistics was, of course, Quételet, whose concept of *l'homme moyen* shaped French statistics for almost a century. The work of Cheysson, Levasseur, de Foville, and Adolphe and Jacques Bertillon continued Quételet's work without introducing any major methodological innovations.[18]

The changes introduced into statistical thinking by English statisticians in the wake of Darwin turned on the relation between norm and mean. This change can be conveniently presented as a contrast between Quételet and Galton. Quételet's work was based on discovery of the regular distribution around the mean, which explained the dispersal of individual cases; hence his emphasis on *l'homme moyen*. Galton, on the other hand, emphasized differences and the unequal distribution of abilities. Following Cournot, he developed the notions of median and quartiles to replace Quételet's mean. Together the two became known as Pearson's standard deviation. Galton's anthropology combined physical, moral, and social characteristics in a common field constituted by differences. The significance of Galton's innovations was finally presented to France in 1910 in a long article by Lucien March on "the manner in which one should set forth the principal elements of statistical theory."[19] March downplayed the importance of English accomplishments and highlighted the French tradition of statistical innovation. The French adopted Galton's emphasis on the statistical field, but shunned what they saw as his deterministic, physicalist cast. The French eugenics movements, generally less influential than their English counterparts, also differed in their emphasis on natalism. March proposed supplementary aid to workers' families in which the fathers belonged to mutualist societies and hence were stable and productive French citizens. The agenda called for new techniques for regulating and strengthening healthy social forces.

While Durkheim was speculating on the need for occupational bonds in modern society, others were getting exactly these sorts of structures in place. The Conseil Supérieur du Travail, created in 1891 (and reorganized in 1899 by Millerand), brought together employers, workers, legislators, and law professors to discuss and prepare legislation on working conditions which would create new contractual ties between workers and patrons. Before 1945, the Office du Travail was the major scientific-administrative institution in France. Directed by Arthur Fontaine, a friend of Lucien Herr and Albert Thomas, it employed a variety of different methods: statistics were collected and monographs written on salaries, unemployment, workers' budgets, work regulations, hygiene, security, professional associations, and mediatory groups. In 1901, François Simiand, through his socialist connections, was appointed librarian at the Ministry of Commerce. Over the course of the next decade he brought in Halbwachs and then Henri Hubert and Georges Bourgin, all contributors to L'Année sociologique. The Office du Travail was transformed by Lucien March (1859–1933), who established a sophisticated statistical analysis of the five-year census figures. March, a former engineer, introduced the Hollerith "electric census-taking machine" using perforated punch cards, improving on them with his own "classicounter-printer," which was used until the 1940s.

The institutional role of statistics was advanced during the First World War. Painlevé, a mathematician, headed the War Ministry; his colleague, the probabilist statistician Emile Borel, occupied a post which coordinated activities among various ministries. Borel strongly advocated a larger role for the Statistique Générale de la France. Simiand, Halbwachs, and the other members of the socialist-normalian group worked on standardizing procedures, a major step forward in the creation of state management. Although these procedures were eliminated after 1918, with the triumph of Loucheur, they would reappear under Vichy and be definitively institutionalized after the liberation. Simiand, French secretary for the Comité Interallié de Statistique des Fabrications de Guerre from 1918 to 1919, urged Millerand to consolidate French statistical services. Millerand agreed, arguing more strongly than the statisticians themselves for the separation of pure and applied research. The seeds of the national statistics agency, INSEE, created twenty-five years later, are found here.

The importance of statistical methods had been demonstrated during the war; probability theory was finally being accepted. The Institut de Statistique of the University of Paris was created in 1920 and animated by probabilitist mathematicians as well as by March and Halbwachs. Simiand and Halbwachs became active members of the Société Statistique de Paris (Simiand was elected its president in 1921). In 1924 Halbwachs collaborated on the first French course manuals treating probability theory.

When the new University of Strasbourg was created in 1919, the French government sought to make it among the most prestigious in Europe, especially since it replaced an earlier German university. The chair in sociology was a symbolic one in this regard, as its previous incumbent was Georg Simmel. Hence, the committee charged with distributing chairs and appointing candidates—of which Thomas was a prominent member—chose carefully. The first chair in pure sociology in France was given to Halbwachs. Millerand, as Commissioner General of Alsace-Lorraine, was pleased to confirm the nomination. Halbwachs took on his duties on March 1, 1922.[20] Strasbourg was indeed a prestigious academic setting, with a faculty that included Marcel Gueroult, Charles Blondel, Marc Bloch, Lucien Febvre, and Georges Lefebvre. Halbwachs spent sixteen years at Strasbourg producing major sociological studies such as *Les Cadres sociaux de la mémoire* [The social framework of memory] in 1925, and *L'Evolution des besoins dans les classes ouvrières* [The evolution of working-class needs] in 1933. Strangely, he directed only two doctoral theses (one by an American and the other by a Turk), and his political activity remained limited. Thus, after the war, both Thomas and Halbwachs were far from the Parisian political scene; Sellier remained to carry the banner.

Social Reconstruction: Laws and Projects

For many years, the Musée Social had collected and publicized planning legislation in other European countries. Previous French legislative efforts had been almost completely stymied by the Conseil d'Etat's strict respect for private-property rights, liberal economic doctrines, and the financial autonomy of the communes. After the war, housing and urban-planning legislation was finally passed by the French parliament. As limited as it was, this legislation established a legal basis for all intervention in these domains until Vichy. The massive demographic and industrial changes taking place in the Parisian region had not gone unnoticed. In addition to the efforts of the Musée Social itself, the decade preceding passage of the laws was marked by a consolidation of forces among France's technical experts, most visible in the formation of the Association Générale des Hygiénistes et Techniciens Municipaux and reform movements in the parliamentary and extra-parliamentary center left. The First World War catalyzed these forces; the massive destruction of urban quarters and rural villages, it was argued, necessitated planning.[21]

Beauquier's modified bill was reintroduced in November 1912. Joseph Cornudet, a deputy from the Paris region, introduced further modifications in June 1913. A new parliament and the war delayed its adoption by the Chamber of Deputies until May 1915. The Senate then buried it in a committee, and the drafts of the bill were lost when its chairman died. Finally, after the war, a revised version was agreed upon and became law in March 1919.[22] The final version, differing little from Beauquier's original, required towns over 10,000 to develop plans for their future growth, taking into account streets, open spaces, sites for public buildings, public-health regulations, water, and sewage. The commune remained the administrative and legal base. The bill contained no credits and no sanctions. Cornudet, a moderate and a pragmatist, backing off from what he considered to be a losing confrontation and, preferring a law without sanctions to no law at all, agreed to separate expropriation from planning. As one deputy put it: "This law is aesthetic, a law of clouds."[23]

The law of November 6, 1918 (building on the public-health law of February 12, 1912) extended expropriation procedures to the level of the zone, a particularly important addition for circulation planning. Urbanists were optimistic that this provision would open the way for major expropriation. It soon became apparent that the Cornudet law was insufficient, and Siegfried and his allies proposed a series of amendments. A new law of July 19, 1924 required that a plan be deposited at the town hall before building permits were issued; increased, but still limited, powers of enforcement were given to both the mayor and the prefect. More technical precision was specified; at least one quarter of the area had to be devoted to either roads or to public services. There was a provision for the protection of artistic buildings and monuments. Many loopholes remained, and between 1924 and 1928 the same basic pattern of uncontrolled building occurred as that immediately following the war. Lax interpretation of these laws and their elementary provisions for such things as wells (one well for three hectares) meant that the laws were effectively ignored. Some of the largest building organizations in France (e.g., the Sociétés d'Epargne) were basically exempt. The technical dimensions of the required plans were not specified in any detail in the legislation and hence were subject to open-ended interpretation. Between 1917 and 1920 there was only one technical bureau in France in a position to advise municipalities on these matters. Nonetheless, as modest as these procedures were in themselves, they opened the way for transferring technical competence to the central state.

Two important changes were slowly being institutionalized in these legal battles: first, the legitimation and institutionalization of pairs of expert urbanists and administrators; second, a shifting conception of society. What had begun as a predominantly hygienist and philanthropic concern for acquiring land for workers' housing gradually expanded to a debate about the nature of the modern city, public services, and the role of the state as an agent of social transformation. In these proliferating discourses, as in the changing social formations themselves, a new spatial schema for society arose: one in which work and housing were separated, and in which experts claimed legitimacy based on technical competence. Finally, urbanists' complaints of defeat must be situated. Planners, claiming to speak in the name of the common good and of scientific rationality, have consistently expressed frustration with political constraints. Obviously this was a highly ambiguous discourse, and should not be taken at face value. Even Lyautey and Prost frequently lamented their inability to achieve sufficient control over speculation, but they never complained about authoritarian procedures.[24] While it would be an exaggeration to call Sellier anti-democratic, the political stalemate in France, the economic problems, and the logic of planning in the name of the public good led him down a similar path.

Beyond the Musée Social: Sellier's Agglomeration

Elegant and comprehensive images of the city were easiest to produce when the city was built from scratch, as in Morocco. An architect, Gaston Rambert, argued that although the French public habitually associated the colonies with Khmer temples, noisy and picturesque processions, and piles of colonial products, this image was outdated. Morocco was absolutely modern, as witnessed in the 1922 colonial exhibition at Marseilles. All the new Moroccan cities had plans: beauty and hygiene ruled, and comprehensive documentation was standard. Rambert praised the utility and beauty not only of the exquisite maps but of the systematic use of photographs demonstrating the progress of construction. The coherence and beauty of these plans was best revealed by the aerial photographs. The modernity of Casablanca and Rabat in terms of *équipement*, specialization of quarters, and circulation planning surpassed anything in France.[25]

The problem of bringing order to an existent situation was more complex. Postwar urban discourse vacillated between organic and mechanical metaphors.[26] The term "function," taken over from biologists and geographers, shakily bridged the metaphoric field. On the mechanist side, Léon Jaussely argued that the economic organization of the city should be considered as "the large-scale Taylorization of a vast workshop where, for very specific reasons, everything must have a definite place and cannot occupy any other."[27] Jaussely provided a kind of manifesto in the first issue of *La Vie Urbaine*. Urbanism grew out of geography, which provided two essential tools: the detailed and comprehensive analysis of *genres de vie* and the technical means of representing these data in a standard form. Jaussely claimed that the life of a city in its entirety could be reproduced through graphic means, in a series of plans drawn at the same scale.[28] Jaussely produced maps of climatic conditions, topography, demography, historical influence, social and professional locations, ethnic groups, population movement, economic activity, circulation patterns, public and private spaces, construction, overcrowded housing, death and morbidity rates, and traffic accidents. Combining this swirl of variables into a single plan required a complexity of presentation that Jaussely barely intuited.

On the organicist side, Louis Bonnier compared the city with a living organism evolving in space and time. Bonnier proposed to study Paris as a grouping of populations, ignoring older, arbitrary administrative distinctions drawn up for historical reasons and related to political or military considerations.[29] Bonnier presented a series of remarkable maps of the spatial growth of the Parisian *agglomération* and of the changing densities of specific areas. Population, Bonnier argued, occupied a different space from politics; Jaussely would have made the same point for economics. Uniting all variables in a common field required new conceptions of space and society.

After the war Sellier and his allies fought for a planned, socially hygienic, and aesthetically coordinated series of garden cities developed in conjunction with public housing in Paris itself. Sellier's strategy for the Parisian *agglomération* was based on communes acquiring land and a coordination of all efforts at the departmental level by his office. This implied two important innovations: state intervention in the definition of change and identification of the need to invent and then plan for the placement of new social unities. Paris's population in 1920 was numerically the same as before the war: the 200,000 men killed in the war had been replaced by an influx of industrial workers. If the population had remained quantitatively stable, its social characteristics had altered. For example, the number of inhabitants in the Parisian region occupying single rooms or hotels rose to 1 out of every 13. There was almost no private construction after the war. The reasons were largely economic: from 1914 to 1920 the price of construction materials had nearly quintupled, labor costs had tripled, and the price of putting up a building in Paris had increased fourfold. Even with the help of the prewar public-housing laws (HBM), which reduced taxes and lent money to private builders at lower rates, it was still economically unfeasible to build for the working classes. The war had fundamentally altered the situation in which the HBM legislation had been passed, and the laws had not been changed to meet these new conditions.

As early as 1913, Sellier had proposed state intervention in the housing market. The passage of laws, a product of pressure from the Musée Social and fashioned after foreign examples, had given the communes limited power to coordinate action, but no real financial basis on which to act. Sellier, frustrated and angered by the minimal success of Siegfried's model, reacted strongly against it. Sellier argued for a larger public-service arena as the only adequate means of responding to the crisis. After the war, the prefecture of the Seine, advised by Jaussely and Sellier, created a technical bureau to aid the eighty-four communes surrounding Paris in developing plans. The bureau provided technical aid and helped coordinate statistics and planning in three areas: evolution of population, circulation needs, and open space. The bureau was the first experiment in state tutelage over the communes (even if this was not exactly the authors' intent).[30]

The lead article of the 1923 issue of La Vie Urbaine was a report by Sellier on the International Conference on Garden Cities and Urban Planning held in Paris in October 1922.[31] Sellier urged the creation of a series of satellite garden-city settlements. Although never offering an exact definition, Sellier's conception of garden cities was drawn directly from Raymond Unwin's *Plans de villes,* as well as from the many inspection tours he and his architects made throughout Europe. Sellier admired the English accomplishments but was opposed to literal imitations, especially of the ideal of self-contained satellite cities. Howard's vision, he said, could not serve as a direct model for France because it planned for cities separate from large agglomerations. Sellier thought of the suburb as urban. One might say that for him, the English put too much emphasis on the garden and not enough on the city. It is worth noting that as early as 1920, Sellier codified the use of three basic terms, made famous later by Le Corbusier—*demeurer, travailler, passer* (reside, work, circulate)—as the essential, interconnected functions of modern city life.

Despite its sociological inconvenience, Sellier favored retaining the commune as a basic unit because of its historical significance and the social and political anchor it provided for *la cité:* "As feeble as may be the local life of the suburban communes, it nonetheless exists."[32] For political reasons, Sellier opposed the creation of a single, unified commune, which he feared would drown out the voices of elected officials and give a free hand to administration. Democracy required a local, socially grounded counterpart to government bureaucracy. When such a counterweight was weak, it should be strengthened; when it was absent entirely, it should be created. This implied an agenda separate from that of the reorganization of *la cité.* The pathos of attempting to glue the two together was typical.

Rehumanized Matter

Although its importance was primordial, Sellier paid little explicit attention to industry.[33] The images he did provide of work were largely negative: it was tiring, polluted, noisy, ugly, and unhealthy. Just as he did not valorize working-class sociality or revolutionary politics, so too he devised no reform project for industry. Sellier's counter-image was peace and calm *after* work: "At the entrance to the city the prospective inhabitant ceases to be a worker and becomes once more a man." This humanism was meant to be a refusal of working-class isolation and brutalization as well as an affirmation of a modern, socialist, Republican citizenry. To situate this compensatory, rehabilatory stance toward modern work, we turn to Halbwachs.

Halbwachs, in his "Matière et société" (Matter and Society), presented one of the first French theories of alienation, basing his argument in good Durkheimian fashion on social rather than economic alienation. Halbwachs defined industrial workers as that group of men who, "in order to carry out [*s'acquitter de*] their jobs, must orient themselves toward matter and leave society."[35] He proceeded to demonstrate how industrial workers' representations of themselves and others were mediated by matter, and how this mediation deformed the workers' representations of both nature and society. The natural tendency to value the picturesque in nature grasped as a whole, and the inherent value of social relations in a social whole, were reduced to "a series of mechanically associated sensations that close in on themselves."[36] The opposite of this situation, the norm of social health, was social life at its most intense—urban life—where the social worth of both nature and culture were appreciated fully.

The supposed advances in industrial relations were accelerating, rather than reversing, this negative process. The introduction of Taylorism refined the decomposition of social relations. On the one hand, it enforced a standardization of individuality among workers; on the other hand, the introduction of management specialists who did not share skills or social life with the workers resulted in an important loss of autonomy for industrial workers. The result was increased desocialization. The industrial worker in modern society increasingly formed representations of himself along an axis of inanimate matter, which led him away from society. The situation of salaried employees was only marginally better. Halbwachs showed how their status was determined by their general lack of independence, initiative, and responsibility. Along with that of the rest of the emerging middle classes, their work was characterized by an ambiguous technicity.[37] These people applied fixed rules to specified situations but little else was demanded of or permitted them. The plight of this *humanité materialisée* followed the great tides of social change. Their situation was ambiguous; they were neither fully dominated nor dominant. Halbwachs quotes de Tocqueville on the spirit of the middle classes as a mixture of that of the people and that of the aristocracy; though capable of producing miracles, by itself it would never produce a government or civilization of virtue and grandeur.[38] Clearly, Halbwachs felt that a vision of social justice and the techniques to implement it were needed to save the new employees from mediocrity or worse.

Socialist Social Space

Sellier's concern for creating new forms of social bonds—in many ways parallel to Lyautey's conceptions of pacification, except that the group to be pacified did not yet exist—was explicitly developed in a 1922 article in *La Vie Urbaine,* on "social centers in rural regions of the United States." Sellier pointed to American small-town or rural innovations which he believed could be applied in France to *agglomérations urbaines.*[39] Sellier was enthusiastic about the American experience of rural civic centers. They were excellent devices for the development of social life, promising to preserve and revitalize rural habitation. Sellier valorized the intensifying of social activity per se. As in pacification, once a combination of economic activity and civic administration were present, and once a space was created, new, healthy social unities would emerge, and older ones would be stabilized and regenerated. Although the functioning and financing of these civic centers varied a great deal, they shared a number of common features. Each contained an auditorium available for purposes ranging from banquets to speeches and a kitchen; a larger town would include a cafe, billiards room, library, a visiting room for the county health officer and agricultural agent, and the Chamber of Commerce. Sellier knew that parallel spaces existed in French cities.

The *Maison Commune* or *Maison Pour Tous* was a transformation of the social spaces of the socialist *Bourse du Travail* or Social Catholic *Foyer.* It became a characteristic form of new

French cities between the wars, especially (if not uniquely) in socialist municipalities, and has been called the major socialist contribution to *équipement*.[40] Its evolution was such that Agache and his associates, in their 1915 manual *Comment reconstruire nos cités détruites* [How to rebuild our destroyed cities], included a *Maison Pour Tous* as an essential part of any urban plan. The simply constructed, large building (in small towns placed next to sports facilities) would house a library, a sewing room for women, childcare facilities and *une buvette de tempérance* (a non-alcoholic refreshment stand).[41] Often placed at the city's symbolic center, the *Maison* embodied hopes for modern civilization: the best of politics, education, and culture. The idea of an autonomous social space, neither a governmental building nor a private mercantile amusement space, had a complex history in the nineteenth century. Jean-Louis Cohen (in the spirit of Halbwachs) argues that it would be naive to reduce the production of these spaces entirely to reformers' projects; they corresponded to social demands as well. The displacement of union activity to a broader and more diffuse place of sociability (and of education) occurred slowly but surely, as the left was assimilated into the Third Republic.[42]

A Healthy Agglomeration

Sellier's aim was to provide the cadre for a renewed modern sociality. His consistent goal (which he never achieved) was to make garden cities complete social cells composed of inhabitants from a wide range of social categories, thus avoiding an unhealthy isolation stemming from the irrational development of cities and their consequent class hostility, of that accentuated and exaggerated social differentiation of thoughts and practices which leads to "a sad and monotonous effect, producing ugliness."[43] Sellier fully accepted the principle of different classes of housing for different social categories. Sellier was not alone in accepting the spatial separation of classes. The only two French projects in the first half of the century that did not explicitly acknowledge class differences were Garnier's Cité Industrielle and Le Corbusier's Cité Radieuse. Garnier only accommodated one class, while Le Corbusier's standards applied to a universal, *homme-type*.[44]

Sellier, following Halbwachs, was guided by a norm of social life in which the mixing of classes intensified the representations of society. Sellier thought that the working class, the salaried employees, and the lower-middle classes were the social groups most in need of a rich, independent, and picturesque social setting.[45] He envisioned garden cities as quarters or neighborhoods, capable of serving specific needs in the best possible manner but not cut off from the city.[46] This principle was important: neither Sellier nor the Conseil Général de la Seine sought to destroy Paris, only to preserve it by relieving the conditions of congestion, by creating urban suburbs as part of a new *agglomération*. The garden cities were to be neither complete cities nor a suburban scattering of individual houses, but social unities attached to an urban center, improved according to the latest principles, assembling divers social categories and devoted to strengthening social exchanges, solidarity, and moral bonds. Sixteen garden cities were built around Paris in the interwar period, of which Plessis-Robinson with 5,500 dwellings, Drancy with 1,060, Suresnes with 2,735, and Stains with 1,655 were the largest.

Suresnes

As Sellier was mayor of Suresnes, it was an obvious candidate for the implementation of his plans. For over a thousand years the village of Suresnes, on the western outskirts of Paris, had survived on its vineyards. During the seventeenth century it was a fashionable site of aristocratic houses; the Rothschilds built a mansion there in the nineteenth century. By the end of the nineteenth century, a railroad linked Suresnes (and other suburbs) to Paris, and the village was being transformed into an industrial site. The Rothschilds built a steel tube factory; a bicycle factory was erected, and in 1905 Darraca, the first car manufacturer, arrived. Other industry followed: aviation motors, Westinghouse electrical industry, Hewitt, a biscuitry, and an important perfume factory. By 1900 Suresnes's population had grown to 11,000. Although some vineyards were still active, its future lay elsewhere.[47]

Suresnes's *Plan d'aménagement* was not completed until 1927. Following Sellier's ideas, it sought to direct an existing evolutionary development. The garden city of Suresnes was to be built on 30 hectares acquired by the Department of the Seine adjacent to the existing town. The study of the site was followed by a general design of the whole. Within this whole, elements (streets, squares, edifices, houses, trees, sports fields, schools, shops, and communal buildings) were distributed according to the urbanist's art. Services were housed in functionally specific buildings deployed as morphological elements. Social services were assigned a symbolic central location, forming the focus of the city's circulation system and substituting for monuments. Sellier's team paid particular attention to educational and hygienic services as well as to the creation of new spaces for modern social life.

Although the concept of zoning was only officially recognized in French plans after 1932, it had been used for quite some time. For Suresnes, three main zones were delimited: an industrial zone in which housing was discouraged; a residential zone reserved for individual houses and small businesses; and a model garden city guided by strict, modern health considerations of maximum light and building controls. The plan called for 1300 lodgings distributed in 550 individual houses grouped around gardens, and 750 lodgings in collective houses of three to four stories, grouped along the main thoroughfares. The plan allowed for three to five rooms for each family, with running water, electricity, gas, a garage, and in some cases central heating.[48] In Suresnes, Sellier introduced cooperatives of consumption and production, restaurants, and mutualist pharmacies. Community centers were included in the plans for almost all the garden cities, although only a few were built by the late 1930s. The first postwar *Maison Pour Tous* was built in 1924 in Genevilliers by Ernest Hébrard.

History as Science and Consensus
It was no accident that most of the proposed garden-city sites were located adjacent to older towns. Whenever Sellier spoke of the "cities of tomorrow" he evoked an older, preserved core and a periphery organized along modern planning principles but maintaining strong ties with the older city. In the first issue of the *Bulletin de la Société Historique de Suresnes* (1920) Sellier argued the importance of preserving some of the old quarters

of Suresnes so as to conserve a sense of its identity. The old city played a historical, touristic role as well as keeping the character, the specificity of the city's culture, alive. Given "inevitable, hideous, effects of modern industrial civilization," an enlightened municipal administration understood that in urban evolution, as in biology, there was a high price to be paid for a brutal rupture of past and present.[49] It followed that scientific understanding of history was the key to constructing a healthy future. This belief firmly rooted Sellier in what we have been calling *techno-cosmopolitanism.*

Historical discourse also had additional roles. The Historical Society of Suresnes was used by Sellier as a means of achieving consensus, or at least of communicating with potentially hostile social groups and local notables. It also served to establish him as a historical figure in his own right.[50] During a period of intense change, the discourse of history became a privileged medium of communication. Both the change and the historical valorization of the locale had begun before Sellier's arrival: the first history of Suresnes was written in 1890 and a historical society formed in 1901. However, bitter fights during the Dreyfus affair had destroyed the town's consensus. By the 1920s diverse circles in Suresnes, as elsewhere in France, were independently returning to local history: the parish published documents on the town's religious history, and secular teachers collected documents on its past. In 1926, Sellier enthusiastically supported local initiatives for an artistic and historical society. He welcomed the idea of a *fête municipale,* and the municipality funded these efforts to achieve a common view of Suresnes's past and present. However, Sellier refused to give the association municipal status, preferring that it retain its local social affiliation. Although former comrades in the Communist Party actively criticized Sellier's participation with church leaders and industrialists, he remained conscious of the need to broaden his political and social base; his support of the historical society was related to these considerations. The members of the society were prosperous older men from Suresnes; a number of his adversaries were members of its directing committee.

Historical discourse, as a promoter of both unity and division, has played a central role in French life.[51] Sellier had learned, and learned to practice, a "heroic" history focusing on exemplary figures of the left. He transformed this mode of historical moralizing into a discourse legitimizing for his own social policies. He often cited Saint Vincent de Paul's charitable works in Suresnes and frequently referred to his namesake Henri IV. Sellier appeared in the pages of the association's bulletin as the patron of Suresnes, without mention of his political party. The society contributed to making him a legend, hoping to form a consensus around his person if not his ideas.

However, Sellier also practiced another kind of history. He and his friend Marcel Poëte had together established a course on urbanism and the history of Paris at the Ecole Pratique des Hautes Etudes which stressed the importance of local historical determinants in the definition, growth, and future of cities. Although this historical approach also had its rhetorical functions, Sellier took its scientific importance quite literally. Before elaborating his plan for Suresnes, he undertook a detailed study of the commune's evolution. He wrote an article for the first issue of the Société Historique's annual bulletin entitled "l'Avenir de Suresnes lié à son passé" [The future of Suresnes tied to its past], chronicling the town's growth and its periods of health and decline. Sellier presented his program of reform as the logical end point of the commune's historical development, in conformity with the town's particularities and le tempérament suresnois. For Sellier, Suresnes' deep history, its long durée, was the key to unifying the town through elaborating a common historical memory, a common identity. Sellier's scheme for combining technological modernization with local historical and environmental anchors was not prophetic of the future; it proved even less stable, and more pathetic, than Lyautey's version.

The Socio-Technical Environment: Middling Modernism

The economic depression and hardening ideological climate, as well as the political splintering of France during the 1930s, stymied implementation of social legislation. Taken literally, Sellier's project of urbanism as civilizing technique was a failure. His vision of a modern *agglomération* of regionally distributed garden cities in which tired employees returned each night to restorative islands of green and social peace, while perversely prophetic of other social worlds to come, was truncated in practice; housing goals, to mention only one aspect of the plan, were not even approached, much less met. Private builders constructed the vast majority of housing during the interwar period, independent of any larger, explicit, coordinated plan. Those like Sellier whose humanist-socialist vision was dying became increasingly bitter; the complement to Sellier's practical failure can be found in the ambiguous apogee of this vision of humanity, the Front Populaire's 1937 International Exposition on Art and Technique—specifically its construction of the Musée de l'Homme. The quieter articulation of a middling modernist discursive field, in which a set of functionally oriented technologies were invented and freed from the moorings of history, locale, and socially saturated environment, was occurring simultaneously.

During the course of the 1920s and 1930s, intervention slowly shifted from city planning to the management of *la matière sociale*. Instead of a functionally harmonized urbanity, Sellier and his team were constrained by political weakness and worsening economic conditions to gradually limit the scope of their interventions to the perfecting of specific social spaces and social sciences. The loss involved—the diminishing of a social and socialist vision—was clearer to Sellier than to his followers. Sellier's assistants became almost evangelistic spokesmen for the creation of modernized tools for the sociological analysis of needs and norms of life, as well as enthusiastic participants in the creation of social actors to implement such techniques. This transition was aptly characterized by one of Sellier's assistants as a move from a *plan de ville* (city plan) to a *plan de vie* (life plan). Georges Canguilhem, analyzing a parallel change in psychology, characterized it as a shift from utilitarianism—utility for man—to instrumentalism, i.e., man as a means of utility. The sea change in techniques, objects, and goals caused theorists to seek laws of adaptation to a socio-technical, rather than a historico-natural, milieu.[52] The change constitutes an important element in the transition, in certain specified domains, to what could plausibly be called sociological and middling modernism.

Administrators of Normal Life

In 1938 Louis Boulonnois, one of Sellier's chief counselors in
Suresnes, published a book which can be considered an official
presentation of Sellier's program in its final form.[53] Boulonnois, who referred to Sellier as *Maître,* had been a schoolteacher
in Suresnes before joining Sellier's administration. Married to
one of Suresnes' new corps of social workers, he might be characterized as a fully integrated member and apostle of the new,
reformist-socialist administration. Although by 1938 Sellier
himself was bitter, Boulonnois remained optimistic. The goal
was no longer limited to meeting housing needs or even to the
systematic distribution of welfare institutions throughout the
city, although, as Sellier was keenly aware, these objectives were
far from having been attained. By the mid-thirties, a complementary task (present in rough form in Sellier's earlier projects) had been brought to center stage: offering public support
in instituting a comprehensive program of physical and moral
preventive care to alleviate social ills. The isolation and
rectification of islands of pathology no longer held priority;
rather, the new program amounted to a blueprint for the
scientific administration of modern life as a whole.

For Boulonnois and Sellier, the objectives of municipal organization were to predict and prepare for accidents and to
specify needs—put most broadly, to prepare the instruments of
social defense. In their view, although their programs served
the public good and their responsibility was regulating the community's well-being, their role was not so much political as technical.[54] Care of the collectivity fell to administration, these
technicians argued with beguiling understatement, because the
ordinary citizen, preoccupied with the details of day-to-day life,
all too frequently neglected to plan ahead. Administration's
role as arbiter and planner might not always be appreciated by
the average citizen, but such ingratitude was the price to be
paid in achieving broader public good. *Prévoyance* was no
longer the individual moral virtue par excellence, to be incul-
cated by discipline and surveillance but rather a normalizing
administrative function guided by science and operating on an
entire population.

The transition to technocratic modernism would be completed when the population's norms of health became functions of the instruments of measurement themselves. Boulonnois argued that the role of administration was the scientific arbitration of social conflict. Successful management entailed more comprehensive and sophisticated knowledge of the population (particularly its range of differences and its future development) as well as more flexible, continuous, and farsighted means of administering services. The ideal target population for scientific administration, according to Boulonnois, was still in a molten social state (i.e., not fixed in its historical, geographical or social milieu). The inhabitants of Suresnes, consisting of skilled laborers, "where social classifications had not yet emerged, where the ties of neighborliness, of solidarity, and of friendship were clear, quickly perceived, and quickly accepted,"[55] fit Boulonnois's bill. Public service was charged with producing and directing a new social solidarity among these men. The "plan" provided Boulonnois with a metaphoric bridge connecting social organization and the individual. His penchant for slogans served him well; he defined the task as "To bestow on the allotments a city plan (*plan de ville*) and, symmetrically, on the assisted families a life plan (*plan de vie*)."[56] Presented here, bluntly and to the point of caricature, was a project of middling modernist totalization and individualization. It was no longer a matter of regulating and ameliorating a locale and its inhabitants, but rather of treating both as matter to be formed and normed at will—or, more accurately, through a thoroughly voluntarist program.

Boulonnois's faith in positivist science could not have been more robust: "Everything that exists, visible or invisible, has a plan."[57] In this discourse, society, the state, and the individual were potentially transparent to one another. In order to articulate these institutions and the population, social facts had to be brought into a standardized grid. This entailed an objective and objectifying vocabulary for individual and social needs, as well as a functionalist understanding of institutions. To this technician's vision of social reality was attached a conception of the state as a set of bureaus whose job was to deliver functionally specific public services—roads, water, agriculture, hygiene, and housing—and to provide, as Habermas is fond of saying, "steering mechanisms" for the whole society. While Boulonnois's proposals were formed as part of a socialist-humanist project, Vichy and subsequent French regimes carried out parallel projects for the state, though with different aims.

The locus of intersection of the macro- and micro-knowledges and powers was probably housing, although it is important to emphasize that social housing was in the process of being redefined as an abstract question of technical spaces and scientifically established needs, rather than as a specifically disciplinary concern. In 1934, for example, an international project sought to establish a homogeneous typology of housing. These standards were adopted for the census, permitting a standardized analysis of needs and a more substantial base for provision. Concurrent with the establishment of these technical standards, a set of normalizing and organizing criteria was outlined. Norms and means were now joined. These norms of sociability were based on *la famille normale moyenne:* a stable and rational household. The norms not only classified families, but served as the basis of intervention to hasten their creation and stabilization. However, the criteria for identifying normality were not static; the scientific definition of needs was constantly being reevaluated. Furthermore, families who failed to qualify for housing were not definitely eliminated from the pool but, rather, were offered the possibility of consulting with social workers and reapplying. Once such families aligned their practices with those of the scientifically defined and selected normal community, they might qualify for housing.

Boulonnois urged his colleagues to replace the older, humiliating *quasi-policières* investigations with a more precise understanding of community needs; they were also encouraged to generate feelings of solidarity among and toward those who failed to meet the standards.[58] The links between the administration, its technical experts, and the population whose welfare it protected operated as a new social division of work, and constituted the norm and means of a new social solidarity. The scientific advice on living conditions established a means of extending the normalization process. The administration defined the normal use of a house, and used this to prescribe the necessary conditions for occupation: e.g., rooms with specified functions, apartment size as a function of family size (with specified upper limits); modernized equipment like gas and electricity; regular payment of rent, but also gas bills; the right of social workers to enter the house to check hygiene; and obligatory inscription in an insurance plan. All these improvements and regulations implied and reinforced a regular salary and regular habits. Once the normalized *mode de vie* (style of life) became a category defined in terms of *niveau de vie* (quality of life) the added surpluses became indications of status. The older class and "type" understanding was giving way to a grid of stratification and "distinction."[59]

Many of these criteria were not new, but given the new administrative structure, they led gradually to state measures (in relation to a normal family) used to establish rent, state subventions, and so on. Various systems of control reinforced these normalized and scientific standards: visits to the public baths were obligatory, as were weekly visits from social workers who established typical household budgets. Katherine Burlen characterizes these developments as a regulated "dramatization of daily life."[60] Universalizing social norms and economic stratification gradually displaced the disciplinary tactics of hygiene and environmentalist localisms in defining and enforcing social reality. The *plan de vie* was passing from a bacteriological and class phase to a functionalist and normalizing sociological one, the middling modernist.[61]

Beyond Urban Suburban

It was only after 1926, with the advent of the Poincaré administration, that the plans of cities and housing needs were accorded serious attention. But by 1929, the first effects of the world economic crisis clamped restraints back in place.[62] As housing costs rose (doubling between 1919 and 1926 and tripling by 1930), more compact formulas were developed. The English romantic style was abandoned and slowly replaced by a minimalist functionalism. At Drancy, for example, one found "a strict geometric alignment of three to five story apartment blocks, punctuated by five identical and regularly spaced six-teen story towers."[63] By the 1930s, the picturesque had been forgotten. The moralizing effects of historically and regionally rooted stylistic features were replaced by universalistic stan-dards of air, space, and functionality. While the cause for these changes was predominantly economic, they also reflected the broader changes in social practices and understandings dis-cussed above.

An unsigned article on "housing and modern urbanism in recent World's Fairs" in the 1930 issue of *La Vie Urbaine* defen-sively presented two housing expositions recently held in Paris. The first, held in 1928, once again demonstrated France's back-wardness. The second, which took place the following year, was organized to promote the Loucheur housing law; the stumbling block was its financing, even for the middle-class housing. Al-though the French record was not glorious, some noteworthy advances had been made in improving norms of health and comfort; a variety of communally shared services were now standard in HBM and industrial workers' accommodations. A tone of annoyance, however, marked an anonymous evaluation of such dwellings as "sad and monotonous, barracks-like."[64] The proposed solution to this perceived mediocrity was unim-aginative: the government should assign different buildings to different architects, a solution that would be reused in the 1970s during another period of doubt. The aesthetic medioc-rity of the new garden-city complexes demonstrated that health measures alone did not constitute social art. Confronting the dismal picture at the end of the decade, the editors advised— with a touch of shrillness—against adopting merely technical solutions. The danger was that mass-produced housing would eliminate the role of architect-urbanist. This hesitant and ambi-valent message was hardly a paean of praise to Taylorism or the glories of industrial production popular with the high mod-ernists; standardization alone could easily produce new ug-liness and exclude men of art.[65]

In 1935 Sellier, looking back on his accomplishments since the war, sarcastically remarked that since the Loucheur law on housing was almost inoperative, it was time to evaluate its in-fluence. Despite its authors' intentions, Sellier warned that the law had increased the role of technicians and technical standards at the expense of men of art and science, thus threatening architectural progress.[66] The Prefecture of the Seine had contributed to the problem by adopting the most minimal and retrograde conceptions of housing. If the technician and economist had produced a mediocre standardization, the efforts of the free market were equally dismal; handymen-surveyors calling themselves architects had produced a series of spectacular disasters. Sellier bitterly lamented that much of the French working class seemed to prefer to live piled up on each other in the worst conditions rather than spend a little more on hygiene and comfort—an attitude, he added, that was shared by most of the elected officials of the communes surrounding Paris. Still, some progress had been made. Before the war the mere introduction of a WC and running water on each floor was considered almost revolutionary. These amenities, along with gas and electricity, were now considered, if not necessary, at least desirable. In the next period elevators and bathtubs were destined to become equally common. But after two decades of effort, Sellier's sense of defeat was unmitigated.

Reluctantly acknowledging economic and political realities, Sellier's office began concentrating on complexes of collective buildings.[67] Sellier accepted the elimination of regional styles in favor of architectural formulas in which aesthetics were dictated by utilitarian concerns. Remembering that earlier he had argued that collective buildings inevitably became barracks, Sellier now defended modernist architecture for its more rational use of space and its efficient provision of services. The result, by the late 1930s, was the almost complete abandonment of the model of the individual house: construction of fifteen-story buildings was under way in the garden cities of Drancy and Châtenay-Malabry.

Socialist Modern

The most ambitious of the socialist projects actually built was just outside Lyons, in Villeurbanne.[68] An independent commune, Villeurbanne had formerly been a workers' city attached to a factory. In 1903, Lyons' socialist mayor, Victor Augagneur, attempted to incorporate Villeurbanne into Lyons. Although meeting strong local resistance, Augagneur had support on the national level, and would certainly have succeeded if he had not accepted the post of governor-general of Madagascar. His famous successor, Edouard Herriot, let the incorporation effort drop.[69] Villeurbanne had voted for reformist-socialist candidates since 1892. Dependent on the larger city of Lyons in a manner parallel to Suresnes and Paris, Villeurbanne underwent major changes between the wars, as its population doubled. Goujon was elected mayor in 1924 (winning over 90 percent of the vote, with communist support). The employee and working-class elite of Villeurbanne came to dominate the city in the interwar period. These groups formed the backbone of Goujon's electoral support and profited most directly from his policies. While Goujon shared Sellier's broad conceptions of socialist municipal organization, he was more successful than Sellier in devising original formulas of state, private, and municipal financing. During his mandate (1924–1934), two-thirds of the commune's territory was transformed; more than a quarter of the commune's land was acquired by the municipality and used for social purposes.[70]

Villeurbanne is famous for its pair of nineteen-story skyscrapers at the new core of the city, which rise above the monumental Palace of Work and stand across the vast Place Albert Thomas from the new city hall. The towers were designed by an architect named Morice Leroux, whom Goujon had met in Morocco.[71] The complex, built using American techniques, contained 1500 apartments arranged in 6 blocks of 11 stories and the 2 towers of 19 stories. They observed the most advanced hygienic standards, allowing the maximum amounts of light and air. Other innovative features included common garbage disposal, central heating, and common hot water supplies; advanced stair and elevator design permitted both vertical and horizontal movement, promoting active conviviality; and stores occupied the bottom level. The Palais du Travail was almost at the center of the urban arrangement, adjacent to the real center of power—the mayor's office. The large town hall, grouping all the municipal services, was designed by Robert Giroud, a student of Garnier. His project, with its large clock tower and massive columns, was designed to symbolize the strength and vitality of the city, as well as its democratic availability to the citizenry. The style was functional, distinguishing it from the regional styles of the garden cities, although the Art Deco details situated it historically.[72]

Dr. Goujon was emphatic about the socialist goals of the new center city. In his 1927 presentation of the project for the Palace of Work, he underlined the weakening of workers' sociability and their consequent increased vulnerability to private (above all, religious) organizations. He called for the creation of a "secular temple," a center for the intellectual, moral, and artistic activity indispensable to the democratic development of *la cité* and the education of the working class, the fundamental road to improving their conditions.[73] The palace contained a pool, a theater with 1,500 sets, a *radio-synthétique* organ, hygiene services, and meeting halls for unions, cooperatives, mutual-aid societies, and artistic and sporting groups. The ground floor was devoted to an immense "democratic" brasserie. Inauguration of the complex in June 1934 was marked by twenty days of festivities; a National Conference of Socialist Municipalities alternated with a cycle of operettas.[74] The center was slow to take hold; it was only after World War II that land prices rose, commerce was attracted, and living in skyscrapers became generally accepted. After the war, the didactic socialist culture was replaced by more popular and commercial forms. The center first attracted employees, minor bureaucrats, skilled workers, and schoolteachers to its 1500 units of housing.

The Museum of Man: All Difference United

After the First World War, French ethnologists were faced with the task of redefining their ties with the naturalist traditions within which nineteenth-century anthropology and museology had been squarely located, as well as with Durkheimian sociology.[75] The problem that Paul Rivet (1876–1958) and Georges-Henri Rivière (1897–1985) posed for themselves was double: how, on the one hand, could one maintain a synthetic vision of man in face of the ever-increasing scientific specialization; and how, on the other hand—given a strong politico-ethical commitment to enlightened progress through science—could one represent scientific advances in a form capable of reaching the broadest possible public? How, in other words, could one reconstitute anthropology as a science and bring it into public view for the greater edification of the French people and nation?

Their efforts to modernize the most human of the human sciences reveal the same ambivalence and hesitation between the techno-cosmopolitan understanding of history, nature, and reform and a background synthetic, universalizing, and decontextualized middling-modernist understanding parallel to that confronting Sellier and his assistants. In the anthropological sciences, the latter alternative would triumph only after the Second World War, although, as in the case of Sellier, some of its preconditions were already laid. Those preconditions, however, did not guarantee success. A debased International style became the official style of France's vast, postwar building program; a universal science of structure, based in the practices of bricolage, would emerge to unite analytically all cultural differences. It is worth underlining once again the historically contingent relation of these formal and scientific developments to the political affiliations of their instigators.

French anthropology underwent major institutional changes in the 1920s. Impetus was provided by the arrival of the Cartel des Gauches in 1924 and the support offered by none other than Garnier's patron, Herriot. Anthropology's modern institutional base, the Institut d'Ethnologie, was created in 1925, jointly directed by the philosopher-anthropologist Lucien Lévy-Bruhl, naturalist and doctor Paul Rivet, and Durkheim's nephew and intellectual heir, Marcel Mauss. Political ambiguities and contradictions were present from the start. Lévy-Bruhl, professor at the Sorbonne, promoted a reformed colonial role for France, an interest shared by the three founders (who were all reformist socialists). While its neo-Lamarckianism made French scientific racism less virulent than that found elsewhere, the other side of the coin is that anti-colonialism among social scientists developed late in France.[76] The complexity of contemporary politics and its relations with ethnography was indicated by Rivet's attempts to merge the

Institute of Ethnology with the older and more prestigious
Société d'Ethnologie, which was run by the conservative, neo-
Le Playist Minister Louis Marin, the man Lyautey had asked
to organize the ethnographic exhibits at the 1931 Colonial
Exposition.[77]

In 1928 Rivet was elected to the chair of anthropology in
Paris. The post carried with it the directorship of the Trocadero anthropological collections of bones and curios. One of
Rivet's first actions was to arrange the transfer of administrative
control of the Trocadero museum from the Ministry of Beaux-
Arts to that of Public Instruction. In this setting, the regenera-
tive scientific and popular role he envisioned for the museum
could be more readily combined. There was much to be done.
In a 1930 article announcing a campaign for the museum's
rescue, Rivet described its advanced state of deterioration—the
institution lacked heat, security, and personnel. Within two
years, with the help of the government and an active private
fund-raising drive, the budget had increased twenty times, and
attendance had quadrupled. Rivet and Rivière practiced a cultural and scientific politics of diffusion and vulgarization
through radio broadcasts, interviews in the press, and well-
publicized expositions, of which the Dakar-Djibouti scientific
expedition, financed by a prize fight in Paris with Museum
guards as "seconds," is the most celebrated example.[78]

Rivet and Rivière approached museology through a con-
textualization of objects based on extensive ethnographic
documentation. The museum's scientific role consisted of
promoting technical and sociological studies of objects and peoples cast broadly within a Maussian *fait total* (total fact) perspective in which each object was illuminated by—and metonymic
of—a whole society. Each society was juxtaposed with neighboring regions and areas; the sum of these represented the
whole world. Rivet and Rivière were not culturalists emphasizing radical uniqueness, nor did they attempt to overthrow their
naturalist ancestors. Rather, concerned that the degree of
specialization attained by modern science would prevent synthetic judgments and comprehensive presentations of conclusions, the two experimented with new forms of totalizing and
individualizing representation, adopting a rather literal meto-

nymic approach to the problem. By grouping scholars working on the same geographical area and placing them close to other groups working on other areas, they hoped that the spatial layout of the museum would facilitate communication within and across specializations. In this manner, each group could keep up with the latest advances in all areas.

Unity and progress would be assured through this holistic spatial organization—what Rivet called its *encyclopédiste* dimension. Of course, the discursive ground upon which the Enlightenment project of representation had rested had long since disappeared. Rivet's encyclopedic grid would literally structure a different understanding of the world. One indication of the distance traveled since the Enlightenment is captured by juxtaposing a 1792 statement, "the Museum: one understands by this word the bringing together of everything nature and art have produced that is most rare and perfect. A museum is the Temple of Nature and Genius," with Marcel Mauss's famous claim that "canned food represents our society better than the most sumptuous jewel or the rarest stamp."[79] The Musée de l'Homme displays emphasized unfamiliar but everyday objects, not masterpieces. Society had replaced nature and art, although Mauss was more of a bricoleur than a triumphant structuralist.

The museum's popular educational role was second only to its scientific mission. The most "typical" objects of different civilizations were to be presented to a large public with elaborate, edifying explanations. Rivet proposed Musée de l'Homme as the first museum accessible to "the collectivity, since it [would] be open at night, when manual and intellectual laborers, freed from their professional obligations, had the right to devote their leisure to education, while escaping the preoccupations of their jobs."[80] Here he echoes Charles Gide's celebration of the modern worker-citizen. Politically, Rivet sought to make the museum a bastion of anti-racism. However, anti-racism and anti-fascism in France at that time did not mean anti-colonialism; Jean Jamin describes the politics of these socialist scientists as at best "neo-colonial before its time." Ethnographic museums had a national role as "incomparable instruments of colonial propaganda (the Musée d'Anvers) and cultural propaganda (the many museums created by the Soviet Union)."[81] Rivet's statement, written in 1931, might well have been a defense of Lyautey's colonial exposition, except that by 1931 Lyautey was far less sanguine about the future.[82]

The 1937 Universal Exposition devoted to "Art et Technique" included plans for a new museum to house Rivet and Rivière's modern anthropological vision: the Musée de l'Homme. Projects for an International Exposition with permanent buildings began appearing almost as soon as Lyautey's colonial exposition in the Vincennes woods closed its Orientalist doors in 1931. The urban projects advocated by Sellier and Musée Social loyalists were soon put aside. Many urbanists were disappointed with the siting of the Front Populaire's exposition on "Art et Technique," on the centrally located Champ de Mars near the Seine, the site of nineteenth-century expositions. The August issue of L'Architecture d'aujourd'hui asked leading architects, critics, and urbanists to evaluate the exposition plans. The chief architect, Jacques Gréber, defended his choice of an inner-city site as inevitable, given the short (three-year) lead time. Sellier was acerbic; the choice of the site was indefensible. No discussion with urbanists had preceded it: politicians and restaurant owners, still bitter over the placement of the Exposition Coloniale in Vincennes, had simply dictated the decision. Sellier insisted that Lyautey's example had been positive, since Paris had benefited from a park, a road system, and the renovation of part of a neighborhood adjacent to the exposition grounds. Alfred Agache proclaimed that the chief cause of the debacle was a lack of unified and responsible direction: "Where we needed a technical dictator like Lyautey, we contented ourselves with appointing powerless administrators and impotent commissions."[83]

The decision to build a complex of theaters and museums on the Trocadero site facing the Champ de Mars set in motion a cascade of projects. On top of the Chaillot hill (first chosen as a monumental site by Napoleon I, later leveled and adorned with gardens and a 125-meter rotary by Napoleon III), overlooking the Seine, the Champ de Mars, and the Eiffel Tower, sat an eclectic Orientalist fantasy built for the 1878 World's Fair. It housed the Trocadero ethnographic museum, the Museum of

Indochina, the Museum of Comparative Sculpture (proposed by Viollet-Le-Duc shortly before his death), and a popular theater designed to accommodate 10,000 (reducing an earlier design for a 100,000-seat coliseum). The first rounds of the site competition, in 1932, required preservation of the existing Trocadero building by means of camouflage. Two architects who had worked in Morocco entered the competition: Albert Laprade proposed a central tower (a campanile in one version) rising from the hill; Joseph Marrast made the hill a Provençal mountain and planned to convert the existing building into an imitation of the Casablanca cathedral. These rather desperate attempts at symbolism reveal the fatigue of this decontextualized, representational eclecticism.

In January 1935, the commission named Jacques Carlu (1890–1976) chief architect of the Trocadero. Carlu, a winner of the Grand Prix de Rome in 1919 for a highly neoclassical palace for the League of Nations in Geneva, had recently returned from nine years spent in Pittsburgh, New York, and Boston. Through his brother Jean, a poster designer and member of the Union des Artistes Modernes, Jacques met Robert Mallet-Stephens. In September 1934 this team of Beaux-Arts architect and modernist trendsetter submitted sketches for a Museum of the Republic: a tentative meeting of International *style moderne* and Beaux-Arts neoclassicism. Once appointed, Carlu was assigned the task of making the definitive camouflage drawings and overall plan. He argued vigorously and successfully for abandoning the camouflage entry. He proposed leaving the central space of the Trocadero hill empty, so as not to compete with the Eiffel Tower.[84] Carlu presented a project for two museums and a Haussmannian, ceremonial esplanade he described as modern but "well within the French monumental tradition." In 1936 a futile, last-minute, impassioned petition to save the old building—with its Turkish baths, fake Lebanese style, and other "Moorish abominations," as a later critic put it—was signed by Picasso, Matisse, Rouault, Chagall, and Braque, as well as by leading art critics, who protested that the overall renovation plans lacked unity. The entire, frantic race to complete the new buildings and gardens in time for the opening was filmed continuously by crews in the Eiffel Tower.

Jacques Gréber, seeking to establish the complex as an official showcase of French art, supported a state patronage program. The Trocadero and the Museum of Modern Art were to use the greatest number of artists, while preserving the stylistic unity of the monuments. A commission headed by the eminent architectural historian Louis Hautecoeur selected seventy-one artists to participate. The commission was eclectic, and chose a vast array of talents and approaches ranging from the state-sanctioned Grand-Prix-de-Rome winners to designers like the Martel brothers, whose work approached cubism. An architectural committee attempted to harmonize these disparate efforts in time for the opening of the exposition of 1937. The results were not uniformly successful; decorative sculptural motifs—Arts of the Five Continents, the Navy—stuck, in the eyes of one critic, to the walls like postage stamps.[85] Another critic evaluated the result as more Assyrian than Greek.

In retrospect, the whole enterprise embodies the last full-blown expression of Gaudet's insouciant definition of eclectic classicism as everything worth preserving. The museum and its architecture bring the pathos Canguilhem has spoken of to its limit. Against the grain of their own intentions, the actors themselves provided the possibility of their project being radically transformed. Others would soon take up elements of the schemata, recasting them in what we can now recognize as an unambiguously modernist project of social and spatial decontextualization.

Post-Urban

In 1935, an architect named Maurice Rotival proposed a bold new solution to the housing problem: "To create inexpensive housing, one must go outside the urban tradition, one must rethink the problem from the very beginning."[86] He called for new conceptions of urban rationality, order, and health. The planning movement had failed: "To the city's ordinary decadence of old age we have added the premature decadence of the suburbs."[87] The solution was to construct only where all variables could be fully controlled: a regional plan taking into account major roads and wooded sites, with public services nested in nodes along the major roadways and not in the center of the city. These *grandes ensembles* (his phrase) should be sited away from existing cities; the multiplication of sports terrains would keep the youth out of the big cities: "In a word this would amount to superimposing upon the present suburban grid of Paris a new and entirely different one which would have to be separated from the first by a veritable Great Wall of China."[88] This schema did not envision either an urbanized suburb or a pastoral rural environment: there was no representational nostalgia, grass but not fields. The site had become abstract; all reference to older modes of life, to history, to the sedimented place of memory, and to sociality had been eliminated. Both in the garden cities and in the colonies, the symbolic central point of the city had been reserved for public administration. Administration was evolving from an organizing symbol to a technical consideration. Rotival proposed grouping administrative services alongside the highway; the social environment had become middling modernist.

Notes

Introduction

1. *Oeuvres de Descartes*, ed. Samuel S. de Sacy (Paris, 1966), 2: 723.

2. Richard F. Kuisel, *Capitalism and the State in Modern France: Renovation and Economic Management in the Twentieth Century* (Cambridge, Eng., 1981), 135; Robert Paxton, *Vichy France: Old Guard and New Order, 1940–44* (New York, 1972); Jean Bouvier and François Bloch-Lainé, *La France restaurée 1944–54: dialogue sur les choix d'une modernisation* (Paris, 1986).

3. Kuisel, *Capitalism and the State*, 128.

4. Michel Ecochard, "Problèmes d'urbanisme au Maroc," *Bulletin économique et social du Maroc* 15, no. 52(October–December 1951): 28. On the Charter of Athens and the modernist movement see Leonardo Benevolo, *The History of Modern Architecture: The Modern Movement* (Cambridge, 1977), vol. 2.

5. Jean Dethier, "60 ans d'urbanisme au Maroc," *Bulletin économique et social du Maroc* 32, nos. 118–119(July–December 1970): 34.

6. Jean Delorme, "Casablanca de Henri Prost à Michel Ecochard," *Architecture, mouvement, continuité* 42(June 1977): 10; Janet L. Abu-Lughod, *Rabat: Urban Apartheid in Morocco* (Princeton, N.J., 1980), 216–36.

7. Robert Auzelle, *Technique de l'urbanisme* (Paris, 1953); idem., "Conditions et impératifs de l'urbanisme," *Le Vie urbaine* (April–June 1961).

8. Paul-Henry Chombart de Lauwe, *Paris: essais de sociologie, 1952–1964* (Paris, 1965).

9. Annelise Gérard, "Quartier et unité de voisinage dans la pratique urbanistique française 1919–1973." (Thèse de 3e cycle, Université de Paris VII, 1977), 309.

10. Cf. Maurice Roncayolo, *Histoire de la France Urbaine* (Paris: Seuil, 1985), 5: 370.

11. Charles Baudelaire, "Conseils aux jeunes littérateurs," *Oeuvres complètes de Charles Baudelaire: L'Art romantique* (Paris, 1868), 286.

12. E.H. Gombrich, "Norm and Form: The Stylistic Categories of Art History and Their Origins in Renaissance Ideals," *Norm and Form, Studies in the Art of the Renaissance* (London, 1966), 83.

13. Carl Schorske, *Fin-de-Siècle Vienna: Politics and Culture* (New York, 1980); T.J. Clark, *The Painting of Modern Life: Paris in the Art of Manet and His Followers* (New York, 1985); Hans Blumenberg, *The Legitimacy of the Modern Age* (Cambridge, 1983); Manfredo Tafuri, *The Sphere and the Labyrinth: Avant-Gardes and Architecture from Piranesi to the 1970s* (Cambridge, 1987); Jurgen Habermas, *The Philosophical Discourse of Modernity: Twelve Lectures* (Cambridge, 1987); Reyner Banham, *A Concrete Atlantis: U.S. Industrial Building and European Modern Architecture, 1900–1925* (Cambridge, 1986).

14. Georges Canguilhem, "Le Normal et le pathologique," *Le Normal et le pathologique* 2d ed. (Paris, 1966), 182–83.

15. Georges Canguilhem, *La connaissance de la vie*, 2d ed. (Paris, 1965).

16. Hans Blumenberg, *The Legitimacy of the Modern Age* (Cambridge, 1983), 422.

17. Hannah Arendt, *The Life of the Mind* (New York, 1981), 104–9. The troubled relations of word and image are adroitly analyzed in W. J. T. Mitchell, *Iconology, Image, Text, Ideology* (Chicago, 1986).

18. On "specific" versus "universal" intellectuals, see Michel Foucault, "Truth and Power," *Power/Knowledge: Selected Writings and Other Writings 1972–1977*, ed. Colin Gordon (New York, 1980), 126–33. The definition of technocrats comes from Gérard Brun, *Technocrates et technocratie en France, 1914–1945* (Paris, 1985), 8–9.

19. Pierre Bourdieu, "Fieldwork in philosophy," *Choses dites* (Paris, 1987).

Chapter 1

1. Alexandre Le Maître, *La Métropolitée* (Amsterdam, 1682).

2. Hugues Neveux, "Les Discours sur la ville," *Histoire de la France urbaine*, vol. 3, *La Ville classique de la Renaissance aux révolutions*, ed. Emmanuel Le Roy Ladurie (Paris, 1981), 20.

3. The literature on Louis XIV, Versailles, and related matters is, in the strict sense of the term, enormous. Directly related to the concerns of this book are: Philippe Beausant, *Versailles, Opéra* (Paris, 1981); Norbert Elias, *The Court Society*, trans. Edmund Jephcott (New York, 1983); as well as Norbert Elias, *The Civilizing Process*, 2 vols., trans. Edmund Jephcott (New York, 1978); Louis Marin, *Le Portrait du roi* (Paris, 1981).

4. Michel Foucault, "The Eye of Power," *Power/Knowledge: Selected Interviews and Other Writings by Michel Foucault, 1972–1977*, ed. Colin Gordon (New York, 1980), 152.

5. Michel Foucault, *The Order of Things: An Archaeology of the Human Sciences* (New York, 1973), 322.

6. Foucault, *The Order of Things*, 312, 319.

7. Raymond Williams, *Culture and Society: 1780–1950* (New York, 1983), xviii.

8. George W. Stocking, Jr., "French Anthropology in 1800," *Race, Culture, and Evolution: Essays in the History of Anthropology* (New York, 1968), 15; Jean Jamin and Jean Copans, *Aux Origines de l'anthropologie française: les mémoires de la société des observateurs de l'homme en l'an VIII* (Paris, 1979); Gerard Leclerc, *L'Observation de l'homme: une histoire des énquêtes sociales* (Paris, 1979); Joseph-Marie de Gérando, *The Observation of Savage Peoples*, trans., ed. and intro. F.G.T. Moore (London, 1969).

9. Georges Gusdorf, *La Conscience révolutionnaire: les idéologues* (Paris, 1978); Michèle Duchet, *Anthropologie et histoire au siècle des lumières* (Paris, 1971).

10. de Gérando, *Savage Peoples*, 63.

11. Ibid., 70.

12. Michèle Duchet in *Anthropologie et histoire* draws the colonialist conclusions from Enlightenment anthropology; Edward Said in *Orientalism* (New York, 1978) makes even stronger claims for the insidious implications of Napoleon's scientific mission to Egypt; Jean Jamin and Jean Copans in *Aux Origines de l'anthropologie française* warn against the presentist fallacy in reading later consequences into these treatises.

13. Jamin and Copans, *Aux Origines*, 54.

14. On Cuvier, see William Coleman, *Georges Cuvier, Zoologist: A Study in the History of Evolution Theory* (Cambridge, Mass., 1964); Dorinda Outram, *Georges Cuvier: Vocation, Science and Authority in Post-Revolutionary France* (Dover, N.H., 1984); Joseph-Marie de Gérando, *Le Visiteur du Pauvre* (Paris, 1920). On the emergence of modern attention to the poor, see Giovanna Procacci, *Le Gouvernement de la misère, la question sociale entre les deux révolutions 1789–1848* (thèse de doctorat de troisième cycle, Université de Paris VIII, 1983).

15. This rigorous separation of the life sciences from the physical sciences earned Bichat a place of honor in Auguste Comte's Positivist Calendar, as the patron saint of the modern sciences. Auguste Comte, *Système de politique positive*, vol. 4 (Paris, 1854), 402, insert B, as cited in Martin S. Staum, *Cabanis: Enlightenment and Medical Philosophy in the French Revolution* (Princeton, N.J., 1980), 255.

16. Michel Foucault, *The Order of Things*, 268.

17. Georges Canguilhem, "Du Social au vital," *Le Normal et le pathologique*, 4th ed. (Paris, 1979), 188–89.

18. On the definition of utopias in urbanism, see: Françoise Choay, *La Règle et le modèle* (Paris, 1980).

19. René Rémond, *The Right Wing in France: From 1815 to de Gaulle*, 2d ed. (Philadelphia, 1966).

20. Félicité de Lamennais, "Progrès de la révolution," *Oeuvres complètes* (Brussels, 1839), 2: 241.

21. Frank E. Manuel and Fritzie P. Manuel, *Utopian Thought in the Western World* (Cambridge, Mass., 1979).

22. Manuel and Manuel, *Utopian Thought*, 601. Saint-Simon, "Du Système industriel," *Oeuvres de Saint-Simon et d'Enfantin*, vol. 22 (Paris, 1865–78).

23. Frank E. Manuel, *The New World of Henri Saint-Simon* (Cambridge, Mass., 1956), 314.

24. Theodore Zeldin, *France 1848–1945*, vol. 1, *Ambition, Love and Politics* (Oxford, 1973), 431.

25. François Delaporte, *Disease and Civilization: The Cholera in Paris, 1832*, trans. Arthur Goldhammer, pref. Paul Rabinow (Cambridge, Mass., 1985).

26. Georges Canguilhem, "Le Vivant et son milieu," *La Connaissance de la vie* (Paris, 1965), 129.

27. F.-J. Double, *Rapport sur le choléra-morbus, lu à l'Académie royale de Médecine le 13 septembre 1831* (Paris, 1831), 156–57.

28. For a detailed description of Enlightenment anthropologies, see Michèle Duchet's classic *Anthropologie et histoire au siècle des lumières* (Paris, 1971).

29. D.J. Larrey, *Mémoire sur le choléra-morbus* (Paris, 1831), 27–33.

30. J. Sarazin, *Le Choléra pestilentiel* (Paris, 1831), 19–20.

31. The classic work is Louis Chevalier, *Classes laborieuses et classes dangereuses à Paris pendant la première moitié du XIXe siècle* (Paris, 1958); also see Chevalier's *Le Choléra: La Première épidémie du XIXe siècle* (Paris, 1958); *Histoire de la France urbaine*, vol. 4, *La Ville de l'âge industriel: le cycle haussmannien*, ed. Maurice Agulhon (Paris, 1983).

32. Dr. Malouin, *Mémoires de l'Académie des sciences* (Paris, 1753), as cited in Blandine Barret-Kriegel, "Les Demeures de la misère: le choléra-morbus et l'émergence de l'habitat," *Politiques de l'habitat, 1800–1850*, ed. Michel Foucault (Paris, 1977), 86.

33. For more details see Delaporte, *Disease and Civilization*, and Erwin Ackerknecht, "Villermé et Quételet," *Bulletin of the Journal of the History of Medicine* 26 (1952).

34. Benoiston de Châteauneuf, *Rapport sur la marche et les effets du choléra-morbus dans Paris* (Paris, 1834).

35. Chevalier, *Classes laborieuses*, 13.

36. Louis-René Villermé, "Note sur les ravages du choléra-morbus," *Annales d'hygiène publique et de médecine légale* 11(1834).

37. Michel Chevalier, *Société des amis du peuple: de la civilisation* (Paris, 1832), 2–6.

38. Charles Beranger, as cited in Barret-Kriegel, "Les Demeures de la misère," 113.

39. Dr. Ange Guépin, *Histoire de Nantes* (Nantes, 1835); also Dr. Ange Guépin and Charles E. Bonamy, *Nantes au XIXe siècle: statistique, topographie industrielle et morale* (Nantes, 1835), reprint, ed. Philippe Le Pichon and Alain Supiot, preceded by "De l'Observation de la ville comme corps social," (Nantes, 1981). Pages are listed first for the original edition and second for the excellent re-edition and commentary.

40. Guépin and Bonamy, *Nantes au XIXe siècle*.

41. Ibid., 31/65.

42. Ibid., 455/277.

43. Guépin, *Histoire de Nantes,* 107, 42.

44. Jean-Claude Perrot, "Urbanisme et commerce au XVIIIe siècle dans les ports de Nantes et Bordeaux," *Actes du Colloque 'Villes et compagnes, XVe–XXe siècle'* (Lyons, 1977). For additional historical material see Pierre Lelièvre, *L'Urbanisme et l'architecture à Nantes au XVIIIe siècle* (Nantes, 1972); Paul Rabinow, "Ordonnance, Discipline, Regulation: Some Reflections on Urbanism," *Humanities in Society* 5, nos. 3–4(Summer and Fall 1982); *Iconographie de Nantes* (Nantes, 1978), 98.

45. This literalization of representation at the end of the Classical age is best seen in the work of Ledoux and Boullée.

46. See: *Mathurin Crucy, 1749–1826: architecte nantais néo-classique* (Nantes, 1986).

47. César Daly, "Discours prononcé au nom des anciens élèves de Félix Duban," *Funérailles de Félix Duban,* ed. César Daly (Paris, 1871), 33, as quoted in Neil A. Levine, "The Romantic Idea of Architectural Legibility: Henri Labrouste and the Neo-Grec," *The Architecture of the Ecole des Beaux-Arts,* ed. Arthur Drexler (New York, 1977), 328.

48. Levine, "Romantic Idea of Architectural Legibility," 328.

49. Anthony Vidler, "The Idea of Type," *Oppositions* 8(Spring 1977).

50. Joseph Rykwert, *On Adam's House in Paradise: The Idea of the Primitive Hut in Architectural History* (Cambridge, Mass., 1972). See also Louis Hautecoeur, *Histoire de l'architecture classique en France,* vol. 5 (Paris, 1953), 1–3.

51. Marc-Antoine Laugier, *Essai sur l'architecture* (Paris, 1753), xx.

52. Antoine Quatremère de Quincy, "Caractère," *Encyclopédie méthodique d'architecture,* vol. 1 (Paris, 1788), as cited in Vidler, "The Idea of Type," *Oppositions* 8(Spring, 1977) 104.

53. See Alberto Perez-Gomez, *Architecture and the Crisis of Modern Science* (Cambridge, Mass., 1983).

54. As quoted by Benevolo, *History of Modern Architecture,* 1: 31.

55. Hautecoeur, *Histoire,* 5: 110.

56. Richard Chafee, "The Teaching of Architecture at the Ecole des Beaux-Arts," Drexler, ed., *The Architecture of the Ecole des Beaux-Arts,* 61. Joseph Rykwert, *The First Moderns: The Architects of the Eighteenth Century* (Cambridge, Mass., 1972).

57. David Van Zantan, "Architectural Composition at the Ecole des Beaux-Arts from Charles Percier to Charles Garnier," Drexler, ed., *Architecture of the Ecole des Beaux-Arts,* 112.

58. Reyner Banham, *Theory and Design in the First Machine Age,* 2d ed. (Cambridge, Mass., 1982), 16. Thomas Kuhn, *The Structure of Scientific Revolutions,* 2d ed. (Chicago, 1970), 192.

59. Neil A. Levine, "Architectural Reasoning in the Age of Positivism: The Neo-Grec

Idea of Henri Labrouste's Bibliothèque Sainte-Geneviève," 5 vols., Ph.D. diss. (Cambridge, Mass., 1975).

60. Ibid., 357.

61. Antoine Quatremère de Quincy, *Essai sur la nature, le but et les moyens de l'imitation dans les beaux-arts* (Paris, 1923).

62. Levine, "The Romantic Idea of Architectural Legibility," 367.

63. Ibid., 370.

Chapter 2

1. George Rosen, *A History of Public Health* (New York, 1958), 131–91. Jacqueline Hecht, "L'Idée du dénombrement jusqu'à la Révolution," *Pour une histoire de la statistique*, vol. 1(Paris, 1986); Theodore M. Porter, *The Rise of Statistical Thinking, 1820–1900* (Princeton, N.J., 1986); Stephen M. Stigler, *The History of Statistics: The Measurement of Uncertainty before 1900* (Cambridge, Mass., 1986); Jacques Dupâquier and Michel Dupâquier, *Histoire de la démographie* (Paris, 1985). George Rosen, "Medical Care and Social Policy in Seventeenth Century England," *Bulletin of the New York Academy of Medicine*, 2d ser., no. 29(1953). George Rosen, "Problems in the application of statistical analysis to questions of health: 1700–1880," *Bulletin of the History of Medicine* 29(1955). I would like to thank Bernard-Pierre Lecuyer as well as François Ewald for their separate help in these matters.

2. Keith Michael Baker, *Condorcet: From Natural Philosophy to Social Mathematics* (Chicago, 1975); Ian Hacking, *The Emergence of Probability: A Philosophical Study of Early Ideas about Probability, Induction and Statistical Inference* (Cambridge, Eng., 1975).

3. Philippe Pinel, "Résultats d'observations et construction des tables pour servir à déterminer le degré de probabilité de la guérison des aliénés," *Mémoires de la classe des sciences mathématiques et physiques de l'Institut National de France* (Paris, 1807), 169–205.

4. Marie-Noëlle Bourguet, "Décrire, compter, calculer: The debate over statistics during the Napoleonic period," *The Probabilistic Revolution*, ed. Lorraine Daston, Michael Heidelberger and Lorenz Kruger, vol. 1, *Ideas in History* (Cambridge, Eng., 1986).

5. Institut Royal de France, *Académie royale des sciences: programme du prix de statistique proposé par l'Académie Royale des Sciences pour l'année 1818* (Paris, 1817).

6. Harold Westergaard, *Contributions to the History of Statistics* (London, 1932), 136. The movement was not without its opponents: conservatives charged statisticians with a materialistic determinism which ignored man's spiritual and moral qualities; liberal economists like Jean-Baptiste Say criticized the scattered and unsystematic manner in which statistical studies were being piled up; mathematicians and activists accused statisticians of using a weak notion of causality and of collecting misleading decontextualized numbers. See Michelle Perrot, "Premières Mesures des faits sociaux: les débuts de la statistique criminelle en France, 1780–1830," *Pour une histoire de la statistique*, vol. 1 (Paris, 1986), 134.

7. Bernard-Pierre Lecuyer, "Démographie, statistique, et hygiène publique sous la monarchie censitaire," *Annales de démographie historique* (1977). Bertrand Gille, *Les*

Sources statistiques de l'histoire de France: des enquêtes du XVIIe siècle à 1870 (Geneva, 1964), 170.

8. Prospectus, *Annales d'hygiène publique et de médecine légale*, no. 1 (1829): v.

9. Bernard-Pierre Lecuyer, "Médecins et observateurs sociaux: Les Annales d'hygiène et de médecine légale, 1820–1850," *Pour une histoire de la statistique*, vol. 1 (Paris, 1986); Ann La Berge, "Popular Health Publications: Periodicals, Pamphlets and Books," in her "Public Health in France and the French Public Health Movement, 1815–1848," Ph.D. diss., University of Tennessee, 1974.

10. William Coleman, *Death Is a Social Disease: Public Health and Political Economy in Early Industrial France* (Madison, 1982). On Villermé and other leading figures such as Parent-Duchâtelet, see Alain Corbin, *Les Filles de noce: Misère sexuelle et prostitution, 19e et 20e siècles* (Paris, 1979).

11. Louis-René Villermé, "Mémoire sur la mortalité dans la classe aisée et dans la classe indigente," *Mémoires de l'Académie Royale de Médecine* 1(1828), 51–98.

12. La Berge, "Public Health in France," 45. See also Coleman, *Death Is a Social Disease*.

13. Louis-René Villermé, *Tableau de l'état physique et moral des ouvriers employés dans les manufactures de coton, de laine et de soie*, 2 vols. (Paris, 1840).

14. Bernard-Pierre Lecuyer and Anthony P. Oberschall, "Sociology, III: The Early History of Social Research," *International Encyclopedia of the Social Sciences*, ed. David L. Sills, vol. 15 (New York, 1968).

15. William M. Reddy, "Visions of subsistence," *The Rise of Market Culture, the Textile Trade and French Society, 1750–1900* (Cambridge, 1984), ch. 6.

16. Maurice Halbwachs, *La Théorie de l'homme moyen: essai sur Quételet et la statistique morale* (Paris, 1913), 72. Joseph Lottin, *Quételet: statisticien et sociologue* (Paris, 1912); Bernard-Pierre Lecuyer, "Quételet," *Encyclopedia Universalis* (Paris, 1985).

17. Adolphe Quételet, "Recherches sur la loi de la croissance de l'homme," *Nouveaux mémoires de l'académie des sciences et belles-lettres de Bruxelles* (Brussels, 1832); *Recherches sur le penchant au crime aux differents âges* (Brussels, 1831); Porter, *Rise of Statistical Thinking*, 46 for the last point. Stigler's judgment is even more negative, *History of Statistics*, 161.

18. Simeon Denis Poisson, *Recherches sur la probabilité des jugements en matière criminelle et en matière civile* (Paris, 1837); on Poisson, see Stigler, *History of Statistics*, 182–94.

19. Adolphe Quételet, "Sur l'appréciation des documents statistiques," *Bulletin de la Commission Centenaire de Statistique* (1844), 2: 258.

20. Quételet, *Recherches sur le penchant au crime*, 2: 274.

21. Ibid., 29–30. Buffon, *De l'homme, Oeuvres complètes*, ed. A. Richard (Paris, 1835), 8: 386–88.

22. Georges Canguilhem, "Norme et moyenne," *Le Normal et le pathologique*, 4th ed. (Paris, 1979), 100.

23. Adolphe Quételet, *Etudes sur l'homme* (Paris, 1842), 21.

24. Porter, *Rise of Statistical Thinking*, 54–55.

25. Stigler, *History of Statistics*, 215.

26. Anthony Vidler, "News from the Realm of No-Where," *Oppositions* 1(September 1973): 87.

27. Léonce Reynaud, *Traité d'architecture*, 2 vols. (Paris, 1850 and 1858).

28. Julien Gaudet, *Eléments et théorie de l'architecture*, 4th ed., 4 vols. (Paris, 1915), 1: 80–81.

29. Kenneth Frampton, *Modern Architecture: A Critical History* (New York, 1980), 64.

30. Viollet-Le-Duc, *Discourses on Architecture*, 2 vols. (Paris: 1860; Boston: 1875).

31. Michel Foucault, *The Order of Things: An Archaeology of the Human Sciences* (New York, 1971), 319.

32. Although Viollet-Le-Duc does sometimes say this. Cf. *Discourses on Architecture*, 2: 1.

33. Ibid., 14.

34. Ibid., 57.

35. Sir John Summerson, "Viollet-Le-Duc and the Rational Point of View," in "Architectural Design Profiles: Eugène Emmanuel Viollet-Le-Duc, 1814–1879," *Architectural Design* 50: no. 3/4(1980): 1–14.

36. Through these connections he was kept busy with commissions to design chateaux; best known is the Chateau at Pierrefonds, commissioned in 1858.

37. Louis Vitet, Eugène Viollet-Le-Duc, *A Propos de l'enseignement des arts du dessin* (Paris, 1863, republished with a preface by Bruno Foucart, Paris, 1984).

38. Pierre Lavedan, "Paris à l'arrivée d'Haussmann," *La Vie Urbaine*, n.s., nos. 3–4 (July–December 1953).

39. Louis Chevalier, *La Formation de la population parisienne au XIXe siècle* (Paris, 1950); Emile Levasseur, *La Population française*, vol. 2 (Paris, 1889–1892).

40. As quoted in Ann-Louise Shapiro, *Housing the Poor of Paris, 1850–1902* (Madison, 1985), 6.

41. Anne Thalamy, "Réflexions sur la notion d'habitat aux XVIIIe et XIXe siècles," *Politiques de l'habitat, 1800–1850*, ed. Michel Foucault (Paris, 1977).

42. Michel Foucault, "La Politique de la santé au XVIIIe siècle," *Les Machines à guérir: aux origines de l'hôpital moderne*, ed. Foucault (Paris, 1979).

43. Maurice Halbwachs, "Les Plans d'extension et d'aménagement de Paris avant le XIXe siècle," *La Vie Urbaine*, 2 (1920).

44. The major works on the subject include Georges Haussmann, *Mémoires du Baron Haussmann*, 3 vols., 3d ed. (Paris, 1890); David H. Pinkney, *Napoleon III and the Rebuild-*

ing of Paris (Princeton, N.J., 1958); Jeanne Gaillard, *Paris la Ville, 1852–1870* (Paris, 1977); Louis Girard, *La Politique des travaux publiques du Second Empire* (Paris, 1951); Anthony Sutcliffe, *The Autumn of Central Paris: The Defeat of Town Planning 1850–1970* (Montreal, 1971); Françoise Choay, *The Modern City: Planning in the 19th Century* (New York, 1969); *Histoire de la France urbaine*, vol. 4, *La Ville de l'âge industriel: le cycle haussmannien*, ed. Maurice Agulhon (Paris, 1983); Pierre Lavedan, *Histoire de l'urbanisme*, 3 vols. (Paris, 1952–66); Leonardo Benevolo, *History of Modern Architecture*, vol. 1, *The Tradition of Modern Architecture* (Cambridge, Mass., 1971).

45. Françoise Choay, "Pensées sur la ville, arts de la ville," *Histoire de la France urbaine*, 4: 198.

46. Benevolo, *History of Modern Architecture*, 1: 78.

47. For the political point, see David Harvey, *Consciousness and the Urban Experience: Studies in the History and Theory of Urbanization* (Baltimore, 1985); idem, *The Urbanization of Capital: Studies in the History and Theory of Capitalist Urbanization* (Baltimore, 1985); T.J. Clark, *The Painting of Modern Life: Paris in the Art of Manet and his Followers* (New York, 1985).

48. Marcel Roncayolo, "Logiques urbaines," *Histoire de la France urbaine*, vol. 4, ed. Agulhon, 103.

49. Bernard-Pierre Lecuyer, "Historiens et enquêteurs sociaux: quelques réflexions sur leur ignorance mutuelle sous la monarchie censitaire," *Historiens et sociologues aujourd'hui*, ed. François Furet (Paris, CNRS, 1986).

50. Anthony Sutcliffe, *The Autumn of Central Paris*, 182. On history see Stephen Bann, *The Clothing of Clio: A Study of the Representation of History in Nineteenth-century Britain and France* (Cambridge, Eng., 1984); Donald R. Kelley, *Historians and the Law in Post-revolutionary France* (Princeton, N.J., 1984); Hayden White, *Metahistory: Historical Representation in Nineteenth-century Europe* (Baltimore, Md., 1973); Anthony Vidler, "Architecture in the Museum: Didactic Narratives from Boullée to Lenoir," *The Writing of the Walls: Architectural Theory in the Late Enlightenment* (Princeton, N.J., 1987).

51. Ann Lorenz Van Zantan, "Form and Society: César Daly and the 'Revue Générale de l'Architecture,' " *Oppositions* 8(Spring 1977). Hélène Lipstadt and Harvey Mendelsohn, *Architectes et ingénieurs dans la presse: polémique, débat, conflit* (Paris, 1980).

Chapter 3

1. Michelle Perrot, ed., *L'Impossible prison, Recherches sur le système pénitentiaire au XIXe siècle, débat avec Michel Foucault* (Paris, 1980); "The Three Ages of Industrial Discipline in Nineteenth-Century France," *Consciousness and Class Experience in France*, ed. John M. Merriman (New York, 1979).

2. Maurice Halbwachs, *Les Expropriations et le prix des terrains à Paris de 1860 à 1900* (Paris, 1909). Between 1853 and 1870 Paris' debt rose from 163 million francs to 2,500 million, and by 1870 debt charges made up 44.14 percent of the city budget. Anthony Sutcliffe, *The Autumn of Central Paris: The Defeat of Town Planning, 1850–1970* (Montreal, 1971), 42.

3. The most complete treatment of the whole issue of Paris' suburban development remains Jean Bastié, *La Croissance de la banlieue parisienne* (Paris, 1964). See also Roger-

H. Guerrand, *Les Origines du logement social en France* (Paris, 1967). For a contemporary Marxist view, see David Harvey, *The Urbanization of Capital: Studies in the History and Theory of Capitalist Urbanization* (Baltimore, 1985). A form of Haussmannization had been followed in other major French cities (Lyons, Montpellier, Bordeaux, and Lille) with similar results. Marcel Roncayolo, "Logiques urbaines," *Histoire de la France urbaine*, vol. 4, *La Ville de l'âge industriel, le cycle haussmannien*, ed. Maurice Agulhon (Paris, 1983), 120.

4. Yves Lequin, "Discussion," *Construire la ville*, ed. Maurice Garden and Yves Lequin (Lyons, 1983), 167; Christian Topalov, *Le Logement en France, Histoire d'une marchandise impossible* (Paris, 1987), part 2.

5. Guerrand, *Les Origines du logement social en France* (Paris, 1967), ch. 3.

6. As cited in Monique Eleb-Vidal and Anne Debarre-Blanchard, *Architecture domestique et mentalités: les traités et les pratiques au XIXe siècle*, published as an issue of *In Extenso, recherches à l'Ecole d'Architecture Paris-Villemin* (1985), 102.

7. Stephan Jonas, *Construire la ville*, ed. Garden and Lequin (Lyons, 1983), 164.

8. Louis-René Villermé, "Sur les cités ouvrières," *Annales d'hygiène publique et de médecine légale* 43(1850): 8. See also Bullock and Read, *Movement for Housing Reform*.

9. Ann-Louise Shapiro, *Housing the Poor of Paris*, 53, citing Henry Fougère, *Les Délégations ouvrières aux expositions universelles sous le Second Empire* (Montlucon, 1905), 20–21.

10. N. Harou-Romain, "Des Cités ouvrières," *Annales de la charités* 5(1849): 737.

11. There are two recent studies of Le Play in English. One reads him as a major forerunner of empirical social science: Catherine Bodard Silver's extended introduction to the collection of his writings entitled *Le Play: On Family, Work, and Social Change*, ed., trans., and intro. Catherine Bodard Silver (Chicago, 1982). The other emphasizes his technical and reform accomplishments: Michael Brooke, *Le Play: Engineer and Social Scientist* (London, 1970).

12. Silver, introduction, *Le Play*, 1.

13. Ibid., 18.

14. Frédéric Le Play, *La Constitution essentielle* (Paris, 1893), 3–4, as cited in Silver, introduction, *Le Play*, 16.

15. Frédéric Le Play, preface, *Programme de gouvernement et d'organisation sociale d'après l'observation comparée de divers peuples* (Paris, 1881), vi.

16. Frédéric Le Play, *Vues générales sur la statistique* (Paris, 1840).

17. Luigi Einaudi, "The Doctrine of Original Sin and the Theory of the Elite in the Writings of Frédéric Le Play," *Essays in European Economic Thought*, trans. and ed. Louise Sommer (Princeton, N.J., 1960), 169.

18. Frédéric Le Play, *Les Ouvriers européens*, 2d ed. (Tours, 1877–79), 53.

19. Ibid., 1: 223.

20. Ibid., 11.

21. Ibid., 20.

22. Ibid., 446.

23. Le Play, *La Constitution essentielle* (Tours, 1893), 230.

24. Frédéric Le Play, *La Méthode de la science sociale* (Tours, 1879).

25. Madeleine Rébérioux, "Les Ouvriers et les expositions universelles de Paris au XIXe siècle," 199, as cited in *Le Livre des expositions universelles, 1851–1989* (Paris: Union Centrale des Arts Décoratifs, 1983).

26. Utopian solutions were still the only site of discursive experimentation and Guise the only practical French experiment. Jean-Pierre Epron et al., *L'Usine et la ville, 1839–1986: 150 ans de l'urbanisme* (Neuilly-sur-Seine, 1986).

27. Stephan Jonas, "Structures industrielles et politique urbaine à Mulhouse au XIXe siècle, 1798–1870," *Construire la ville*, ed. Lequin and Garden, 88.

28. Dr. A. Penot, "Des Institutions de prévoyance sociale fondées par les industriels du Haut-Rhin en faveur de leurs ouvriers," *Bulletin de la Société industrielle de Mulhouse* 26 (1855).

29. Leonardo Benevolo, *The History of Modern Architecture*, vol. 1, *The Tradition of Modern Architecture* (Cambridge, Mass., 1971), 128.

30. Jean-Baptiste Duroselle, *Les Débuts du catholicisme social en France (1822–1870)* (Paris, 1951).

31. Monique Eleb-Vidal and Ann Debarre-Blanchard, *Architecture domestique*, 124–28.

32. Guerrand, *Les Origines du logement social en France*, 125.

33. Michelle Perrot, "The Three Ages," 160.

34. The exemplar of the inflationist position is Lion Murard and Patrick Zylberman, *Le Petit Travailleur infatigable: villes-usines, habitat et intimités au XIXe siècle* (Paris, 1976). A more complex understanding is found in Jean-Pierre Frey, *La Ville industrielle et ses urbanités: la distinction ouvriers/employés, Le Creusot 1870–1930* (Brussels, 1985); Christian Devillers and Bernard Huet, *Le Creusot: naissance et développement d'une ville industrielle, 1782–1914* (Seyssel, 1981). On the location of industry and related questions see Jean-Pierre Epron et al., *L'Usine et la ville, 1836–1986: 150 ans de l'urbanisme* (Neuilly-sur-Seine, 1986).

35. Emile Cheysson, "Le Creusot: condition matérielle, intellectuelle et morale de la population: institutions et relations sociales," *Bulletin de l'Association internationale pour le développement du commerce et des expositions*, 19 July 1869, 12. On the historical sociology of the schools, see Frey, *La Ville industrielle*, 86–98.

36. An excellent discussion of these developments can be found in Georges Teyssot, "La casa per tutti, per una genealogia dei tipi," *Le Origini della questione delle abitazioni in Francia, 1850–1894*, ed. Roger-H. Guerrand (Rome, 1981).

37. Later developments will be slightly more flexible and individualized, seeking a more *petit bourgeois* clientele.

38. Frey, *La Ville industrielle*, 158–80.

39. By the early years of the nineteenth century many of these requirements are taken over by state regulations and one by one are withdrawn from the local level. The Schneiders included a clause in the deeds they sold waiving rights to damages from *dégâts* caused by their industrial activities.

40. Fernand L'Huillier, *La Lutte ouvrière à la fin du Second Empire* (Paris, 1957), 21. Jean-Baptiste Dumay, *Mémoires d'un militant ouvrier du Creusot, 1841–1905* (Paris, 1976).

41. As cited in L'Huillier, *La Lutte ouvrière*, 52.

Chapter 4

1. Claude Digeon, *La Crise allemande de la pensée française, 1870–1914* (Paris, 1959); Allan Mitchell, *Bismarck and the French Nation 1848–1890* (New York, 1971).

2. Edgar Quinet, *Lettres d'exil*, vol. 3 (Paris, 1885–86), 123–60.

3. Hubert Lyautey, *Le Rôle social de l'officier suivi de textes et de lettres autour de 'Le Rôle social de l'officier'* (Paris, 1984), 15–16.

4. André Maurois, *Lyautey* (Paris, 1931), is the standard biography of its generation. There are many others: the most recent and comprehensive although still hagiographic is André Le Révérend, *Lyautey* (Paris, 1983). Le Révérend has published two other illuminating books on Lyautey: *Lyautey, l'écrivain (1854–1934)* (Paris, 1976), and *Un Lyautey inconnu: correspondance et journal inédits, 1874–1934* (Paris, 1980).

5. Benoist-Méchin, *Lyautey l'africain ou le rêve immolé, 1854–1934*, reprint (Paris, 1978), 16.

6. Ibid., 25.

7. Le Révérend, *Un Lyautey inconnu*, 50.

8. Benjamin F. Martin, *Albert de Mun: Paladin of the Third Republic* (Chapel Hill, N.C., 1978).

9. Ibid., 12–13.

10. Theodore Zeldin, *France 1848–1945*, vol. 5, *Anxiety and Hypocrisy* (Oxford, 1981), 252.

11. Le Révérend, *Un Lyautey inconnu*, 43–44.

12. Ibid., 51.

13. Ibid., 59.

14. Colonel Laronde, "Villes et villages de colonisation à plan régulier en Algérie," *L'Urbanisme aux colonies et dans les pays tropicaux*, ed. Jean Royer, vol. 1 (La Charité-sur-Loire, 1932).

15. Le Révérend, *Un Lyautey inconnu*, 95.

16. Hubert Lyautey, *Lettres du Tonkin et de Madagascar, 1894–1899* (Paris, 1920), 467.

17. Le Révérend, *Un Lyautey inconnu,* 106.

18. Ibid., 83.

19. Ibid., 80.

20. Ibid., 100.

21. Vincent Crapanzano, "Goethe in Italy," *Writing Culture: The Poetics and Politics of Ethnography,* ed. James Clifford and George E. Marcus (Berkeley, 1986).

22. Lyautey, *Journal de Tours* (Paris, 1886), as quoted in Le Révérend, *Un Lyautey inconnu,* 165–66.

23. Lyautey's criticism of the Le Playist heritage was shared by others. Jean-Baptiste Duroselle identifies it as one of the major causes for the failure of the movement. Jean-Baptiste Duroselle, *Les Débuts du catholicisme social en France (1822–1870)* (Paris, 1951), 708.

24. Richard D. Challener, *The French Theory of the Nation in Arms, 1866–1939,* 2d ed. (New York, 1965); Alain Ehrenberg, *Le Corps militaire: politique et pédagogie en démocratie* (Paris, 1983); Joseph Montheilhet, *Les Institutions militaires de la France* (Paris, 1932); Raoul Girardet, *La Société militaire dans la France contemporaine, 1815–1939* (Paris, 1953); Paul-Marie de la Gorce, *The French Army: A Military-Political History,* trans. Kenneth Douglas (London, 1963); Vincent Monteil, *Les Officiers* (Paris, 1960); William Serman, *Les Officiers français dans la nation, 1848–1870* (Paris, 1982); Allan Mitchell, *Victors and Vanquished: The German Influence on Army and Church in France after 1870* (Chapel Hill, N.C., 1984).

25. Ehrenberg, *Le Corps militaire,* 73.

26. Charles Lyautey, *Réflexion qui a fait naître chez un vieillard médaillé de Sainte-Hélène la brochure intitulé 'L'Armée française en 1867'* (Paris, 1867).

27. Martin, *Albert de Mun.* See also the important work of Robert Nye, *Crime, Madness and Politics in Modern France: The Medical Concept of National Decline* (Princeton, N.J., 1984).

28. Girardet, *La Société militaire,* 168–69.

29. Jean Jaurès, *L'Armée nouvelle,* pref. Lucien Lévy-Bruhl (Paris, 1915).

30. For details of the long debates over how to reform the French army during this period, see Allan Mitchell, *Victors and Vanquished.*

31. Girardet, *La Société militaire,* 31.

32. Lyautey, *Lettres du Tonkin et de Madagascar,* 450.

33. Lyautey, letter to Henry Beranger, 4 December 1891, as cited in Lyautey, *Le Rôle social,* 120.

34. Ibid., 123.

35. Ibid., 124.

36. Ibid., 201.

Chapter 5

1. Linda L. Clark, *Social Darwinism in France* (Birmingham, Ala., 1984), 30. Also see Claude Digeon, *La Crise allemande de la pensée française, 1870–1914* (Paris, 1959) and Claude Nicolet, *L'Idée républicaine en France: essai d'histoire critique, 1789–1924* (Paris, 1982).

2. Clark, *Social Darwinism*, 32. Michel Foucault takes up this idea of zoological wars in *The History of Sexuality*, vol. 1, *An Introduction*, trans. Robert Hurley (New York, 1978), 133–47.

3. Yvette Conry, *L'Introduction du darwinisme en France au XIXe siècle* (Paris, 1974). In 1972 no full edition of Darwin's works was yet available in France.

4. For the peculiarities of the translator, Clemence Royer, and the inaccuracies of the translation, see Clark, *Social Darwinism*, ch. 2.

5. The Paris Municipal Council voted funds in 1886 for the creation of a chair in the "Evolution des Etres Organisés." This was the second chair for which they had provided money; the first was "Histoire de la Révolution française." The deputies were concerned that too much metaphysics was still being taught at the Sorbonne and that France was falling behind other countries. Marc Vire, "La Création de la chaire d'Evolution des Etres Organisés' à la Sorbonne en 1888," *Revue de synthèse historique* 100, nos. 95–96 (July–December 1979).

6. Clark comments that even Darwin did not fully qualify as a Darwinist by Conry's criteria.

7. Jacques Roger, "Présentation," special issue "Les Néo-Lamarckians français," *Revue de synthèse historique* 100, nos. 95–96 (July–December 1979): 281.

8. Georges Canguilhem, "Le Vivant et son milieu," *La Connaissance de la vie* (Paris, 1965), 134.

9. Ibid., 136.

10. Antoine Cabaton, *Dictionnaire de bio-bibliographie générale, ancienne et moderne de l'Indochine française* (Paris, 1935), 222.

11. In addition to de Lanessan's own works cited below, see Linda L. Clark, *Social Darwinism*; Alan Lagarde, "Jean de Lanessan (1843–1911): analyse d'un transformiste," *Revue de Synthèse historique* 100, nos. 95–96 (July–December, 1979), 337–51.

12. Ibid., 144.

13. In his 1884 editions of *Oeuvre complète de Buffon*, Jean de Lanessan reissued Buffon's *L'Histoire naturelle, générale et particulière*, the first volume which had appeared in 1749. De Lanessan contributed a 400-page preface to the new edition.

14. Michèle Duchet, *Histoire et anthropologie au siècle des lumières* (Paris, 1971).

15. For biographical details: L.J. Jordanova, *Lamarck* (Oxford, 1984), 1–10. For additional bibliography, see Jacques Roger, "Lamarckiana," *Revue de synthèse historique* 100, nos. 95–96 (July–December 1979).

16. François Delaporte, *Nature's Second Kingdom: Explorations of Vegetality in the Eighteenth Century*, trans. Arthur Goldhammer (Cambridge, Mass., 1982). Coleman claims the word appeared first, in 1800, in an obscure German medical publication. William Coleman, *Biology in the Nineteenth Century: Problems of Form, Function, and Transformation* (New York, 1971), 1.

17. Dorinda Outram, *Georges Cuvier: Vocation, Science and Authority in Post-Revolutionary France* (Dover, N.H., 1984).

18. Jordanova, *Lamarck*, 45.

19. Jean-L. de Lanessan, *Le Transformisme: évolution de la matière et des êtres vivants* (Paris, 1883), 5

20. Jean-L. de Lanessan, *La Lutte pour l'éxistence et l'association pour la lutte: étude sur la doctrine de Darwin*, 2d ed. (Paris, 1882).

21. Jean-L. de Lanessan, *L'Expansion coloniale de la France: étude économique, politique et géographique sur les établissements français d'outre-mer* (Paris, 1886), iv.

22. Vincent Berdoulay, *La Formation de l'école française de géographie* (Paris, 1981), and André Meynier, *Histoire de la pensée géographique en France, 1872–1969* (Paris, 1969). On the place of military geography as well as the history of military cartography, see Yves Lacoste, *La Géographie: ça sert, d'abord, à faire la guerre*, 2d ed. (Paris, 1982), 19–41.

23. Charles-Robert Ageron, *France coloniale ou parti colonial?* (Paris, 1978), ch. 3.

24. Alfred Fierro, *La Société de Géographie 1821–1946* (Geneva, 1983), 3–50.

25. Donald Vernon McKay, "Colonialism in the French Geographical Movement, 1871–1881," *Geographical Review* 33(April 1943).

26. Jean-Pierre Nardy, "Levasseur, géographe," *Annales littéraires de l'Université de Besançon* 93 (1968).

27. Emile Levasseur, *L'Etude et l'enseignement de la géographie* (Paris, 1872). The ground for some of these changes had been laid by a prewar reform association seeking to modernize, through the introduction of science, the Enseignement Secondaire des Jeunes Filles, founded in 1867. Its members included: Levasseur, Paul Bert, Milne-Edwards, Viollet-Le-Duc, Ernest Lavisse and Vidal de la Blache. On Republican ideology see: Jacques and Mona Ozouf, "Le Thème du patriotisme dans les manuels primaire," *Le Mouvement social* 49(October–December 1964); Catherine Rhein, "La Géographie: discipline scolaire et/ou science sociale?, 1860–1920," *Revue française de sociologie* 23(1982).

28. Rhein, "La Géographie," 229.

29. Pierre Lyautey, *Gallieni* (Paris, 1959), 13.

30. Hubert Deschamps and Paul Chauvet, eds., *Gallieni pacificateur: écrits coloniaux de Gallieni* (Paris, 1949), 21.

31. Ibid., 20–21.

32. Jean Ganiage, *L'Expansion coloniale de la France* (Paris, 1968), 118–20.

33. David Marr, *Vietnamese Anti-Colonialism 1885–1925* (Berkeley, 1971). Alexander Woodside locates the beginnings of the transition at the beginning of the nineteenth century. See his *Vietnam and the Chinese Model: A Comparative Study of Vietnamese and Chinese Government in the First Half of the Nineteenth Century* (Cambridge, Mass., 1971).

34. Jean Ganiage, professor at the Sorbonne and author of the standard French history text, said as late as 1968 that "le plus dangereux chef de bandes, le De-Tham, ne soumit pas avant 1897" (the most dangerous leader, De-Tham, did not give in until 1897). *L'Expansion coloniale*, 139. The Vietnamese court used the term "pirate" with perhaps even more condescension than did the French. Thanks to Pierre Brocheux for this point.

35. Hubert Lyautey, *Lettres du Tonkin et de Madagascar, 1894–1899*, vol. 7 (Paris, 1920). The literature on De-Tham is large. See Nguyen Van Phong, *La Société vietnamienne de 1882 à 1902* (Paris, 1971), 20–26.

36. "Colonel Gallieni should prove to be the principal assistant of Monsieur de Lanessan in this task of pacification and organization." Joseph S. Gallieni, *Gallieni au Tonkin, 1892–1896, par lui-même* (Paris, 1941), viii–ix.

37. Joseph S. Gallieni, *Trois Colonnes au Tonkin, 1894–1895* (Paris, 1899), 154.

38. Gallieni, *Gallieni au Tonkin*, 71.

39. Ibid., 66.

40. Norbert Elias, *The History of Manners*, trans. Edmund Jephcott (New York, 1978). See also Orvar Lofgren, "Our Friends in Nature: Class and Animal Symbolism," *Ethnos* 50, nos. 3–4 (1985).

41. Stephen Ellis, *The Rising of the Red Shawls: A Revolt in Madagascar, 1895–1899* (Cambridge, Eng., 1985).

42. Alexander Woodside, *Vietnam and the Chinese Model: A Comparative Study of Vietnamese and Chinese Government in the First Half of the Nineteenth Century* (Cambridge, Mass., 1971); David Marr, *Vietnamese Anti-Colonialism 1885–1925* (Berkeley, 1971). For Morocco without the missionary success but with economic parallels, see Jean-Louis Miège, *Le Maroc et L'Europe, 1830–1894*, 4 vols. (Paris, 1961–63).

43. Ellis, *Rising of the Red Shawls*, 22–26, 156.

44. Jean Ganiage, *L'Expansion coloniale de la France* (Paris, 1968), 184–97.

45. Alfred Grandidier, *Rapport sur une mission à Madagascar 1869–1871* (Paris, 1872), 473.

46. On Le Bon and associated thinkers and social context, see Robert A. Nye, *The Origins of Crowd Psychology: Gustave Le Bon and the Crisis of Mass Democracy in the Third Republic* (Beverly Hills, 1975); Susanna Barrows, *Distorting Mirrors: Visions of the Crowd in Late Nineteenth-Century French* (New Haven, 1981); Serge Moscovici, *L'Age des foules* (Paris, 1985); Catherine Rouvier, *Les Idées politiques de Gustave Le Bon* (Paris, 1986).

47. In Madagascar in the 1890s, the leading spokesman for comparative soul psychology was a certain Jean Carol, later recognized as an expert on colonial psychology. Gallieni reserved a particularly strong hatred for the man, suppressing his post as editor of the *Journal Officiel.* Bouillion, *Le Colonisé et son âme: Madagascar* (Paris: Harmattan, 1981), 90.

48. P.F. Cazeux, "Les Sakalaves et leurs pays," *Bulletin de la Société de géographie commerciale de Bordeaux* (21 May 1888); Dr. L. Catat, *Voyage à Madagascar 1889–1890* (Paris, n.d.).

49. C. Buet, *Madagascar: la reine des îles africaines; histoire, religion, flore* (Paris, 1883), 399.

50. Michel Massiot, citing E.F. Gautier, *Trois Héros* (Paris, 1931) in *L'Administration publique à Madagascar* (Paris, 1971), 72.

51. Joseph S. Gallieni, *Neuf ans à Madagascar* (Paris, 1908), 27. For the parallel French interpretation of Vietnam see Nguyen Van Phong, *La Société vietnamienne de 1882 à 1902* (Paris, 1971). For Morocco, see Edmund Burke III, *Prelude to Protectorate in Morocco: Precolonial Protest and Resistance, 1860–1912* (Chicago, 1976).

52. General Joseph S. Gallieni, *La Pacification de Madagascar: Opérations d'octobre 1896 à mars 1899*, ed. F. Hellot (Paris, 1900), iv–vi.

53. O. Hatzfeld, *Madagascar* (Paris, 1952), 39–40.

54. Georges Condominas, *Fokon'olona et collectivités rurales en Imerina* (Paris, 1960), 92.

55. Gallieni, *Neufs ans à Madagascar*, 55.

56. Ibid., 49.

57. The double administration system instituted by Gallieni remained basically in place until 1960. Personally, Gallieni supported an active formative role for Malgache personnel. By 1905, official statistics, listed 23,500 students in lay schools and 16,000 in missionary schools. This figure would be almost ten times higher if the schools directed by a *non-diplomé* teacher were taken into account. For Tunisia, see Ganiage, *L'Expansion coloniale de la France*, 340.

58. Maurice Bloch, *Placing the Dead: Tombs, Ancestral Villages and Kinship Organization in Madagascar* (New York, 1971).

59. Condominas, *Fokon'olona*, 22–24.

60. Ellis, *Rising of the Red Shawls*, cautions a salutary prudence on this point.

61. André Le Révérend, *Lyautey* (Paris, 1983), 257.

62. Hubert Lyautey, *Dans le Sud de Madagascar: pénétration militaire, situation politique et économique 1900–1902* (Paris, 1903), 234.

63. Lyautey, *Dans le Sud de Madagascar*, 379.

64. Ibid., 379. Housing types and their civilizational correlates had been synthesized by Viollet-Le-Duc for the International Exposition of 1889.

65. Ibid., 40–41.

66. Lyautey, "Du Rôle colonial de l'armée," *Dans le Sud de Madagascar*, 274.

67. Ibid., 285.

68. Ibid., 227.

69. Ibid., 208.

70. Arnold Van Gennep, *Tabou et totemisme à Madagascar: étude déscriptive et théorique* (Paris, 1904), 1.

71. Lucien Lévy-Bruhl, *La Morale et la science des moeurs* (Paris, 1903; Reprint, 1971).

72. Ibid., 272.

Chapter 6

1. Alexis de Tocqueville, *De la Démocratie en Amérique* (Paris, 1840; Reprint, 1961, 1: 308–15.

2. Jean-Baptiste Martin, *La Fin des mauvais pauvres: de l'assistance à l'assurance*, pref. Madeleine Rébérioux (Seyssel, 1983), 13. For the institutional history see Henri Hatzfeld, *Du Pauperisme à la securité sociale* (Paris, 1971). See William M. Reddy, *The Rise of Market Culture: The Textile Trade and French Society, 1750–1900* (New York, 1984) for the discourse of liberalism versus its practices.

3. François Ewald, *L'Etat providence* (Paris, 1986); Christian Topalov, "Invention du chômage et politiques sociales au début du 20e siècle: une comparaison France-Grande Bretagne-Etats Unis," unpublished paper, Centre de Sociologie Urbaine, March 1986; Gérard Noiriel, *Les Ouvriers dans la société française XIXe–XXe siècle* (Paris, 1986), chs. 2, 3.

4. Arpad Ajtony et al., *Assurance, prévoyance, securité: formation historique des techniques de gestion sociale dans les sociétés industrielles* (Paris, 1979), 54.

5. Antoine Savoye, "Les Continuateurs de Le Play au tournant du siècle," *Revue française de sociologie* 22, no. 3 (July–September, 1981).

6. Emile Cheysson, "Notice biographique," *Oeuvres choisies*, vol. 2 (Paris, 1911).

7. Emile Cheysson, "Le Rôle social de l'ingénieur," *Oeuvres Choisies*, vol. 2 (Paris, 1911), 25. Alain Desrosières, "L'Ingénieur d'état et le père de famille: Emile Cheysson et la statistique," *Annales des Mines: Gérer et Comprendre* 2(March 1986).

8. Desrosières, "L'Ingenieur"; Stephen M. Stigler, *The History of Statistics: The Measurement of Uncertainty before 1900* (Cambridge, Mass., 1986), chs. 8, 9, 10; Donald A. MacKenzie, *Statistics in Britain, 1865–1930: The Social Construction of Scientific Knowledge* (Edinburgh, 1981).

9. Desrosières, "L'Ingénieur," 76.

10. Emile Cheysson, "Les Méthodes de la statistique," *Oeuvres choisies*, vol. 1 (Paris, 1911), 156.

11. Ibid., 158.

12. Emile Cheysson, "L'Economie sociale à l'exposition universelle de 1889," *La Réforme sociale*, 3d ser., nos. 3–4 (13 June 1889): 692.

13. Ibid., 228.

14. Ibid., 229.

15. Ibid., 235.

16. Michelle Perrot, *Les Ouvriers en grève: France 1871–1890* (Paris, 1974).

17. See *Annuaire statistique de la ville de Paris et du département de la Seine* (1886), as cited in Ann-Louise Shapiro, *Housing the Poor of Paris, 1850–1902* (Madison, 1985), 55.

18. A *Congrès International d'Hygiène* was held at the International Exposition in Paris in 1889. J. Bertillion declared that "la santé doit être le guide et le juge de l'urbaniste" (good health should be the guide and judge of the urbanist). As cited in Roger-H. Guerrand, *Les Origines du logement social en France* (Paris, 1967), 227.

19. Henri Rollet, *L'Action sociale des catholiques en France, 1871–1901* (Paris, 1947).

20. Nicholas Bullock and James Read, *The Movement for Housing Reform in Germany and France, 1840–1914* (Cambridge, Eng., 1985).

21. Ibid., 278.

22. Georges Picot, "La question des logements ouvriers à Paris et à Londres," *La Réforme sociale* 10(15 September 1885), 247–61.

23. Emile Muller and Emile Cacheux, as cited in Bullock and Read, *The Movement for Housing Reform*, 414.

24. Sanford Elwitt, "Social Reform and Social Order in Late Nineteenth-Century France: The Musée Social and its Friends," *French Historical Studies* 11, no. 3 (Spring 1980): 437.

25. Jules Siegfried, *La Misère: son histoire, ses causes, ses remèdes* (Le Havre, 1880), 195–99.

26. See *Exposition universelle de 1889. Rapports du jury international, Groupe d'économie sociale*, vol. 2 (Paris, 1891), as cited in Elwitt, "Social Reform," 433.

27. Charles Gide, *Les Institutions de progrès social*, 4th ed. (Paris, 1912), 152.

28. Emile Cheysson, *Le Musée social* (Paris, 1906), 11.

29. Theodore Zeldin, *France 1848–1945*, vol. 1, *Ambition, Love and Politics* (Oxford, 1973), 645.

30. J.E.S. Hayward, "The Official Social Philosophy of the French Third Republic: Léon Bourgeois and Solidarism," *International Review of Social History* 6(1961): 32.

31. Ibid.

32. J.E.S. Hayward, "Solidarist Syndicalism: Durkheim and Duguit, I," *The Sociological Review* 8, no. 1 (July 1960): 17.

33. Léon Bourgeois, Alfred Croiset (Dean of the Faculté des Lettres de l'Université de Paris), Darlu (Inspecteur Général de l'Instruction publique), Devinat (Director of the Ecole Normale d'Instituteurs de la Seine), Charles Gide (Professor of the Faculté de Droit de Montpellier), Xavier Léon (Director of the *Revue de Métaphysique et de Morale*), Georges Renard (Professor at the Conservatoire National des Arts et Métiers).

34. Ibid., xi.

35. Léon Bourgeois, "La justice sociale, première conférence faite à l'Ecole des Hautes Etudes sociales, 6 nov. 1901," *Solidarité* (Paris, 1912), 159 ff.

36. M.F. Rauh, "Propriété individuelle et propriété solidaire," *Essai d'une philosophie de la solidarité: conférences et discussions*, ed. Léon Bourgeois and Alfred Croiset (Paris, 1902).

37. Ibid., 175.

38. Rauh claimed that his idea was shared by many modern French socialists. He listed Andler, Fournière, Jaurès, Georges Renard, Rouanet, Georges Sorel.

39. Charles Gide, "La Solidarité Economique" (1902), *Philosophie de la solidarité*, ed. Bourgeois and Croiset. See Rosalind H. Williams, *Dream Worlds: Mass Consumption in Late Nineteenth Century France* (Berkeley, 1982).

40. Williams, *Dream Worlds*, 231.

41. J.E.S. Hayward, "Solidarity: The Social History of an Idea in Nineteenth Century France," *International Review of Social History* 2(1959): 272.

42. Evélyne Pisier-Kouchner, *Le Service public dans la théorie de l'état de Léon Duguit* (Paris, 1972).

43. Léon Duguit, "Le Droit constitionnel et la sociologie," *Revue internationale de l'enseignement* 17 (1889).

44. J.E.S. Hayward, "Solidarist Syndicalism: Durkheim and Duguit, II," *The Sociological Review* 8, no. 2 (December 1960), 189.

45. Léon Duguit, *Le Droit social: le droit individuel et la transformation de l'état*, 2d ed. (Paris, 1911).

46. Ibid., 79.

47. It was not until 1884 that professional organizations were legalized and 1901 that all associations were legalized. J.E.S. Hayward, "Solidarist Syndicalism, II," 186.

48. Georges Canguilhem, "Le Vivant et son milieu," *La Connaissance de la vie* (Paris, 1965); Anne Buttimer, *Society and Milieu in the French Geographic Tradition* (Chicago, 1971); Lucien Febvre, *La Terre et l'évolution humaine: introduction géographique à l'histoire* (Paris, 1922); Louis Poirier, "L'Evolution de la géographie humaine," *Critique* 8, 9 (January–February 1947); Yvette Conry, *L'Introduction du Darwinisme en France au XIXe*

siècle (Paris, 1974); Numa Broc, "La Géographie française face à la science allemande, 1870–1914," *Annales de Géographie* 86, no. 473 (January–February 1977).

49. Paul Vidal de la Blache, "La Géographie humaine: ses rapports avec la géographie de la vie," *Revue de synthèse historique* 7 (1903): 225.

50. Yves Lacoste, *La Géographie: ça sert, d'abord, à faire la guerre* (Paris, 1982) with a 1986 postface discussing Vidal's shift of interest.

51. Paul Vidal de la Blache, *Principes de géographie humaine* (Paris, 1905; Reprint, 1922), 7; Vincent Berdoulay, "The Vidal-Durkheim Debate," *Humanistic Geography: Prospects and Problems*, ed. David Ley and Marwyns Samuels (Chicago, 1978), 77–90.

52. F. Luckermann, "The 'Calcul des Probabilités' and the Ecole française de géographie," *The Canadian Geographer* 9, no. 3 (1965): 128.

53. Paul Vidal de la Blache, "L'Ecole Normale," *Revue internationale de l'enseignement* 8 (1884): 534.

54. Thiebault Flory, *Le Mouvement régionaliste français: sources et développement* (Paris, 1966); Howard Clyde Payne, "French Regionalism, 1851–1914: A Study of the Principal Alternatives to Administrative Centralization," Ph.D. diss., University of California, Berkeley, 1947.

55. Flory, *Mouvement régionaliste*, 3.

56. The National Assembly nominated a committee to study decentralization on April 24, 1871. The Waddington report offered another plan for departmental organization which, when stripped of its chief decentralist features, became the basis for the Law of August 10, 1871, the cornerstone of the Third Republic's departmental administration.

57. Jean-L. de Lanessan, in his exposé "proposition de loi municipale" (proposition of law on municipal organization), *Journal officiel*, ser. e, annex no. 1687 (10 February 1883): 413.

58. An unpublished text of Proudhon, cited in *L'Action régionaliste* (January–March 1955), as cited in Flory, *Mouvement régionaliste*, 26. Pierre-Joseph Proudhon, *Du Principe fédératif* (Paris, 1863), 83. Maurice Prélot, *Histoire des idées politiques*, 2d ed. (Paris, 1966), 566.

59. Frédéric Le Play, *La Réforme sociale en France*, 6th ed., vol. 4 (Paris, 1878).

60. Maurice Barrès, *Les Lézardes sur la maison*, 2d ed. (Paris, 1904), 41, 50; Zeev Sternhell, *Maurice Barrès et le nationalisme français* (Paris, 1972); Eugen Weber, *The Nationalist Revival in France, 1905–1914* (Berkeley, 1959).

61. Maurice Barrès, *Scènes et doctrines du nationalisme* (Paris, 1902), 490.

62. André Mellerio, "La Société pour la protection des paysages de France," *La Réforme sociale* 48 (1–16 September 1904): 430, as cited in Payne, "French Regionalism," 296.

63. The word "regionalism" was coined in 1874 by a Provençal poet, M. de Berluc-Perusis. The regionalists' main organ was *L'Action régionaliste*, founded in 1902. Flory, *Mouvement régionaliste*, 2–4.

64. Jean-Charles Brun, "Le Play et la vie provinciale," *La Réforme sociale* 61(1 December

1906): 781; also see Emile Faguet, "Une Etude sur Le Play," *Revue des Deux Mondes*, 6th ser., no. 11(15 December 1912).

65. Charles Beauquier, "L'Allocution du president d'honneur," *L'Action régionaliste* 12, nos. 2–3 (February–March 1913): 18–19.

66. Paul Vidal de la Blache, "Régions françaises," *Revue de Paris* 5, no. 17 (15 December 1910).

67. Henri Hauser, "Les Régions économiques," *Le Fait de la semaine* 27(9 November 1918): 27–28.

68. Clinics and municipal hospitals increased in England after the Public Health Act of 1875 and in Germany after 1900. Zurich offered free medical care for all residents. German cities built a certain amount of public housing for municipal workers. Municipalities were granted slum clearance rights throughout Europe, as early as the late 1860s in England and in a much weakened form in France with the public health bill of 1902.

69. Michael McQuillen, "The Development of Municipal Socialism in France, 1880–1914," Ph.D. diss., University of Virginia, 1973.

70. Michelle Perrot and Annie Kriegel, *Le Socialisme français et le pouvoir* (Paris, 1966); Jules Guesde, *Services publics et socialisme* (Paris, 1883).

71. César de Paepe, "De l'organisation des Services Publics dans la Société future," *Compte-rendu officiel du VIIe congrès général de l'Association Internationale des Travailleurs* (Bruxelles, 1874; Verviers, 1875); reprinted in *Revue socialiste* 10 (September–December 1889); David Stafford, *From Anarchism to Reformism: A Study of the Political Activities of Paul Brousse within the First International and the French Socialist Movement, 1870–1890* (Toronto, 1971), 59.

72. Paul Brousse, *La Propriété collective et les services publics* (Paris, 1883).

73. Adrien Veber, "Le Socialisme communal," *Revue socialiste* 17 (June 1893): 664.

74. Maurice Dommanget, *Edouard Vaillant: un grand socialiste, 1840–1915* (Paris, 1956).

75. Ibid., 152. The only really successful attempt was in Lyons in 1904 under Victor Augagneur. The next year, 1905, saw the formation of the *Section Française de l'International Ouvrière* (S.F.I.O.). Millerand, Briand, Viviani, and Augagneur formed a breakaway party, *Parti socialiste française*–really radicals. At the S.F.I.O.'s eighth congress at Saint-Quentin in 1911, there was a resurgence of municipalists led by Adrien Veber, Edgar Milhaud and Albert Thomas. The Guesdists continued to oppose municipalism.

76. Tyler Stovall's thesis presents this case in a relatively sympathetic light. "The Urbanization of Bobigny 1900–1939." Ph.D. diss., University of Wisconsin-Madison, 1984.

77. Pierre Mimin, *Le Socialisme municipal* (Paris, 1911), 136.

78. Communes had been authorized to operate markets (1790), cemeteries (1804), savings banks (1835), slaughterhouses (1838), pawnshops (1851), baths and lavatories (1861), crematories and funeral parlors (1889), some municipal gasworks (Tourcoing, 1880), and a municipal tramway (Tourcoing, 1885). Mimin, *Socialisme municipal*, 60; Adrien Veber, *Le Socialisme municipale* (Paris, 1908), 48. On August 7, 1896, and Febru-

ary 1, March 29, 1901, the Conseil set forth three crippling conditions: "first, if private initiative were lacking; second, if that initiative was demonstrably insufficient; and third, if the existence of a *monopole de fait* could be proven unavoidable." McQuillen, "Municipal Socialism," 136.

79. Robert de Boyer Montegut, "Les Bureaux de placement municipaux et les bourses du travail," *Revue socialiste* 4 (November 16, 1912): 534. In 1906 municipalities were granted the right to make loans to societies for the construction of low-cost housing. This ruling was extended in 1912 to allow them to construct such housing themselves. Charles W. Pipkin, *Social Politics and Modern Democracies*, vol. 2 (New York, 1931), 156–58.

Chapter 7

1. A parallel could be drawn with another significant cohort of prize-winning architects present in Rome in 1827–28: Labrouste, Vaudoyer, Duc, and Duban. Van Zantan, *Designing Paris: The Architecture of Duban, Labrouste, Duc, and Vaudoyer* (Cambridge, 1987), 1.

2. Françoise Choay, *The Modern City: Planning in the Nineteenth Century* (New York, 1969), 104. George Collins and Christiane Crasemann Collins, *Camillo Sitte and the Birth of Modern City Planning* (New York, 1965), 11.

3. Collins and Collins, *Camillo Sitte*, 63–64.

4. Ibid.

5. Charles Buls, *Esthétique des villes* (Brussels, 1893). Anthony Sutcliffe, *The Autumn of Central Paris: The Defeat of Town Planning, 1850–1970* (Montreal, 1971).

6. Julien Gaudet, *Eléments et théories de l'architecture* (Paris, 1915), 4 vols.

7. Richard Chafee, "The Teaching of Architecture at the Ecole des Beaux-Arts," *The Architecture of the Ecole des Beaux-Arts*, ed. Arthur Drexler (New York, 1977).

8. Gaudet, *Eléments et théories de l'architecture*, 135–36.

9. Reyner Banham, *Theory and Design in the First Machine Age* (Cambridge, Mass., 1960), 16.

10. Auguste Choisy, *Histoire de l'architecture*, 2 vols. (Paris, 1899).

11. Choisy, *Histoire de l'architecture* 1: 25.

12. Reyner Banham: "Outside the contribution of engineers like Freyssinet, France gave to the developing practice of a new architecture before 1914, only the work of two members of the academic succession to Gaudet, Auguste Perret and Tony Garnier." *Theory and Design*, 35; René Jullian, *Histoire de l'architecture moderne en France, de 1889 à nos jours, un siècle de modernité* (Paris, 1984); Françoise Choay, "Pensées sur la ville, arts sur la ville," *Histoire de la france urbaine*, vol. 4, *La Ville de l'âge industriel: le cycle haussmannien*, ed. Maurice Agulhon (Paris, 1983). Siegfried Giedion, *Bauen in Frankreich Eisen Eisenbeton*, as quoted in Jean-Louis Cohen, "Prima del purismo: un costruttivismo mediterraneo," *Rassegna* 17 (March 1984): 4.

13. Christophe Pawlowski, *Tony Garnier et les débuts de l'urbanisme fonctionnel en France* (Paris, 1967), 66.

14. The original drawings seem to have disappeared altogether. The earliest extant set dates from 1917. Dora Wiebenson, *Tony Garnier: The Cité industrielle* (New York, 1969), 12–13.

15. Michel Roz, "Tony Garnier, un monumento lionese," *Rassegna* 17 (March 1984): 30.

16. Pierre Lavedan, *L'Histoire de l'urbanisme*, vol. 3, *Epoch contemporaine* (Paris, 1966), 293.

17. Two important professional journals, *Construction lyonnaise* and *Lyon touriste*, played an active role in promoting these ideas. Alain Charre, "Lione: l'invenzione di une citta industriale," *Rassegna* 17 (March 1984): 26.

18. Sylviane Leprun, *Le Théâtre des colonies: scénographie, acteurs et discours de l'imaginaire dans les expositions, 1855–1937* (Paris, 1986), 168.

19. Jean Badovici and Albert Morancé, eds., *L'Oeuvre de Tony Garnier* (Paris, 1938), introduction, as cited in Banham, *Theory and Design*, 36.

20. Maria Rovigatti, "Tony Garnier e la didattica dell'Ecole des Beaux-Arts," *Rassegna* 17 (March 1984); Pierre Pinon, "Gli 'envois de Rome': tradizione e crisi," *Rassegna* 17 (March 1984).

21. Henri Prost won a competition for a hospital in 1899 with a pavilion solution. Pawlowski, *Tony Garnier*, fig. 12, p. 41.

22. Ibid., 45.

23. Ibid., 54.

24. "Although translations of Howard, Sitte appeared in 1902/03, neither Howard's nor Stubben's work would " 'enter the library of the Ecole.' " Pierre Pinon, "Gli 'envois de Rome,' " 19.

25. Pawlowski, *Tony Garnier*, 65.

26. The program Jaussely attached to his "democratic city" read: "The progress and application of science and modern technology will modify the present conditions of society (allowing man more independence and leisure)—advancing humanity toward the realization of spiritual liberation through social education. In each city some large place should be created where citizens will be able not only to expand their education but also to discuss the organization and conditions of their work, and to hold demonstrations freely. In the metropolis of a great democratic state that is truly worthy of this title, these new functions require durable, utilitarian and humanitarian structures expressing the progress of mankind." On Jaussely's plan and its relations to Garnier, see Pawlowski, *Tony Garnier*, 49–50; also Wiebenson, *Tony Garnier*, 25.

27. Wiebenson, *Tony Garnier*, 29.

28. Garnier included model farms in the surrounding countryside.

29. Claude-Nicolas Ledoux, *L'Architecture considérée sous le rapport de l'art, des moeurs et de la législation*, vol. 1 (Paris, 1804), 1: "On verra des usines importantes, filles et mères de l'industrie donner naissance à des réunions populeuses. Une ville s'élèvera pour les enceindre et les courroner." ("We shall see large factories, daughters and mothers of industry, give birth to populous reunions. A city will rise up to encompass and to crown them.") As cited in Pawlowski, *Tony Garnier*, 74.

30. On the connection to Zola, see Alain Lagier, "Da Emile Zola à Tony Garnier," *Rassegna* 17(March 1984).

31. Originally Garnier had planned to put a large, covered market near the administrative grouping, but later situated it next to the railway station.

32. This attention to memory was quite typical of the Third Republic. Pierre Nora, ed., *Les Lieux de mémoire*, 3 vols. (Paris, 1984–87).

33. Van Zantan, *Designing Paris*, 30–31.

34. François Ewald, *L'Etat providence* (Paris, 1986); parallel versions are found in Jean-Baptiste Martin, *La Fin des mauvais Pauvres* (Seyssel, 1983) and Jacques Donzelot, *L'Invention du social: essai sur le déclin des passions politiques* (Paris, 1984).

35. Léon Bourgeois, *La Politique de la prévoyance sociale*, vol. 2 (Paris, 1919), 321.

36. As cited in Ewald, *L'Etat providence*, 328.

37. Emile Cheysson, as quoted in Donzelot, *L'Invention du social*, 137. Germany under Bismarck, with its 1883 law on health insurance and 1884 law on work accidents, set the standards. From the first *Congrès International des Accidents du Travail*, held at the Parisian 1889 Exposition Universelle, until 1914, regular international congresses were held.

38. Wiebenson, *Tony Garnier*, 19.

39. Edouard Herriot led a delegation (including Garnier) to Germany in 1909 to visit the Dresden exhibit on hygiene. Cf. Alain Charre, "Lionne: l'invenzione di una citta industriale," *Rassegna* 17 (March, 1984): 28. He praised the German conception of town planning, including its juridical approach to the direct municipal administration of services. In 1912, Herriot formed a commission to plan the expansion and improvement of Lyons, preceded by an international city planning exhibit. Although Garnier never succeeded in building his Cité Industrielle, he was able to construct several major projects in Lyons; his slaughterhouse and stadium were major accomplishments and received international recognition. In 1909, Garnier asked that Herriot be put in charge of reconstructing Lyons' hospitals. He joined a municipal study mission which went to Denmark and Germany to visit new hospitals. His report of February, 1910 was close to those in the Cité Industrielle. Alain Lagier, "L'ospedale a Grange-Blanche," *Rassegna* 17: 54. The final plans—for a Garden City for the sick, with southern exposure and symmetrical distribution of pavilions—was similar to a Rothschild hospital in Paris. Although construction of the hospital began in 1915, it was not officially inaugurated until 1934 with the help of a loan from the Rockefellers. Garnier's design for an entire quarter for low-income housing—les Etats-Unis—also parallels his Cité Industrielle project, especially in its full *équipement* of the quarter with schools, carefully planned streets, and an associated factory. Although the roughly 1700 units Garnier planned in 1919 were built, they occupied an area one-fifth as large as he had projected.

40. Louis Hautecoeur, "Henri Prost à la Villa Medici," *L'Oeuvre d'Henri Prost: architecte et urbaniste* (Paris, 1960).

41. Ibid., 16.

42. Ibid., 18.

43. Prost and Jaussely were assigned to survey Italy's squares and other urban structures for a work on urban art which never appeared. Cohen, "Prima del purismo," 6.

44. Hautecoeur, "Henri Prost à la Villa Medici," 209.

45. Ibid., 211.

46. Henri Prost, "L'Urbanisme." Unpublished ms., Archives de l'Académie d'Architecture, n.d.

47. Françoise Choay, *La Régle et le modèle* (Paris, 1980), 285.

48. Ibid., 1.

49. Ibid., 5.

50. For details of the concours see Anvers, "Programme du Concours," *L'Oeuvre d'Henri Prost*, 211–13. Twenty-seven projects were submitted to the competition, with names like "cité-jardins for ever" and "vérité." Prost was the winner. The only published criticism was a sense on the part of some of the jury members that perhaps the squares were disproportionately large and that not enough care was given to *lotissements*.

51. Ibid., 35.

52. Henri Prost, "L'Anneau d'or," *L'Oeuvre d'Henri Prost*, 215.

53. Paul Rabinow and Gwen Wright, "Savoir et pouvoir dans l'urbanisme moderne colonial d'Ernest Hébrard," *Les Cahiers de la recherche architecturale* 9(January 1982).

54. Ernest M. Hébrard and Henrik Christian Andersen, *Creation of a World Center of Communication*, vol. 1, *Great Monumental Conceptions of the Past* (Paris, 1913), iii–x.

55. For a detailed discussion of the history of architects' views on the origins of architecture, see Joseph Rykwert, *On Adam's House in Paradise: The Idea of the Primitive Hut in Architectural History* (New York, 1972; 2d ed., Cambridge, Mass., 1981).

56. Hébrard and Andersen, *Creation of a World Center*, 125.

57. Ibid., 47.

58. Ibid., 49.

59. Ibid., 71. Readers familiar with the Lenin memorial will be struck by the similarities.

60. For details see Giuliano Gresleri and Dario Matteoni, *La Citta' Mondiale: Andersen, Hébrard, Otlet, Le Corbusier* (Venis, 1982), 21–45.

Chapter 8

1. Pascal Ory, *Les Intellectuals en France: de l'Affaire Dreyfus à nos jours* (Paris, 1986). Charles Prochasson, "Le Socialisme normalien, Recherches et réflexions autour du Groupe d'Etudes socialistes et de l'Ecole Socialiste, 1907–1914, "Mémoire de Maîtrise, Université de Paris I, 1981. Max Lazard, a member of the Groupe and close friend of Lyautey's, aided the Groupe in finding funding.

2. Jean-Pierre Gaudin, "Prévision, aménagement et gestion locale: l'émergence des plans d'urbanisme en France 1900–1940," thèse de doctorat d'état, University of Montpellier I, 1983.

3. Thanks to Christian Topalov for his insights on these matters.

4. Jean Bastie, *La Croissance de la banlieue parisienne* (Paris, 1964); Louis Chevalier, *Classes laborieuses et classes dangereuses à Paris pendant la première moitié du XXe siècle* (Paris, 1958), 182; Christian Topalov, *Le Logement en France, Histoire d'une marchandise impossible* (Paris, 1987). By 1931 the population of the suburbs came close to equaling that of Paris, which was beginning to decline: Paris had 2,891,000 inhabitants, the suburbs 2,016,000. Figures from Norma Evenson, *Paris: A Century of Change, 1878–1978* (New Haven, Conn., 1979), 221; J.H. Clapham, *The Economic Development of France and Germany, 1815–1914* (Cambridge, Eng., 1951), 158–70; Tyler Stovall, "The Urbanization of Bobigny, 1900–1939," Ph.D. diss., University of Wisconsin-Madison, 1984. I would like to thank Professor Stovall for his generous help in sharing his understanding of the growth of Paris suburbs with me.

5. Susanna Magri, *Politique du logement et besoins en main-d'oeuvre* (Paris, 1972), 65; Louis Chevalier, *La Formation de la population parisienne au 19e siècle* (Paris, 1950), 130–44.

6. For a general discussion of suburbs which highlights the particularity of the French case, see Robert Fishman, *Bourgeois Utopias: The Rise and Fall of Suburbia* (New York, 1987).

7. John P. McKay, *Tramways and Trolleys: The Rise of Urban Mass Transport in Europe* (Princeton, N.J., 1976), 149–50.

8. Maurice Halbwachs, *Les Expropriations et le prix des terrains à Paris* (Paris, 1909); Jacques Bertillion, *Essai de statistique comparée du surpeuplement des habitations à Paris et dans les capitales européenes* (Paris, 1894). Topalov gives a detailed explanation for the specificity of this conjunctural crisis in *Le Logement en France*, 103–228.

9. Eugène Hénard, *Etudes sur les transformations de Paris et autres écrits sur l'urbanisme*, ed. Jean-Louis Cohen (Paris, 1982), originally published between 1903 and 1909 with continuous pagination.

10. Peter Wolf, *Eugène Hénard and the Beginning of Urbanism in Paris, 1900–1914* (The Hague, 1968).

11. Hénard, *Etudes*, 223–24. Not all of his projects were brilliant; among his more disastrous ideas was a major street cutting through the Palais Royale and an X-shaped bridge.

12. Ibid., 123.

13. Jean François Chiffard, "Les H.B.M. et la ceinture de Paris," *Architecture, mouvement, continuité* 43(1977): 15.

14. Léon Jaussely, for example, adopted Hénard's *boulevard à redans triangulaires* as an addition to his Barcelona plan, thereby providing a direct view of the sea for every house on the new street.

15. Originally published under a slightly different title. See Robert Fishman, *Urban Utopias in the Twentieth Century: Ebenezer Howard, Frank Lloyd Wright, Le Corbusier* (New York, 1977), 23.

16. Edward Gibbon Wakefield, *Art of Colonisation* (London, 1849).

17. Georges Risler, "Les Cités jardins," *Mémoires et documents du Musée social* (December 1909).

18. Charles Andler, *La Vie de Lucien Herr* (Paris, 1977), 120.

19. Maurice Halbwachs, *Classes sociales et morphologie*, ed. and intro. Victor Karady (Paris, 1972), 12.

20. Henri Sellier, "En Mémoire d'Albert Thomas," as cited in Ginette Baty-Tornikian, *Architecture et social démocratie: un projet urbain idéal typique, agglomération parisienne 1919–1939* (Paris, 1980), 4. The other major secondary sources are: Thierry Leroux, "L'Urbanisme social-démocrate: Henri Sellier," Thèse de 3e cycle, Ecole des Hautes Etudes en Sciences Sociales, 1981; Katherine Burlen, ed., *La Banlieue oasis: Henri Sellier et les cités-jardins, 1900–1940* (Paris, 1987). I would particularly like to thank Katherine Burlen for her insights on these matters.

21. Madeleine Rébérioux, "Un Milieu socialiste à la veille de la grande guerre: Henri Sellier et le réformisme d'Albert Thomas," *La Banlieue Oasis*, ed. Burlen.

22. Madeleine Rébérioux, "Le Socialisme français 1875–1914," *Histoire générale du socialisme*, ed. J. Droz (Paris, 1975), vol. 2.

23. René Sordes, *Histoire de Suresnes: des origines à 1945* (Suresnes, 1965), 526.

24. Yves Lequin, *Les Ouvriers de la région lyonnaise, 1848–1914* (Lyons, 1977).

25. Catholic workers' unions were among the first to be successful in these circles.

26. Henri Sellier, *Les Banlieux urbaines*, pref. Albert Thomas (Paris, 1920).

27. Ibid., 60.

28. Jean-Pierre Gaudin, ed., *Les Premiers urbanistes français et l'art urbain, 1900–1930* (Paris, 1987).

29. Georges Risler, "Les Plans d'aménagement et d'extension des villes," *Mémoires et documents du Musée social* 11(1912): 304.

30. Cf. *Annales du Musée social* 32(1912): 32–36.

31. Agache (not a Prix-de-Rome winner) won third place in the competition for the planning of Canberra. In 1915, he inaugurated the first professional course in France on urbanism at the Ecole Libre des Sciences Sociales. Jean-Christophe Tougeron,

"Donat-Alfred Agache: un architecture urbaniste," *Les Cahiers de la recherche architecturale* 8(April 1981). Wolf, *Eugène Hénard*, 85.

32. Jean-Pierre Gaudin, "Prévision, aménagement et gestion locale," 135ff., for these and following details.

33. Robert de Souza, *Nice: capital d'hiver* (Paris, 1913). Also, Donat-Alfred Agache, J.M. Aubertin, and E. Redont, *Comment reconstruire nos cités détruites: notions d'urbanisme s'appliquant aux villes, bourgs, et villages* (Paris, 1915).

34. Ibid., 405.

35. Emile Benard won Phoebe Hearst's competition for an expanded campus in 1899, and the regents adopted the plan in 1900. After Benard refused to come to Berkeley, John Galen Howard modified Benard's monumental plan between 1903 and 1924. Verne A. Stadtman, ed., *Centennial Record of the University of California* (Berkeley, 1967), 48, 79, 392.

36. Ibid., 389.

37. Gaudin, *L'Avenir*, 151.

38. Jean-Claude Vigato, "Notes sur la question stylistique," *Les Cahiers de la recherche architecturale* 15–17(1985). More detail is contained in Vigato's thesis, "L'Architecture du régionalisme, Les Origines du débat, 1900–1950," Ecole d'Architecture de Nancy, 1982; Jean-Louis Cohen, "Les Architectes français et l'art urbain, 1900–1914," Gaudin, *Les Premiers urbanistes*.

39. Agache et al., *Comment reconstruire*, 5.

40. Leon Rosenthal, *Villes et villages français après la guerre: aménagement, restauration, embellissement, extension*, intro. Louis Bonnier (Paris, 1918).

41. Roger Marx, *L'Art social*, pref. Anatole France (Paris, 1918). On Roger Marx see Debora Silverman, *The Origins of French Art Nouveau 1889–1900: Nature, Neurology, and Nobility* (Berkeley, 1989).

42. Poëte, the leading contemporary practitioner of urban history, emphasized neither the static nor the cyclical in urban change but rather sought to understand the mutation and evolution of urban forms.

43. Rosenthal, *Villes et villages français*, 19, 28.

44. Ibid., 28.

Chapter 9

1. Melvin Knight, "French Colonial Policy—The Decline of 'Association,'" *Journal of Modern History* 5, no. 2 (June, 1933): 215.

2. Hubert Lyautey, "Congress of Moroccan Higher Education Speech" (Rabat, May 26, 1921), Hubert Lyautey, *Paroles d'Action, 1900–1926* (Paris, 1927), 340–41.

3. For a full account not only of French tactics but of Moroccan resistance to them, see

Edmund Burke III, *Prelude to Protectorate in Morocco: Precolonial Protest and Resistance, 1860–1912* (Chicago, 1976).

4. His *chef de cabinet* was the son of ex-Governor General Rousseau, who had replaced de Lanessan in Indochina.

5. Letter of August 19, 1918 to Barrucand, as cited in André Le Révérend, *Lyautey* (Paris, 1983), 386.

6. Letter to Joseph Reinach, July 1915, as cited in Le Révérend, *Lyautey*, 388. Gallieni, just before his death, held the post of Minister of War, and organized the defense of Paris.

7. Hubert Lyautey, "Eloge de l'élite," *Revue hebdomadaire* (July 12, 1930), as cited in Le Révérend, *Lyautey, l'écrivain*, 334.

8. Letter of November 12, 1915 to Desjardins, as cited in Le Révérend, *Lyautey, l'écrivain*, 335.

9. Letter of September 17, 1920 to Desjardins, as cited in *Lyautey, l'écrivain*, 337.

10. Georges Hardy, *Portrait de Lyautey* (Paris, 1949), 308.

11. For further discussion of this point see: Michel Foucault, interview with Paul Rabinow and Hubert Dreyfus, "On the Genealogy of Ethics: An Overview of Work in Progress," *The Foucault Reader*, ed. Paul Rabinow, 340–72.

12. Le Révérend, *Lyautey, l'écrivain*, 311.

13. Ibid., 325. For the invention of the "traditional" Moroccan government, the *Makhzen*, see Daniel Rivet, *Lyautey et l'institution du protectorat français au Maroc, 1912–1925*, Doctorat d'Etat en Histoire et Sciences Sociales, Université de Paris (Val-de-Marne), 1985, 214ff.

14. Letter of May 13, 1919 to Jonnart, as cited in André Le Révérend, *Un Lyautey inconnu: correspondance et journal inédits, 1874–1934* (Paris, 1980), 288.

15. Hubert Lyautey, *Lettres du Tonkin et de Madagascar, 1894–1899* (Paris, 1920), 71.

16. One of his officers called him "Swann à épaulettes," as cited in Rivet, *Lyautey*, 183.

17. Lyautey, *Lettres du Tonkin*, 296.

18. Letter of August 6, 1919 to Wladimir D'Ormesson, as cited in Le Révérend, *Un Lyautey inconnu*, 292.

19. Georges Hardy, *Portrait de Lyautey*, 262.

20. André Gide quoting Lyautey in "Pages retrouvées," *Nouvelle Revue Française* (January 1970), as quoted in Le Révérend, *Lyautey, Ecrivain*, 339.

21. Jacques Berque, "Medinas, villes neuves, et bidonvilles," *Cahiers de Tunisie* 21–22 (1958).

22. Louis Sablayrolles, *L'Urbanisme au Maroc: les moyens d'action, les résultats* (Albi, 1925), 109.

23. Rivet, *Lyautey*, 924.

24. Jean Marrast, "Maroc," *L'Oeuvre d'Henri Prost: Architecture et urbanisme* (Paris, 1960), 49–119; Commissaire Résident Général au Maroc, *La Renaissance du Maroc: Dix années de protectorat, 1912–1922* (Rabat, 1923); Jean Dethier, "Soixante ans d'urbanisme au Maroc, l'évolution des idées et des réalisations," *Bulletin Economique et Social du Maroc* 32, Double no. 118–119 (July–December 1970): 5–56; Henri Descamps, "L'Architecture française au Maroc, L'Urbanisme: L'Oeuvre de M. Prost," *La Construction Moderne*, 46(December 20, 1930).

25. Jean Marrast, ed., *Prost* (Paris, 1960), 119.

26. Ibid., 59.

27. Ibid., 63.

28. Lamented but not documented by Janet L. Abu-Lughod, *Rabat: Urban Apartheid in Morocco* (Princeton, 1980) 163ff.

29. Hubert de la Casinière, *Les Municipalités marocaines, leur développement, leur législation* (Casablanca, 1924), 88.

30. Guillaume de Tarde, "Rapport général sur Afrique du Nord," *L'Urbanisme aux colonies et dans les pays tropicaux*, vol. 1, ed. Jean Royer (La Charité-sur-Loire and Paris, 1932–35), 29.

31. Ibid.

32. Casinière, *Municipalités marocaines*, ix.

33. Casinière, *Municipalités marocaines*, 6. On the repeated use of California imagery at this period, see Will Swearingen, "In Search of the Granary of Rome: Irrigation and Agricultural Development in Morocco, 1912–1982," Ph.D. diss., University of Texas, Austin, 1984.

34. Casinière, *Municipalités marocaines*, 11.

35. Knight, "French Colonial Policy," 216.

36. Hubert Lyautey, letter of December 30, 1913, as cited in Pierre Lyautey, ed. *Lyautey l'Africain, textes et lettres du Maréchal Lyautey*, vol. 1, *1912–1913* (Paris, 1953), 176.

37. Letter of December 5, 1913, ibid., 179.

38. Henri Prost, "Le Développement de l'urbanisme dans le protectorat du Maroc de 1914 à 1913," Royer, ed., *L'Urbanisme aux colonies et dans les pays tropicaux*, 1: 62.

39. Sylviane Munoz, "Monographie historique et économique d'une capitale coloniale: Rabat de 1912 à 1939," 2 vols., thèse pour le Doctorat d'état es-lettres et sciences humaines, Université de Nice, 1986. This massive thesis contains a detailed description of the social, economic, and political life of Rabat. Thanks are due to Professor Munoz for her insights and generosity.

40. Munoz, "Monographie historique et économique," 352.

41. Prost had been recommended to Lyautey by J.C.N. Forestier, the Conservateur des

Promenades de Paris, an associate of the Musée Social. He consulted with Prost on Rabat's parks. Details in Munoz, "Monographie historique et économique," 96.

42. Prost, "Développement de l'urbanisme," 66.

43. Brian Taylor, "Discontinuité planifiée, villes coloniales modernes au Maroc," *Les Cahiers de la Recherche Architecturale* 9 (January 1982): 62.

44. Abu-Lughod makes clear the consequences of this planning mistake. *Rabat: Urban Apartheid in Morocco,* 160–61.

45. Munoz, "Monographie historique et économique," 140–43.

46. François Béguin, et al., *Arabisances, décor architectural et trace urbain en Afrique du Nord, 1830–1950* (Paris, 1983), 119.

47. Edmund Burke III, "La Mission scientifique au Maroc: science sociale et politique dans l'âge de l'impérialisme," *Bulletin Economique et Social du Maroc,* nos. 138–139 (1978): 37–56; idem., "The First Crisis of Orientalism, 1890–1914," *Connaissances du Maghreb, sciences sociales et colonisation* (Paris, 1984).

48. Louis Mercier, "Rabat: Déscription topographique," *Archives Marocaines* 7(1906): 296–349.

49. Lyautey, introduction, *L'Islam et la politique contemporaine* (Paris, 1927), as quoted in Knight, "French Colonial Policy," 224; Clifford Geertz, *Islam Observed: Religious Development in Morocco and Indonesia* (Chicago, 1971).

50. Henri Descamps, "L'Architecture française au Maroc, L'Urbanisme: L'Oeuvre de M. Prost," *La Construction Moderne* 46(December 14, 1930): 173.

51. E. Pauty, "Rapport sur la défense des villes et la restauration des monuments historiques," *Hesperis* 2, nos. 1–2(1922): 449.

52. Descamps, "L'Architecture française au Maroc," 174.

53. Munoz mentions the Ocean, Kebibat, and Grand Agueda quarters. "Monographie historique et économique," 154.

54. Abu-Lughod, *Rabat: Urban Apartheid in Morocco,* 156–57.

55. Abu-Lughod fails to establish how much land was expropriated during this period but cites Knight as saying that it was only after Lyautey left that large chunks were grabbed.

56. Prost went on to do regional planning on the Côte d'Azur, and to devise the first regional circulation plan for the Parisian region before becoming the chief urban planner in Istanbul.

57. Urban planning was hardly unknown in pre-Protectorate Morocco: it is worth remembering that in the eighteenth century, the Moroccan sultan had commissioned a Portuguese architect to build the port-fortress city of Mogador. Henri Terrasse, *Histoire du Maroc des origines à l'établissement du protectorat français,* vol. 2 (Casablanca, 1950), 298.

58. Under Malekite Islamic law, the land in Casablanca belonged to the *Makhzen*; it fell into the category of land reconquered from the Christians. Louis Milliot, *Introduction à l'étude du droit musulman* (Paris, 1953), 491ff.

59. André Adam, *Casablanca: essai sur la transformation de la société marocaine au contact de l'Occident* (Paris, 1968), 15.

60. Hubert Lyautey, letter of August 20, 1919 to André Lazard, as cited in Le Révérend, *Un Lyautey inconnu*, 294.

61. See *Encyclopédie coloniale et maritime* (Paris, 1948), 435–44.

62. Maurice Zimmermann, *Paysages et villes du Maroc* (Lyons, 1923), 34.

63. There was a "Plan Agache" for Casa, reproduced in Michel Ecochard, *Casablanca: le roman d'une ville* (Paris, 1955). Apparently Agache had merely cleaned up an army engineer's drawings. Personal communication, Jean-Louis Cohen.

64. Prost, "Développement de l'urbanisme," 78.

65. François Béguin et al., *Arabisances, décor architectural et trace urbain en Afrique du Nord, 1830–1950* (Paris, 1983), 11.

66. Jean-L. de Lanessan: saving a pagoda was worth twenty columns. *Principes de colonisation* (Paris, 1897), 62.

67. Hubert Lyautey, "Allocution d'ouverture," *Paroles d'action, 1900–1926* (Paris, 1927), 451.

68. Brian Taylor, "Discontinuité Planifiée," 54.

69. Albert Laprade, "Une Ville créée spécialement pour les indigènes," *L'Urbanisme dans les colonies*, ed. Jean Royer.

70. Annelise Gérard, "Quartier et unité de voisinage dans la pratique urbanistique française, 1919–1973," Thèse de 3e cycle, Université de Paris VII, 1977.

71. Jean-Paul Charnay, "La Guerre de Rif, dernière campagne coloniale ou première guerre révolutionnaire?" *Téchnique et Géosociologie: la guerre du Rif, le nucleaire en Orient* (Paris, 1984). See also: David S. Woolman, *Rebels in the Rif: Abd el-Krim and the Rif Rebellion* (Berkeley, 1968); *Abd el-Krim et la République du Rif*, Actes du colloque international d'études historiques et sociologiques, 18–20 January 1973 (Paris, 1976).

72. Lottman claims that Lyautey had hatched a plot, stopped by Pétain, to overthrow Herriot. Herbert R. Lottman, *Pétain* (Paris, 1984), 130. Lottman curiously adds that Lyautey had spent all the war years in Morocco.

73. Ibid., 134.

74. Charnay, "Guerre du Rif," 58.

75. Ibid., 86.

76. For details see Henri Prost, "Rapport general," Royer, ed. *Urbanisme dans les colonies*.

Chapter 10

1. Henri Sellier, *Les Banlieux urbaines et la réorganisation administrative du département de la Seine* (Paris, 1920), 23–24.

2. Susanna Magri and Christian Topalov, "De la Cité jardin à la ville rationalisée: un tournant du projet réformateur, 1905–1925; une étude comparative France, Grande Bretagne, Italie, Etats-Unis," unpublished ms., June 1986.

3. Georges Teyssot, "Civilisation du salarié et culture de l'employé: variations sur Siegfried Kracauer, Ernst Bloch et Walter Benjamin," *Les Cahiers de la recherche architecturale*, 15–17(1985).

4. For a detailed discussion of neo-socialist alternatives see Zeev Sternhell, *Ni Droite ni gauche: l'idéologie fasciste en France* (Paris, 1983).

5. Charles S. Maier, "Between Taylorism and Technocracy: European Ideologies and the Vision of Industrial Productivity in the 1920s," *Journal of Contemporary History* 5, no. 2 (1970); Henri Le Châtelier, *Le Taylorisme*, 2d ed. (Paris, 1934). For workers' resistance, see Albert Thomas, preface to Paul Devinat, *Scientific Management in Europe* (Geneva, 1927). Thanks to Professor Mary McLeod for her thesis and articles cited below and for her helpful comments and discussions.

6. Richard F. Kuisel, *Capitalism and the State in Modern France: Renovation and Economic Management in the Twentieth Century* (Cambridge, Eng., 1981); Martin Fine, "Toward Corporatism: The Movement for Capital-Labor Collaboration in France, 1914–1936," Ph.D. diss., University of Wisconsin, 1971; John F. Godfrey, *Capitalism at War: Industrial Policy and Bureaucracy in France, 1914–1918* (Leamington Spa, U.K., 1987).

7. Godfrey, *Capitalism at War*, 6–7.

8. Madeleine Rébérioux et Patrick Fridenson, "Albert Thomas, pivot du réformisme français," *Le Mouvement social* 87(April–June 1974).

9. Godfrey, *Capitalists at War*, 187–88.

10. As cited in Jacques Amoyal, "Les Origines socialistes et syndicalistes de la planification en France," *Le Mouvement social* 87(April–June 1974): 137.

11. Gerd Hardach, "La Mobilisation industrielle en 1914–1918: production, planification et idéologie," *Cahiers du Mouvement social*, no. 2, *1914–1918: L'autre front*, ed. Patrick Fridenson (Paris, 1977), 102.

12. Godfrey, *Capitalists at War*, 85.

13. Kuisel, *Capitalism and the State*, 46. See also Henri Hauser, *Le Problème du régionalisme* (Paris, 1924).

14. Godfrey, *Capitalists at War*, 91.

15. Charles S. Maier, *Recasting Bourgeois Europe: Stabilization in France, Germany and Italy in the Decade after World War I* (Princeton, N.J., 1975), 73–74.

16. Louis Loucheur, "Rapport de la commission chargée par le Ministère de l'Hygiène

et de la Prévoyance sociale d'étudier les mesures les plus propres à remédier la crise du logement," *La Vie urbaine* 4(September–October 1919): 494–96.

17. Alain Desrosières, "Histoires de formes: statistiques et sciences sociales avant 1940," *Revue française de sociologie* 26, no. 26 (May–June 1985): 277; Laurent Thèvenot, "La Mesure de la qualité des personnes: généalogie des enquêtes de mobilité," *Pour une histoire de la statistique,* vol. 2 (Paris, 1986); Jean Bouvier, "François Simiand: la statistique et les sciences humaines," *Pour une histoire de la statistique,* vol. 1 (Paris, 1986); Donald A. MacKenzie, *Statistics in Britain, 1865–1930: The Social Construction of Scientific Knowledge* (Edinburgh, 1981); Maurice Halbwachs, "L'Expérimentation statistique et les probabilités" and "La Méthodologie de François Simiand: un empirisme rationaliste," *Classes sociales et morphologie,* ed. and intro. Victor Karady (Paris, 1972).

18. Institutional advances, however, were made; Adolphe Bertillon (1821–1883) directed the Bureau de Statistique de la Ville de Paris, compiling massive studies of housing, crime, and health. His two sons achieved a perfect division of labor: one quantitative, the other qualitative. Jacques (1851–1922) followed his father in directing the Bureau de Statistique. His brother Alphonse (1853–1914) directed the Service d'Identité Judiciaire de la Préfecture de la Police, where the developed procedures for the identification of individuals, including fingerprinting (a technique borrowed from Galton).

19. Desrosières, "Histoire de formes," 295.

20. John E. Craig, "Maurice Halbwachs à Strasbourg," *Revue française de sociologie* 20, no. 1 (January–March 1979).

21. Jean-Pierre Gaudin, *L'Avenir en plan: technique et politique dans la prévision urbaine, 1900–1930* (Seyssel, 1985), 94.

22. Anthony Sutcliffe, *Towards the Planned City: Germany, Britain, the United States, and France, 1780–1914* (New York, 1981), 152–53.

23. Typically, even Bastié cites Swedish and British legislation as preceding this law but neglects to mention that of Morocco. Jean Bastié, *La Croissance de la banlieue parisienne* (Paris, 1964), 279.

24. Albert Grillet, *Les Alignements en droit marocain* (Paris, 1936).

25. Gaston Rambert, "La Cartographie à l'Exposition coloniale de Marseille," *Annales de Géographie* (15 November 1922): 433–48.

26. Annelise Gérard, "Quartier et unité de voisinage dans la pratique urbanistique française, 1919–1973" (Thèse de troisième cycle, Université de Paris VII, 1977), 23.

27. Leon Jaussely, preface to Raymond Unwin, *L'Etude pratique des plans de ville* (Paris, 1922), vii.

28. Leon Jaussely, "Chronique de l'urbanisme," *La Vie Urbaine* 1–2(March–June 1919): 184–85.

29. Louis Bonnier, "La Population de Paris en mouvement, 1800–1861," *La Vie Urbaine* 1–2 (March–June 1919): 8. The principal organ of urbanist discourse during the interwar period was *La Vie Urbaine.* The review had both scientific and more directly utilitarian goals. Its original board included figures from science and politics: Louis

Bonnier, Marcel Poëte, Emmanuel de Margerie, Georges Espinas, Camille Jullian, Brunhes, Demangeon, Forestier, Charles Gide, Jaussely, Georges Risler. Collaborators included Patrick Abercrombie, Agache, Aubertin, Augustin Bernard, Raoul Blanchard, Charles Brun, Lucien Febvre, Maurice Halbwachs, Henri Hauser, René Maunier, Henri Prost, Léon Rosenthal, Henri Sellier.

30. The law of May 14, 1932 instituted a *plan d'aménagement* for the Parisian region. From 1928 to 1934 Henri Prost directed studies of the region leading to a regional transportation plan. This plan coordinated 656 communes, a procedure generalized by the law of July 25, 1935.

31. Henri Sellier, "Conférence internationale des cités-jardins et de l'aménagement des villes," *La Vie Urbaine* 18(15 February 1923).

32. As cited in Thierry Leroux, "L'Urbanisme social-démocrate: Henri Sellier," thèse de 3e cycle, Ecole des Hautes Etudes en Sciences Sociales, 1981, p. 89.

33. On the history of this theme see Epron, ed., "L'Usine et la ville 1836–1986: 150 ans d'urbanisme," special issue of *Culture technique* (Spring 1986).

34. Leroux, "L'Urbanisme social-démocrate: Henri Sellier," 186.

35. Maurice Halbwachs, "Matière et société," *Classes sociales et morphologie*, ed. and intro. Victor Karady (Paris, 1972), 60.

36. Ibid, 68.

37. Maurice Halbwachs, "Les Caractéristiques des classes moyennes," Karady ed., *Classes sociales et morphologie*, 105.

38. Ibid., 111.

39. Henri Sellier, "Les Centres sociaux dans les régions rurales aux Etats-Unis," *La Vie urbaine* (1922): 1.

40. Ginette Baty-Tornikian, *Architecture et social démocratie* (Paris, 1980), 100.

41. Donat-Alfred Agache, J.M. Auburtin, and E. Redont, *Comment reconstruire nos cités détruites: notions d'urbanisme s'appliquant aux villes, bourgs et villages* (Paris, 1915), 33. The 1919 law imposing a work day of eight hours introduced the question of free time and reinforced the campaign for the creation of alternatives to the bistro and cabaret.

42. Jean-Louis Cohen, "Des Bourses du travail au temps des loisirs, les avatars de la sociabilité ouvrière," *Architectures pour le peuple: maisons du peuple—Belgique, Allemagne, Autriche, France, Grande-Bretagne, Italie, Pays-Bas, Suisse* (Brussels, 1984), 159.

43. Leroux, "L'Urbanisme social-démocrate: Henri Sellier," 180. Only the city of Stains accommodated a range of social classes.

44. Gérard, "Quartier et unité," 23.

45. For a romanticized tour of the exotic suburbs, see Léandre Vaillat, *Seine: chef-lieu Paris* (Paris, 1937).

46. Leroux, "L'Urbanisme social démocrate: Henri Sellier," 169. The technical term "neighborhood" was first introduced in 1909 by C.H. Cooley, in his work on social

organization, and picked up by American planners. In 1923 C.A. Perry, and in 1925 R.E. Park and E.W. Burgess, used the term. Gérard, "Quartier et unité," 9–182.

47. René Sordes, *Histoire de Suresnes: des origines à 1945* (Suresnes, 1965), 460–75.

48. The first Union des Coopératives (bread, charcuterie, hardware, and coal) was established in France in 1910.

49. Henri Sellier, "L'Avenir de Suresnes lié à son passé," *Bulletin de la Société historique de Suresnes* 1(1929): 1–2.

50. Christian Betron, "A la Recherche d'un consensus: Henri Sellier et la Société historique de Suresnes," *La Banlieue oasis: Henri Sellier et les cités-jardins, 1900–1940*, ed. Katherine Burlen (Paris, 1987).

51. For an extensive literature, see Pierre Nora, ed., *Les Lieux de mémoire*, vol. 1, *La République* (Paris, 1984).

52. Georges Canguilhem, "Qu'est-ce que la psychologie," *Etudes d'histoire et de philosophie des sciences* (Paris, 1983), 378–79.

53. Louis Boulonnois, *L'Oeuvre municipale de M. Henri Sellier à Suresnes* (Paris, 1938).

54. The medical community resisted the emphasis on preventive medicine: antidiphtheria vaccination campaigns, cancer checkups, dispensaries of the Office Public d'Hygiène Sociale. For more details see Henri Hatzfeld, *Du Pauperisme à la securité sociale: essai sur les origines de la securité sociale en France, 1850–1940* (Paris, 1971).

55. Boulonnois, *L'Oeuvre municipale*, 15.

56. Ibid., 80. The attempt to extend the arts of government to the whole population was international in scope and generously supported by the Rockefeller Foundation. Lion Murard and Patrick Zylberman, "La Raison de l'expert ou l'hygiène comme science sociale appliqué," *Archives européenne de sociologie* 26(1985). Murard and Zylberman, "Robert-Henri Hazemann, Urbaniste Social," *Urbi*, 10(Winter, 1986). Despite the authors' erudition, their interpretation seems ahistorical and inflationist. For a more incisive interpretation see Burlen, *La Banlieue oasis*.

57. Boulonnois, *L'Oeuvre municipale*, 1.

58. Louis Boulonnois, "Correction annuelle des dénombrements de population," *La Vie urbaine*, n.s. 6 (15 November 1930).

59. Pierre Bourdieu, *La Distinction, critique sociale du jugement* (Paris, 1979).

60. Burlen, "Sciences du logement," *La Banlieue oasis*, 110.

61. Henri Sellier and Robert-Henri Hazemann, "La Santé publique et la collectivité," *Rapport de la commission d'hygiène du service social* (Paris, 1936).

62. Evenson, *Paris: A Century of Change, 1878–1978*, 222. Two of these planned garden cities (Drancy and Champigny) were built by the railway workers' union. Suresnes, Stains, and Gennevilliers were built to house local populations; two others (Chatenay-Malabry, Plessis-Robinson) were built around plots sold at low prices. Six of these localities had socialist mayors, the most famous of whom were Sellier at Suresnes, and Albert Thomas at Champigny.

63. Ibid., 226.

64. Anonymous, "L'Habitation et l'urbanisme modernes d'après les expositions récentes," *La Vie Urbaine*, n.s. 1(15 February 1930): 66.

65. An interesting case study of the crossing of these fields can be found in Brian Brace Taylor, *Le Corbusier: The City of Refuge, Paris, 1929/33* (Chicago, 1987).

66. Henri Sellier, "Le Logement ouvrier contemporain," *L'Architecture d'aujourd'hui* 6, no. 6 (June 1935): 7.

67. Henri Sellier, "L'Oeuvre de l'Office Public d'Habitations à Bon Marché du Département de la Seine," *L'Architecture d'aujourd'hui* 8, nos. 5–6 (June 1937): 45.

68. Marc Bonneville, *Naissance et métamorphose d'une banlieue ouvrière: Villeurbanne, processus et formes d'urbanisation* (Lyons, 1978).

69. Bernard Meuret, "Le Problème du centre comme mode de différentiation d'une commune socialiste: Villeurbanne," Burlen ed., *La Banlieue oasis*.

70. Dr. Lazare Goujon, *Villeurbanne 1924–1934: dix ans d'administration* (Lyons, 1934). Finance methods are detailed in Bonneville, *Naissance et métemorphose*, 77–111.

71. For architectural criticisms, see Dominique Boudier, Didier François, and Michel Reynaud, "Villeurbanne, 1924–1934, un centre urbaine," *Architecture, mouvement, continuité* 39(1976): 57–62. In 1919, Tony Garnier proposed a Métropole du Travail of 1,000,000 people. He placed a vast Bourse du Travail, comprising all the social services and activities of the city, at the city's center.

72. The construction of a metal and glass Maison du Peuple in Clichy in 1939 marked "without doubt the typological conclusion of the history of *maisons du peuple*." Jean-Louis Cohen, "Des Bourses du travail au temps des loisirs: les avatars de la sociabilité ouvrière (France 1914–39)," *Architectures pour le peuple: maisons du peuple—Belgique, Allemagne, Autriche, France, Grande-Bretagne, Italie, Pays-Bas, Suisse* (Brussels, 1984), 179.

73. Bonneville, *Naissance et métamorphose*, 73.

74. Cf. *Dix années de réalisations des municipalités socialistes* (Lyons, 1934), 19.

75. Paul Rivet, P. Lester, and Georges-Henri Rivière, "Le Laboratoire d'anthropologie du museum," *Archives du Museum National d'Histoire Naturelle* 12, no. 2 (June 1935): 507. Donald Bender, "The Development of French Anthropology," *Journal of the History of the Behavioral Sciences*, 1(1965): 139–51; Michael Hammond, "Anthropology as a Weapon of Social Combat in Late-Nineteenth-Century France," *Journal of the History of the Behavioral Sciences*, 16(1980): 118–32; Elizabeth A. Williams, "Anthropological Institutions in Nineteenth Century France," *Isis* 76(1985): 331–48; Francis Schiller, *Paul Broca: Founder of French Anthropology, Explorer of the Brain* (Berkeley, 1979); Herman Lebovics, "Conservative Anthropology and the End of the Third Republic," unpbd. ms., 1988. Thanks to Jean Jamin for his insights on these and so many other issues, and to Richard Gringeri, who has generously shared knowledge of these events and actors.

76. Michel Leiris, "L'Ethnographe devant le colonialisme," *Les Temps modernes* 6, no. 58 (August 1950), is the first systematic statement.

77. Lubovics, "Conservative Anthropology."

78. Paul Rivet and Georges-Henri Rivière, "La Réorganisation du Musée d'Ethnographie du Trocadéro," *Bulletin du museum national d'histoire naturelle*, 2d ser., vol. 2, no. 5 (June 1930). On the Dakar-Djibouti expedition see Jean Jamin, "Objets trouvés des paradis perdus: à propos de la mission Dakar-Djibouti" *Collections passion: exposition du 5 juin au 31 dec.*, eds. Jacques Hainard and Roland Kaehr (Neuchâtel, 1982).

79. A.-G. Kersaint, *Discours sur les monuments publics* (Paris, 1792), as cited in Anthony Vidler, *The Writing of the Walls: Architectural Theory in the Late Enlightenment* (Princeton, 1987), 165.

80. Paul Rivet, "Ce que sera le Musée de l'Homme," *L'Oeuvre*, June 14. 1936.

81. Archives of the Musée de l'Homme, as cited in Jean Jamin, "Du Musée de l'Homme considéré comme un Laboratoire des representations," unpublished ms., December 5–6, 1986, 20. Rivet, elected as a socialist deputy from Paris in 1935, had belonged since 1927 to the Ligue Contre l'Oppression Coloniale et l'Impérialisme, whose president was Albert Einstein; he was a co-founder of the 1934 Comité de Vigilance des Intellectuels Antifascistes. Martin Blumenson, *The Vilde Affair: Beginnings of the French Resistance* (Boston, 1977).

82. The dream of enriching the national heritage through reviving popular culture was carried forward by Rivière with the creation of the Musée des Arts et Traditions Populaires in 1937. On Rivière see Isac Chiva, "Georges-Henri Rivière: Fifty Years in the Ethnology of France," *Social Science Information* 25, no. 3 (1986).

83. Alfred Agache, "La Leçon de l'exposition de 1937, Enquête de l'Architecture d'Aujourd'hui," *L'Architecture d'aujourd'hui*, no. 8 (August 1937): 7.

84. Bruno Foucart, "The Inspired Hilltop," *The New Trocadéro*, ed. Isabelle Gournay (Brussels, 1985), 63.

85. Jean Favier, *L'Exposition internationale* (Paris, 1937), as quoted in "An Official Showcase for French Art," *The New Trocadéro*, ed. Isabelle Gournay (Brussels, 1985), 100.

86. Maurice Rotival, "Les Grands ensembles," *Architecture d'aujourd'hui* 5, no. 6 (June 1935): 57.

87. Ibid., 61.

88. Ibid., 72.

Bibliography

Abd el Krim et la République du Rif. Actes du Colloque international d'etudes historique et sociologiques, 18–20, January 1973. Paris: Maspero, 1976.

Abu-Lughod, Janet. *Rabat: Urban Apartheid in Morocco.* Princeton, N.J.: Princeton University Press, 1980.

Ackerknecht, Erwin. "Villermé et Quételet." *Bulletin of the Journal of the History of Medicine* 26(1952).

Arendt, Hannah. *The Life of the Mind.* Rev. ed. New York: Harcourt Brace Jovanovich, 1981.

Actes du colloque 'Villes et compagnes, XVe–XXe siecle'. Lyons, 1977.

Adam, André. *Casablanca: essai sur la transformation de la société marocaine au contact de l'Occident.* Paris: C.N.R.S., 1968.

Agache, Donat-Alfred. "La Leçon de 1937, Enquête de *L'Architecture d'aujourd'hui.*" *L'Architecture d'aujourd'hui* 8(August 1937).

Agache, Donat-Alfred, J.M. Aubertin, and E. Redont. *Comment reconstruire nos cités détruites: notions d'urbanisme s'appliquant aux villes, bourgs et villages.* Paris: Colin, 1915.

Agéron, Charles-Robert. *France coloniale ou parti colonial?* Paris: Presses Universitaires de France, 1978.

Agulhon, Maurice, ed. *Histoire de la France urbaine,* vol. 4: *La Ville de l'age industriel: le cycle haussmannien.* Paris: Seuil, 1983.

Ajtony, Arpad, et al. *Assurance, prévoyance, securité: formation historique des techniques de gestion sociale dans les sociétés industrielles.* Paris, 1979.

Amoyal, Jacques. "Les Origines socialistes et syndicalistes de la planification en France." *Le Mouvement social* 87(April–June 1974).

Andler, Charles. *La Vie de Lucien Herr.* Paris: Rieder, 1932; Paris: Maspero, 1977.

Bibliography

Ansart, Pierre. *Sociologie de Saint-Simon*. Paris, Presses Universitaires de France, 1970.

Augagneur, Victor. *Erreurs et brutalités coloniales*. Paris: Montaigne, 1927.

Auzelle, Robert. "Conditions et impératifs de l'urbanisme." *La Vie Urbaine* (April–June 1961).

Auzelle, Robert. *Technique de l'urbanisme*. Paris: Presses Universitaire de France, 1953.

Badovici, Jean, and Albert Morancé, eds. *L'Oeuvre de Tony Garnier*. Paris: Morancé, 1938.

Baker, Keith Michael. *Condorcet: From Natural Philosophy to Social Mathematics*. Chicago: University of Chicago Press, 1975.

Banham, Reyner. *A Concrete Atlantis: U.S. Industrial Building and European Modern Architecture*. Cambridge, Mass.: M.I.T. Press, 1986.

Banham, Reyner. *Theory and Design in the First Machine Age*. New York: Praeger, 1960, 1967. Rev. ed. Cambridge Mass.: M.I.T. Press, 1980.

Bann, Stephen. *The Clothing of Clio: A Study of the Representation of History in Nineteenth-century Britain and France*. New York: Cambridge University Press, 1984.

Barrès, Maurice. *Les Lézardes sur la maison*. 2nd ed. Paris: Sansot, 1904.

Barrès, Maurice. *Scènes et doctrines du nationalisme*. Paris: Juven, 1902.

Barrows, Susanna. *Distorting Mirrors: Visions of the Crowd in Nineteenth-century France*. New Haven, Conn.: Yale University Press, 1981.

Bastié, Jean. *La Croissance de la banlieue parisienne*. Paris: Presses Universitaires de France, 1964.

Baty-Tornikian, Ginette. *Architecture et social démocratie: un projet urbain idéal typique, agglomération parisienne 1919–1939*. Paris: Institut d'Etudes et de Recherches Architecturales et Urbaines (I.E.A.R.U.), 1980.

Baudelaire, Charles. "Conseil aux jeunes littérateurs." *Oeuvres complètes de Charles Baudelaire: l'art romantique*. Paris: Michel Lévy, Frères, 1868.

Baudoui, Remy. "Planification territoriale et reconstruction, 1940–1946." Thèse de 3e cycle, Université de Paris (Val-de-Marne), 1984.

Bender, Donald. "The Development of French Anthropology." *Journal of the History of the Behavioral Sciences* 1(1965).

Beausant, Philippe. *Versailles, opéra*. Paris: Gallimard, 1981.

Béguin, Francois, et al. *Arabisances, décor architectural et trace urbain en Afrique du Nord, 1830–1950*. Paris: Dunod, 1983.

Belgrand, Eugène. *Les Travaux souterrains de Paris*. 4 vols. Paris: Dunod, 1972–87.

Benevolo, Leonardo. *The History of Modern Architecture*. 2 vols. Cambridge, Mass.: M.I.T. Press, 1971.

Benevolo, Leonardo. *The Origins of Modern Town Planning.* Cambridge, Mass.: M.I.T. Press, 1967.

Benoist-Mechin, Jacques G. P. *Lyautey l'africain ou le rêve immolé, 1854–1934.* Lausanne: Clairfontaine, 1966. Reprint. Paris: Perrin 1978.

Benoiston de Chateauneuf. *Rapport sur la marche et les effets du choléra-morbus dans Paris.* Paris: Imprimerie Royale 1834.

Berdoulay, Vincent. *La Formation de l'école française de géographie, 1870–1914.* Paris: Bibliothèque nationale, 1981.

Berque, Jacques. "Medinas, villes neuves et bidonvilles." *Cahiers de Tunisie* 21–22(1958).

Bertillion, Jacques. *Essai de statistique comparée du surpeuplement des habitations à Paris et dans les capitales européennes.* Paris, 1894.

Besnard, René, and C. Aymard. *L'Oeuvre française au Maroc.* Paris, Hachette, 1914.

Bianchi, Serge, et al. *Histoire d'un domaine: du château seigneurial de Draveil à la cité coopérative Paris-Jardins.* Le Neubourg: Association des Amis de l'Histoire du Domaine, 1984.

Bichat, Xavier. *Recherches physiologiques sur la vie et sur la mort.* 3d ed. Paris: Brosson, 1805.

Bloch, Maurice. *Placing the Dead: Tombs, Ancestral Villages and Kinship Organization in Madagascar.* London and New York: Seminar Press, 1971.

Bloch-Lainé, François, and Jean Bouvier. *La France restaurée 1944–1954: dialogue sur les choix d'une modernisation.* Paris: Fayard, 1986.

Blumberg, Hans. *The Legitimacy of the Modern Age.* Cambridge, Mass.: M.I.T. Press, 1983.

Blumenson, Martin. *The Vilde Affair: Beginnings of the French Resistance.* Boston: Houghton-Mifflin, 1977.

Bonald, Louis, vicomte de. *Oeuvres complètes.* Ed. Abbe Migne. 3 vols. Paris: Migne, 1859–64.

Bonald, Louis, vicomte de. *Théorie du pouvoir politique et religieux.* Ed. Colette Capitan. Paris: 1796. Reprint. Paris: Union générale d'éditions, 1966.

Bonneville, Marc. *Naissance et métamorphose d'une banlieue ouvrière: Villeurbanne, processus et formes d'urbanisation.* Lyons: Presses Universitaire de Lyon, 1978.

Bonnier, Louis. "La Population de Paris en mouvement, 1800–1861." *La Vie Urbaine* 1–2(March 1919).

Boudier, Dominique, Didier François, and Michel Reynaud "Villeurbanne; 1924–1934, un centre urbain." *Architecture, mouvement, continuité* 39(1976).

Boudon, Philippe. *Pessac de Le Corbusier, 1927–1967: étude socio-architecturale.* Paris: Dunod, 1969.

Boudon, Philippe. *Richelieu, ville nouvelle: essai d'architecturologie.* Paris: Dunod, 1978.

Bougle, Célestin, and Elie Halévy, eds. *Doctrine de Saint-Simon.* Paris: Rivière, 1924.

Bouillon, Antoine. *Le Colonisé et son âme: Madagascar.* Paris: Harmattan, 1981.

Boulonnois, Louis. "Correction annuelle des dénombrements de population." *La Vie Urbaine* n.s. 6(15 November 1930).

Boulonnois, Louis, *L'Oeuvre municipale de M. Henri Sellier à Suresnes.* Paris, Berger-Levrault 1938.

Bourdieu, Pierre. *Choses Dites.* Paris: Minuit, 1987.

Bourdieu, Pierre. *La Distinction, critique sociale du jugement.* Paris: Minuit, 1979.

Bourgeois, Léon. *La Politique de la prévoyance sociale.* 2 vols. Paris: Charpentier, 1914–1918.

Bourgeois, Léon. *L'Idée de solidarité et ses conséquences sociales, 1901–1903.* Repr. in *Solidarité.* 7th ed., rev. and engld. Paris: Colin, 1912.

Bourgeois, Léon, and Alfred Croiset, eds. *Essai d'une philosophie de la solidarité: conférence et discussions.* Paris, 1902.

Bourguet, Marie-Noëlle. "Race et folklore: l'image officielle de la France en 1800." *Annales: économies, sociétés, civilisations* 4(July–August 1975).

Brebion, A. *Dictionnaire de bio-bibliographie générale, ancienne et moderne de l'Indochine française.* Annales de l'Académie des Sciences coloniales, vol. 8. Paris: Société d'editions géographiques, maritimes et coloniales, 1935.

Broc, Numa. "La Géographie française face à la science allemande, 1870–1914." *Annales de géographie* 86, no. 473 (January–February 1977).

Brooke, Michael. *Le Play: Engineer and Social Scientist.* London: Longmans, 1970.

Brousse, Paul. *La Propriété collective et les services publics.* Paris, 1883.

Brun, Gérard. *Technocrates et technocratie en France, 1914–1945.* Paris: Albatros, 1985.

Brun, Jean-Charles. "Le Play et la vie provinciale." *La Reforme sociale* 61(1 December 1906).

Buet, Charles. *Madagascar: la reine des îles africaines; histoire, religion, flore.* Paris: Palmé 1883.

Buffon, Georges Louis Leclerc. *Oeuvres complètes de Buffon.* Rev., ann., intro. by Jean-L. de Lanessan, 14 vols. Paris: Le Vasseur, 1884–85.

Bullock, Nicholas, and James Read. *The Movement for Housing Reform in Germany and France 1840–1914.* Cambridge: Cambridge University Press, 1985.

Buls, Charles. *Esthétique des villes.* Brussels: Bruylard, 1893.

Burke, Edmund III. "La Mission scientifique au Maroc: science sociale et politique dans l'âge de l'impérialisme." *Bulletin éonomique et sociale du Maroc* 138–139 (1978).

Burke, Edmund III. "The First Crisis of Orientalism, 1890–1914." Jeane-Claude Vatin, ed." *Conaissances du Maghreb: sciences sociales et colonisation.* Paris: Centre National de la Recherche Scientifique, 1984.

Burke, Edmund III. *Prelude to Protectorate in Morocco: Precolonial Protest and Resistance, 1860–1912.* Chicago: University of Chicago Press, 1976.

Burlen, Katherine, ed. *La Banlieue oasis: Henri Sellier et les cités-jardins, 1900–1940.* Paris: Presses Universitaires de Vincennes, 1987.

Buttimer, Anne. *Society and Milieu in the French Geographic Tradition.* Chicago: Rand McNally for the Association of American Geographers, 1971.

Cabanis, Georges. "De l'influence des tempéraments sur la formation des idées et des affections morales." *Institut de France, Académie des sciences morales et politiques, Mémoires,* series 1, vol. 2. Paris: 1804.

Canguilhem, Georges. *Etudes d'histoire et de philosophie des sciences.* Paris: Vrin, 1983.

Canguilhem, Georges. *La Connaissance de la vie.* 2d ed. Paris: Vrin, 1965.

Canguilhem, Georges. *Le Normal et le pathologique.* 4th ed. Paris: Presses Universitaires de France, 1979.

Carmille, René. *La Mécanographie dans les administrations.* Paris: Receuil Sirey, 1942.

Casinière, Hubert de la. *Les Municipalités marocaines: leur développement, leur legislation.* Casablanca: Imprimerie de la Vigie marocaine 1924.

Castel, Robert. *La Gestion des risques: de l'anti-psychiatre à l'après-psychoanalyse.* Paris: Minuit, 1981.

Catat, Louis. *Voyage à Madagascar 1889–1890.* Paris: Administration de l'Univers illustré, 189–?.

Cayol, J. B. "Considérations pratiques dur le choléra-morbus de Paris," *Journal de médecine et de chirurgie pratiques* 3(1834).

Cazeux, P. F. "Les Sakalaves et leurs pays." *Bulletin de la Société de géographie commerciale de Bordeaux* (21 May 1888).

Certeau, Michel de. *The Practice of Everyday Life.* Trans. Steven F. Rendall. Berkeley: University of California Press, 1984.

Challener, Richard D. *The French Theory of the Nation in Arms, 1866–1939.* 2d ed. New York: Russell and Russell, 1965.

Charnay, Jean-Paul. "La Guerre de Rif: dernière compagne coloniale ou première guerre révolutionnaire?" *Technique et géosociologie; la guerre du Rif, le nucleaire en Orient.* Paris: Anthropos, 1984.

Charre, Alain. "Lione: l'invenzione di una citta industriale." *Rassegna* 17(March 1984).

Bibliography

Chevalier, Louis. *Le Choléra: la première épidemie du XIXe siècle.* La Roche-sur-Yon: Imprimerie centrale de l'ouest, 1958.

Chevalier, Louis. *Classes laborieuses et classes dangereuses à Paris pendant la première moitié du XIXe siècle.* Paris: Plon, 1958.

Chevalier, Louis. *La Formation de la population parisienne au XIXe siècle.* Paris: Presses Universitaires de France, 1950.

Chevalier, Michel. "Etudes sur les questions politiques et sociales," *Revue des deux mondes* 6(April–June 1850).

Chevalier, Michel. "Les Questions politiques et sociales; l'Assistance et la prévoyance politiques—rapport de la Commission." *Revue des Deux Mondes* 6(April–June 1850).

Chevalier, Michel. *Société des amis de peuple: de la civilisation.* Paris: 1832.

Cheysson, Emile. "Le Creusot: condition matérielle, intellectuelle et morale de la population; institutions et relations sociales." *Bulletin de l'Association internationale pour le développement du commerce et des expositions* (19 July 1869).

Cheysson, Emile. "L'Economie sociale à l'exposition universelle de 1889." *La Réforme sociale,* 3rd ser., no. 4(13 June 1889).

Cheysson, Emile. *Le Musée social.* Paris, 1906.

Cheysson, Emile. *Oeuvres choisies.* 2 vols. Paris: Rousseau, 1911.

Chiffard, Jean François. "Les H.B.M. et la ceinture de Paris." *Architecture, mouvement, continuité.* 43(1977).

Chiva, Isac. "Georges-Henri Rivière: Fifty Years in the History of Ethnology." *Social Science Information* 25, no. 3 (1986).

Choay, Françoise. "Haussmann et le système des éspaces verts parisiens," *Revue d l'art* 29(1975).

Choay, Françoise. *The Modern City: Planning in the Nineteenth Century.* Trans. Marguerite Hugo and George R. Collins. New York: Braziller, 1969.

Choay, Françoise. *La Règle et le modèle: sur la théorie de l'architecture et de l'urbanisme.* Paris: Seuil, 1980.

Choisy, Auguste. *Histoire de l'architecture.* 2 vols. Paris: Gauthier-Villars, 1899.

Chombart de Lauwe, Paul-Henry. *Paris: essais de sociologie, 1952–1964.* Paris: Ouvrières, 1965.

Clapham, J.H. *The Economic Development of France and Germany, 1815–1914.* Cambridge: Cambridge University Press, 1951.

Clark, Linda L. *Social Darwinism in France.* Birmingham, Ala.: University of Alabama Press, 1984.

Clark, T. J. *The Painting of Modern Life: Paris in the Art of Manet and his Followers.* New York: Knopf, 1985.

Clifford, James, and George E. Marcus, eds. *Writing Culture: The Poetics and Politics of Ethnography.* Berkeley: University of California Press, 1986.

Cohen, Jean-Louis. "Des Bourses du travail au temps des loisirs: les avatars de la sociabilité ouvrière (France 1914–39)." *Architectures pour le peuple: maisons du peuple— Belgique, Allemagne, Autriche, France, Grande-Bretagne, Italie, Pays-Bas, Suisse.* Brussels: Archives de l'architecture moderne, 1984.

Cohen, Jean-Louis. "Prima del purismo: un costrutivismo mediterraneo." *Rassegna* 17(March 1984).

Cohen, Stephen S. *Modern Capitalist Planning: the French Model.* Updated ed. Berkeley: University of California Press, 1977.

Coleman, William. *Biology in the Nineteenth Century, Problems of Form, Function, and Transformation.* New York: Wiley, 1971.

Coleman, William. *Death is a Social Disease: Public Health and Political Economy in Early Industrial France.* Madison, Wis.: University of Wisconsin Press, 1982.

Coleman, William. *Georges Cuvier, Zoologist: A Study in the History of Evolution Theory.* Cambridge, Mass.: Harvard University Press, 1964.

Collins, George, and Christiane Casemann Collins. *Camillo Sitte: The Birth of Modern City Planning.* Reprint. New York: Rizzoli, 1965.

Commissaire Resident General au Maroc. *La Renaissance du Maroc: dix ans de protectorat, 1912–1922.* Rabat: Résidence générale de la République française au Maroc, 1923.

Comte, Auguste. *Système de politique positive.* Paris: Baillière, 1854.

Condominas, Georges. *Fokon'olona et collectivités rurales en Imerina.* Pref. Hubert Deschamps. Paris: Berger-Levrault, 1960.

Conry, Yvette. *L'Introduction du darwinisme en France au XIXe siècle.* Paris: Vrin, 1974.

Coqueau, Claude-Philibert *Essai sur l'établissement des hôpitaux, dans les grandes villes.* Paris: Pierres, 1787.

Corbin, Alain. *Les Filles de noce: misère sexuelle et prostitution: 19e et 20e siècles.* Paris: Aubier Montaigne, 1979.

Cottereau, Alain. "Les Débuts de planification urbaine dans l'agglomération parisienne." *Sociologie du travail* 4, special issue "Politique urbaine" 4(1970).

Craig, John E. "Maurice Halbwachs à Strasbourg." *Revue française de sociologie* 20, no. 1 (January–March 1979).

Cuvier, Georges. *Rapport historique sur le progrès des sciences naturelles depuis 1789, et sur l'état actuel.* Paris: Imprimerie impériale, 1810.

Daly, César, ed. *Funérailles de Félix Duban.* Paris: Ducher, 1871.

Daston, Lorraine, Michael Heidelberger and Lorenz Kruger, eds. *The Probabilistic Revolution.* 2 vols. Cambridge: Cambridge University Press, 1986.

Bibliography

de Sacey, Samuel Silvestre, ed. *Oeuvres de Descartes*. 2 vols. Paris: Club français du livre, 1966.

de la Gorce, Paul-Marie. *The French Army: A Military-Political History*. Trans. Kenneth Douglas. London: Weidenfeld and Nicholson, 1963.

de la Tour du Pin. *Vers un ordre social chrétien*. Paris: 1929. Reprint.

de Gérando, Joseph-Marie. *The Observation of Savage Peoples (considérations sur les méthodes à suivre dans l'observations des Peuples Sauvages;* Paris, 1800). Ed., trans. and intro. F.G.T. Moore. London: Routledge & Kegan Paul, 1969.

de Gérando, Joseph-Marie. *Le Visiteur du pauvre*. Paris: Colas, 1820.

Delambre, Jean Baptiste. ed. *Rapport historique sur les progrès des sciences mathématiques depuis 1789 et sur leur état actuel*. Paris: Imprimerie impériale, 1810.

Delaporte, François. *Disease and Civilization: The Cholera in Paris*. Trans. Arthur Goldhammer. Pref. Paul Rabinow. Cambridge, Mass.: M.I.T. Press, 1985.

Delaporte, François. *Nature's Second Kingdom: Explorations of Vegetality in the Eighteenth Century*. Trans. Arthur Goldhammer. Cambridge, Mass.: M.I.T. Press, 1982.

Delorme, Jean. "Casablanca de Henri Prost à Michel Ecochard." *Architecture, mouvement, continuité* 42(June 1977).

Demangeon, Alain, and Bruno Fortier. *Les Vaisseaux et les villes: l'Arsenal de Cherbourg*. Brussels: Mardaga, 1978.

Descamps, Henri. "L'architecture française au Maroc; L'urbanisme: l'oeuvre de M. Prost." *La Construction moderne* 46(December 20, 1930).

Deschamps, Hubert Jules. *Histoire de Madagascar*. Paris: Berger-Levrault, 1965.

Deschamps, Hubert, and Paul Chauvet, eds. *Gallieni pacificateur: écrits coloniaux de Gallieni*. Paris: Presses Universitaire de France, 1949.

Desrosières, Alain. "Histoires de formes: statistiques et sciences sociales avant 1940." *Revue française de sociologie* 26, no. 26 (May–June 1985).

Desrosieres, Alain. "L'Ingénieur d'état et le père de famille: Emile Cheysson et la statistique." *Annales des mines: gérer et comprendre* 2(March 1986).

Déthier, Jean. "Soixante ans d'urbanisme au Maroc, l'evolution des idées et des réalisations," *Bulletin économique et sociale du Maroc* 32, no. 118–119 (July–December 1970).

Devillers, Christian, and Bernard Huet. *Le Creusot: naissance et développement d'une ville industrielle, 1782–1914*. Seyssel: Champ Vallon, 1981.

Devinat, Paul. *Scientific Management in Europe*. Pref. Albert Thomas, Geneva: International Labor Office 1927.

Digeon, Claude. *La Crise allemande de la pensée française, 1870–1914*. Paris: Presses Universitaires de France, 1959.

Dommanget, Maurice. *Edouard Vaillant: un grand socialiste, 1840–1915.* Paris: Table ronde, 1956.

Dix ans de réalisations des municipalités socialistes. Lyons, 1934.

Donzelot, Jacques. *L'Invention du social: essai sur le déclin de passions politiques.* Paris: Fayard, 1984.

Double, François-Joseph. *Rapport sur le choléra-morbus, lu à l'Académie Royale de Médecine le 13 septembre 1831.* Paris: 1831.

Drexler, Arthur, ed. *The Architecture of the Ecole des Beaux-Arts.* New York: Museum of Modern Art, 1977.

Dreyfus, Hubert L., and Paul Rabinow. *Michel Foucault: Beyond Structuralism and Hermeneutics.* 2d ed., enl. Chicago: University of Chicago Press, 1983.

Duchet, Michèle. *L'Anthropologie et l'histoire au siècle des lumières.* Paris: Maspéro, 1971.

Duguit, Léon. "Le Droit constitutionnel et la sociologie." *Revue internationale de l'enseignement* 17(1889): 484–505.

Duguit, Léon. *Le Droit social: le droit individuel et la transformation de l'état.* 2d ed. Paris: Alcan, 1911.

Dumay, Jean-Baptiste. *Mémoires d'un militant ouvrier du Creusot, 1841–1905.* Intro. and notes by Pierre Ponsot. Paris: Maspéro, 1976.

Dumont, Louis. *Homo Hierarchicus: The Caste System and Its Implications.* Trans. Mark Saintsbury. Chicago: University of Chicago Press, 1970.

Dupâquier, Jacques, and Michel. *Histoire de la démographie: la statistique de la population des origines à 1915.* Paris: Perrin, 1985.

Durkheim, Emile. *De la division du travail social.* Paris: Alcan, 1893.

Duroselle, Jean-Baptiste. *Les Débuts du catholicisme social en France, 1822–1870.* Paris: Presses Universitaires de France, 1951.

Ecochard, Michel. *Casablanca: le roman d'une ville.* Paris: Editions de Paris, 1955.

Ecochard, Michel. "Problèmes d'urbanisme au Maroc," *Bulletin économique et sociale du Maroc* 15, no. 52 (October–December 1951).

Ehrenberg, Alain. *Le Corps militaire: politique et pédagogie en démocratie.* Paris: Aubier-Montaigne, 1983.

Einaudi, Luigi. "The Doctrine of Original Sin and the Theory of the Elite in the Writings of Frederic Le Play." *Essays in European Economic Thought.* ed. and trans. Louise Sommer. Princeton, N.J.: Princeton University Press, 1960.

Eleb-Vidal, Monique, and Anne Debarre-Blanchard. *Architecture domestique et mentalités: les traités et les pratiques au XIXe siècle.* No. 5 in series: *In Extenso: recherches à l'Ecole d'architecture Paris-Villemin.* Paris: Ecole d'Architecture Paris-Villemin, 1985.

Bibliography

Elias, Norbert. *The Civilizing Process.* Vol. 1, *The History of Manners.* Trans. Edmund Jephcott. New York: Urizen, 1978.

Elias, Norbert. *The Court Society.* Trans. Edmund Jephcott. New York: Urizen, 1969. Reprint, 1983.

Ellis, Stephen. *The Rising of the Red Shawls: A Revolt in Madagascar, 1895–1899.* Cambridge: Cambridge University Press, 1985.

Elwitt, Sanford. "Social reform and Social Order in Late Nineteenth-Century France: The Musée Social and its Friends." *French Historical Studies* 11, no. 3 (Spring 1980).

Elwitt, Sanford. *The Third Republic Defended: Bourgeois Reform in France, 1880–1914.* London and Baton Rouge, La.: University of Louisiana Press, 1986.

Emangard, F.-P. *Dissertation sur le choléra-morbus épidémique.* Paris: L'Aigle, 1832.

Epron, Jean-Pierre, et al. *L'Usine et la ville, 1836–1986: 150 ans de l'urbanisme.* Special issue, *Culture Technique.* Neuilly-sur-Seine, 1986.

Ernouf, Alfred Auguste, and Alphonse Alphand. *L'Art des jardins.* 3rd ed., rev. Paris: Rothschild, 1868.

Evenson, Norma. *Paris: A Century of Change, 1878–1978.* New Haven, Conn.: Yale University Press, 1979.

Ewald, François. *L'Etat providence.* Paris: Grasset, 1986.

"Exposition de la cité moderne, Nancy, 4–17 mai 1913." *Bulletin de la Chambre de commerce de Nancy* (July–August 1913).

Faguet, Emile. "Une Etude sur Le Play." *Revue des deux mondes,* 6th ser., no. 11 (15 December 1912).

Febvre, Lucien. *La Terre et l'évolution humaine: introduction géographique à l'histoire.* Paris: Renaissance du livre, 1922.

Fierro, Alfred. *La Société de géographie 1821–1946.* Geneva: Droz, 1983.

Fine, Martin. "Towards Corporatism: The Movement for Capital-Labor Collaboration in France, 1914–1936," Ph.D. diss. University of Wisconsin, 1971.

Fishman, Robert. *Bourgeois Utopias: The Rise and Fall of Suburbia.* New York: Basic Books, 1987.

Fishman, Robert. "Suburbia and the Metropolis in Comparative Perspective: Paris and London in the Nineteenth Century" (Paper at AHA meeting, San Francisco, December 1983).

Fishman, Robert. *Urban Utopias in the Twentieth Century: Ebenezer Howard, Frank Lloyd Wright, and Le Corbusier.* New York: Basic Books, 1977.

Flory, Thiebaut. *Le Mouvement régionaliste français: sources et développement.* Paris: Presses Universitaires de France, 1966.

Foucault, Michel. *The Birth of the Clinic: An Archaeology of Medical Perception*. Trans. A.M. Sheridan Smith. New York: Pantheon, 1973.

Foucault, Michel. *Discipline and Punish: The Birth of the Prison*. Trans. Alan Sheridan. New York: Pantheon, 1978.

Foucault, Michel. *Histoire de la folie à l'âge classique*. Paris: Plon, 1961.

Foucault, Michel. *Histoire de la sexualité*. Vol. 1, *La Volonté de savoir*. Paris: Gallimard, 1976.

Foucault, Michel. *The History of Sexuality*. vol. 1, *An Introduction*. Trans. Robert Hurley. New York: Vintage, 1978.

Foucault, Michel. *Madness and Civilization: A History of Insanity in the Age of Reason*. Trans. Richard Howard. New York: Pantheon, 1965.

Foucault, Michel. *Les Mots et les choses: une archéologie des sciences humaines*. Paris: Gallimard, 1966.

Foucault, Michel. *Naissance de la clinique: une archéologie du regard medical*. Paris: Presses Universitaires de France, 1963.

Foucault, Michel. "Omnes singulatim: vers une critique de la raison politique." *Le Débat: histoire, politique, société*. 41(September–November 1986).

Foucault, Michel. "On the Geneology of Ethics," *The Foucault Reader*. ed. Paul Rabinow. New York: Pantheon, 1984.

Foucault, Michel. "On Governmentality." *Ideology and Consciousness* 6(Autumn 1979).

Foucault Michel. *The Order of Things: an Archaeology of the Human Sciences*. New York: Pantheon, 1971; Vintage, 1973.

Foucault, Michel. *Power/Knowledge: Selected Interviews and Other Writings 1972–1977*. Ed. Colin Gordon. Trans. Colin Gordon et al. New York: Pantheon, 1980.

Foucault, Michel. "The Subject and Power." Hubert L. Dreyfus and Paul Rabinow, *Michel Foucault: Beyond Structuralism and Hermeneutics*. 2d ed., enl. Chicago: University of Chicago Press, 1983.

Foucault, Michel. *Surveiller et punir: naissance de la prison*. Paris: Gallimard, 1975.

Foucault, Michel, ed. *Les Machines à guérir: aux origines de l'hôpital moderne*. Brussels: Mardana, 1979.

Foucault, Michel, ed. *Politiques de l'habitat (1800–1850)*. Paris: C.O.R.D.A., 1977.

Fougère, Henry. *Les Délégations ouvrières aux éxpositions universelles sous le Second Empire*. Montlucon: Herbin, 1905.

Frampton, Kenneth. *Modern Architecture: A Critical History*. New York: Oxford University Press, 1980.

Frey, Jean-Pierre. *La Ville industrielle et ses urbanités: la distinction ouvriers/employés, Le Creusot 1870–1930.* Brussels: Mardaga, 1985.

Fridenson, Patrick, ed. *1914–1981: l'autre front: études.* Paris: Ouvrières, 1977.

Gaillard, Jeanne. *Paris, la ville, 1852–1870: l'urbanisme parisien à l'heure d'Haussmann.* Paris: Champion, 1977.

Gallieni, Joseph S. *Gallieni au Tonkin (1892–1896) par lui-même.* Paris: Berger-Levrault, 1941.

Gallieni, Joseph S. *Neuf Ans à Madagascar.* Paris: Hachette, 1908.

Gallieni, Joseph S. *La Pacification de Madagascar: opérations d'octobre 1896 à mars 1899.* Ed. F. Hellot, Paris: Chapelot, 1900.

Gallieni, Joseph S. *Trois Colonnes au Tonkin, 1894–1895.* Paris: Chapelot, 1899.

Gallois, Louis. "Les Noms de pays." *Annales de géographie* 18(15 January 1909).

Ganiage, Jean. *L'Expansion coloniale de la France.* Paris: Presses Universitaires de France, 1968.

Garden, Maurice, and Yves Lequin, eds. *Construire la ville, XVIIe-XVIIIe siècles.* Lyons: Presses Universitaires de Lyon, 1983.

Gaudet, Julien. *Eléments et théories de l'architecture, cours professé à l'Ecole Nationale et Spéciale des Beaux-Arts.* 4 vols. 4th ed. Paris: Libraire de la construction moderne, 1915.

Gaudin, Jean-Pierre. "Prévision, aménagement et guestion locale: l'emergence des plans d'urbanisme en France 1900–1940." Thèse de Doctorat d'Etat en Sciences Politiques, Université de Montepellier I, 1983.

Gaudin, Jean-Pierre. *L'Avenir en plan: téchnique et politique dans la prévision urbaine, 1900–1930.* Seyssel: Champ Vallon 1985.

Gaudin, Jean-Pierre, ed. *Les Premiers urbanistes français et l'art urbain, 1900–1930.* No. 11, in ser. *IN EXTENSO, recherches à l'école d'architecture Paris-Villemin.* Paris: Ecole d'architecture Paris-Villemin, 1987.

Gaultier, Louis. *Rapport général sur l'Exposition de 'la cité reconstitué' (25 mai–15 août 1916).* Paris: Association générale des hygiènistes et techniciens municipaux, 1917.

Gautier, Emile Felix. *Figures de conquètes coloniales: Trois héros: le générale Laperrine, le père de Foucauld, Prince de la Paix.* Paris: Payot, 1931.

Geertz, Clifford. *Islam Observed, Religious Development in Morocco and Indonesia.* Chicago: University of Chicago Press, 1971.

Gennep, Arnold van. *Tabou et totémisme à Madagascar: étude descriptive et théorique.* Paris: Leroux, 1904.

Gérard, Annelise. "Quartier et unité de voisinage dans la pratique urbanistique française, 1919–1973." Thèse de troisième cycle, Université de Paris VII, 1977.

Gide, Charles. *Les Institutions de progrès social.* 4th ed. Paris, 1912. 5th ed. Paris: Tenin, 1920.

Giedion, Sigfried. *Space, Time and Architecture: The Growth of a New Tradition.* 4th ed. Cambridge, Mass.: Harvard University Press, 1962.

Gille, Bértrand. *Les Sources statistiques de l'histoire de France: des enquêtes du XVIIe siècle à 1870.* Geneva: Droz, 1964.

Girard, Louis. *La Politique des travaux publiques du Second Empire.* Paris: Colin, 1952.

Girardet, Raoul. *La Société militaire dans la France contemporaine, 1815–1939.* Paris: Plon 1953.

Godfrey, John F. *Capitalism at War: Industrial Policy and Bureaucracy in France 1914–1918.* Leamington, Spa, U.K., 1987. New York: Berg, 1987.

Gombrich, E. H. "Norm and Form: The Stylistic Categories of Art History and Their Origins in Renaissance Ideals." *Norm and Form: Studies in the Art of the Renaissance.* London: Phaidon, 1966.

Gouhier, Henri. *La Jeunesse d'August Comte et la formation du positivisme.* Paris: Vrin, 1933–41.

Goujon, Lazare. *Villeurbanne 1925–1934: dix ans d'administration.* Lyons, 1934.

Gournay, Isabelle, ed. *The New (Le Nouveau) Trocadéro.* Bilingual ed. Institut Français d'Architecture. Brussels: Mardaga, 1985.

Grandidier, Alfred. *Rapport sur une mission à Madagascar 1869–1871.* Paris, 1872.

Gresleri, Giuliano, and Dario Matteoni. *La Citta' Mondiale: Andersen, Hébrard, Otlet, Le Corbusier.* Venise: Poli/Marsilio, 1982.

Grillet, Albert. *Les Alignements en droit marocain.* Paris: Receuil Sirey 1936.

Guépin, Ange. *Histoire de Nantes.* Nantes: Prosper Sebire, 1835.

Guépin, Ange and Charles Eugène Bonamy. *Nantes au XIXe siècle: statistique, topographique, industrielle et morale.* Nantes, 1835. Reprint. Nantes: University of Nantes, 1981.

Guérnier, Eugène, and G. Froment-Guieysse, eds. *Encyclopédie Coloniale et Maritime.* 2 vols. Paris, 1936; 11 vols. Ser. *Encyclopédie de l'empire français.* Paris, 1948.

Guerrand, Roger-H. *Les Origines du logement social en France.* Paris: Ouvrières, 1967.

Guesde, Jules. *Services publics et socialisme.* Paris: Oriol, 1883.

Gusdorf, Georges. *La Conscience révolutionnaire: les Idéologues.* Paris: Presses Universitaires de France, 1978.

Gusdorf, Georges. *Introduction aux sciences humaines: essai critique sur leurs origines et leur développement.* Paris: Belles Lettres, 1960.

Habermas, Jurgen. *The Philosophical Discourse of Modernity: Twelve Lectures.* Cambridge, Mass.: M.I.T. Press, 1987.

Bibliography

"L'Habitation et l'urbanisme moderne d'après les éxpositions récentes." *La Vie Urbaine,* n.s., 1(15 February 1930).

Hacking, Ian. *The Emergence of Probability: A Philosophical Study of Early Ideas about Probability, Induction and Statistical Inference.* Cambridge: Cambridge University Press, 1975.

Halbwachs, Maurice. *Classes sociales et morphologie.* Ed. and intro. Victor Karady. Paris: Minuit, 1972.

Halbwachs, Maurice. *Les Expropriations et le prix des terrains à Paris (1860–1900).* Paris: Rieder, 1909.

Halbwachs, Maurice. "Les Plans d'extension et d'aménagement de Paris avant le XIXe siècle." *La Vie urbaine* 2(1920).

Halbwachs, Maurice. *La Théorie de l'homme moyen: essai sur Quételet et la statistique morale.* Paris: Alcan, 1913.

Hammond, Michael. "Anthropology as a Weapon of Social Combat in Late Nineteenth Century France." *Journal of the History of the Behavioral Sciences* 16(1980).

Hardy, Georges. *Portrait de Lyautey.* Paris: Bloud and Gay, 1949.

Harou-Romain, N. "Des Cités ouvrières," *Annales de la Charités* 5(1849).

Harvey, David. *Consciousness and the Urban Experience: Studies in the History and Theory of Urbanization.* Baltimore, Md.: The Johns Hopkins University Press, 1985.

Harvey, David. *The Urbanisation of Capital: Studies in the History and Theory of Capitalist Urbanization.* Baltimore, Md.: The Johns Hopkins University Press, 1985.

Hatzfeld, Henri. *Du Pauperisme à la sécurité sociale: essai sur les origines de la sécurité sociale en France, 1850–1940.* Paris: Colin, 1971.

Hatzfeld, Olivier. *Madagascar.* Paris: Presses Universitaires de France, 1952.

Hauser, Henri. "Les Régions économiques." *Le Fait de la semaine* 27(9 November 1918).

Hauser, Henri. *Le Problème du régionalisme.* Paris: Presses Universitaires de France, 1924.

Haussmann, Georges. *Mémoires du Baron Haussmann.* 3 vols. 3d ed. Paris: Victor-Harvard, 1890–93.

Hautecoeur, Louis. *Histoire de l'architecture classique en France.* 7 vols. Paris: Picard, 1943–57.

Hayward, J. E. S. "The Official Social Philosophy of the French Third Republic: Léon Bourgeois and Solidarism." *International Review of Social History* 6(1961).

Hayward, J. E. S. "Solidarist Syndicalism: Durkheim and Duguit, I." *The Sociological Review* 8, nos. 1–2 (July 1960).

Hayward, J. E. S. "Solidarist Syndicalism: Durkheim and Duguit, II." *The Sociological Review* 8, no. 2 (December 1960).

Hayward, J. E. S. "Solidarity: The Social History of an Idea in Nineteenth Century France." *International Review of Social History* 2(1959).

Hazemann, Robert-Henri. *Le Service social municipal et ces relations avec les oeuvres privées.* Paris: Le Mouvement sanitaire, 1928.

Hébrard, Ernest M., and Hendrik Christian Andersen. *Creation of a World Center of Communication.* 2 vols. Paris: 1913.

Hecht, Jacqueline. "L'Idée de dénombrement jusqu'à la Révolution." *Pour une histoire de la statistique.* Vol. 1. Paris: Institut National de la Statistique et des Etudes Economiques, 1977.

Hénard, Eugène. *Etudes sur les transformations de Paris et autres écrits sur l'urbanisme.* Paris: Librairies-imprimeries réunis, 1903. Reprint. Ed. Jean-Louis Cohen. Paris: L'Equerre, 1982.

Hénard, Eugène, and Robert de Souza. "Les Espaces libres à Paris." *Mémoires et documents du Musée social* (July 1908).

Heuschling, Xavier *Manuel de statistique éthnographique universelle.* Brussels: Société typographique belge, 1847.

L'Huillier, Fernand. *La Lutte ouvrière à la fin du Second Empire.* Paris: Colin, 1957.

Hunt, Lynn. *Politics, Culture and Class in the French Revolution.* Berkeley; University of California Press, 1984.

Iconographie de Nantes d'après les collections de musée. Nantes: Musées départementaux de Loire-Atlantique—Musée Dobrée, 1978.

Institut Royal de France. Académie Royale des Sciences. *Programme du prix de statistique proposé par l'Académie Royale des Sciences pour l'année 1818.* Paris: 1817.

Jamin, Jean. "A la recherche des paradis perdus: à· propos de la Mission Dakar-Djibouti." *Collections passion: exposition du 5 juin à 28 décembre.* Ed. Jacques Hainard and Roland Kaehr. Neuchâtel: Musée d'ethnographie, 1982.

Jamin, Jean. "Du Musée de l'homme considéré comme un laboratoire de représentations." Unpublished ms., December 5-6, 1986.

Jamin, Jean, and Jean Copans. *Aux Origines de l'anthropologie française: Les mémoires de la societé des observateurs de l'homme en l'an VIII.* Paris: Sycomore, 1979.

Jaurès, Jean. *L'Armée nouvelle.* Pref. Lucien Lévy Bruhl. Paris: Humanité, 1915.

Jaussely, Léon. "Chronique de l'urbanisme." *La Vie Urbaine* 1-2(March 1919).

Jordanova, L. J. *Lamarck.* New York: Oxford University Press, 1984.

Jullian, René. *Histoire de l'architecture moderne en France de 1889 à nos jours: un siècle de modernité.* Paris: Sers, 1984.

Justi, Johann H.G. von. *Eléments généraux de police.* Paris: Rozet, 1769.

Kaufmann, Emil. *Architecture in the Age of Reason: Baroque and Post-Baroque in England, Italy, and France.* Cambridge, Mass.: Harvard University Press, 1955.

Kelley, Donald R. *Historians and the Law in Postrevolutionary France.* Princeton, N.J., Princeton University Press, 1984.

Knight, Melvin. "French Colonial Policy—the Decline of 'Association.' " *The Journal of Modern History* 5(June 1933).

Kuhn, Thomas S. *The Structure of Scientific Revolutions.* Chicago: University of Chicago Press, 1962. 2d ed. Enl., 1970.

Kuisel, Richard F. *Capitalism and the State in Modern France: Renovation and Economic Management in the Twentieth Century.* Cambridge: Cambridge University Press, 1981.

La Berge, Ann F. "Public Health in France and the French Public Health Movement, 1815–1848." Ph.D. diss. University of Tennessee, 1974.

Lacoste, Yves. *La Géographie: ça sert, d'abord, à faire la guerre.* 1st ed. Paris Maspéro, 1976. 2nd ed., 1982.

Lacouture, Jean. *Charles de Gaulle.* 3 vols. Paris: Seuil, 1965.

Lacouture, Jean. *Pierre Mendès France.* Paris: Seuil, 1981. Trans. George Holoch. Paris: Holmes and Meier, 1984.

Lagier, Alain. "Da Emile Zola a Tony Garnier." *Rassegna* 17(March 1984).

Lamennais, Hugues Félicité Robert de. *Oeuvres complètes.* 2 vols. Brussels: Société Belge de Librairie, 1839.

Lanessan, Jean-L. de. *L'Expansion coloniale de la France: étude économique, politique et géographique sur les établissements français d'outre-mer.* Paris: Alcan, 1886.

Lanessan, Jean-L. de. *La Lutte pour l'éxistence et l'association pour la lutte: étude sur la doctrine de Darwin.* 2d ed. Paris: Doin, 1882.

Lanessan, Jean-L. de. *Principes de colonisation.* Paris: Alcan, 1897.

Lanessan, Jean-L. de. *Le Transformisme: évolution de la matière et des êtres vivants.* Paris: Doin, 1883.

Larrey, Dominique Jean. *Mémoire sur le choléra-morbus.* Paris: Huzard, 1831.

Laugier, Marc-Antoine. *Essai sur l'architecture.* Paris: Duschesne, 1753.

Lavedan, Pierre. *Histoire de l'urbanisme.* Vol. 3, *Epoch contemporaine.* 2d ed., rev. Paris: Laurens, 1966.

Lavedan, Pierre. "Paris à l'arrivée d'Haussmann." *La Vie Urbaine,* n.s., nos. 3–4 (July–December 1953).

Le Châtelier, Henri. *Le Taylorisme.* 2d ed. Paris: Dunod, 1934.

Le Maître, Alexandre. *La Métropolitée.* Amsterdam: Boekhilt, 1682.

Le Pichon, Phillipe, and Alain Suppiot. "De l'observation de la ville comme corps sociale." Introduction, Guépin and Bonomy. *Nantes au XIXe Siècle: statistique, topographique, industrielle et morale.* Eds. Le Pichon and Supiot. Nantes: Université de Nantes, 1981.

Le Play, Pierre Guillaume Frédéric. *La Constitution essentielle de l'humanité: éxposé des principes et des coutumes qui créent la prosperité ou la souffrance des nations.* Tours: Mame, 1893.

Le Play, Frédéric. *Frederic Le Play: On Family, Work, and Social Change.* Ed., trans., and intro. Catherine Bodard Silver. Chicago: University of Chicago Press, 1982.

Le Play, Frédéric. *La Méthode de la science sociale.* Tours: Mame, 1879.

Le Play, Frédéric. *Les ouvriers européens; études sur les travaux, la vie domestique, et la condition morale des populations ouvrières de l'Europe.* Paris: Imprimerie impériale, 1855. 2d ed. Tours: Mame, 1877–79.

Le Play, Frédéric. *Programme de gouvernement et d'organisation comparée de divers peuples.* Paris: Tardieu, 1881.

Le Play, Frédéric. *La Réforme sociale en France déduite de l'observation comparée des peuples européens.* 2 vols. Paris: Plon, 1864. 6th ed. 4 vols. Tours: Mame, 1878.

Le Play, Frédéric. *Vues générales de statistique.* Reprint from *L'Encyclopédie nouvelle.* Paris: Bourgogne et Martinet, 1840.

Le Réverend, André. *Lyautey.* Paris: Fayard, 1983.

Le Réverend, André. *Lyautey écrivain: 1854–1934.* Paris: Ophrys, 1976.

Le Réverend, André, ed. *Un Lyautey inconnu: correspondance et journal inédits, 1874–1934.* Paris: Perrin, 1980.

Le Roy Ladurie, Emmanuel, ed. *Histoire de la France urbaine.* Vol. 3, *La Ville classique de la Renaissance aux révolutions.* Paris: Seuil, 1981.

Lebovics, Herman. "Conservative Anthropology and the End of the Third Republic." Unpbd. ms. (1988).

Leclerc, Gerard. *L'Observation de l'homme: une histoire des enquêtes sociales.* Paris: Seuil, 1979.

Lecuir, Jean. "Criminalité et moralité. Montyon, statisticien du Parlement de Paris." *Revue d'histoire moderne et contemporaine* 21(July–September 1974).

Lecuyer, Bernard-Pierre. "Démographie, statistique, et hygiéne publique sous la monarchie censitaire." *Annales de demographie historique* (1977). Ecoles des Hautes Etudes en Sciences Sociales. Paris: Mouton, 1977.

Lecuyer, Bernard-Pierre. "Historiens et enquêteurs sociaux: quelques réflexions sur leur ignorance mutuelle sous la monarchie censitaire." *Historiens et sociologues aujourd'hui.* Paris: CNRS, 1987.

Bibliography

Lecuyer, Bernard-Pierre. "Médecins et observateurs sociaux: les Annales d'Hygiène et de Médecine Legale, 1820–1850." *Pour une histoire de la statistique.* Vol. 1. Paris: Institut National de la Statistique et des Etudes Economiques, 1977.

Lecuyer, Bernard-Pierre. "Quételet." *Encyclopaedia Universalis.* Paris: Encyclopaedia Universalis, 1985.

Lecuyer, Bernard-Pierre, and Anthony P. Oberschall. "Sociology, III: The Early History of Social Research." *International Encyclopedia of the Social Sciences.* Vol. 15. Ed. David L. Sills. New York: 1968.

Ledoux, Claude-Nicolas. *L'Architecture considerée sous le rapport de l'art, des moeurs, et de la législation.* 2 vols. Paris: Auteur, 1804.

Lehec and Jean Cazeneuve, eds. *Corpus des philosophes français.* Vol. 2. Paris: Presses Universitaires de France, 1956.

Lehideux, Francois. "Reconstruction 1941." *Urbanisme* 71(January–May 1941).

Leiris, Michel. "L'Ethnographe devant le colonialisme." *Les Temps modernes* 6, no. 58 (August 1950).

Lelièvre, Pierre. *L'Urbanisme et l'architecture à Nantes au XVIIIe siècle.* Nantes: Durancé, 1972.

Leprun, Sylviane. *Le Théâtre des colonies: scénographie, acteurs et discours de l'imaginaire dans les expositions, 1855–1937.* Paris: Harmattan, 1986.

Lequin, Yves. *Les ouvriers de la région lyonnaise, 1848–1914.* Lyons: Presses Universitaires de Lyon, 1977.

Leroux, Thierry. "L'Urbanisme Social-democrate: Henri Sellier." Thése de 3e cycle. Ecole des Hautes en sciences sociales, Paris, 1981.

Leroy, Maxime. *La Vie véritable du Comte Henri de Saint-Simon (1760–1825).* Paris: Grasset, 1925.

Leroy-Beaulieu, Paul. *De l'Etat moral et intellectuel des populations ouvrières et de son influence sur le taux des salaires.* Paris: Guillaumin, 1868.

Levasseur, Emile. *L'Etude de l'enseignement de la géographie.* Paris: 1872.

Levasseur, Emile. *La Population française.* 3 vols. Paris: Rousseau, 1889–92.

Levine, Neil A. "Architectural Reasoning in the Age of Positivism: The Neo-Grec Idea of Henry Labrouste's Bibliothèque Saint-Geneviève." 5 vols. Ph.D. diss. Yale University, 1975.

Lévy-Bruhl, Lucien. *La Morale et la science des moeurs.* Paris, 1903. Reprint Paris: Presses Universitaire de France, 1971.

Ley, David, and Marwyn Samuels, ed. *Humanistic Geography: Prospects and Problems.* Chicago: University of Chicago Press, 1978.

Lipstadt, Hélène. "Housing the Bourgeoisie: César Daly and the Ideal Home." *Oppositions* 8(Spring 1977).

Lipstadt, Hélène, and Harvey Mendelsohn. *Architectes et ingènieurs dans la presse: polémique, débat, conflict*. Paris C.O.R.D.A., 1980.

Lofgren, Orvar. "Our Friends in Nature: Class and Animal Symbolism," *Ethos* 50, nos. 3–4 (1985).

Lottin, Joseph. *Quételet: statisticien et sociologue*. Louvain: Institut supèrieur de philosophie, 1912.

Lottman, Herbert R. *Pétain*. Trans. Beatrice Vierne, Paris: Seuil, 1984.

Loubet del Bayle, Jean-Louis. *Les Non-Conformistes de années 30: une tentative de renouvellement de la pensée politique française*. Paris: Seuil, 1969.

Loucher, Louis. "Rapport de la Commission chargée par le Ministère de l'hygiène et de la prévoyance sociale d'étudier les mesures les plus propres à remedier la crise du logement." *La Vie Urbaine* 4(September–October 1919).

Luckermann, F. "The 'Calcul des probabilites' and the Ecole française de géographie." *The Canadian Geographer* 9, no. 3 (1965).

Lyautey, Charles. *Réflexion qui a fait naître chez un vieillard médaillé de Sainte-Hélène la brochure intitulé 'L'Armée française en 1867'*. Paris: 1867.

Lyautey, Louis Hubert Gonsalve. *Dans le Sud de Madagascar: pénétration militaire, situation politique et économique, 1900–1902*. Paris: Charles-Lavauzelle, 1903.

Lyautey, Louis Hubert Gonsalve. *Lettres du Tonkin et de Madagascar, 1894–1899*. 7 vols. Paris: Colin, 1920.

Lyautey, Louis Hubert Gonsalve. *Lyautey l'africain: textes et lettres du Marechal Lyautey*. Ed. and intro. Pierre Lyautey. Vol. 1, 1912–1913. Paris: Plon, 1953.

Lyautey, Louis Hubert Gonsalve. *Paroles d'action—Madagascar, Sud-Ouranais, Oran, Maroc (1900–1926)*. Paris: Colin, 1927.

Lyautey, Louis Hubert Gonsalve. "Du rôle de l'officier dans le service universel." *La Revue des deux mondes* (March, 1891). Reprint. *Le Rôle social de l'officier suivi de textes et de lettres autour de (Le Rôle social de l'officier)*. Paris: Albatros, 1984.

Lyautey, Pierre. *Gallieni*. Paris: Gallimard, 1959.

McKay, Donald. "Colonialism in the French Geographical Movement, 1871–1881." *Geographical Review* 33(1843).

McKay, John P. *Tramways and Trolleys: The Rise of Urban Mass Transport in Europe*. Princeton, N.J.: Princeton University Press, 1976.

McLeod, Mary. "Urbanism and Utopia: Le Corbusier from Regional Syndicalism to Vichy." Ph.D. diss., Princeton University, 1985.

McQuillen, Michael. "The Development of Municipal Socialism in France, 1880–1914." Ph.D. diss., University of Virginia, 1973.

MacKenzie, Donald A. *Statistics in Britain 1865–1930: The Social Construction of Scientific Knowledge*. Edinburgh: Edinburgh University Press, 1981.

Magri, Susanna. *Politique du logement et besoins en main-d'oeuvre.* Reprint. Paris: Centre de sociologie urbaine, 1972.

Magri, Susanna, and Christian Topalov. "De la Cité jardin à la ville rationalisée: un tournant du projet réformateur, 1905–1925; une étude comparative France, Grande-Bretagne, Italie, Etats-Unis." Unpublished ms., June 1986.

Maier, Charles S. "Between Taylorism and Technocracy; European Ideologies and the Vision of Industrial Productivity in the 1920's." *Journal of Contemporary History* 5, no. 2 (1970).

Maier, Charles S. *Recasting Bourgeois Europe: Stabilization in France, Germany and Italy in the Decade after World War I.* Princeton, N.J.: Princeton University Press, 1975.

Manuel, Frank E. *The New World of Henri de Saint-Simon.* Cambridge, Mass.: Harvard University Press, 1956.

Manuel, Frank E. and Fritzie P. Manuel. *Utopian Thought in the Western World.* Cambridge, Mass.: Harvard University Press, 1979.

Marin, Louis. *Le Portrait du roi.* Paris: Minuit, 1981.

Marr, David. *Vietnamese Anti-Colonialism, 1885–1925.* Berkeley: University of California Press, 1971.

Martin, Benjamin F. *Albert de Mun: Paladin of the Third Republic.* Chapel Hill, N.C.: University of North Carolina Press, 1978.

Martin, Jean-Baptiste. *La Fin des mauvais pauvres: de l'assistance à l'assurance.* Pref. Madeleine Rébérioux. Seyssel: Champ Vallon, 1983.

Marx, Roger. *L'Art social.* Pref. Anatole France. Paris: Charpentier, 1918.

Massiot, Michel. *L'Administration publique à Madagascar.* Pref. Hubert Deschamps. Paris: Librairie générale de droit et de jurisprudence, 1971.

Mathurin Crucy, 1749–1826: architecte nantais néo-classique. Nantes: Musées départementaux de Loire-Atlantique, 1986.

Maurois, André. *Lyautey.* Paris: Plon, 1931.

Mauss, Marcel. "Divisions et proportion des divisions de la sociologie." *Essais de sociologie.* Ed. Victor Karady. Paris: 1971.

Mayer, Arno. *The Persistence of the Old Regime: Europe to the Great War.* New York: Pantheon, 1981.

Mellerio, André. "La Société pour la protection des paysages de France." *La Réforme sociale* 48(1–16 September, 1904): 430.

Mercier, Louis. "Rabat: description topographique." *Archives marocaines* 7(1906).

Meynier, André. *Histoire de la pensée géographique en France, 1872–1969.* Paris: Presses Universitaires de France, 1969.

Bibliography

Miège, Jean-Louis. *Le Maroc et l'Europe (1830–1894)*. 4 vols. Paris: Presses Universitaires de France, 1961–63.

Milliot, Louis. *Introduction à l'étude du droit musulman*. Paris: Receuil Sirey, 1953.

Mimin, Pierre. "Le Socialisme municipal devant le conseil d'état." *Revue socialiste* 51(May 1910).

Mimin, Pierre. *Le Socialisme municipal devant le Conseil d'Etat: critique juridique et politique des régies communales*. Paris: Sirey, 1911.

Mitchell, Allan. *Bismarck and the French Nation*. New York: Pegasus, 1971.

Mitchell, Allan. *Victors and Vanquished: The German Influence on Army and Church in France after 1870*. Chapel Hill, N.C.: University of North Carolina Press, 1984.

Mitchell, W. J. T. *Iconology: Image Text, Ideology*. Chicago: University of Chicago Press, 1986.

Moheau. *Recherches et considérations sur la population de la France*. Ed. René Gonnard. Reprint. Paris: Guethner, 1912.

Montegut, Robert de Boyer. "Les Bureaux de placement municipaux et les bourses du travail." *Revue socialiste* 4(16 November 1912).

Monteil, Vincent. *Les Officiers*. Paris: Seuil, 1960.

Monteilhet, Joseph. *Les Institutions militaires de la France, 1814–1932: de la paix armée à la paix désarmée*. Paris: Alcan, 1932.

Munoz, Sylviane. "Monographie historique et économique d'une capitale coloniale: Rabat de 1912 à 1939." 2 vols. Thése pour le Doctorate d'état es-lettres et sciences humaines, Université de Nice, 1986.

Murard, Lion, and Patrick Zylberman. *Le Petit Travailleur infatigable: villes-usines, habitats et intimités au XIXe siècle*. Paris: Recherches, 1976. 2d ed. 1980.

Murard, Lion, and Patrick Zylberman. "La Raison de l'expert ou l'hygiéne comme science sociale appliqué." *Archives européennes de sociologie* 26(1985).

Murard, Lion, and Patrick Zylberman. "Robert-Henri Hazeman, urbaniste sociale." *Urbi* 10(Winter 1986).

Moscovici, Serge. *L'Age des foules, un traité historique de psychologie des masses*. Brussels: Complexe, 1985.

Nardy, Jean Pierre, and Paul Clanal. "Pour le Cinquantenaire de la mort de Paul Vidal de la Blache." *Annales littéraires de l'Université de Besançon* 93(1968).

Nguyen Van Phong. *La Société viétnamienne de 1882 à 1902 d'après les écrits des auteurs français*. Paris: Presses Universitaires de France, 1971.

Nicolet, Claude. *L'Idée républicaine en France: essai d'histoire critique, 1789–1924*. Paris: Gallimard, 1982.

Nisbet, Robert. *The Social Group in French Thought.* Ph. D. diss., University of California, Berkeley, 1939. Reprint. New York: Arno, 1980.

Noiriel, Gérard. *Les Ouvriers dans la société française au XIXe siècle.* Paris: Seuil, 1986.

Nora, Pierre, ed. *Les Lieux de la mémoire.* 3 vols. Paris: Gallimard, 1984–87.

Nye, Robert A. *Crime, Madness and Politics in Modern France: The Medical Concept of National Decline.* Princeton, N.J.: Princeton University Press, 1984.

Nye, Robert A. *The Origins of Crowd Psychology: Gustave Le Bon and the Crisis of Mass Democracy in the Third Republic.* London and Beverly Hills: Sage, 1975.

L'Oeuvre d'Henri Prost: architecture et urbanisme. Paris: Académie d'architecture, 1960.

Ory, Pascal. *Les Intellectuels en France, de l'affaire Dreyfus à nos jours.* Paris: Colin, 1986.

Outram, Dorinda. *Georges Cuvier: Vocation, Science and Authority in Post-Revolutionary France.* Dover, N.H.: Manchester University Press, 1984.

Ozouf, Jacques and Mona Ozouf. "Le Thème du patriotisme dans les manuels primaires." *Le Mouvement social* 49(1964).

Paillard, Y. G. "Victor Augagneur: socialisme et colonisation." *Bulletin academique malgache* 52, nos. 1–2 (1976).

"Paris 1937." Special issue, *L'Architecture d'aujourd'hui* 8, nos. 5–6 (June 1937).

Pauty, E. "Rapport sur la defense des villes et la restauration des monuments historiques." *Hesperis* 2, nos. 1,2 (1922).

Pawlowski, Krzysztof. *Tony Garnier et les débuts de l'urbanisme fonctionnel en France.* Paris: Centre de recherche d'urbanisme, 1967.

Paxton, Robert. *Vichy France: Old Guard and New Order, 1940–44.* New York: Knopf, 1972.

Payne, Howard Clyde. "French Regionalism, 1815–1914: A Study of the Principal Alternatives to Administrative Centralization." Ph.D. diss. University of California, Berkeley, 1947.

Penot, Dr. A. "Des Institutions de prévoyance sociale fondeés par les industriels du Haut-Rhin en faveur de leurs ouvriers." *Bulletin de la Société industrielle de Mulhouse* 26(1855).

Perez-Gomez, Alberto. *Architecture and the Crisis of Modern Science.* Cambridge, Mass.: M.I.T. Press, 1983.

Perrot, Michelle. *Les Ouvriers en grève: France 1871–1890.* 2 vols. Paris: Mouton, 1974.

Perrot, Michelle. "Premières mesures des faits sociaux: les débuts de la statistique criminelle en France (1780–1830)." *Pour une histoire de la statistique.* Vol. 1. Paris: Institut National de la Statistique et des Etudes Economiques, 1977.

Perrot, Michelle. "Three Ages of Industrial Discipline." *Consciousness and Class Experi-*

ence in Nineteenth Century France. Ed. John Merriman. New York: Holmes and Meier, 1979.

Perrot, Michelle and Annie Kriegel. *Le Socialisme français et le pouvoir.* Paris: Etudes et documentations internationales, 1966.

Pevsner, Nikolaus. *Pioneers of Modern Design: From William Morris to Walter Gropius.* 2d ed., rev. Harmondsworth, England: Penguin, 1960.

Piarron de Chamousset, C. H. *Plan d'une Maison d'Association pour se procurer des secours dans les cas de maladie, suivis d'additions et d'éclaircissement et de deux lettres critiques sur ce projet.* Paris, 1754.

Picot, Georges. "La Question des logements ouvriers à Paris et à Londres." *La Réforme sociale* 10(15 September 1885).

Pierrard, Pierre. *L'Eglise et les ouvriers en France, 1840–1940.* Paris: Hachette, 1984.

Pinel, Philippe. "Resultats d'observations et construction des tables pour servir à déterminer le degré de probabilité de la guérison des aliénés." *Mémoires de la classe des sciences mathématiques et physiques de l'Institut National de France.* Paris: 1807.

Pingusson, G. H. "L'Esprit de 1937." *L'Architecture d'aujourd'hui* 6, no. 6 (June 1935).

Pinkey, David H. *Napoleon III and the Rebuilding of Paris.* Princeton: Princeton University Press, 1958.

Pinon, Pierre. "Gli 'envois de Rome': tradizione e crisi." *Rassegna* 17(March 1984).

Pipkin, Charles W. *Social Politics and Modern Democracies.* 2 vols. New York: Macmillan, 1931.

Pisier-Kouchner, Evélyne. *Le Service public dans la théorie de l'état de Léon Duguit.* Paris: Librairie générale de droit et de jurisprudence, 1972.

Poirier, Louis. "L'Evolution de la géographie humain." *Critique* 8, no. 9 (January–February 1947).

Poisson, Siméon Denis. *Recherches sur la probabilité des jugements en matière criminelle et en matière civile.* Paris: Bachelier 1837.

Porter, Theodore M. *The Rise of Statistical Thinking, 1820–1900.* Princeton, N.J.: Princeton University Press, 1986.

Pour une histoire de la statistique. 2 vols. Paris: Institut National de la Statistique et des Etudes Economiques, 1976–77. Reprint. 1st vol. only. Paris: INSEE, 1986.

Prelot, Marcel. *Histoire des idées politiques.* Paris, 1961. 2d ed. 1966.

Premier Rapport des commissaires chargés par l'Académie du projet d'un nouvel Hôtel-Dieu. Paris: 1785.

Prendre la ville: ésquisse d'une histoire de l'urbanisme d'état. Paris: Anthropos, 1977.

Procacci, Giovanna. "Le Gouvernement de la misère: la question sociale entre les deux révolutions, 1789–1848." Thèse de doctorat de troisième cycle, Université de Paris VIII, 1983.

Prochasson, Charles. "Le Socialisme normalien, recherches et reflexions autour du Groupe d'Etudes Socialiste et de l'Ecole Socialiste, 1907–1914." Mémoire de Maîtrise, Université de Paris I, 1981.

Prost, Henri. "L'Urbanisme." Unpublished ms.. Archives de l'Académie d'architecture.

Proudhon, Pierre-Joseph. *Du Principe fédératif et de la nécessité de reconstituer le parti de la révolution.* Paris: Dentu, 1863.

Quatremère de Quincy, M. *Essai sur la nature, le but et les moyens de l'imitation dans les beaux-arts.* Paris: Treuttel et Wurtz, 1823.

Quételet, Lambert-Adolphe-Jacques. "Recherches sur la loi de la croissance de l'homme." *Nouveaux mémoires de l'académie des sciences et belles-lettres de Bruxelles* 7(1832).

Quételet, Lambert-Adolphe-Jacques. *Recherches sur le penchant au crime au differents ages.* 2d ed. Brussels: Hayez, 1833.

Quételet, Lambert-Adolphe-Jacques. "Sur l'appréciation des documents statistiques." *Bulletin de la Commission centenaire de statistique* 2(1844).

Quételet, Lambert-Adolphe-Jacques. *Sur l'homme et le développement de ses facultés, ou essais de physique sociale.* Paris: Chatelier, 1835. 2d ed. 2 vols. Brussels: Hauman, 1836.

Quinet, Edgar. *Lettres d'exil à Michelet et à d'autres amis.* 4 vols. Paris: Calmann-Lévy, 1885–86.

Rabinow, Paul. "Ordonnance, Discipline, Regulation: Some Reflections on Urbanism." *Humanities in Society* 5, nos. 3–4 (Summer and Fall, 1982).

Rabinow, Paul, and Gwen Wright. "Savoir et pouvoir dans l'urbanisme moderne colonial d'Ernest Hébrard." *Les Cahiers de la recherche architecturale* 9(January 1982).

Rambert, Gaston. "La Cartographie à l'Exposition coloniale de Marseille." *Annales de géographie* 31(15 November 1922): 433–48.

Rébérioux, Madeleine. "Les Ouvriers et les expositions universelles de Paris au XIXe siècle." *Le Livre des expositions universelles 1851–1889.* Paris: Union Centrale des Arts Décoratifs, 1983.

Rébérioux, Madeleine. "Le Socialisme français, 1875–1914." *Histoire générale du socialisme.* Ed. Jacques Droz. 4 vols. Paris: Presses Universitaires de France, 1972–78.

Rébérioux, Madeleine, and Patrick Fridenson. "Albert Thomas: pivot du réformisme français." *Le Mouvement social* 87(April–June 1974).

Reddy, William M. *The Rise of Market Culture: The Textile Trade and French Society, 1750–1900.* Cambridge and New York: Cambridge University Press, 1984.

Remond, René. *The Right Wing in France: From 1815 to de Gaulle.* 2d ed. Philadelphia: University of Pennsylvania Press, 1966.

Résidence Générale de la Republique Française au Maroc. *La Renaissance du Maroc: Dix années de protectorat, 1912–1922.* Poitiers: 1922.

Reybaud, Louis. *La Fer et la houille.* Paris: Lévy et Frères, 1874.

Reynaud, Léance. *Traité d'architecture.* 2 vols. Paris: Carlian-Godury Dalmont, 1850. 2d. ed. 1858.

Rhein, Catherine. "La Géographie: discipline scolaire et/ou science sociale?, 1860– 1920." *Revue française de sociologie* 23(1982).

Risler, Georges. "Les Cités jardins." *Mémoires et documents du Musée social* (December 1909).

Risler, Georges. "Les Plans d'aménagement et d'extension des villes." *Mémoires et documents du Musée social* 11(1912).

Rivet, Daniel. "Lyautey et l'institution du protectorat français au Maroc, 1912–1925." Thèse de Doctorat d'Etat en Histoire et Sciences-Sociale, Université de Paris (Val-de-Marne), 1985.

Rivet, Paul. "Ce que sera le Musée de l'Homme." *L'Oeuvre* (14 June 1936).

Rivet, Paul, and Georges-Henri Rivière. "La Réorganisation du Musée d'éthnographie du Trocadéro," *Bulletin du Museum national d'histoire naturelle.* 2nd ser. nos. 2,5 (June 1930).

Rivet, Paul, P. Lester, and Georges-Henri Rivière. "Le Laboratoire d'Anthropologie du Museum," *Archives du Museum national d'histoire naturelle* 12, no. 2 (June 1935).

Roger, Jacques, ed. "Les Néo-Lamarckiens français." *Revue de synthèse historique* 100, nos. 95–96 (July–December 1979).

Rollet, Henri. *L'Action sociale des catholiques en France, 1871–1901.* Paris: Boivin, 1947.

Roncayolo, Marcel, ed. *Histoire de la France urbaine.* Vol. 5, *La Ville aujourd'hui, croissance urbaine et crise du déclin.* Paris: Seuil, 1985.

Rosanvallon, Pierre. *Le Moment Guizot.* Paris: Gallimard, 1985.

Rosen, George. *A History of Public Health.* New York: MD Publications, 1958.

Rosen, George. "Medical Care and Social Policy in Seventeenth-Century England." *Bulletin of the New York Academy of Medicine* 29(1953).

Rosen, George. "Problems in the Application of Statistical Analysis to Questions of Health: 1700–1880." *Bulletin of the History of Medicine* 29(1955).

Rosenthal, Léon. *Villes et villages, français après la guerre: aménagement, restauration, embellissement, extension.* Pref. Louis Bonnier, Paris: Payot: 1918.

Rotival, Maurice. "Les Grands Ensembles." *L'Architecture d'aujourd'hui* 5, no. 6 (June, 1935): 57–72.

Rouvier, Catherine. *Les Idées politiques de Gustave Le Bon.* Paris: Presses Universitaires de France, 1986.

Rovigati, Maria. "Tony Garnier e la didattica dell'Ecole des Beaux Arts.' " *Rassegna* 17(March 1984).

Royer, Jean, ed. *L'Urbanisme aux colonies et dans les pays tropicaux*. 2 vols. La Charité-sur-Loire and Paris, 1932–35.

Roz, Michel. "Tony Garnier, un monumento lionese." *Rassegna* 17(March 1984).

Rykwert, Joseph. *The First Moderns: The Architects of the Eighteenth Century*. Cambridge, Mass.: M.I.T. Press, 1980.

Rykwert, Joseph. *On Adam's House in Paradise: the Idea of the Primitive Hut in Architectural History*. New York: Museum of Modern Art, 1972. Reprint. Cambridge, Mass.: M.I.T. Press, 1981.

Sablayrolle, Louis. *L'Urbanisme au Maroc. Les Moyens d'actions. Les Résultats*. Albi: Imprimerie cooperative du sud-ouest, 1925.

Said, Edward. *Orientalism*. New York: Pantheon, 1978.

Saint-Simon, Henri de. *Oeuvres de Saint-Simon et d'Enfantin*. 47 vols. Paris: Dentu, 1865–1878.

Sarazin, Jean. *Le Choléra pestilentiel*. Paris: Barbaet Levasseur, 1831.

Savoye, Antoine. "Les Continuateurs de Le Play au tournant du siècle." *Revue française de sociologie* 22, no. 3 (July–September 1981).

Schiller, Francis. *Paul Broca, Founder of French Anthropology, Explorer of the Brain*. Berkeley: University of California Press, 1979.

Schorske, Carl. *Fin-de-Siècle Vienna, Politics and Culture*. New York: Vintage, 1981.

Sellier, Henri. "L'Avenir de Suresnes lié à son passé." *Bulletin de la Societe historique de Suresnes* 1(1929).

Sellier, Henri. *Les Banlieues urbaines et la réorganisation administrative du Département de la Seine*. Paris: Rivière 1920.

Sellier, Henri. "Les Centres sociaux dans les régions rurales aux Etats-Unis." *La Vie Urbaine* 4(1922).

Sellier, Henri. "Conférence internationale des cités-jardins et de l'aménagement des villes." *La Vie Urbaine* 18(15 February 1923).

Sellier, Henri. "Divers aspects de la politique anglaise en matière d'habitation." *La Vie Urbaine* 3(1921).

Sellier, Henri. "Essai sur les évolutions comparées du logement et la population dans le département de la Seine de 1896 à 1811." *La Vie Urbaine* 3(1921).

Sellier, Henri. "Le Logement ouvrier contemporain." *L'Architecture d'aujourd'hui* 6, no. 6 (June).

Sellier, Henri. "L'Oeuvre de l'office publique d'habitations à bon marché du département de la Seine." *L'Architecture d'aujourd'hui* 8, nos. 5–6 (June 1937).

Sellier, Henri, and Robert-Henri Hazemann. "La Santé publique et la collectivité." *Rapport de la commission d'hygiène du service social.* Paris, 1936.

Sherman, William. *Les Officiers français dans la nation, 1848–1914.* Paris: Aubier-Montaigne, 1982.

Shapiro, Ann-Louise. *Housing the Poor of Paris, 1850–1902.* Madison, Wis.: University of Wisconsin Press, 1985.

Siegfried, Jules. *La Misère: son histoire, ses causes, ses remèdes.* 4th ed. Le Havre: Poinsignon, 1880. 1st ed. Paris: Ballière, 1877.

Silverman, Debora. *The Origins Art Nouveau in France, 1889–1900: Nature, Nobility and Neurology.* Berkeley: University of California Press, 1989.

Sordes, René. *Histoire de Suresnes: des origines à 1945.* Suresnes: Société historique de Suresnes, 1965.

Souza, Robert de. *Nice: capital d'hiver.*Ser. *L'Avenir de nos villes, études pratiques d'esthétique urbaine.* Paris: Berger-Levrault, 1913.

Stadtman, Verne A., ed. *Centennial Record of the University of California.* Berkeley, Calif.: University of California Print Department, 1967.

Stafford, David. *From Anarchism to Reformism: A Study of the Political Activities of Paul Brousse within the First International and the French Socialist Movement, 1870–1890.* Toronto: University of Toronto Press, 1971.

Staum, Martin S. *Cabanis: Enlightenment and Medical Philosophy in the French Revolution.* Princeton, N.J.: Princeton University Press, 1980.

Sternhell, Zeev. *Maurice Barrès et le nationalisme français.* Paris: Colin, 1972.

Sternhell, Zeev. *Ni droite ni gauche: l'idéologie fasciste en France.* Paris: Seuil, 1983.

Stigler, Stephen M. *The History of Statistics: The Measurement of Uncertainty before 1900.* Cambridge, Mass.: Belknap Press of Harvard University Press, 1986.

Stocking, George W., Jr. *Race, Culture and Evolution: Essays in the History of Anthropology.* New York: Free Press, 1968.

Stovall, Tyler. "The Urbanization of Bobigny, 1900–1939." Ph.D. diss., University of Wisconsin-Madison, 1984.

Summerson, Sir John. "Viollet-Le-Duc and the Rational Point of View." "Architectural Design Profile: Eugène Emmanuel Viollet-Le-Duc, 1814–1879." *Architectural Design* 50, nos. 3–4 (1980).

Sutcliffe, Anthony. *The Autumn of Central Paris: The Defeat of Town Planning 1850–1970.* Montreal: McGill-Queen's University Press, 1971.

Sutcliffe, Anthony. *Towards the Planned City: Germany, Britain, the United States and France, 1780–1914.* New York: St. Martin's, 1981.

Swearingen, Will Davis. "In Search of the Granary of Rome: Irrigation and Agricultural Development in Morocco, 1912–1982." Ph.D. diss., University of Texas at Austin, 1984.

Tafuri, Manfredo. *The Sphere and the Labyrinth, Avant-gardes and Architecture from Piranesi to the 1970s.* Cambridge, Mass.: M.I.T. Press, 1987.

Taine, Hyppolite. *De l'idéal dans l'art.* Paris: Baillière, 1867.

Taine, Hyppolite. *Philosophie de l'art.* Paris: Baillière, 1865.

Taylor, Brian Brace. "Discontinuité planifiée: villes coloniales modernes au Maroc." *Les Cahiers de la recherche architecturale* 9(1982).

Taylor, Brian Brace. *Le Corbusier, the City of Refuge: Paris, 1929–1933.* Chicago: University of Chicago Press, 1987.

Tenon, Jacques-René. *Memoires sur les hôpitaux de Paris.* Paris: Pierres, 1788.

Terrassee, Henri. *Histoire du Maroc des origines à l'établissement du protectorat français.* 2 vols. Casablanca: Atlantides, 1849–50.

Teyssot, Georges. "Civilisation du salarié et culture de l'employé: variations sur Siegfried Kracauer, Ernst Bloch et Walter Benjamin." *Les Cahiers de la recherche architecturale* 15–17(1985).

Thiry, Jean Baron. *Bonaparte en Egypte: décembre 1797—24 aôut 1799.* Paris: Berger-Levrault, 1973.

Tocqueville, Alexis de. *De la Démocratie en Amérique.* 2 vols. Brussels: L'Hauman, 1835. Rev. ed. 2 vols. Paris: Gallimard, 1961.

Topalov, Christian. "Invention du chômage et politiques sociales au début du 20e siècle: une comparaison France—Grande Bretagne—Etats-Unis." Unpublished ms. Centre de Sociologie Urbaine, March 1986.

Topalov, Christian. *Le Logement en France, Histoire d'une marchandise impossible.* Paris: Presses de la Fondation National des Sciences Politique, 1987.

Tougeron, Jean-Christophe. "Donat-Alfred Agache: un architecte urbaniste." *Les Cahiers de la recherche architecturale* 8(April 1981).

Unwin, Raymond. *L'Etude pratique des plans de ville.* Paris: Librairie centrale des beaux-arts, 1922.

Vaillat, Léandre. *Seine: chef-lieu Paris.* Paris: Arts et metiers graphiques, 1937.

Van Zanten, Ann Lorenz. "Form and Society: César Daly and the 'Revue Generale de l'Architecture.'" *Oppositions* 8(Spring 1977).

Van Zanten, David. *Designing Paris: The Architecture of Duban, Labroste, Duc and Vaudoyer.* Cambridge, Mass.: M.I.T., 1987.

Veber, Adrien. "Le Socialisme communal." *Revue socialiste* 17(June 1893).

Veber, Adrien. *Le Socialisme municipale.* Paris: Giarde et Brière, 1908

Vera, Andé. "Le Style nouveau." *Urbanisme* 98(January 1944).

Vidal de la Blache, Paul Marie-Joseph. "L'Ecole Normale." *Revue internationale de l'enseignement* 8(1884).

Vidal de la Blache, Paul Marie-Joseph. "La Géographie humaine: ses rapports avec la géographie de la vie." *Revue de synthèse historique* 7(1903).

Vidal de la Blache, Paul Marie-Joseph. "Les Pays de France." *La Réforme sociale* 48(1–16 September 1904).

Vidal de la Blache, Paul Marie-Joseph. *Principes de géographie humaine.* Paris: Colin, 1922.

Vidal de la Blache, Paul Marie-Joseph. "Régions françaises." *Revue de Paris* 5, no. 17 (15 December 1910).

Vidler, Anthony. "The Idea of Type." *Oppositions* 8(Spring 1977).

Vidler, Anthony. "News From the Realm of No-Where." *Oppositions* 1(September 1973).

Vidler, Anthony. *The Writing of the Walls: Architectural Theory in the Late Enlightenment.* Princeton: Princeton University Press, 1987.

Vigato, Jean-Claude. "L'Architecture du Régionalisme; les origines du débat (1900–1950)." Rapport de Fin d'Etude. Ecole d'Architecture de Nancy, 1982.

Vigato, Jean-Claude. "Notes sur la question stylistique." *Les Cahiers de la recherche architecturale* 15–17(1985).

Villermé, Louis-René. "Mémoire sur la mortalité dans la classe aisée et dans la classe indigente." *Mémoire de l'Académie Royale de Médecine* 1(1828).

Villermé, Louis-René. "Note sur les ravages du choléra-morbus." *Annales d'hygiène publique et de médecine légale* XI(1834).

Villermé, Louis-René. "Sur les cités ouvrières," *Annales d'hygiène publique et de médecine légale* 43(1850).

Villermé, Louis-René. *Tableau de l'état physique et moral des ouvriers employés dans les manufactures de coton, de laine et de soie.* 2 vols. Paris: Renouard, 1840.

Eugène Emmanuel Viollet-Le-Duc, 1814–79. London: Academy, 1980.

Viollet-Le-Duc, Eugène Emmanuel. *Discourses on Architecture.* Boston: Ticknor, 1875.

Vire, Marc. "La Création de la chaire d' 'Evolution des Etres Organisés' à la Sorbonne en 1888." *Revue de synthèse historique* 100, nos. 95–96 (July–December 1979).

Vitet, Louis, and Eugène Viollet-le-Duc. *A Propos de l'Enseignement des Arts du Dessin.* Paris, 1863. Reprint. Pref. Bruno Foucart. Paris: Ecole Nationale Supérieure des Beaux-Arts, 1984.

Wakefield, Edward Gibbon. *Art of Colonisation.* London, 1849.

Weber, Eugen. *The Nationalist Revival in France, 1905–1914*. Berkeley: University of California Press, 1959.

Weill, Georges. *Un Précurseur du socialisme: Saint-Simon et son oeuvre*. Paris: Perrin, 1894.

Westergaard, Harald Ludwig. *Contributions to the History of Statistics*. London: King, 1932. 2d ed. New York: Agathon, 1968.

White, Hayden. *Metahistory: The Historical Imagination of Nineteenth Century Europe*. Baltimore: The Johns Hopkins University Press, 1973.

Wiebenson, Dora. *Tony Garnier: The Cité industrielle*. New York: Braziller, 1969.

Williams, Elizabeth A. "Anthropological Institutions in Nineteenth Century France." *Isis* 76(1985).

Williams, Raymond. *Culture and Society, 1780–1950*. New York: Columbia University Press, 1958. Reprint. 1983.

Williams, Rosalind H. *Dream Worlds: Mass Consumption in Late Nineteenth Century France*. Berkeley: University of California Press, 1982.

Wolf, Peter M. *Eugène Hénard and the Beginning of Urbanism in Paris 1900–1914*. The Hague: International Federation for Housing and Planning (The Hague) and the Centre de Recherche d'Urbanisme (Paris), 1968.

Woodside, Alexander. *Vietnam and the Chinese Model: A Comparative Study of Nguyen and Ch'ing Civil Government in the First Half of the Nineteenth Century*. Cambridge, Mass.: Harvard University Press, 1971.

Woolman, David S. *Rebels in the Rif: Abd el-Krim and the Rif Rebellion*. Stanford, Calif.: Stanford University Press, 1968.

Zeldin, Theodore. *France 1848–1945*. Vol. 1, *Ambition, Love and Politics*. Oxford: Oxford University Press, 1973.

Zeldin, Theodore. *France 1848–1945*. Vol. 5, *Anxiety and Hypocrisy*. Oxford: Oxford University Press, 1981.

Zimmermann, Maurice. *Paysages et villes du Maroc*. Lyons: Lyon colonial, 1923.

Index

Selected Index of Names

Selected Index of Names

Selected Index of Names